# BRUN FAMILY
# NAPA VALLEY • FROM 1874


WILLIAM ALEXANDER HEWITT
– EDITOR –

GRANDSON OF
JEAN ADOLPHE BRUN

SON OF
EDWARD THOMAS HEWITT


# HEWITT FAMILY
# SAN FRANCISCO • FROM 1882

Privately printed in the U.S.A. by
William A. Hewitt
Rutherford, Napa Valley, California



Library of Congress Catalog Number: 89-83256

ISBN 0-86691-126-X

# BRUN FAMILY • NAPA VALLEY • FROM 1874
# HEWITT FAMILY • SAN FRANCISCO • FROM 1882

## CONTENTS

# PREFACE

During recent years various members of my family have expressed an interest in learning more about the roots of the Hewitt family on my father's side, and the Brun family from which my mother descended. Younger family members, who are currently in their twenties and thirties, have been especially eager to learn more about their forebears.

Regrettably, records and photographs relating to our family history have never been organized into a single body of information. Instead, items of interest to my parents and other family members have accumulated over the years in scattered bottom drawers and musty boxes. Other pieces of historical documentation have been stored in the deep recesses of household closets and various other elusive places for safekeeping.

About two years ago I decided to gather as much information as possible to allow me to put together a book on the Brun and Hewitt family history. The material I have gathered has been organized and put into book form so I can present a copy to each living descendant of my two grandfathers, Jean Adolphe Brun and William Alexander Hewitt.

I also plan to send copies of this book to libraries and historical societies that are interested in the early days of the vineyards and wineries of the Napa Valley of California. Additionally, copies will be sent to libraries that are interested in the period when motor trucks were manufactured by many small regional companies such as my father's. Since the advent of the internal combustion engine at the turn of the century, there have been more than 1,500 manufacturers of automobiles and motor trucks in the United States. Today, the great majority of those types of vehicles are manufactured by only a relatively few major producers.

Most of the early material I gathered during my research was focused on the lives of my grandfather, Jean Adolphe Brun, 1845-1894, and my father, Edward Thomas Hewitt, 1868-1933. For the period of 1912-1946, the material we found was mostly related to the activities of the Hewitt children, my brother Ed, my sister Adrienne (Deets), and the editor of this book. The disproportionate representation of the activities of those few members of our family is at least partly due to the fact that my father almost always had his camera within easy reach. Other family members took few photographs between 1900 and the early 1930s. Consequently I truly regret that this book does not contain a wider assortment of photographs related to other branches of our family.

Please note that when a photo caption refers to an uncle, or an aunt, or a cousin, or a grandparent, it indicates the relationship of that person to my brother, Ed, my sister, Adrienne, and to me.

Finally, let me say to each family member who might become interested in this book, I hope you will build on the nucleus I am offering. I hope that you will gather photographs and documents related to the activities of your immediate families, and keep those treasures in albums, where you can easily find them. Additionally, I plaintively urge each of you to write names and dates on all photographs you may have that you wish to keep, and in the process make an effort to throw away the less attractive photographs you have been accumulating, and keep only the best ones. This may be difficult for some of you, but it makes the "keepers" even more attractive.

I have arbitrarily selected the end of World War II as the cut-off point for this chronicle of our family. I have chosen 1946 as the best time to conclude this book because the documentation of our activities has greatly escalated since the late 1940s due to the ever increasing use of cameras and personally written records.

This book begins with a focus on family members who left Switzerland, France and England more than one hundred years ago to find their futures in the United States of America. The book then traces the lives of the direct descendants of our early ancestors in the U.S. and tells how they fared during subsequent years. Much of my own story, especially the period of my Navy years during World War II, has been woven into the fabric of the overall presentation in order to convey a personal feeling of what our family life was like during the first half of the 20th century.

From 1946 on, each of you can record the activities of your immediate family from the vantage point of your own personal experience, and interest in perpetuating the ongoing history of our family.

*William A. Hewitt - 1989*
*Editor*

# INTRODUCTION

Although some of us may be residing elsewhere today, all living descendants of my two grandfathers, Jean Adolphe Brun and William Alexander Hewitt, have strong family ties to San Francisco.

The oldest family ties to San Francisco belong to Pamela Hewitt and her sister, Christine Hewitt Morrison, daughters of my brother, Edward Thomas Hewitt, and his wife of more than fifty years, Viola Koster Hewitt.

Both Pam and Tina Hewitt were born in San Francisco and can claim direct San Francisco lineage back to 1847 and 1849. One of their great-great-great-grandfathers, Immanuel Charles Christian Russ, and his immediate family, arrived in San Francisco from New York in 1847 aboard the sailing ship Loo Choo, a U.S. military transport. Soon after they settled, the Russ family built a house on the block of land on Montgomery Street, bordered by Bush and Pine Streets. I.C.C. Russ' granddaughter, Lilly Russ Bruckmann, was the grandmother of Viola Koster Hewitt, the mother of Pam and Tina.

Louis Mermoud, a paternal great-great-grandfather of Pam and Tina Hewitt, arrived in San Francisco from Poliez Le Grand near Lausanne, Switzerland, in 1849. Louis Mermoud's daughter, Emma, was born in San Francisco in 1860 and married Jean Adolphe Brun in 1880. The newlyweds, who were Pam and Tina's great-grandparents, and also my grandparents, established their residence in Oakville in the Napa Valley, where Jean Brun and his partner, Jean Chaix, had built a winery in 1877. A few years later, Brun and Chaix planted a vineyard and then built their second winery in 1886 on Howell Mountain, on the east slope of the Napa Valley.

At the time of my birth in San Francisco, in August 1914, World War I erupted with the "guns of August." My personal memories of that tumultuous war are rather minimal, but I do remember Aunt Julie in her long white Red Cross uniform with its white veil that was highlighted by a bright red cross on the front of it. She served in a canteen in the Ferry Building where she helped cheer soldiers who were about to leave San Francisco for the fighting front in France.

She and the other Red Cross volunteers offered the soldiers coffee, doughnuts and cigarettes.

I also remember an occasion soon after the end of World War I when our whole family boarded a San Francisco Bay ferry boat to go to the Oakland Mole, the steam train terminal where Uncle Jack arrived from France via the East coast. The war was over and Uncle Jack was returning home from battles at Chateau Thierry, Verdun, the Argonne front, and the San Mihiel front, with a detachment of California soldiers who were about to be mustered out of the U.S. Army. I was so proud to be seen with him in his khaki wool uniform, complete with wrap-around leggings, and broadbrim soldier's hat.

In the early 1920s many of the fire engines of San Francisco were horse-drawn. Brother Ed and I often walked two and a half blocks from home to the nearest firehouse to admire the horses that stood in stalls that were alongside an early model steam boiler fire wagon. The horses' harness hung from the ceiling in front of the fire wagon, which was aimed at the wide open doors of the firehouse. The harness was precisely located so it could be lowered by lines and pulleys as soon as the horses were out of their adjacent stalls and were standing in front of the fire wagon. Ed and I always hoped an alarm would sound while we were in the firehouse so we could watch the excitement of the horses being quickly hitched up, and then see them dash out the door with firemen clinging to the back of the wagon. The boiler on the wagon emitted a billowing trail of smoke behind as it raced to the fire.

In the early 1920s San Francisco still used cobblestones for pavement on many of its streets, to give dray horses more traction as they pulled delivery wagons up and down the hills of the city. As boys, Ed and I were fascinated when we saw sparks fly from the iron shoes of the horses as they struggled uphill over those basalt block cobblestones.

During those years, many areas of San Francisco were still illuminated at night by gas lamps atop cast iron pedestals, planted in the sidewalks alongside the granite curbstones. Everyday, as twilight approached, men who worked as lamplighters would start to walk their routes to light the gas lamps that were housed in large, clear glass bowls about ten or twelve feet above the sidewalk. Each lamplighter carried a slim wooden pole which was topped by a starter flame protected from the wind by a perforated metal cylinder. There also was a hook at the end of the pole that was used to open the gas valve when the starter was ready to light the jet inside the glass bowl.

As children, on summer vacation, one of our favorite events was to make a small expedition with our parents aboard the "Crookedest Railway in the World," to the top of Mount Tamalpias. A picturesque little steam engine pulled open-sided passenger cars, each with a surrey-type roof. These cars featured full-length running boards so passengers could easily climb up to the rows of benches that extended across the full width of each car.

The Muir Woods-Tamalpias Railway had its base terminal in the town of Mill Valley in Marin County. Our favorite time for traveling on that little train was in the early evening when it would leave the main street of Mill Valley in time to snake up to the top of the mountain while there was still daylight. Then we would have dinner, en famille, in the tavern near the top of the peak and enjoy the panoramic view which included the east bay area and the city of San Francisco, plus a bit of the Pacific Ocean and its coast line. After dinner, when darkness had set in, we descended the mountain in an open gravity car that silently rolled down the mountain through the moonlit darkness. Those gravity cars had no engines and, of course, they were steered by the steel railroad tracks. The only useful piece of manual control equipment was a set of brakes, operated by the conductor.

On a slightly sloping plateau about halfway down the mountain, the tracks followed an unusual pattern called the "Bow Knot," which resembled a very large figure eight with irregular sides. The only way the gravity cars got through the uphill stretches of the "Bow Knot" was by momentum. Those fantastic little cars offered a joyful thrill that we will always remember. The whole mountainside was a captivating fun park, especially after dark.

Incidentally, during those relatively uncomplicated days, there was almost no fear of burglars or housebreakers in San Francisco. Consequently, my parents did not feel it necessary to lock the front door of our house while we were in residence; however, as a mild precaution, they did lock the doors and close windows each summer when we went, en famille, to Marin County during the eight-week school vacations. Father commuted to San Francisco by electric train and ferry boat during those weeks, since the Golden Gate Bridge didn't exist until 1937.

In the mid-1920s I listened to a radio for the first time. It was a simple crystal set Ed and I assembled from "do-it-yourself" materials. We used a Quaker Oats carton as the cylinder around which we wrapped thin, cotton-covered copper wire. There was also a condenser, a crystal, a "cat's whisker," and an earphone headset. The antenna was a single strand of heavy, bare copper wire that we strung from our house to a post at the back of the garden. What a triumph it was when we actually heard voices and music come through the earphones, after we had searched with the "cat's whisker" for a sensitive spot on the crystal.

Another significant event of those times was the stock market crash in October 1929. During the booming bull market of the late 1920s even some of us children in high school bought shares in companies such as Transamerica, which at that time was the holding company that owned the San Francisco-based Bank of Italy, now Bank of America. We also liked the Wrigley Chewing Gum Company. We felt Wrigley was a good stock because it paid a monthly dividend and sent each shareholder a carton containing about ten assorted packs of chewing gum at Christmas time. The retail price of gum then was five cents for a pack of five sticks.

The big economic depression that followed the crash of October 1929 lasted for several years. Because of that depression, and because I was only 16 years old when I graduated from Lowell High School in 1931, I chose to work for two years before I started college. In many ways that deep economic depression was a crucible that made survivors out of most of us who were working, or in school during that period.

In 1932 the assassination of two members of the Longshoremen's Union (ILWU), in front of their union headquarters near the waterfront, sparked a general strike in San Francisco. Martial law was declared and the National Guard was called out in full battle regalia to "preserve the peace." Streetcars did not operate and public services were minimal; however, business, of sorts, continued.

While martial law was in effect, sandbag revetments were built in the financial district of San Francisco at strategic intersections, such as Montgomery and California Streets. Uniformed members of the National Guard manned machine guns within the shelter of the revetments.

Graduates of Stanford and Cal were working at starting salaries of $65 a month at the American Trust Company (now the Wells Fargo Bank) where I had the same type of messenger job as they had in the early 1930s, before I enrolled in the University of California. After I had worked for American Trust for about a year, the depression began to hurt more deeply. The lowest paid employees of the bank then received a five percent pay cut, which netted us $61.75 per month, and the top officers received 20 percent pay cuts. Unemployed men were selling fresh apples on the streets at five cents each in order to earn a bit of money. Yes, times were tough, but we were survivors.

In the fall of 1933 I entered the University of California in Berkeley, and spent four wondrous years there until my graduation in 1937, with an AB degree in economics and a minor in political science. I learned a lot, both in and out of class, and made friends who are still good friends now, fifty years later.

In 1940 Wally Haas, my college roommate, invited me to be one of his ushers in the wedding ceremony that would join him in marriage with Evelyn Danzig in New York. This event was very special in many ways. It had a warm family feeling and the accompanying events were great fun. Even getting to New York from San Francisco was memorable. It was my first transcontinental trip on a commerical airliner, thanks to Walter Haas Sr.

The plane in which I traveled was a United Airlines DC-3 sleeper, which boasted about ten or twelve berths, in double-decker arrangement, somewhat similar to the accommodations offered on a railroad Pullman car. Our first refueling stop was Salt Lake City. We arrived there in the late evening, greeted by the news that radio reports indicated stormy weather ahead. Consequently, an airline decision was made to wheel our DC-3 into the hangar where the passengers could sleep in their berths while waiting for the storm to dissipate. Incidentally, as was the custom in those days, our United Airlines stewardess was a registered nurse. She tucked us in very nicely and eventually we arrived in New York.

While in New York for Wally and Evie's wedding, I enjoyed an unexpected dividend. For the first time I saw a television set in action. It was in the Manhattan apartment of Evie's parents, and it was housed in a mahogany case about five-feet tall, full of vacuum tubes. The dimensions of the picture screen were about five by seven inches, to the best of my recollection. What an exciting world I lived in.

During late 1940 and early 1941, Pete Burgess, another of my college roommates, and I decided to take flying lessons under a government-sponsored program. The flight instruction was at Mills Field, now known as San Francisco International Airport, and the ground instruction classes were held during evening sessions at San Mateo Junior College.

After eight hours of dual flights with the instructor, I was ready to fly "solo." Then, after twenty-seven hours of "solo" in that high-wing, single engine Luscombe, it was time for me to be tested for my pilot's license. I well remember that Saturday morning. The weather was fair, the sky was blue and the breezes were light.

The C.A.A. (Civil Aeronautics Agency) inspector and I took off and I responded to his requests to perform the usual test maneuvers, which included several stalls, tight vertical turns, a spin, a simulated emergency landing, a bit of cross-country flying and, lastly, a series of three spot landings. The spot landings required me to fly several big half-circles of the field at different altitudes. At an appropriate moment during each of those short flights, the instructor would reach for the throttle and shut off the gasoline supply to the engine. At that point, I was obliged to glide the aircraft to a proper landing without using any power.

My first two spot landings were okay. During my takeoff for the third one, the engine started to cough when the plane had climbed to an altitude of about 150 feet. We were out of gas.

The model of Luscombe I was flying was designed so the instructor was sitting on my right side and there was a single control stick between us. He quickly told me he was taking control as he grabbed the stick and shut off the ignition switch. He immediately swung the control stick from side to side which wagged the plane's tail sufficiently to make it act as a sort of air brake, which slowed us down a bit. Simultaneously, he pushed the stick forward to make the plane descend, as steeply as was safe, for a landing on the runway which, fortunately, was still directly below us. Once we touched ground he applied the brakes hard, and we came to a full stop only about twenty-five feet short of the end of the pavement. Beyond that was a swamp full of tall marsh grass between the end of the runway and the open water of San Francisco Bay. It would have been difficult to rescue persons who might have landed in that marsh.

Perhaps you are wondering why we were so negligent as to let our little airplane run out of gas. Here is our explanation. The Luscombe Silvaire we were flying was designed before tricycle landing gear was popular. It was a tail-down model and its gas gauge was designed to be read in straight and level flight. Consequently, the gauge was not accurate when the plane was on the ground with its tail below a level flight position. The C.A.A. inspector was not aware of that point and neither was I, since it hadn't been taught to me during the course of instruction.

Incidentally, before the last takeoff the inspector and I both read the gas gauge as indicating the tank was a quarter full. We then agreed that there was sufficient fuel for a short trip around the field, since the weather was clear and calm and there was virtually no air traffic that morning.

Consequently, the inspector did not penalize me. We merely had the plane towed to the gas pump where we filled its tank with fuel. Then we made our final takeoff and spot landing and I was awarded my coveted pilot's license.

World War II is a long story. Suffice to say, on Monday morning, December 8, 1941, the day after Pearl Harbor was attacked, I went directly to headquarters of the Twelfth Naval District in San Francisco, and started to make inquiries as to whether the Navy could use a 27 year old officer candidate. About two months later in early February 1942, I was commissioned as an Ensign USNR. The esprit in the Navy during my service was excellent, and four years after I joined I completed my naval duty with the rank of Lieutenant Commander. During most of those four years I was on sea duty in the South Pacific; first on the light cruiser, USS St. Louis, and then on the battleship, USS California. Both of those ships engaged in considerable action while I served aboard them.

On being commissioned as an Ensign USNR, I was assigned to active duty in the Operations Office of the Twelfth Naval District, based in San Francisco. My office duties in that department were so minimal I felt I could do a week's work in less than one day, if my duties could come to the surface in a more rapid sequence. It was a very dull job. I felt almost like an imposter when I went to work wearing a naval officer's uniform.

I felt a naval officer should be serving aboard a ship. My itch for sea duty came to a head one day when I read an Alnav from the Secretary of the Navy. It was a dispatch addressed to all naval personnel, and its principal message was "Officers are urgently needed at sea."

I wasted no time in showing the Secretary's dispatch to the Captain in charge of District Operations, and I simultaneously requested that I be transferred to sea duty. I was amazed when he responded, "Hewitt, you might not like sea duty." I couldn't believe what I had heard, but I was too new on the job to press my point. Consequently, after a short discussion, I withdrew from the Captain's office, wondering why he wanted me to remain on his staff while officers were needed aboard naval ships that were fighting the Japanese in the Pacific.

About two months later, another Alnav came through. This time the message was that certain categories of officers were eligible to participate in a two-month training session at the U.S. Naval Base in Newport, Rhode Island. Here was another opportunity to escape boredom and, hopefully, have another shot at being assigned to sea duty. Again, I carried the dispatch to my Captain and asked if I could be assigned to the training session. This time his reply was a bit more encouraging. He said, "O.K., Hewitt, if you agree to return to duty in this office after the training session has been completed."

The schooling at Newport was a worthwhile exercise and, in due course, I returned to the naval operations office in San Francisco. Nothing much had changed there even though the Navy and the Marines in the Pacific were taking over various Japanese military bases, such as Tarawa, Eniwetok and Kwajalein, plus part of Guadalcanal in the Solomon Islands.

After a few more weeks of the dull office grind, a local dispatch advised our office that the USS St. Louis, a light cruiser then anchored in San Francisco Bay, was scheduled to engage in target practice outside the Golden Gate on the following day. This meant she would fire her six-inch main battery guns at a large canvas target mounted on a sea sled, towed by a tug. This intrigued me, so I went to the Captain's office and plaintively stated I had been an officer in the Navy for more than eight months and had not yet witnessed the firing of a naval gun. "Sir," I said, "may I have your permission to spend tomorrow aboard the St. Louis?" I was pleased when the Captain replied, "Permission granted."

Unfortunately, on the following morning San Francisco and the adjacent coastline were covered by a heavy blanket of low fog. With the thought in mind that San Francisco fog often lifts in the late morning, I drove to the Embarcadero where I found a St. Louis shore boat. Once aboard the St. Louis I talked with one of the ship's officers who was still hopeful that target practice would be possible that day.

Several other officers made me feel at home in the wardroom where we relaxed while waiting for a final decision regarding target practice. Eventually, the deadline was reached and the decision was negative because the fog hadn't lifted.

Sadly, I had to return ashore without having witnessed a firing of the ship's main battery guns. The motor whaleboat that took us to the San Francisco waterfront had a crew of two sailors and there was only one other passenger aboard besides myself. He was the ship's gunnery officer, a lieutenant commander.

We struck up a conversation during which he lamented the fact that two ensigns assigned to duty in the gunnery department of the St. Louis were not expected to arrive before the scheduled departure of the ship in two days. Naturally, my response was, "How about me?" The gunnery officer had no objection and suggested I ask my Captain to send a priority dispatch to the Navy Department in Washington requesting immediate orders that would transfer me to the USS St. Louis. "Good idea," I replied.

Once ashore I went immediately to the Naval Operations Office in the Federal Building and explained the situation to my Captain, concluding with, "The St. Louis needs me." At last the Captain's reaction was favorable. "You have my permission to be transferred if you also can get permission from the District Personnel Officer."

I walked briskly to the Personnel Office where I explained everything to the Captain in charge, concluding with, "If you grant my request, I already have my Captain's permission." The personnel captain was a jovial Irishman who had no objection to my request. In fact, he seemed pleased and said he would send the priority dispatch to Washington immediately.

Twenty-four hours later an affirmative reply was received and I was instructed to gather my health and payroll records and report to the St. Louis before seven o'clock the next morning.

I celebrated my departure with several friends at dinner in the Palm Court of the Palace Hotel and then went home a little after midnight to pack a suitcase. At about 2:30 A.M. a Navy car arrived to drive me to the waterfront pier where the St. Louis was tied up, ready for departure. I kissed my mother au revoir and I was off to sail aboard the St. Louis to the South Pacific. The ship departed promptly at 7:00 A.M. and we sailed non-stop to Noumea, New Caledonia. After a few days there, we headed for Guadalcanal. Our approach to that island was after dark and we were greeted by the sight of streams of anti-aircraft tracer bullets that were aimed at Japanese aircraft that were bombing American positions in the Henderson

Airfield area. I finally had first-hand evidence that the Japanese and the Americans were literally trying to kill each other. It was not a real surprise, but it made quite an impression on me.

My first taste of action was when the USS St. Louis participated in a number of shore bombardments in the Solomon Islands in June 1943. Those actions included midnight bombardments by our task force of U.S. cruisers and destroyers, aimed at the Japanese-held Munda Airfield and its adjoining army barracks. Our objectives also included other military targets on New Georgia and Kolombangara Islands which were located midway between Guadalcanal and Bouganville, in the Solomons.

The St. Louis also participated in two major surface battles in the Solomon Islands. The first was in late June 1943 when the "Tokyo Express," a task force of Japanese cruisers and destroyers, dashed down from the Bouganville, their decks laden with fresh troops, to replace the casualties suffered during our bombardment of Munda Airfield and its barracks twenty-four hours earlier. The USS Helena, our sister ship, which was cruising 1,000 yards ahead of the St. Louis in our battle formation, was sunk during that engagement. Fortunately, more than 750 of the Helena's 1,100-man crew were rescued.

One week later, on the fourth of July 1943, during our second battle with Japanese warships in the "slot" of the Solomon Islands, the bow of the St. Louis was blasted by a torpedo that was shot at us by a Japanese cruiser or destroyer. The resulting damage sent our ship to the Mare Island Navy Yard in San Francisco Bay for major repairs, after some extensive patch-up work was done by a Navy repair ship in Espiritu Santo, New Hebrides.

On arrival at Mare Island, I was immediately transferred to the USS California, one of the older battleships, built in 1922, which was the pride of the fleet before World War II. The California had been sunk in very shallow water during the Japanese raid on Pearl Harbor on December 7, 1941. Soon after she was sunk, the California was raised and towed to Bremerton Navy Yard in Puget Sound, near Seattle, where she was substantially modernized. A new gadget called radar was installed for surface and air search. This equipment later enabled us to track enemy ships and aircraft that were beyond visual contact. Fire control radar for putting the ship's big guns on target was also installed.

At the time of the attack on Pearl Harbor in 1941, the USS California's only anti-aircraft weapons were 50-caliber machine guns. These were replaced during the modernization work at Bremerton by 20-and 40-millimeter gun emplacements plus six twin mounts of five-inch dual purpose guns that could be used against both surface and air targets. The then newest type of five-inch projectile featured a proximity fuse, which meant such projectiles would explode into heavy pieces of shrapnel when their proximity fuses sensed they were near enough to target aircraft to allow the shrapnel to do serious damage. The effectiveness of this innovative type of projectile greatly improved the Navy's success rate in knocking down enemy aircraft.

Due to a lack of officers with radar experience aboard the California, the ship's Executive Officer quickly sent me to Pearl Harbor for a two-month course in radar training at Camp Catlin, which was under the auspices of the U.S. Marine Corps. On completing the course I returned to the California, where I supervised the installation of new equipment in the ship's Combat Information Center (C.I.C).

A few days before the refurbished California sailed out of Puget Sound, on January 31, 1944, for its shake-down cruise in the waters off southern California, the lieutenant in charge of the ship's radar operations was not able to pass the vision test which was part of his annual physical exam. Consequently, he was immediately transferred to shore duty, and I was assigned to replace him as officer in charge of radar operations and the ship's C.I.C. Obviously, I was a rookie in that type of responsibility, so I immediately engaged in absorbing a lot of individual study and on-the-job training. The well-trained petty officers in my division were very helpful during that period.

After several weeks of shake-down, the California headed west into the Pacific. Our first action aboard BB-44, affectionately known as the "Prune Barge," was the bombardment of Japanese military positions on Saipan in the Mariana Islands, followed by intensive bombardments of neighboring Guam and the Tinian Islands. All of these bombardments were in support of the amphibious landings that were made by U.S. Marines and U.S. Army units, to secure those Japanese-held islands for occupation by U.S. military forces.

From the Marianas we sailed to the Philippines where our first action was to bombard the Japanese positions on the shores of Leyte in order to soften their resistance sufficiently to allow General MacArthur to wade ashore and announce, "I have returned."

Not long after American military forces established a beachhead on the island of Leyte, the Japanese admiralty decided to make a three-pronged attempt to retake their former military bases on Leyte. They organized three strong naval task forces to act simultaneously in an effort to accomplish their basic objective. One of the three Japanese task forces headed east toward Leyte Gulf through San Bernardino Straits, which is a passage through the Philippines, a bit north of the entrance to Leyte Gulf.

The second Japanese task force was to approach Leyte from the east coast of Luzon, the northernmost island of the Philippines. That approach was blocked by a task force of U.S. aircraft carriers and battleships under the command of Admiral Halsey.

The third Japanese task force steamed through the Sulu Sea, so it could approach Leyte Gulf from the south, through Surigao Straits. This group of ships included two major Japanese battleships, the Fuso and the Yamashiro, plus a strong contingent of cruisers and destroyers.

The American Naval Command quickly assigned U.S. warships to cope with each of the three approaching Japanese task forces. The USS California, together with five other U.S. battleships, plus cruisers, destroyers and P.T. boats, was ordered to block the passage of the Japanese ships through Surigao Straits.

U.S. cruisers, destroyers and P.T. boats were positioned on both sides of Surigao Straits in a sleeve formation, and the capital ships formed a battle line that cruised back and forth across the top of the Straits. This latter formation was a classic one which, in naval circles, is called "crossing the T." It was a formation that enabled the U.S. battleships, in a "battle line," to fire full broadsides at the Japanese ships steaming in a single file column up the Straits toward the U.S. ships, with the Fuso and Yamashiro at the head of the column. The best the Japanese could do, under those circumstances, was to fire only from their forward main battery turrets against full broadsides from our ships.

Of the two Japanese battleships that entered Surigao Straits, the Fuso and the Yamashiro were both sunk by U.S. Navy gunfire and torpedoes. U.S. ships also sunk two Japanese destroyers, Yamagumo and Michishio. Consequently, the enemy task force withdrew from battle and headed back home through the Sulu Sea with two of their cruisers, Mogami and Asagumo, heavily damaged. Only one U.S. ship, a destroyer, was damaged in the Battle of Surigao Straits. Unfortunately, most of that damage was caused by friendly U.S.

ships, when the ill-fated U.S. destroyer became adventurous and approached too close to the Japanese warships. Consequently, she was damaged during the melee.

"Crossing the T" in the Battle of Surigao Straits was one of the most memorable events of my life, especially since the surface search radar in our Combat Information Center successfully provided the USS California's main battery radar control with the range and bearing information that enabled our ship's guns to get on target during a dark night, at a range of twenty-six thousand yards. The California shot sixty-three rounds of 14-inch armor-piercing projectiles which significantly helped sink the enemy battleships.

Volume Twelve of Admiral Samuel Eliot Morison's *History of the United States Naval Operations in World War II,* entitled *Leyte, June 1944-January 1945,* devotes a full chapter of thirty-six pages to "The Battle of Surigao Straits, 24-25 October 1944."

The following brief excerpts from that chapter capture the historic significance of that battle in the annals of naval history. On page 240 of *Leyte,* Morison states: "The Battle of Surigao Straits marks the end of an era in naval warfare. It was the last naval battle in which air power played no part, except in the pursuit. It was the last engagement of a battle line. Here an old sailor may indulge in a little sentiment."

On page 241 of *Leyte,* Morison continues, "Battle line was first successfully employed in 1655 by James, Duke of York, against the Dutch Admiral Opdum in the Battle of Lowestoft. Standard tactics throughout the days of sail, it was used in all great sea battles, such as Beachy Head, Ushant, the Capes of Chesapeake, the Battle of the Saints, Cape St. Vincent and Trafalgar."

The Battle of Surigao Straits was a key part of the overall battle for Leyte Gulf. Morison describes the latter battle in the preface of his book, *Leyte,* as "...the greatest naval battle of all times; amphibious and aircraft operations up to and including the landings on Leyte; seven weeks of almost continuous fighting on land, sea and in the air until Leyte was secured; ..."

In the 1940s all of my shipmates were proud to be serving in the Navy and they did not complain about being involved in the combat activities in which we participated. Additionally, we had the strong support, with relatively few exceptions, of the American people. Our nation survived Pearl Harbor and the subsequent battles that were perpetrated by the then elite military faction of Japan. And, simultaneously, the United States helped Britain, France and other allies smash the aggressive Hitler regime in Germany. Now, forty-odd years later, our former enemies, Japan and Germany, are democracies and allies of the United States of America.

## ADDENDUM

Looking back over my lifetime, I am greatly impressed by how the overall pace of change has accelerated with dazzling speed during recent years. In the period following World War II the dimensions of the world we live in have shrunk rapidly. In the late 1940s, mass transportation by air started to become commonplace, and television soon brought us instant information related to crises in the most remote corners of the world; whereas, for example, a mere hundred years earlier, it could take weeks, or even months to learn the details about a famine in India.

As a final word in this Introduction, I would like to reflect on several personal experiences which, when linked together, have had considerable impact in driving home to me the force of the accelerated pace of change that has occurred in my lifetime:

1. When I was a young boy in the early 1920s, I enjoyed observing a fire engine in San Francisco that was a horse-drawn vehicle. Gas lamps were still in use to illuminate San Francisco streets, and radio was in its infancy.
2. Then, about fifty years later, when our children, Anna, Adrienne and Sandy were young, Tish and I took them to Cape Kennedy in Florida to watch the launching of Apollo Eleven, which put the first man on the moon. Although Tish and I, together with our children, were three miles from the launching pad, we were as close as spectators were permitted—close enough so we could feel the shock waves from the blast-off in the pits of our stomachs. A relatively short time after the blast-off of Apollo Eleven, we witnessed that unforgettable scene on television when Astronaut Neil Armstrong stepped out of the landing capsule and planted a United States flag on the moon.

So now I wonder, "What will the world be like fifty years after the day our children, Anna, Adrienne and Sandy witnessed the blast-off of Apollo Eleven?"

*William A. Hewitt -1989*
*Editor*

# ACKNOWLEDGMENTS

For his gathering of family information, and early photographs for this book, I owe a considerable debt of thanks to Laurence Jonson. His talent in research and the uncovering of facts that have been buried for generations is indeed impressive.

Larry possesses the ability to obtain copies of items that range from 150-year-old documents that are lodged in the archives of small villages in France, to 100-year-old newspaper articles and census records he uncovered in Napa County and in San Francisco.

He also had success in locating specifications related to chain drive and worm drive motor trucks built by Hewitt-Ludlow in San Francisco just after the beginning of this century.

Larry Jonson is meticulous, imaginative and tireless in his pursuit of pertinent background information. He deserves much credit for his considerable research effort that helped this book come alive.

In the final stages of making this book ready for the printer, Larry Jonson was ably assisted by Lisa Conner, who very capably planned the layout for each page; and by Mary Leonard, who deserves high marks for her skillful work in making the manuscript print-ready.

*William A. Hewitt - 1989*
*Editor*

BOOK I

# BRUN FAMILY
# NAPA VALLEY · FROM 1874

Nouveau Medoc Vineyard and Wine Cellars
BRUN & CHAIX Proprietors
Vineyard and Cellar, Howell Mountain    Shipping Depot, Oakville, Napa Co. Cal.

## Montage of Nouveau Medoc Vineyard and Wine Cellars A Watercolor From the Lithograph Made in 1900.

Prior to his death, Jean Adolphe Brun designed a lithograph of the Brun & Chaix properties to be produced as a sales aid in the large Eastern markets. In 1900, after his death, this artwork to promote his Nouveau Medoc wines of Napa Valley was published as a lithograph in seven colors that measured 26 x 30 inches, an exceptional advertising piece for its day.

Over the years those original lithographs have become quite rare and consequently Mr. Brun's grandson, William Hewitt, was not able to acquire one during an exhaustive search in the 1960s. However, one of Hewitt's friends, Peter Avenali, who resides in San Francisco and the Napa Valley, owns a Brun & Chaix lithograph, and graciously offered Hewitt a photograph of it. Hewitt then commissioned Paul Norton, an Iowa artist, to reproduce the photo in watercolor.

The lithograph is essentially a montage that was intended to illustrate Brun & Chaix activities in the Napa Valley. The upper half shows part of the 190-acre Brun & Chaix vineyard which was located on a slightly rolling plateau on the side of Howell Mountain. The principal building in the background was the winery that Brun & Chaix built to crush the grapes that they produced on their Howell Mountain Vineyard.

Built in 1886, the stone winery is three stories high. Its structure is notched into the hillside in a manner that allows the road to reach entrances on each of the three floor levels. The advantage of this design is that the grapes can be easily hauled to the crusher at the top floor level. The juices then flow by gravity to the vats, barrels and bottles that are located on the second and first floors. Incidentally, grapes are still being crushed on the third floor level since the winery was restored in 1983.

The stonework of the Brun & Chaix Winery was done by Chinese workers who originally had been brought to California to cut the right of way, for the first transcontinental railway, through the solid granite of the Sierra Nevada Mountains. The stone used in the construction of the winery came from a quarry located alongside Angwin Creek. The Chinese worked on the winery under the supervision of an Italian stonemason, Mr. Frank Giungi. Mr. Rice, of St. Helena, was the principal carpenter.

In the lithograph, the winery appears to be a two-story building. This is due to the fact that the first floor is hidden by a contour of the hillside.

The lower half of the montage illustrates the Oakville Crossroads area, with the viewer facing east. The house in the middle foreground, built by Jean Chaix, was actually built on the west side of the railroad tracks. This house still stands in 1989, and is privately occupied as a residence. It is in excellent condition and is easily identified by the nine very tall palm trees that border its east and north sides.

The house behind the Chaix house in the lithograph was built by Jean Adolphe Brun. He lived with his bride of 1880 in that house until he died in 1894. Their six children, Elise, Delphine, Jeannette, Louis, Julie and Jean, were born and raised there, and were young students in the primary grades of Oakville's one-room schoolhouse.

A few years after Jean Adolphe Brun died, his widow moved her family to San Francisco. In 1924 their former Oakville house was completely destroyed by fire. The site of that house now is near the middle of the large Inglenook Winery on the southeast corner of the intersection of Oakville Crossroad and Highway No. 29.

The building in the lower left side of the montage was the Brun & Chaix Oakville Winery which was started in 1877. The wines produced there were made from grapes purchased from nearby vineyards.

The buildings in the lower right side of the montage were Brun & Chaix warehouses located near the Oakville railroad station.

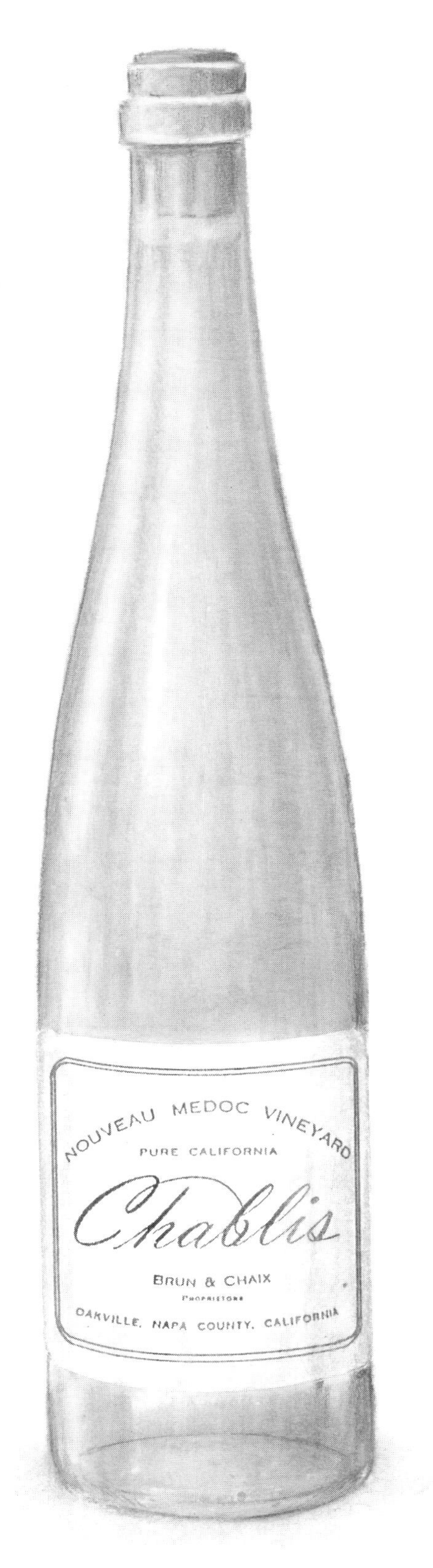


*A bottle of Chablis from the Nouveau Medoc Winery, drawn from a faded old photograph.*

*Brun & Chaix Winery on Howell Mountain. Built in 1886, the winery was restored by Woltner & Co. in 1986. This view shows the top floor of the three-story structure. Photograph by Kevin Roche, 1988.*

*This map highlights the location of the Napa Valley, as related to San Francisco and Sacramento. Note: The Brun and Chaix families lived in Oakville, and the Brun & Chaix partnership operated a winery there. Additionally, the partnership owned and operated a second winery and a vineyard on Howell Mountain, near Angwin.*

## JEAN ADOLPHE BRUN

Lithograph from *History of Napa & Lake Counties California,* published in 1881 by Slocum, Bowen & Co., San Francisco. Lithograph of J.A. Brun on page 525 of that history.

1876. The building is 45x75 feet, and has a capacity of fifty thousand gallons.

*F. Sciaroni's Sherry House.*—Is located in the southern part of St. Helena, and was erected in 1880, the building being two stories high, and 28x37 feet. It has a capacity of thirty thousand. The sherry made both here and at the house on Dr. Crane's place, is an excellent article.

*J. Thomann's Cellar.*—Is situated on the road leading south from St. Helena, at Vineland station, and is one of the most completely arranged cellars in the county. He began business here in 1874, and erected his cellar that year, which is 40x100 feet in size. In 1876 he erected a wing 18x100 feet, and in 1880 he built another wing 30x60 feet, and two stories high. The present capacity of the cellar is one hundred and fifty thousand gallons. He began the business of distilling also in 1874, with a copper still of a capacity of three hundred gallons. In 1880 he put up a wooden still with a capacity of seven hundred and fifty gallons. He has a Heald crusher, and all his machinery is driven by steam. The Heald crusher is a very complete contrivance, as it also stems as well as crushes the grapes. The one owned by Mr. Thomann has a capacity of ten tons an hour.

*J. H. McCord's Cellar.*—Mr. McCord began wine-making in 1871, in partnership with T. A. Gaique, on the place now owned by G. A. Stamer After only a few months the cellar caught on fire, and the building and about thirty thousand gallons of wine were destroyed. He then sold his grapes for the next three years, and in 1874 he made wine in the cellar of W. P. Weaks, at Pine station. For the next four years he used his barn for a cellar, and in 1880 he erected his present building, which is 48x60 feet, and two stories high, having a capacity of one hundred thousand gallons.

*Nouveau Medoc Cellar.*—Is located at Oakville, and is the property of Messrs. Brun & Chaix. They commenced operations in 1877, with a small cellar, only 20x34 feet in size. Since then they have added to this building, until it is now 160x34 feet, and they have another building near by which is 40x54 feet. They now have a total capacity of one hundred and thirty thousand gallons. They have imported nine different varieties of excellent wine-making grapes from Medoc, France, and have a vineyard of twenty acres planted with them on Howell Mountain.

*H. W. Crabb's Cellar.*—Mr. H. W. Crabb is the owner of the "Hermosa Vineyards," situated at Oakville station. He is a careful and very successful grape-grower, and has one of the largest vineyards of the county. In January, 1868, he purchased the present described tract of land, situated at Oakville, on the line of the railroad, twelve miles north of Napa City, containing two hundred and forty acres, without any improvement except a tenement house and barn. He commenced the planting of vines at once,

*Page 224 from* History of Napa & Lake Counties California, *published by Slocum, Bowen & Co., 1881.*

avenue. Mr. Bussenius was united in marriage in Nevada County, at Blue Tent, December 26, 1861, to Miss Johanna Gebhard, daughter of Mrs. Dr. Pfeiffer Stone, Oakland, a native of Mainz, Germany. The names of their children are Robert, Adolph, Lillie, and Ernst.

BRUN, JEAN ADOLPH. This gentlemen, whose portrait appears in the body of this work, was born in France, July 25, 1845, and is the son of Jean Brun and Jeanne Delphine Delaveaux. He resided in France until 1872, having had much experience in his native country in wine, cider, and oil making. In the last-named year he came to Montreal, Canada, where he remained for fourteen months, being engaged in the manufacture of photographic materials. He then went to England, and after a stay of thirty days in that country he sailed for Australia. Here he engaged in the same business, and continued in it for eight months. In September, 1874, he came to California, and shortly afterward came to Napa County, and began as a laborer, being engaged in several cellars as wine-maker. In 1877 he formed a partnership with Mr. Jean Chaix, and began his wine cellar at Oakville, a full description of which will be found in the proper place. In 1870 Mr. Brun took an active part in the great Franco-Prussian war, being in the service for a period of sixteen months. He was married October 23, 1880, to Miss Emma Mermoud, who was born in San Francisco, September 10, 1860.

BERINGER, JACOB L. Was born in Mainz, Germany, May 4, 1845, and is the son of Louis and Marie Gruber Beringer. He resided at his birthplace until he was twenty years of age, receiving in the meantime his education and also learning the cooper's trade and wine-making. In 1865 he went to Berlin and there took charge of a wine cellar for Messrs. Tim & Kloske, in which capacity he spent two years. In 1867 he went back to Mainz and took charge of the wine cellar of J. A. Harth & Co., where he had learned his trade. In 1868 he came to New York and was engaged by Truchess & Winkenbach as foreman in their wine cellar and remained with them for one year. He then opened a depot for German wines and the famous seltzer water, which he maintained until 1872. He then came to California and took charge of Charles Krug's wine cellar and retained that position until 1878. In 1877 he erected his present cellar, and in the following year he moved upon his place and has since then been engaged in the manufacture of wine. A full description of the place will be found elsewhere. The senior member of the firm is Frederick Beringer, the well-known malt dealer of No. 40 Whitehall street, New York. Mr. Beringer was elected to a position on the Board of Trustees of St. Helena in 1878. He was married April 5, 1879, to Miss Agnes Tscheinig, a native of Austria, who was born February 19, 1853. They had one child, which died in its infancy.

*Page 396 from* History of Napa & Lake Counties California, *published by Slocum, Bowen & Co., 1881.*

# Brun & Chaix Nouveau Medoc Winery

BY JOSEPH HENRY JACKSON—1955

As the name suggests, the Nouveau Medoc Winery and Vineyard in the upper Napa Valley was French in its background. Indeed, the proprietors, Messrs. Brun and Chaix, imported thousands of cuttings from the Medoc region of France, whence come the finest Bordeaux wines.

Jean Adolphe Brun, founder of Nouveau Medoc, was born in France in 1845. After the Franco-Prussian War in which he served, it seemed to him he might do better to seek his fortune somewhere else than in France, which had been forced to accept an unfortunate peace. He knew something of making olive oil, cider and wine, and had some knowledge of chemistry. He should be able to find employment almost anywhere.

Young Brun tried Canada first, working for about a year in Montreal for a manufacturer of photographic supplies. Still restless, he moved on to Australia where he got a job in the same trade. There he heard good reports of California and its wines, and decided this might be the place for him. He arrived in 1874, going directly to the Napa Valley.

For two years Brun made wine for various producers in the Yountville area, thriftily saving his money. By 1877 he and his friend, Jean Chaix, who was experienced in growing grapes, formed a partnership and bought a small vineyard on Howell Mountain. Down on the flat in Oakville, close to the railroad, they built a tiny cellar, 20 by 34 feet, and launched Nouveau Medoc.

Because Chaix knew grape-growing and Brun understood both winemaking and business management, the enterprise prospered. By 1881 the firm had expanded astonishingly. Records show that the winery was now 160 by 34 feet, output had increased from 55,000 gallons to 130,000 gallons a year.

Some of this business was in sacramental wines, but on one of his selling trips Brun had discovered that New Orleans particularly liked a fullbodied, slightly sweet red wine. On the warm slopes of Howell Mountain his Medoc grapes developed extra sugar. Picking late and blending judiciously, Brun & Chaix learned to give this special market exactly what it wanted. In two decades the vineyard properties had expanded to 115 acres, the business in Brun's energetic hands had become solidly established, and the wines were winning increased acceptance.

Then in 1894, just short of fifty, Jean Brun died. For a few years his widow and Chaix ran the winery. But by 1901 it seemed wiser to sell. The California Wine Association made the best offer, and Nouveau Medoc passed out of existence. Its labels are excessively rare today among collectors, and the lithograph reproduced herewith is scarce. Perhaps a few oldsters in New Orleans remember the Nouveau Medoc Red, its full body and slight sweetness, but among California's vintners nowadays even the name is virtually forgotten.

Editor's Note: Joseph Henry Jackson was a well-known writer and critic in San Francisco from 1931 until the late 1950s. In 1955 he wrote the above article as part of a series, titled "The Vine in California," for the California Book Club.

Many of his readers may be surprised to know that Joseph Henry Jackson was born and brought up in New Jersey and was not a native Californian, so thoroughly had he identified himself with the Californian scene: first in *Sunset Magazine,* where he rose to be editor-in-chief; then on NBC's "Bookman's Notebook" radio program, which ran eighteen years without a break; and, after 1931, as literary editor of the *San Francisco Chronicle.* He was the author of *Anybody's Gold, Tintypes in Gold* and other books. Additionally he was the editor of several anthologies.

# Napa Valley, California

The following excerpt from Gunther R. Detert's paper on *Charles Krug, 1825-1891,* offers a fine glimpse of Napa Valley history.

The Indian stone age culture, in which the Napa Valley was sleeping for thousands of years, ended in about 1836, a scant 150 years before this writing. At that time George C. Yount became the first person, after the Indians, to settle in the Valley. The California Mexican government mandated him to keep order amongst the Indians and to rid the Valley of its dangerous grizzly bears. Yount was quickly followed by the arrival of his friends, Colonel Chiles and Charles Hopper, both of whom were scouts and guides for pioneers' overland wagontrains, bound for the California and Oregon territory.

At that time Napa Valley was covered with tall, lush grass and acorn-abundant oak trees. Deer, elk, game and wild fowl of all kinds were everywhere. Inevitably the predators—coyote, bear, mountain lions, and especially the grizzly—lurked about the valley ridges and floor.

With the advent of the above new settlement in Yountville, and the small wooden farmhouses near Dr. H.T. Bales' sawmill, near St. Helena, the valley began its agricultural development.

In the early 1860s, less than 30 years after Yount's arrival, the vineyard planting and wine production, which later was to make Napa world renowned, began. Charles Krug was first, and in quick succession H.W. Crabb, Jacob Schram, Gottlieb Groezinger, the Beringer Brothers, Captain Niebaum, and a host of vineyardists and wine producers followed. Now almost every available plantable acre is covered with grapes slowly producing, under the Valley's gentle warm sun and nearly perfect climate, the fine wines for which it is famous.

Charles Krug was the first to break ground for commercial vineyards and wine production. His site was a mile south of the Bale Mill on the northern outskirts of St. Helena, at what came to be known as Krug Station on the railroad.

In 1858 he bought land from Haraszthy in Sonoma, and planted 20 acres of vineyards in the course of the following three years. This developed his interest in winemaking. In the same year, 1858, John Patchett of Napa City contracted with Krug to make wine from Patchett's grapes. Krug started with a modest cider press (it still exists today in the Krug Winery retail room) and proceeded to produce for Patchett 1,200 gallons of wine. It was the first wine ever made in Napa by other than the Spanish process. In the following year, 1859, he produced wine for Louis Bruck on the Bale Mill property, where the W.W. Lyman home was. In 1860 Krug made 5,000 gallons of wine on George C. Yount's farm.

Editor's Note: By 1874, at the time of Jean Brun's arrival, the Napa Valley was an agricultural producer of vegetables, pork, turkey, and fruits. The first wines were being made there, and there were only a few vineyards in production. The valley was a full-day wagon trip from the busy seaport of San Francisco.

With his agricultural background, gained in Bordeaux, 29-year-old Jean Brun made his decision to live in this new land.

In late 1874 he began work in the vineyards of the Yountville area. His experience in winemaking was put to good use when he formed a partnership in 1877 with Jean Chaix. They then built the first segment of their Oakville winery to crush purchased grapes.

Nine years later, in 1886, Brun & Chaix built another winery on Howell Mountain which crushed only the grapes from their newly established vineyard at that location.

## *The heroic builders of yore*

At the beginning, the Napa Valley drew its winery owners and winemakers from every corner of Europe. Gustav Nybom, builder of Inglenook, was a Finn and a retired sea captain. William Bowers Bourn, who launched Greystone, and H. W. Crabb, who owned ToKalon, were Anglo types. The French were represented by a whole series of partnerships, including Debret & Priet and **Brun & Chaix.** But the era 1870-1900 had a predominantly German flavor, one built on solid enough foundations to contribute most of the pioneer names and buildings still enduring today. Charles Krug started commercial winemaking in the valley in 1861 after a short apprenticeship with Agoston Haraszthy in Sonoma. On Krug's heels came the brothers Jacob and Frederick Beringer and Jacob Schram. Now-faded names like J. Thomann, C. J. Beerstecher, and G. Groezinger were major figures in their time.

*Excerpt from* California Wine, *published by the editors of Sunset Books, 1973.*

EDITOR'S NOTE: The text on this page is a reproduction of page 303 from Leon Adams' book, *The Wines of America*. This excerpt is from the chapter titled: "Napa, The Winiest County."



wineries before building this one in 1982. The name Vichon comes from *VI*erra and partners Bru*CH*er and Wats*ON*. A dozen other partners are restaurant and hotelmen whose establishments sell Vichon wines. Only three varieties are made here: Chardonnay, Cabernet, and a Semillon-Sauvignon blend called Chevrier, one of the synonyms of Sémillon.

In Oakville village, there is a stucco-fronted winery on the right that dates from 1886. Originally it was the Nouveau Médoc Vineyard cellar of Brun & Chaix, who were refugees from the troubles in France following the Franco-Prussian war. Jean Adolph Brun knew winemaking, and his partner, Jean Chaix, was experienced in growing grapes. They bought a vineyard and built a stone winery during the 1870s on Howell Mountain east of St. Helena, but then, to be close to the railroad, built this second cellar on the flat at Oakville. By 1889 their vineyards covered 115 acres; their Nouveau Médoc sweetish red wine was the favorite in New Orleans, and their whites were popular in California and the East. But Brun died young, and in 1916 Chaix and his widow sold the property. The buyer was the California Wine Association, which in turn sold to the Covick Company, makers of sacramental wines during Prohibition. In 1940, the cellar was sold at auction to the Napa Wine Company of Louis Stralla. He sold it six years later for $250,000 to the Cella Vineyards of Fresno. Now Heublein crushes and ferments the grapes there for the estate-bottled and coast-counties "vintage" Inglenook table wines. Next door is another cellar, named the Madonna winery when it was built in 1892. It was used after Repeal to make wine and brandy by the Bartolucci Brothers, who owned extensive vineyards nearby, and in 1969 became the winery of Oakville Vineyards, owned by a group of connoisseurs headed by Wilfred E. van Loben Sels, which became defunct in 1977. Then the winery was bought to increase the Napa Valley–produced portion of Inglenook wines.

• 9 •

On your left, a short distance past Oakville, is the mission-style Robert Mondavi Winery, which has multiplied in size to 1.8 million gallons since 1966, when Robert, at the age of fifty-four, left his family's Charles Krug Winery, of which he was part owner, and began building this one for himself and his children.

*Inglenook Chardonnay Cellar in Oakville opened at a Dec. 22, 1986 ceremony.*

EDITOR'S NOTE: The Inglenook Oakville Cellar pictured above stands on the site of the first Brun & Chaix winery built in Oakville in 1877. It is the "stucco-fronted" Inglenook winery that Leon Adams refers to in the excerpt from his book, The Wines of America, that appears on the preceeding page.

As a point of clarification, the 1886 date mentioned by Mr. Adams applies to the second winery by Brun & Chaix, which was the three-story stone winery they built on their vineyard on Howell Mountain, near Angwin.

Jean Adolphe Brun's family house, which stood near his winery in Oakville, was the house in which his wife, Emma, gave birth to their six children during the years that followed their marriage in San Francisco in 1880.

Thirty years after his death in 1894, the house that Jean Brun built in Oakville burned to the ground in 1924. That house was also on the land that is now occupied by the Inglenook Cellar in 1989.

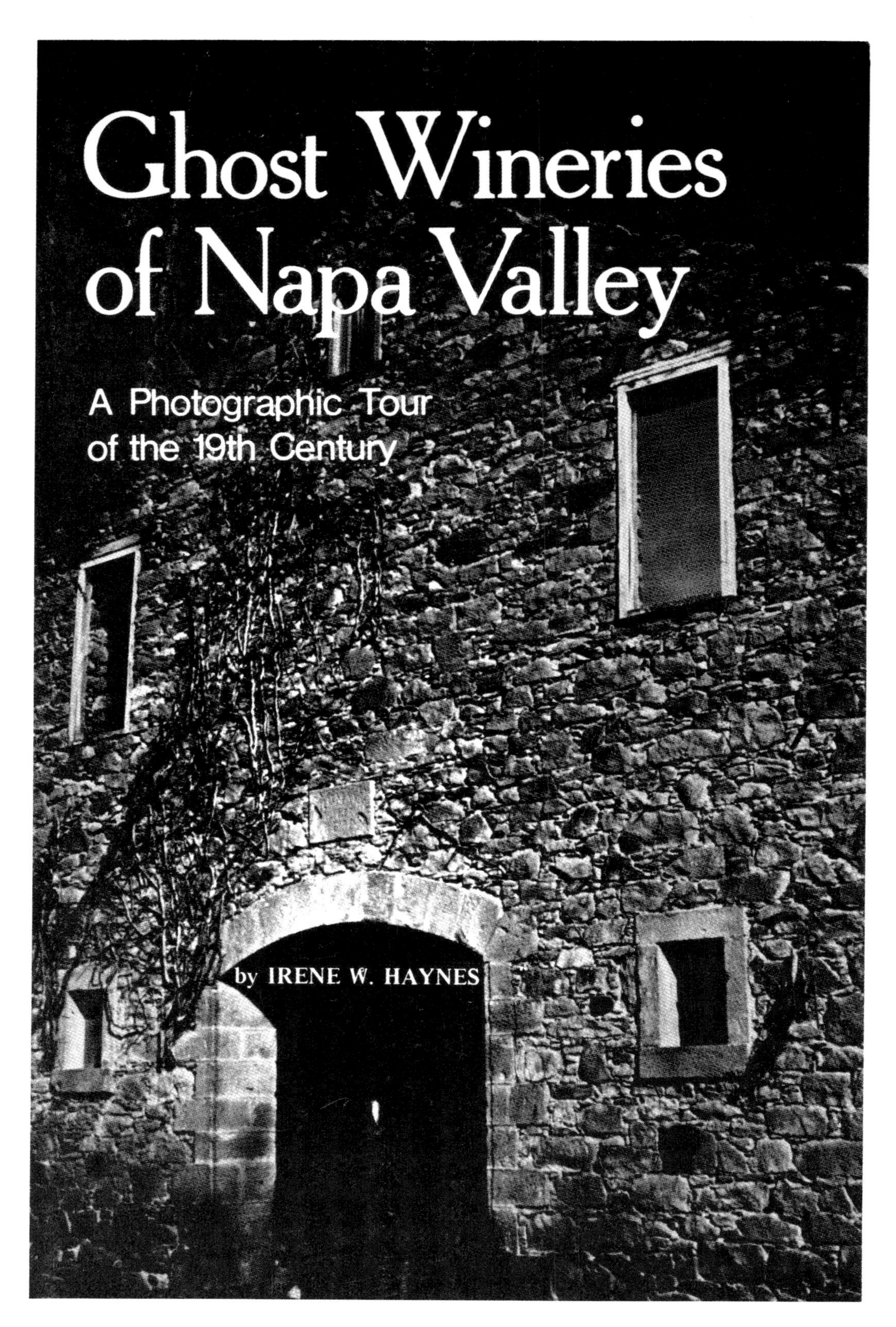

Ghost Wineries of Napa Valley
A Photographic Tour of the 19th Century
by IRENE W. HAYNES


*Cover photograph above, and article on next page, are from* Ghost Wineries of Napa Valley, *by Irene W. Haynes.*

*Howell Mountain*

**St. Helena Star** **October 15, 1886**

Brun and Chaix . . . completed the erection of one of the most convenient and commodious wine cellars in the County with storage up to 150,000 gallons.

**46**

On winding White Cottage Road, which extends north from where Deer Park Road ends, keep a sharp lookout to your left to find the Howell Mountain Winery, a three-story stone cellar nestled behind a knoll. It was built before 1877 by French emigres Jean Adolphe Brun and Jean Chaix, who named it the Howell Mountain Winery, but they soon moved to another cellar on the valley floor at Oakville, which they named Nouveau Medoc Vineyard and where, incidentally, the best Inglenook wines are now produced. Later owners closed the Howell Mountain Winery during Prohibition, but bulk wine was made there sporadically until 1946.

50

EDITOR'S NOTE: See Line 3 above: The name Howell Mountain Winery was used in a familiar way, but Messrs. Brun and Chaix formally named it Nouveau Medoc Vineyard and Wine Cellars. (See the lithograph that immediately follows the introduction to this book.)

The sentence that begins on Line 4 is not correct. The Brun & Chaix Winery on Howell Mountain was built in 1886, not 1877. Brun & Chaix started their Oakville Winery in 1877, nine years before they built their Nouveau Medoc Wine Cellars on Howell Mountain.

*It was traditional among stone masons in the late 1800s to fit a date stone above the keystone of a hand-layed stone building. This 1886 date stone is above the entrance on ground floor level of the Brun & Chaix winery on Howell Mountain. Photograph by William Garnett, 1988.*

*Master label for Nouveau Medoc Vineyard. The specific name of each wine was added to the label at bottling time. The label notes the incorporation of the company which took place in 1900.*

# Nouveau Medoc Vineyard and Wine Cellars

BRUN & CHAIX Proprietors

The following group of newspaper articles, mostly from the *St. Helena Star* and the *Napa Register*, chronicle the activities of the Brun & Chaix partnership, and the growth of their Nouveau Medoc Vineyard and Wine Cellars.

*St. Helena Star*, November 30, 1877

# WINE MAKING

### THE SEASON OF 1877.

[CONTINUED.]

Passing below the immediate vicinity of St. Helena, we come to Oakville and find first in importance the beautiful place and convenient cellars of

H. W. CRABB.

Mr. Crabb is not an old manufacturer, but one of the most observing and inteligent of the class who have made the chemistry of wine in all its subtle transformations a study, and applied to its elucidation the crucible of an active and highly cultured mind. His cellar is a wooden one, with sawdust-filled walls (which he prefers to cement, and holds as this year's product 45,000 gallons of very fine wine. Last year's record was 40,000. He has added this year to his cellar a room holding 12,000 gallons, and built a distillery with a 800-gallon kettle. This is run by steam, as making a better article of spirits and being safer from fire than a direct application of that element. Right at Oakville are two small cellars, the one started last year by

JEAN MONOD.

Jean used to be at Benson's place, a mile below, but sold out early last year and located at town. He made 9,000 gallons, against 10,000 last year. He seems a successful manufacturer. The second cellar at Oakville has been started this year and is the enterprise of Messrs.

BRUN & CHAIX.

They make 10,000 gallons this year, and will doubtless loom up into greater prominence as the years go by.

JOHN BENSON.

Below Oakville about a mile a handsome place with a gilt sign "Far Niente" greets the traveler and is made chiefly conspicuous by a magnificent barn that has been built now a couple of years or more. It is the country home of John Benson, a San Francisco capitalist, who has here a large vineyard and made last year, besides 15,000 gallons of wine, a large quantity of choice raisins. This year he had the misfortune to be stricken by frost—a rare case in this section—and lost his crop so utterly that he made only 500 gallons of wine.

G. GROEZINGER.

A name that will be a familiar one to the Pacific coast is that of G. Grœzinger, of Yountville, whose magnificent establishment and princely enterprise it has been the pleasure of this paper more than once before to write up. Mr. G. we found absent, but were cordially received by his able representative, Mr. L. A. Moore, who combines with multifarious other duties a general supervision of Mr. G.'s affairs during his absence. He showed us around the great cellar and informed us that the amount of wine manufactured this year was only 100,000 gallons, an amount much smaller than heretofore but of improved quality. Its excellence we can personally vouch for.

PAMPEL & GRIGSBY.

At the base of the hills on the west side of the valley, some three miles above and west of Yountville, is a noble cellar and vineyard started by the enterprise of two men—G. S. Burrage and N. W. Tucker—who attained for it in a few years a prominent position among the wine manufacturing industries of the county. The two projectors, by a strange fatality, died within about a year of each other, and their enterprise was left to others' hands. Last year the cellar was idle, its grapes being sent to Van Bever, at Napa. This year, however, it is in the lists again, being taken in hand by two energetic and able managers, Messrs. G. Pampel and Terrill L Grigsby. The former is a young Roumanian who has been making wine in this county four or five years, last year being engaged for J. M. Mansfield, in Brown's Valley. Mr. Grigsby is the well known and public spirited vintner who has made such laudable efforts in behalf of the industry in this county and is this year building a splendid cut stone cellar at his place 3½ miles below the "Burrage & Tucker." The cellar makes this year under these gentlemen 120,000 gallons, and it is already all sold, to B. Dreyfus & Co., New York and San Francisco. They contemplate purchasing this cellar as well as manufacturing largely at Mr. Grigsby's new one.

EDITOR'S NOTE: The first Brun & Chaix Nouveau Medoc Winery was built in 1877, in Oakville. It was the 13th registered commercial winery in California. The first account of this winery was published in the November 30, 1877 issue of the *St. Helena Star*. It is also interesting to note that the *St. Helena Star* was founded in 1874, the year that Jean Brun arrived in the Napa Valley.

St. Helena Star
Published in the heart of the Napa Valley since 1874


*St. Helena Star*
November 30, 1877

Wine Making
The Season of 1877

Right at Oakville are two small cellars. The second cellar at Oakville has been started this year, and is the enterprise of Messrs. Brun and Chaix.

Brun & Chaix

They made 10,000 gallons this year, and will doubtless loom up into greater prominence as the years go by.

EDITOR'S NOTE: For the next three years Jean Brun acquired additional property to expand the original Brun & Chaix cellar. During this early period the two partners made their wine only from purchased grapes.

Editor's Note: The first years of development were paying off. More property was acquired to expand. The small cellar at Oakville was enlarged to 160 x 34 feet. Another building was built nearby, which was 40 x 45 feet.

*St. Helena Star*
January 30, 1880

Napa Valley - Brun Winery
"News of Rutherford"

Mr. Brun of Oakville has purchased of Mrs. Rohlwing an acre of land adjoining the railroad, where, at some future date, he will erect a wine cellar.

Note: Photocopy of original article not available.

*St. Helena Star*
August 13, 1880

BRUN & CHAIX' new cellar, at Oakville, is about completed, and makes, with the old cellar, a capacity of 100,000 gallons—an amount of wine the firm expects to make this fall. We understand that Mr. Brun has bought of Mr Bateman the corner lot at Oakville occupied by the saloon and dwelling, and comprising an acre of ground.

*St. Helena Star*
August 13, 1880

Brun & Chaix' new cellar at Oakville is about completed and makes, with the old cellar, a capacity of 100,000 gallons—an amount of wine the firm expects to make this fall. We understand that Mr. Brun has bought from Mr. Bateman the corner lot in Oakville occupied by the saloon and dwelling, and comprising an acre of ground.

EDITOR'S NOTE: The *St. Helena Star* on October 22, 1880, reported on Brun & Chaix, Oakville, as follows: (Photocopy of original article not available.)

*St. Helena Star*
October 22, 1880

Brun & Chaix Winery has made 100,000 gallons of wine. They have three crushers, a private railroad, a handsome cellar, and are lively men.

Editor's Note: *The San Francisco Chronicle* listed the marriage of Jean Brun to Emma Mermoud of San Francisco on October 23, 1880.

Before her marriage to Jean Brun, Emma Mermoud attended The Young Ladies School, Mills Seminary, Benicia, California. Record of scholarship from the Seminary indicates she was a student in 1872 and 1873. This school became Mills College in 1892, and eventually moved to Oakland. Over the years, Mills has grown to be one of the pre-eminent colleges in California.

*St. Helena Star*
November 26, 1880

**More Vineyard Enterprise.—**
That enterprising winemaking firm, Messrs. Brun & Chaix, at Oakville have just added grape raising to their business, having bought of Mr. W. C. Watson a quarter section of land on Howell Mountain for that purpose. They have already bought lumber for a building on it, and will set out a vineyard next Spring. They made this year at their neat establishment at Oakville 110 to 115,000 gallons of wine, using about 730 tons of grapes. Howell Mountain is becoming a favorite locality with grape growers, and we expect ultimately to see its whole top covered with vineyard. Messrs. Brun & Chaix' location is on Watson's new road across the Mountain, about a mile and a half [illegible]

EDITOR'S NOTE: Brun & Chaix announce that they have bought land on Howell Mountain on which they will start their own vineyard.

*St. Helena Star*
November 26, 1880

More Vineyard Enterprise—

That enterprising winemaking firm, Messrs. Brun and Chaix at Oakville have just added grape raising to their business, having bought of Mr. W.C. Watson a quarter section of land on Howell Mountain for that purpose. They have already bought lumber for a building on it, and will set out a vineyard next spring. They made this year at their neat establishment at Oakville 110 to 115,000 gallons of wine, using about 730 tons of grapes. Howell Mountain is becoming a favorite locality with grape growers, and we expect ultimately to see its whole top covered with vineyard. Messrs. Brun and Chaix' location is on Watson's new road across the mountain about a mile and a half...

(Remainder of article missing)

## Down the Valley.

A ride of a few miles down the Valley after a short absence brings many new sights and ideas. The roads are dusty when you get off the sprinkled street of St. Helena, and are much worn with the immense amount of teaming constantly going on over them. Near Pine Station, C. J.

FIELD'S NEW BARN

Looms up in place of the one lately burned, and the tall seared tree between that and the dwelling shows the mark of the fire.

At Cole's place, next to Griffith's, we find workmen cutting down the row of tall and beautiful poplars that for years have formed an avenue to the house and landmark in the valley.

AT RUTHERFORD

Henry Hortop is busy as usual and his shop full of work. Frye & Nottage are "on deck," attending to the mercantile wants of the community, and doing it so well as to save all in that section the trouble of going elsewhere for goods. Mr. Nottage informed us that

AN INDIAN SKELETON

Had just been found in excavating for the foundations of a barn on Mr. Niebaum's place. It appeared to be that of a female and had around it an immense quantity of beads, as though the woman of that remote period had been not less solicitous of comely appearance than her sisters of to-day. It was fifteen feet below the present surface of the ground, indicating that a land-slide (it is at the base of the foot-hills) had at some period covered it far below its original depth. Below Rutherford,

KREKELER'S NEW DWELLING

Is a conspicuous object and looks very pretty. It is of a novel style of architecture, having a roof that projects all around far enough to form an awning.

AT OAKVILLE

A. Jeanmonod was busy getting out grape stakes. He thinks he shall make no wine this year, on account of the high price of grapes. He met with an accident lately, being capsized with a load of hay and getting his right shoulder dislocated, and is still lame from its effects. He is now building himself a new dwelling, 28x30 feet. He showed us some Mission wine 6 years old which had formed

A NATURAL SHERRY.

It was from hill grapes that had attained 35 per cent. of sugar, a degree that will be appreciated by remembering that 24 is sweet enough for wine-making, and a fact which Mr. J. informs us accounts for the change into sherry.

BRUN & CHAIX

Were busy with their new tank-house, which is being made by J. W. McMillan, of this place. This is a tall and sightly edifice, handsomely built, and will form when completed a prominent feature of the valley. The building itself is 50 feet high, and on this will be the wind-mill—a first-class Napa mill, with 12-foot wheel—towering up 12 to 15 feet higher. The tank is a 10,-000-gallon one, and a railing will be placed around the top of the tank-house to form an observatory. The well is a bored one, 46 feet deep, and has 32 feet of water. Besides the many improvements made at Oakville by this enterprising firm, they have been doing an extensive work on Howell Mountain during the last year. They have cleared and planted 20 acres to vines and have 15 men at work clearing more land, so that they will be able and expect to put out 50 to 60 acres more vineyard next Spring. When these bear they will build a cellar at the vineyard and make the grapes up into wine on the spot. Altogether the progress and improvement made by this firm is remarkable. Starting in only four years ago, on bare ground, they have built up an equipment for making and handling wine that is equaled by few in the valley, and contributed a large share to the general prosperity.

## Pine Station Letter.

Ed. Star:—We still continue to grow a little in the way of improvements. Messrs. Weinberger and Wheeler have put up a tank house 16x16, 28 ft. high, with a tank of 2-000 gallons capacity at their cellar. They also have an engine in connection with the distillery and water works, doing the work for both. The machinery is already on the ground for the distillery, and their cellar and tank house have received a coat of paint. The lower floor of the tank house will be used for a dining room and the upper for a sleeping apartment, the top being tinned to prevent leakage. Work has already been commenced by the above firm steaming tanks, refilling the cellar with tanks and casks fo the coming season's wine making. The warm weather is ripening th grapes very fast and the light colore varieties are getting sweet.

Editor's Note: 1881 was a banner year for Brun & Chaix. Jean Brun's energies and acumen as a visionary businessman were paying off. He imported cuttings of nine different varieties of wine grapes from the Medoc region of France. Twenty acres of the Howell Mountain vineyard were in Medoc grapes. He named his Napa Valley wines "Nouveau Medoc."

*St. Helena Star*
August 5, 1881

Brun & Chaix were busy with their new tankhouse, which is being made by J.W. McMillan, of this place. This is a tall and sightly edifice handsomely built, and will form, when completed, a prominent feature of the valley. The building itself is 50 feet high, and on this will be the windmill—a first class Napa mill, with 12-foot wheel—towering up 12 to 15 feet higher. The tank is a ten thousand gallon one, and a railing will be placed around the top of the tankhouse to form an observatory. The well is a bored one, 46 feet deep, and has 32 feet of water. Besides the many improvements made at Oakville by this enterprising firm, they have been doing extensive work on Howell Mountain during the last year. They have cleared and planted 20 acres to vines and have 15 men at work clearing more land, so that they will be able, and expect, to put out 50 to 60 acres more vineyard next spring. When these bear they will build a cellar at the vineyard and make the grapes up into wine on the spot. Altogether the progress and improvement made by this firm is remarkable. Starting only four years ago on bare ground they have built up an equipment for making and handling wine that is equaled by few in the valley, and contributed a large share to the general prosperity.

*St. Helena Star*
August 12, 1881

A SIGNAL STATION.—We have previously mentioned the tall tank-house of A. Brun & Co., at Oakville, six miles below here. It is now finished, and its top railed around so as to form a lofty and safe observatory. From its roof, over 50 feet above the ground, a grand and beautiful view is had of the Valley from near St. Helena to Yountville, and of the mountain sides from points far beyond. But the principal point of the item is that their mountain vineyard, about 10 miles to the north, on Howell Mountain, is within the range of vision, and the firm propose to establish a system of signals which will be seen by the aid of telescopes, to communicate whatever is desirable from cellar to vineyard and the reverse. This will be equal to a telegraph while daylight lasts, and no doubt a system of flashing lights might carry out the project in the night as well.

EDITOR'S NOTE: This article appeared on the front page of the *St. Helena Star,* August 12, 1881. It was a follow-up on the August 5, 1881 article that appeared in the *Star,* and gives more information on the new landmark tankhouse, built by Jean Brun on his Oakville property.

*St. Helena Star*
August 12, 1881

A Signal Station—We have previously mentioned the tall tankhouse of A. Brun & Co., at Oakville, six miles below here. It is now finished, and its top railed around so as to form a lofty and safe observatory. From its roof, over 50 feet above the ground, a grand and beautiful view is had of the Valley from near St. Helena to Yountville, and of the mountain sides from points far beyond. But the principal point of the item is that their mountain vineyard, about 10 miles to the north, on Howell Mountain, is within the range of vision, and the firm purpose to establish a system of signals which will be seen by the aid of telescopes, to communicate whatever is desirable from cellar to vineyard and the reverse. This will be equal to telegraph while daylight lasts, and no doubt a system of flashing lights might carry out the project in the night as well.

Editor's Note: On the same date, August 12, 1881, another short article in the *St. Helena Star* stated: The junior partner of Brun & Chaix, Oakville, Jean Chaix, will open a branch establishment in Sacramento. The growth of this establishment is among the most rapid in the county, and indicates great ability. Commencing in 1877 with only a small cellar that looked no more pretentious than an ordinary toolhouse, it has grown until it now ranks with the largest in the county.

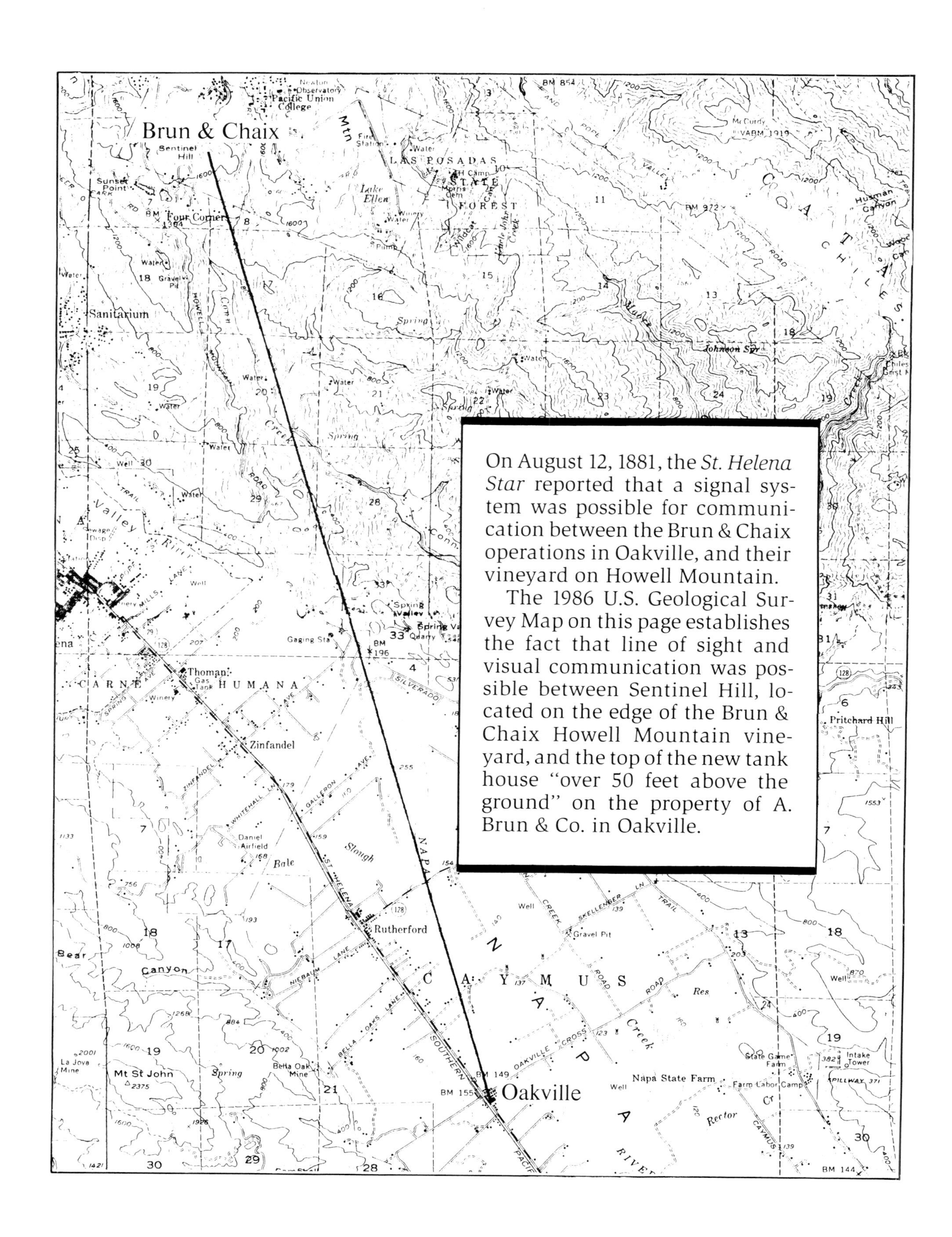


On August 12, 1881, the *St. Helena Star* reported that a signal system was possible for communication between the Brun & Chaix operations in Oakville, and their vineyard on Howell Mountain.

The 1986 U.S. Geological Survey Map on this page establishes the fact that line of sight and visual communication was possible between Sentinel Hill, located on the edge of the Brun & Chaix Howell Mountain vineyard, and the top of the new tank house "over 50 feet above the ground" on the property of A. Brun & Co. in Oakville.

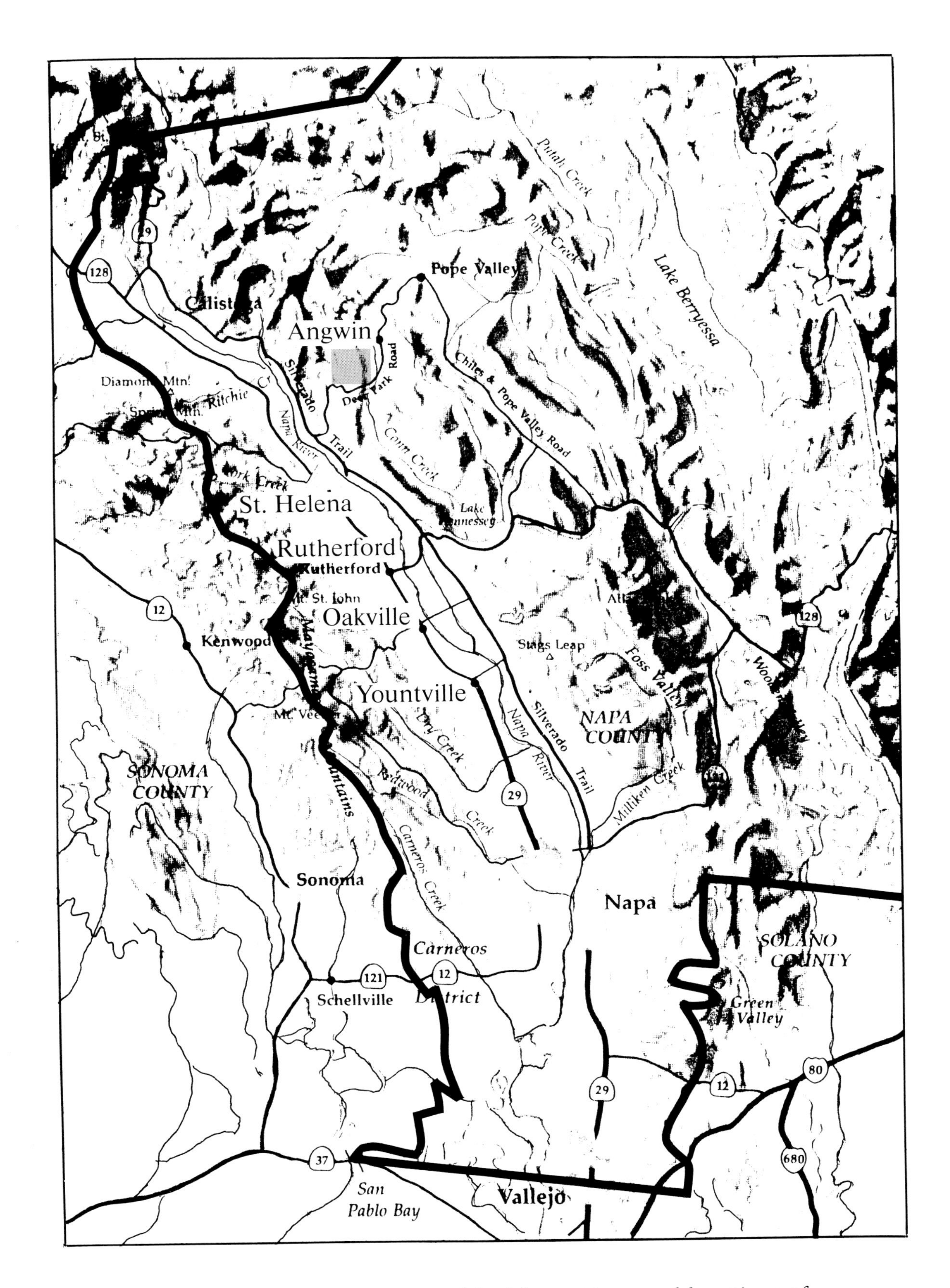


*This Napa Valley map shows topographical formations and locations of major towns in the valley. The Brun & Chaix Howell Mountain property is the shaded area near Angwin.*

*St. Helena Star*, September 16, 1881

## AT THE WINE CELLARS.

### What the Wine Makers are Doing.

A visit to the wineries at this season discloses activity in every department. Bustle and commotion prevail everywhere. The noise of the cooper repairing the immense casks and tanks, banging of boxes and rattling of machinery greet the ear, while the eye is pleased with the busy scene of innumerable laborers hurrying to dispose every article into its place preparatory to working the vintage.

In the vineyards the pickers are gathering the ripened bunches, and on the roadway to the cellars one meets wagons heavily laden bearing the grapes to the crusher.

The first cellar our reporter visited was G. Groezinger's mammoth establishment at Yountville. After a cordial greeting from the gentlemanly proprietor, the reporter was placed in charge of the gentlemanly foreman, who led the way into the cool cellar where lines of oaken casks, on either side of the passage ways, impress one with the immensity of the product of the cellar. With courteous affability he pointed out each improvement or noteworthy feature in the arrangements for wine making. Among the new improvements is the gas generator, by means of which the whole establishment is lighted with gas. A new steam engine of 24 horse power, erected by Heald, will furnish the power to work the crushers and elevators, to which motion is communicated from a shafting over two hundred feet long. A Heald crusher, with a capacity of 80 tons a day, has been added to the establishment. The grapes will be elevated in boxes to the crusher on a slide, by means of an endless belt provided with cleats which catches against the box and hurries it along to the attendant, who empties it into the crusher. As yet the work of wine making at this cellar has not fairly begun, and it is not the intention of the proprietor to manufacture, by many thousand gallons, as much as he did last year.

Journeying along to the vicinity of St. Helena, the first cellar visited was that of Berringer Bros., a short distance north of town. The cellar sits on the side hill west of the road. The buildings are of stone, extensive, ornamental and substantial. The distillery building is finished in Medieval style with towers and bastions. One of the features of this establishment is its underground cellars. Excavations are made in the side hill to a depth of 100 feet, of sufficient capacity for two rows of large casks. Two side chambers are being excavated opening into the main chamber.

Crushing was in active progress, a Heald crusher being used. We learned from the proprietor that the product of this cellar will not exceed 75,000 gallons this year, against 175,000 last year. This falling off is attributed to the high prices at which grapes are held by the growers. Wine makers generally regard the prices asked excessive, and at every cellar visited there is a disposition to manufacture less wine by nearly a half, than was made last year.

At G. Laurent's cellar, two hand crushers were in operation. The quantity of wine made here this year will not exceed 35,000 gallons. The product last year was 55,000 gallons, principally clarets. Mr. Laurent states that the prices asked for grapes render wine making this year a risky industry

At J. C. Weinberger's everything was in readiness to crush. At this cellar none but foreign varieties of grapes are worked. Last year 70,000 gallons were made; this year 45,000 gallons will exceed the intentions of the proprietor.

At Krug's everything was in active operation. This winery is the most extensive in this district, its buildings are tastefully ornamented and provided with all the modern appliances for pursuing the industry. Its enterprising proprietor is keenly on the alert, and no invention or idea is advanced that can improve the quality of grapes or wines, that escapes his observation. A large steam boiler and engine is in position, but through a delay in the machinery, hand crushers were being used. This week, however, two large Heald crushers will be in operation. Krug's vineyard produced last year about 635 tons, which with 1,200 tons purchased from other vinyardists, were crushed. This season the yield of the vineyard will amount to about 600 tons, and about 800 tons will be purchased, which will decrease the wine product many thousand gallons. Thirty men are employed at this cellar.

At Scheffler's, although arrangements were made to manufacture about 300,000 gallons, not more than 250,000 gallons will be made.

Gils Bros. will not make more than 30,000 gallons, which is about half the quantity made last year.

There will also be a proportionate falling off in the quantity of brandy manufactured at all the distilleries of this district.

At John Thomann's cellar about 100,000 gallons of brandy and 40,000 gallons of wine were made last year. Mr. Thomann states that he will not manufacture more than 80,000 gallons this year which will be principally brandy.

Wheeler & Weinburg, above Rutherford, will make about 75,000 gallons of wine, the full capacity of their cellar.

At Oakville Brun & Co. will not manufacture more than one-half the quantity made last year. This firm have leased a cellar at Routier Station, Sacramento county, where the same varieties of grapes are purchased, five to ten dollars a ton less than in this valley. Brun & Co. will work the grape crop of several vineyards in the vicinity of Dry Creek and Oakville.

At Crabb's the product will also fall short of last year. There are many vineyards, the crops of which await purchasers. Wine makers are slow to pay the price demanded. The yield throughout the valley will be somewhat smaller than last year, but as a rule of better quality. The north wind of Sunday and Monday of last week did considerable damage to Riesling varieties on shallow soil, withering them before they ripened. The hot weather of the balance of the week caused the grapes to ripen rapidly, and at many of the cellars the arrangements for crushing and fermenting were far from complete. The high prices asked for grapes has caused wine makers to buy sparingly, as the condition of the wine market scarcely justifies the risk. The prices asked in the vicinity of St. Helena are $30 for foreign varieties and $25 for Mission.

Wine men predict a decline in prices from 20 to 25 per cent. before the close of the week

Editor's Note: The September 16, 1881, issue of the *St. Helena Star* carried a column called "Napa Reporter." It included the following information related to Brun & Chaix.

*St. Helena Star*
September 16, 1881

A visit to the wineries this season discloses activity in every department.

At Oakville, Brun & Chaix will not manufacture more than one-half the quantity made last year. This firm has leased a cellar at Reutier Station, Sacramento County, where the same varieties of grapes are purchased, five to ten dollars a ton less than in this valley. Brun & Chaix will work the grape crop of several vineyards in the vicinity of Dry Creek and Oakville.

There are many vineyards, the crops of which await purchasers. Winemakers are slow to pay the price demanded. The yield throughout the valley will be somewhat smaller than last year, but as a rule better quality.

The high prices asked for grapes have caused winemakers to buy sparingly, as the condition of the wine market scarcely justifies the risk. The prices asked in this vicinity of St. Helena are $30 for foreign varieties and $35 for Mission.

Wine men predict a decline in prices from 20 to 25 percent before the close of the week.

*St. Helena Star*
June 9, 1882

## HOWELL MOUNTAIN.

### The Mountain to California What Medoc is to France.

So much interest is justly felt in the value of Howell Mountain for vineyards—and especially with reference to frost—that the following observations, though now a little late, are still of interest. They are by Mr. C. Ross, a gentleman who has been investigating it with just the object in view that interests our peo-people; namely, its adaptability to vines and liability to frost. Relating the result of a visit to the different vineyards on the mountain immediately after the frosts of May 12th and 13th, he says:

"My first visit was to the vineyards of Messrs. Brun and Chaix, containing as you are aware about 60 acres, part of which was planted last year and the remainder this year; the greater portion of the latter being rooted vines. To my delight I found that the frost had not affected any of the young vines and cuttings except in that particular location lying due east from Mr. Chaix's house forming a small, hollow canyon hedged in on both sides by gradually ascending slopes, and here I ascertained that a few Zinfindels had been lightly touched. Early in the morning of the 13th, the thermometer indicated a temperature of 31 degrees at this point but on the elevated portions of the vineyard the indications were from one to two degrees higher, and the vines in no single instance showed any signs of having been injured, but looked vigorous and strong. This condition of affairs after such a severe test, is not only pleasing to those who ventured to transform Howell Mountain from being one forest of trees to a number of happy homes, but to you in particular, as your theory all along, and your advice to your neighbors has invariably been that, if vines were planted in open and exposed situations, and all hollow places and canyons avoided, there would be no question as to the ultimate success of the project. Science has done considerable to obviate the difficulties of raising grapes and towards lessening the damage caused by late frosts, but it is only by a close study of the matter and a careful selection of location and its exposures that its ravages can entirely be thwarted. For instance on Turner's ranch, adjoining that of Messrs. Brun and Chaix, this principle has recently been clearly demonstrated by our late experience of Jack Frost. On a sunny slope facing due east, different varieties of young vines were materially affected and on a slope facing the west

Editor's Note: In 1882 the public became conscious of the importance of Howell Mountain as a vineyard resource. Mr. C. Ross investigated the adaptability of vines and stated his opinion related to the problems of frost in the elevated vineyards.

*St. Helena Star*
June 9, 1882

## Howell Mountain
## The Mountain To California What Medoc Is To France

So much interest is justly felt in the value of Howell Mountain for vineyards— and especially with reference to frost that the following observations, though now a little late, are still of interest. They are by Mr. C. Ross, a gentleman who has been investigating it with just the object in view that interests our people; namely, its adaptability to vines and liability to frost. Relating the result of a visit to the different vineyards on the mountain immediately after the frosts of May 12th and 13th, he says:

"My first visit was to the vineyards of Messrs. Brun and Chaix, containing as you are aware almost 60 acres, part of which was planted last year and the remainder this year; the greater portion of the latter being rooted vines. To my delight I found that the frost had not affected any of the young vines and cuttings except in that particular location lying due east from Mr. Chaix's house forming a small, hollow canyon hedged in on both sides by gradually ascending slopes, and here I ascertained that a few Zinfandels had been lightly touched. Early in the morning of the 13th, the thermometer indicated a temperature of 31 degrees at this point but on the elevated portions of the vineyard the indications were from one to two degrees higher, and the vines in no single instance showed any signs of having been injured, but looked vigorous and strong. This condition of affairs after such a severe test, is not only pleasing to those who ventured to transform Howell Mountain from being one forest of trees to a number of happy homes, but to you in particular, as your theory all along, and your advice to your neighbors has invariably been that, if vines were planted in open and exposed situations, and all hollow places and canyons avoided, there would be no question as to the ultimate success of the project. Science has done considerable to obviate the difficulties of raising grapes and towards lessening the damage caused by late frosts, but it is only by a close study of the matter and a careful selection of location and its exposures that its ravages can entirely be thwarted."

have been seen about St. Helena for some years were grown on this place, and exhibited a year or two ago at the STAR office. His place is also especially adapted to small fruits and vegetables. It is never troubled with frost, and tomato vines with green fruit can be seen at the present time. Traveling North from Woodworth's we pass through the place of

THOS. WORKOVER,

Who divides his farming operations between growing hay, vines and small fruits. He has several very fine springs with which to irrigate, and supply a small fish pond stocked with German Carp. Farther North, and down the new grade to Pope Valley, is the ranch of

A. J. AUSTIN,

Containing 200 acres, 10 of which were planted to grapes several years ago, which as yet have never been nipped by frost. Fruits of all kinds are a success here, especially the Fig and Apricot. Traveling South, we pass the school-house, located about midway across the mountain plateau, and find ourselves at the home of

JAMES CHILES,

Who owns a tract of 280 acres purchased of D. O. Hunt about 2 years ago. He is making considerable improvement, and expects to plant 5 acres to vines in the Spring.

MR. SUTTON,

A resident of San Francisco, joins Chiles on the East, has several men clearing land and will probably get out 20 acres to vines.

A. P. RUTAN,

With 54 acres, comes next. He has about 12 acres rich garden land cleared, which he will plant to fruits and vegetables. He will plant no grapes this season.

ISAAC SELLERS,

On the North of Chiles, has 160 acres, 85 cleared, 10 of which he will plant to vines this season.

THE JOHNSON BROS.,

Adjoining Chiles on the South, have 100 acres, about 100 of which can be planted to grapes at very little expense for clearing. Thirty of this is seeded to wheat this season.

MARCUS JOHNSON,

Still farther South, has 160 acres. He has a fruit orchard, 5 acres in grapes, and 50 acres of open land finely situated for vineyard and very easily cleared. He will not plant grapes this season.

BRUN & CHAIX.

East of Johnson is the place of Brun & Chaix, containing 191 acres. In 1880, they cleared and planted 20 acres to vines. Last year they planted 40 acres. And so well are they pleased with the results that they will continue their operations and get out 20 acres or more this season. They also have 20 acres in grain, which will be cut and used for hay. They have substantial improvements, good fences, a neat dwelling, and barn. As soon as a sufficient quantity of grapes are raised on the mountain, it is their intention to build a wine cellar and commence the manufacture of wine. They have no fears of frost, as the cold wave of last Spring was the most trying ordeal they ever expect to encounter. And it damaged them but little; only about 2 acres were touched in the lowest ground, which might have been easily prevented by smoking.

B. M. ROKAB

Has purchased 112 acres, adjoining Brun & Chaix on the North, and is aiming to put out 20 acres in vines this season. Adjoining Brun & Chaix on the South is the home of

SAM'L. R. TURNER,

Who has a place of 160 acres. He is an old resident on the mountain, has substantial improvements, with stone walls for fences that will neither decay nor burn. He has a fine little orchard of all kinds of fruits in successful bearing. He has also about 5 acres planted to grapes, and will add more as he is able.

HENRY T. WEGLAND,

Who lives South of Turner, has 150 acres He planted 5 acres to grapes last season, and will plant 5 more this season. Mr. Wegland is an old resident of the mountain; but has been absent about 6 years. He returned about a year ago, however, with a partner to share with him the trials and joys of this life at his mountain home. He has built himself a neat story-and a half dwelling, and has now completed a new barn.

Your correspondent has a comfortable home of 210 acres, lying just west of Marcus Johnson, which he is too modest to say much about. However, he would say that he has 16 acres sowed for hay, has a young orchard of all kinds of fruits which are just coming into bearing; and the results are so promising that he proposes to increase his acres to fruit as fast as he is able, thinking it more profitable than grape growing. As my letter is already too long, I defer my trip to Pope Valley for next week.

THAVELER.

Editor's Note: Another progress report on the development of the Brun & Chaix Howell Mountain property.

*St. Helena Star*
December 22, 1882

East of Johnson is the place of Brun & Chaix, containing 191 acres. In 1880, they cleared and planted 20 acres to vines. Last year they planted 40 acres. So well are they pleased with the results that they will continue their operations and get out 30 acres or more this season. They also have 20 acres in grain, which will be cut and used for hay. They have substantial improvements, good fences, a neat dwelling, and barn. As soon as a sufficient quantity of grapes is raised on the mountain, it is their intention to build a wine cellar and commence the manufacture of wine. They have no fears of frost, as the cold wave of last spring was the most trying ordeal they ever expect to encounter. It damaged them but little, only about 2 acres were touched in the lowest ground, which might have been easily prevented by smoking.

*St. Helena Star*, December 25, 1884

## THE VINTAGE OF 1884

### The "Star's" Annual Report

**[illegible] Gallons, from 97 Wine Cellars of Napa County.**

(Exchanges copying or commenting on this article will please give due credit to the STAR.)

In accordance with its annual custom, the STAR has made a thorough canvass of the county for the wine report of 1884, and takes pleasure in presenting herewith a full and reliable statement of that great industry for the current year. It prides itself and it thinks justly upon this report, which has now been an annual feature of its work for many years and has given to this growing interest in Napa County a distinctiveness, reliability, and prominence which it has enjoyed in no other part of the State, for by no one else in all California is the work undertaken except by this journal, and the work, from its very magnitude, is necessarily confined to the county in which it is published. The enormous increase in the business will be observed rather from the additional cellars engaged in it than from the actual increase in the amount itself, for the latter may be the accident of a year, an abnormally large crop, or unusually favorable conditions of manufacture; but additional places of wine-making show an increased interest in the business and an increased amount of the capital invested therein. The number of cellars this year is an enormous increase over that of any previous one. Not all of them it is true make any considerable amount - many of them only a few hundreds of gallons each - but the fact that they have started in at all shows a commendable interest in the business, and promises well for its future. For the man who starts in to make up his own grapes, is not only learning to make wine - and good wine - but he is learning also what kind of grapes to raise for it; for when he has to face the market itself, he will be put to his mettle to provide for it the very best material possible, to make it rank with the product of other vintners. The number of cellars this year, 97, is a gain of over fifty per cent. over that of last year, which was 63. By a comparison of those making 5,000 gallons or over, we find the number to be 75 to 48, about the same percentage of increase. The number making 10,000 or over is 62 this year, to 37 last year. The number making 100,000 or over is 17 this year to 5 last year, and these 17 make 3,182,000 gallons of the whole. The total amount is more than double that of last year, but of this, it must be borne in mind, a very large portion has been made into brandy, so that nowhere near the amount represented is on the market for sale as wine.

The STAR returns thanks to the vintners of the county for their kindly reception, and many courtesies extended, and hopes to continue the report of their prosperity for many years to come. That prosperity, it may not be necessary to add, has been gained by an intelligent pursuit of the business, and by the making of the very best wine that comes upon the market, a quality that has earned for us just fame among all consumers, and secures for us each year the highest price of all native wines.

Following is a list of the wine makers of Napa County, with the amount of wine manufactured by each.

#### CALISTOGA.

| | GALLONS. |
|---|---|
| L. Kortum | 65,000 |
| H. Zoeller | 5,000 |
| Peter Conter | 1,000 |

#### BETWEEN CALISTOGA AND ST. HELENA.

| | |
|---|---|
| S. P. Connor | 40,000 |
| W. W. Lyman | 15,000 |
| J. Schram | 40,000 |
| E. M. York | 52,000 |
| A. C. Rampendahl | 500 |
| F. H. Rosenbaum (near St. Helena) | 13,000 |

#### ST. HELENA.

| | |
|---|---|
| Jas. Booker | 150 |
| Mrs. H. E. Weinberger | 80,000 |
| J. Laurent | 70,000 |
| Chas. Krug | 365,000 |
| Beringer Bros | 175,000 |
| Mrs. Chas. Lemme | 30,000 |
| F. West | 15,000 |
| W. H. Castner, Jr | *5,000 |
| G. Meredith | 8,600 |
| H. Rampendahl | 7,000 |
| Merriam Bros | 16,500 |
| A. Rossi | 40,000 |
| Frank Kraft | 18,000 |
| D. Martinelli | 250 |
| Louis Sander | 35,000 |
| A. Schweinitzer | 700 |
| B. Tossetti | 30,000 |
| H. Behnke | 200 |
| Tossetti & Guadzatti | 15,000 |
| G. Breitenbuecher | 1,400 |
| N. Degouy | 90,000 |
| Wm. Scheffler | 210,000 |
| H. Hasenmair | 400 |
| H. A. Pellet | 82,000 |
| Ward & Worrell | 60,000 |
| E. Heymann | 42,000 |
| Louis Boniet | 25,000 |
| A. Schranz | 105,000 |
| David Cole | 20,000 |
| F. Sciaroni | 115,000 |
| Henry Sunkler | 7,000 |
| G. C. Fountain | 35,000 |
| Mrs. Wm. Leuthold | 18,000 |

#### BELOW ST. HELENA.

| | |
|---|---|
| John Thomann (and 8,000 brandy) | 116,000 |
| A. L. Williams | 21,000 |
| T. H. Ink | 10,000 |
| M. Furstenfeld | 30,000 |
| John Norton | 21,000 |
| Wm. H. Jordan | 32,000 |
| Chas. Scheggia | 15,000 |
| R. M. Wheeler | 107,000 |
| G. A. Stamer | 130,000 |
| J. H. McCord | 100,000 |
| Vann Bros | 52,000 |
| W. P. Weeks | 72,000 |

#### RUTHERFORD.

| | |
|---|---|
| G. Niebaum | 120,000 |
| C. J. Beerstecher | 1,000 |
| C. P. Adamson | 90,000 |
| S. C. Hastings | 90,000 |
| C. E. Smith | 12,000 |
| H. W. Helms | 28,000 |

#### OAKVILLE.

| | |
|---|---|
| H. W. Crabb (2,400 tons grapes) | 400,000 |
| A. Brun & Co | 150,000 |
| A. Jeanmenod | 25,000 |
| I. Debanne | 72,000 |
| Emil Brenard | 8,000 |
| Geo. Meyer | 6,500 |

#### YOUNTVILLE.

| | |
|---|---|
| G. Groezinger | 300,000 |
| F. Salmina and P. Gambetta | 15,000 |
| F. E. Mielenz | 142,000 |
| Julius Maggetta | 1,000 |

#### NAPA AND VICINITY.

| | |
|---|---|
| H. Hogan | 95,000 |
| Dr. Pettingill | 3,500 |
| Mrs. Ellen E. Hale | 9,000 |
| A. Grossman | 7,500 |
| Marcucci & Salmina | 16,000 |
| C. Anduran & Co. (2400 tons grapes) | 400,000 |
| G. Migliavacca | 145,000 |
| W. Schmolz | 18,000 |
| John Knief | 5,000 |
| Chas. Dell | 6,000 |
| W. Streich | 1,000 |
| Wm. Reed | 3,000 |
| J. Sarts | 340 |
| John Brantle | 200 |
| Chas. Robinson | 10,000 |
| Simonton Cellar (Prof. Hossmann manager) | 20,000 |
| Peter Dado | 250 |
| John Hein | 5,000 |
| Henry Meyer | 3,000 |
| Peter Gartman | 3,000 |
| Furre Fournier | 2,500 |
| — Vorbes | 2,000 |
| F. Borreo | 1,000 |

#### CONN VALLEY.

| | |
|---|---|
| G. Crochet & Co. | 100,000 |
| L. Corthay | 12,000 |

#### CHILES VALLEY.

| | |
|---|---|
| M. Kaltenbach | 16,000 |

#### COLE VALLEY.

| | |
|---|---|
| G. Haug | 2,000 |
| Total, 97 cellars | 4,9[illegible] |

This compares with other years as follows

| | | |
|---|---|---|
| 1883, 68 cellars | 2,300,150 | gallons |
| 1882, 61 " | 2,643,800 | " |
| 1881, 54 " | 2,016,000 | " |
| 1880, 49 " | 2,910,760 | " |

EDITOR'S NOTE: In the 1884 *St. Helena Star* annual report on wine producers, Brun & Chaix was rated as the seventh largest of the 97 wine producers in Napa County, and the second largest in Oakville. This was achieved in seven short years. The *St. Helena Star,* on December 25, 1884, details the listings on the opposite page.

*St. Helena Star*
December 25, 1884

The Vintage Of 1884
The *Star's* Annual Report
1,997,690 Gallons, From 97 Wine
Cellars Of Napa County

In accordance with its annual custom, the *Star* has made a thorough canvas of the county for the wine report of 1884, and takes pleasure in presenting herewith a full and reliable statement of that great industry for the current year. It prides itself—and it thinks justly—upon this report, which has now been an annual feature of its work for many years and has given to this growing interest in Napa County a distinctiveness, reliability, and prominence which it has enjoyed in no other part of the state, for by no one else in all is the work undertaken except by this journal, and the work, from its very magnitude, is necessarily confined to the county in which it is published.

## OAKVILLE

| Winemaker | Gallons |
|---|---|
| H.W. Crabb (2,400 tons grapes) | 400,000 |
| A. Brun & Co. | 150,000 |
| A. Jeanmenod | 25,000 |
| I. Debanne | 72,000 |
| Emil Brenard | 8,000 |
| Geo. Meyer | 6,500 |

*Napa Register*
March 20, 1885

## FROM HOWELL MOUNTAIN.

Napa Reg. 3/20/85

### A Thriving Community—Increase of Vineyards—Improvements.

ED. REGISTER:—From what I can learn and see this season is about five weeks ahead of any season since 1875. Fruit trees are in bloom and grape vines are in leaf. W. J. Chaix, of the firm of Brun & Chaix, will add to their already 95-acre vineyard, 10 more acres. Mr. Chaix who is the pioneer grape grower on Howell Mountain, got about 15 tons of very fine grapes last year, which had the necessary amount of sugar for making good wine. Some of the wine made from Howell mountain grapes was on exhibition at San Francisco and was pronounced by experts to be of the finest quality. For vineyard work Mr. Chaix cannot be surpassed.

Mr. Banks, of Wells, Fargo & Co's Bank, of San Francisco, has a 50-acre vineyard which is very promising. The same gentleman has about 1,000 acres of land for sale. Those in quest of good vineyard land should not fail to see it before purchasing elsewhere.

A Captian De Lano is planting about 20 acres to grapes. W. A. C. Smith, our St. Helena banker, is adding about 25 acres to his already 60 acres. He has a very promising piece of property.

Captain Sutton, of San Francisco, has a 12-acre vineyard. Mr. Aiken, of Berkeley, will set set out three acres to vines and two acres to fruit trees the present season. J. W. Holihan and brother will add about 10 acres to their already 10 acres.

Mr. C. H. Cutler has 5 acres to vines and Capt. Dunbar has 10 acres. Edward S. Hast, of the California Bank has 12 acres in vines. Mr. Colin Ross, who was formerly associated with the San Francisco Savings Union has built himself a fine two story house from which he has as fine a view as can be got in Napa county or any county in the State, and is, with his family enjoying this unsurpassable climate. Mr. Ross, who has been suffering from a multiplication of ailments has, at last, found a place where he is free from pain and enjoys that best of blessings, good health. He has 30 acres in vines and will add 15 acres more. What he is doing is thorough. He has also charge of Mr. Arthur E. Donnell's vineyard, of the California Insurance Co., who has 25 acres in vines.

Next in order comes Charles Krug, the father of the Napa Valley wine trade. We owe more to him for our progress and prosperity in the vine and wine trade than to any other man.

Editor's Note: While Jean Brun's high capabilities in winemaking and business acumen developed Brun & Chaix into a first-rate wine-producing company, Jean Chaix was earning accolades as a grape grower. His crops were eminently successful.

*Napa Register*
March 20, 1885

From Howell Mountain
A Thriving Community - Increase
of Vineyards - Improvements

From what I can learn and see, this season is about five weeks ahead of any season since 1875. Fruit trees are in bloom and grape vines are in leaf. W.J. Chaix, of the firm of Brun & Chaix, will add to their already 95-acre vineyard, 10 more acres. Mr. Chaix who is the pioneer grape grower on Howell Mountain, got about 15 tons of very fine grapes last year, which had the necessary amount of sugar for making good wine. Some of the wine made from Howell Mountain grapes was on exhibition at San Francisco and was pronounced by experts to be of the finest quality. For vineyard work Mr. Chaix cannot be surpassed.

for their fine flavor and keeping qualities. As is well known, Mr. Angwin opened a resort here a few years ago, which has become very popular. Among the many improvements we notice are four large new cottages for guests and a fine new barn, 56x54 feet in size. His place is usually crowded from early spring until Autumn.

We next called on H. Holihan who with his brother, J. W., owns 200 acres, 78 of which they have cleared and planted to vines. J. W. Holihan, who was once in the naval service, has a neat residence in St. Helena where he resides part of his time. We next visited C. W. Banks' place. There being no one to show us around we went alone through the vineyard and found the vines in a healthy and thriving condition and most all in bearing.

We learn he has about 60 acres, all enclosed with a rabbit-proof fence. On the highest elevation he has planted an orchard of apple, pear, prune, peach and English walnut trees, all of which are unusually thrifty. From this point a

MAGNIFICENT VIEW

is had in every direction, extending to the hills of Contra Costa county. Capt. Sutton, adjoining Bank's place on the south, has 30 acres in vines, but few are in bearing as yet. The Captain's business is in San Francisco, but he comes up every Saturday night and returns Monday morning, the year round. His family is spending the summer at their residence near the school house.

They have a good school house here. The school is well attended and is presided over by Miss Katie Newman, said to be an excellent teacher.

W. Aiken resides with his mother adjoining Mr. Sutton's place on the south. He has five acres in vines and will soon commence the erection of a stone residence, and is now having lumber hauled for a new barn.

Mr. Roney, adjoining Mr. Aiken, has about 40 acres cleared and ready to be planted to vines.

W. A. C. Smith, our enterprising St. Helena Banker, has 360 acres adjoining on the west. Ninety-five of this is in vines. A portion of these, three years old, are well loaded with grapes. This is a most promising vineyard.

OTHER PLACES.

The Professor has a very promising young orchard, mostly prunes. One hundred acres were cropped to hay this season. This place promises to make one of the finest estates on the mountain.

Brown & Chaix's place comes next with 191 acres, 105 of which are in vines. Seventy-five acres are now in bearing and Mr. Chaix estimates this season's yield at 250 tons. We never visited a finer appearing vineyard of its age anywhere. They cut 65 acres grain for hay this year have about 5 acres of corn. They building a fine cellar, 60x60. walls are entirely of stone, wh they get from a quarry at the cr ing of Angwin creek. These gen men have also a cellar at Oakville charge of Mr. Brun. Mr. Chaix charge of the Howell Mountain pr erty.

Henry Wegland comes next 8 acres of vines and Samuel Tu with 6 acres. Both vineyards just coming into bearing. A re sentative of the St. Helena *Star* the number of acres planted to v on this mountain at 728. The wr regrets his inability to pay all a who dwell in this mountain distr but hopes to be able to do so at s future time.

We can truthfully say we pleased with our visit, and what saw, and think the prospects of dwellers of this district as promis as those of any part of the county.

JIM SMITH

St. Helena, August 3, 1886.

EDITOR'S NOTE: The Brun & Chaix stone wine cellar and vineyard on Howell Mountain was written up in the *Napa Register*, August 6, 1886.

*Napa Register*
August 6, 1886

Brown (Brun) & Chaix's place comes next with 191 acres, 105 of which are in vines. Seventy-five acres are now in bearing and Mr. Chaix estimates this season's yield at 250 tons. We never visited a finer appearing vineyard of its age anywhere. They cut 65 acres grain for hay this year and have about 5 acres of corn. They are building a fine cellar, 60 x 60. The walls are entirely of stone, which they get from a quarry at the crossing of Angwin creek. These gentlemen have also a cellar at Oakville, in charge of Mr. Brun. Mr. Chaix is in charge of the Howell Mountain property.

*Napa Register*
October 1, 1886

### Busy Times on Howell Mountain

Letters from Howell Mountain, appearing from time to time in these columns, have informed our readers of the great changes that have taken place there during the last five or six years and of the various and costly improvements made on every part of the mountain by property owners.

In many localities the dense growth of fir, pine and other trees, that from time immemorial have shaded this broad plateau have been cleared away and in their places now appear thriving vineyards. The transformation already made is wonderful and yet the work of clearing the forest for vineyard planting is hardly commenced.

All the vineyards planted have made vigorous growth and the older vines are bearing heavily. As in the valley, so on the mountain, grape picking is being prosecuted as rapidly as possible. "This is our harvest time, said one viticulturist, "and we are pushing things." Many of the mountain grapes are hauled to the cellars near St. Helena, but the product of several vineyards has been purchased by

MESSRS. BHUN & CHAIX,

who, at their mountain cellar, now building, will crush these purchased grapes, besides those from their own large vineyard. This cellar is of stone, the front neatly finished, presenting a very attractive appearance. It is situated on the western slope of the mountain, at one side of the 100-acre vineyard belonging to this firm. The building will have three floors: The upper one is to be used for crushing, the second for the fermenting room and the lower one for storage, the capacity of the cellar being 120,000 or 125,000 gallons. One hundred thousand cubic feet of earth was removed from the hillside to make place for the lower story. Eighty acres of vines in the adjacent vineyard are in bearing. Some of the four-year-old vines will, it is estimated, yield four or five tons per acre. Some thirty different varieties of the choicest foreign vines have been planted, all of which are doing well. The vineyard shows that great care has been taken in its cultivation.

We are informed that Judge Hastings will, next year, build a fine stone cellar near his splendid vineyard, formerly the property of C. Krug, and not far from Angwin's summer resort. The vineyards of Jno. Thomann, Mr. Schranz and others promise large returns for labor and time expended.

EDITOR'S NOTE: The *Napa Register* on October 1, 1886, offered a general report on the "great changes" and improvements of the vineyards on Howell Mountain.

*Napa Register*
October 1, 1886

## Busy Times on Howell Mountain

Letters from Howell Mountain, appearing from time to time in these columns, informed our readers of the great changes that have taken place there during the last five or six years and of the various and costly improvements made on every part of the mountain by property owners.

In many localities the dense growth of fir, pine and other trees, that from time immemorial have shaded this broad plateau, have been cleared away and in their places now appear thriving vineyards. The transformation already made is wonderful and yet the work of clearing the forest for vineyard planting is hardly commenced.

All the vineyards planted have made vigorous growth and the older vines are bearing heavily. As in the valley, so on the mountain, grape picking is being prosecuted as rapidly as possible. "This is our harvest time," said one viticulturist, "and we are pushing things." Many of the mountain grapes are hauled to the cellars near St. Helena, but the product of several vineyards has been purchased by

**Messrs. Brun & Chaix,**

who at their mountain cellar, now building, will crush these purchased grapes, besides those from their own large vineyard. This cellar is of stone, the front nearly finished, presenting a very attractive appearance. It is situated on the western slope of the mountain, at one side of the 100-acre vineyard belonging to the firm. The building will have three floors: The upper one is to be used for crushing, the second for the fermenting room and the lower one for storage, the capacity of the cellar being 120,000 or 125,000 gallons. One hundred thousand cubic feet of earth was removed from the hillside to make place for the lower story. Eighty acres of vines in the adjacent vineyard are in bearing. Some of the four-year-old vines will, it is estimated, yield four or five tons per acre. Some thirty different varieties of the choicest foreign vines have been planted, all of which are doing well. The vineyard shows that great care has been taken in its cultivation.

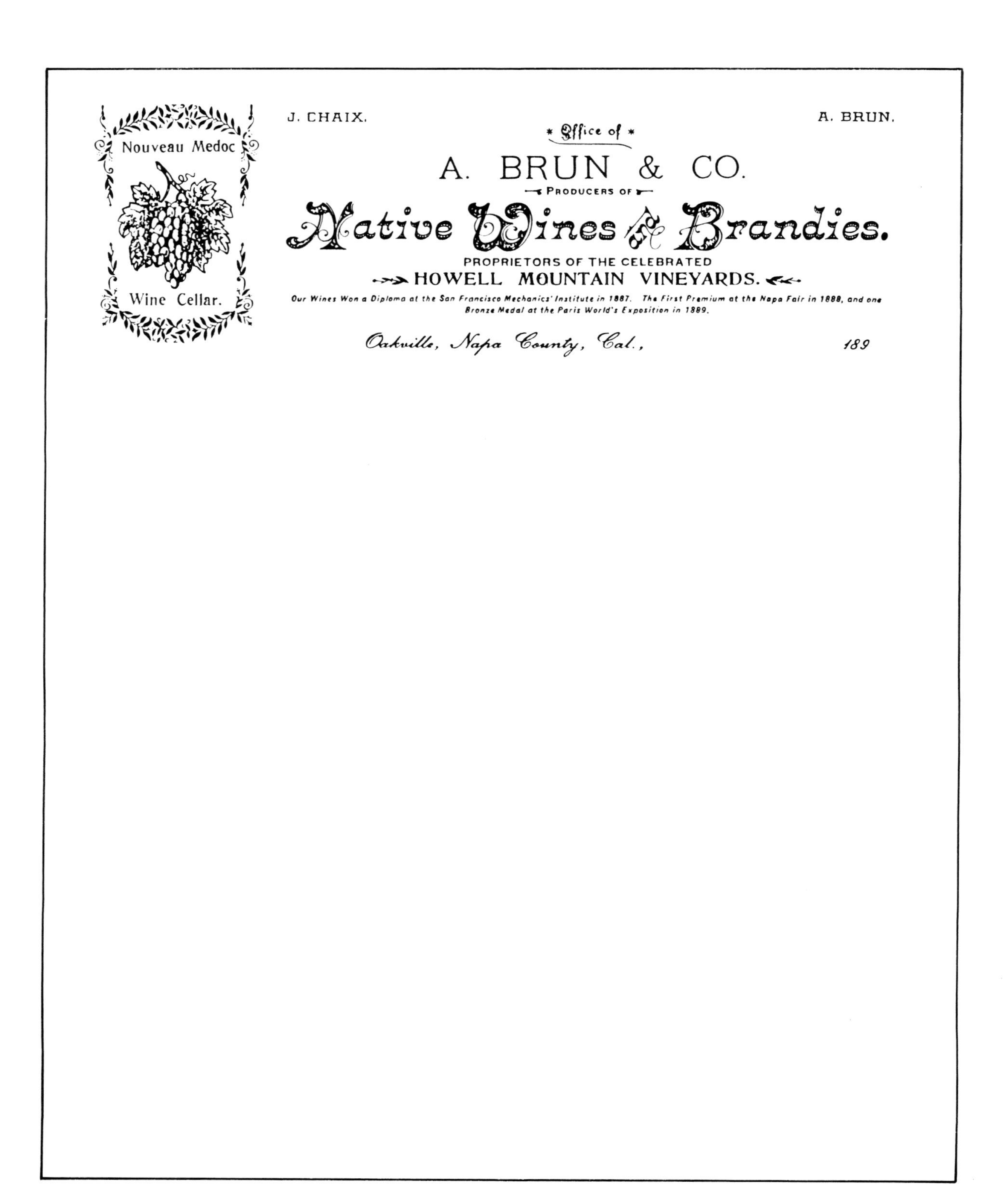

Nouveau Medoc

Wine Cellar.

J. CHAIX. A. BRUN.

Office of

A. BRUN & CO.

PRODUCERS OF

Native Wines and Brandies.

PROPRIETORS OF THE CELEBRATED

HOWELL MOUNTAIN VINEYARDS.

Our Wines Won a Diploma at the San Francisco Mechanics' Institute in 1887. The First Premium at the Napa Fair in 1888, and one Bronze Medal at the Paris World's Exposition in 1889.

Oakville, Napa County, Cal., 189

EDITOR'S NOTE: Letterhead of A. Brun & Co. lists awards from the San Francisco Mechanics Institute in 1887, the Napa County Fair in 1888, and the Paris Wine Exposition in 1889.

Editor's Note: Early drawing of stone cellar built in 1886 by Brun & Chaix on Howell Mountain. This winery was fully restored for production by Francis and Francoise DeWavrin after Woltner & Co. purchased the original Brun & Chaix property in 1980.

*St. Helena Star*, October 15, 1886

# Howell Mountain.

## A PROSPEROUS AND GROWING VINEYARD SECTION.

### Damage Done by Quail—Improvements—Notes, Etc.

HOWELL MOUNTAIN, Oct, 2, 1886.

ED. STAR:—Now that the most laborious part of the work of this season's vintage is about done, we are allowed a short respite from our daily toil, and willingly devote the opportunity to collecting a few items of news appertaining to this section which may interest some of your readers.

It is a generally accepted truism that "eternal vigilance is the price of liberty," but it is also equally worthy of acceptation as an undeniable fact, that the orchardist and vineyardist has to contend with his full share of drawbacks, and that it is only by exercising the most unremitting care and vigilance that he can protect his interests from the depredations of the countless number of enemies that are constantly at work in destroying the fruits of his arduous labors.

The vineyardist's occupation, as a rule, however pleasant and inviting it may appear to the inexperienced in theory, does not in practice furnish such a cornucopia as too many novices in the business are apt to imagine. Without mentioning in detail the various bugs and pests that prey upon our fruit trees and vines, as each season comes round, the ornithological kingdom furnishes its quota of destructive agents. The quail bird is deserving special mention as one of our most inveterate foes, and it is against this last mentioned enemy that we now raise our voices and protest against the State enacting laws for its protection. The loss sustained by vineyardists alone in this particular section from the depredations of this bird can be safely estimated at several tons of fruit, and notwithstanding the fact that the State pays a liberal salary to an appointed officer, whose duty it is to instruct us in the use of remedies for the extermination of the [illegible] and other vermin, at the same time it protects and takes under its sheltering wing our worst foe and tells the farmer, really in effect, that this protege of the State shall be nourished by [illegible] special sport and amusement principally for the members of our sporting clubs, as it is through their influence that such a law is held in force.

As the grape growing industry is also to become one of the most important industries of our State and country, the time has come when all reasonable measures should be adopted for its protection and encouragement, and we look upon the damage done by quail every season as an important factor in retarding its otherwise steady growth and developement. We do not expect that our views upon this important question will receive the approbation of the sporting fraternity, but they ought to view the matter philosophically, and consider what is best for the general good.

Notwithstanding the drawbacks, as above set forth, to our vineyard interests, the season, as a whole, has been most satisfactory to the grower, both as regards quantity and quality. According to Balling's saccharometer, which we have used in making a test, the percentage of sugar reached as high as 24 per cent.—a degree of sweetness that promises a healthier state of fermentation than if the must showed a higher indication, as already proved by the results obtained. Grape growers who are not in a position to crush their own grapes, through the want of proper facilities, sold their grapes at prices ranging from $20 to $22 per ton, a figure that is entirely remunerative and satisfactory to all parties concerned.

The grape growing and the manufacture of wine of a superior quality is no further an experiment in this mountainous district, is evidenced by the fact of the substantial and costly character of the improvements that are gradually being carried on in connection with this industry. Messrs. Brun & Chaix, whose reputation as viniculturists is well known in your valley, have just completed the erection of one of the most convenient and commodious wine cellars in the county, having a storage capacity of upwards of 150,000 gallons of wine. The structure is built entirely of hard, durable stone, three stories in height, roofed with shingles, and being partly dug in the side of a sloping hill, there is easy access by wagons or teams to the three floors. Water is to be abundantly supplied to the whole building from an adjacent spring, the engine supplying the motive power for crushing to do service in pumping water to the necessary elevation. Mr. Frank Giungi did satisfactory work as the mason contractor, and Mr. Rice, of St. Helena, the carpenter work. The firm of Brun & Chaix expect upwards of 250 tons of grapes from their own vineyard this season, which, in addition to the quantity purchased from several of their neighbors, will enable them to manufacture upwards of sixty thousand gallons of wine. The enterprise and perseverance shown by this firm in demonstrating what our elevated regions can accomplish in the way of grape growing is worthy of all praise, and the steady development of the resources of our mountain is due in a great measure to the courage and confidence shown by them in an undertaking which at the outset received but little encouragement and was considered as a risky experiment. Now all doubts are removed on that score, and they are the [illegible] to reap the reward which they justly deserve.

ment, the latter being [illegible] in solid rock and the masonry work carried up to the floor of the third story, where the latter is to be completed with rustic and shingle work in the most modern style. Mr. Aiken being an architect by profession, designed the building, and there is only one opinion as to its elegance and tastefulness. The view to be had from the site where the building is located is very attractive inasmuch as a peep can be had of the Napa valley range of mountains and takes in at a glance a full sweep of the view of the little valley that nestles so cosily on the apex of our own mountain range and is considered one of the important features in our mountain landscape.

Mr. Angwin, the proprietor of the popular summer resort of that name, has added another improvement to the number he has already consummated of late on his property, in the shape of a large barn and stable, at a cost of upwards of $1,500. As Mr. Angwin has to keep a large number of horses on hand for the use and accommodation of his guests, this additional improvement is not only a credit to the mountain but a convenience as well. Like a great many other country resorts, this place has suffered through the migration of its guests to visit the G. A. R. encampment in San Francisco, but since the departure of the veterans to their respective homes, a flow of visitors has set in, which keeps the host not only busy, but leaves him with very few spare apartments.

The politician is abroad, and even in this aerial clime we are favored with frequent visits from the many aspirants for public office. Hand shaking and beaming countenances are now in order.

Although there are now few traces left of the beautiful garb that nature is wont to assume after the fall of the first few showers of rain, still the evergreen tints of the leaves of the madrona and maple trees tend to preserve fresh in our memories the remembrance of the country as it appears to us in the early spring. The dust, which every Californian knows to be an indigenous product, has shrouded every green leaf and shrub with its grey pall, and we now hail with delight the prospect of some refreshing showers being near at hand, as betokened by the overcast appearance of the sky above.

M.

EDITOR'S NOTE: The *Napa Register's* competitor, the *St. Helena Star*, took up the story of success of the Howell Mountain Winery of Brun & Chaix with a major article published October 15, 1886. The "daring experiment" of growing grapes at an elevation of 1,800 feet on Howell Mountain was unheard of. This was an innovation.

*St. Helena Star*
October 15, 1886

## Howell Mountain

### A Prosperous and Growing Vineyard Section

### Damage Done by Quail - Improvements - Notes, Etc.

The grape growing and the manufacture of wine of a superior quality is no further an experiment in this mountainous district, is evidenced by the fact of the substantial and costly character of the improvements that are gradually being carried on in connection with this industry. Messrs. Brun and Chaix, whose reputation as viticulturists is well known in your valley, have just completed the erection of one of the most convenient and commodious wine cellars in the county, having a storage capacity of upwards of 150,000 gallons of wine. The structure is built entirely of hard, durable stone, three stories in height, roofed with shingles, and being partly dug in the side of a sloping hill, there is easy access by wagons or teams to the three floors. Water is to be abundantly supplied to the whole building from an adjacent spring, the engine supplying the motive power for crushing to do service in pumping water to the necessary elevation. Mr. Frank Giungi did satisfactory work as the mason contractor, and Mr. Rice, of St. Helena, the carpenter work. The firm of Brun & Chaix expects upwards of 250 tons of grapes from their own vineyard this season, which in addition to the quantity purchased from several of their neighbors, will enable them to manufacture upwards of sixty thousand gallons of wine. The enterprise and perseverance shown by this firm in demonstrating what our elevated regions can accomplish in the way of grape growing is worthy of all praise, and the steady development of the resources of our mountain is due in great measure to the courage and confidence shown by them in an undertaking which at the outset received but little encouragement and was considered as a risky experiment. Now all doubts are removed on that score and they are the men to reap the reward which they justly deserve.

# THE VINE.

## ITS YIELD IN NAPA VALLEY THIS YEAR.

### Reports of Wine Making From Various Cellars.

Throughout this county grape growers are working hard, early and late, in order to harvest as soon as possible this season's yield—abundant in some vineyards, two-thirds of an average yield in others—but all requiring to be gathered as speedily as may be, while wine men are just as busy at every cellar. According to the estimates of close observers this season's crop in this valley will fall short about thirty per cent. Some vineyards are turning out better than expected earlier in the season. There is a general complaint regarding fermentation, which progresses very slowly, owing, possibly, to an excess of sugar—for grapes are very rich in saccharine matter this fall. Many vineyardists have difficulty in securing help—more than in any previous year. It is almost impossible to get Chinamen. White men are very independent. Wages both in vineyard and cellar are generally one dollar per day and board.

A representative of the REGISTER visited several of the wine cellars at Yountville, Oakville and Rutherford this week and found the work of grape crushing progressing rapidly.

#### At G. Groezinger's

Well known brick cellar crushing commenced about the first of September and will be continued for six weeks or more. The capacity of this cellar is about 750,000 gallons. The amount of wine to be made this season will vary with circumstances. "Our crop is turning out a great deal better than we expected and from our vineyard of 600 acres (150 acres of which are not bearing this year) we expect to make about as much as we did last year," said D. E. Groezinger, who has had charge of the cellar for nearly three years. "We've about one thousand tons to pick yet. We have bought from 600 to 700 tons so far and will probably buy more. Expect to make from 500,000 to 600,000 gallons of wine. Prices range from $10 to $15 per ton." Over forty men are employed on this place—in cellar and in vineyard. Help is unreliable. Many hands will work for a day or two and then resume their tramps again. Mr. Groezinger has planted largely of resistant stock, grafted upon which are the finest varieties of wine grapes.

"We stem all our grapes before we crush them," said the foreman, "thinking this the better plan. Have two hand crushers and crush about 80 tons of grapes per day." Three hydraulic presses, which can be run up to a pressure of 100,000 pounds to the square inch, are used to press the grapes.

One and a half miles back of the cellar is a reservoir containing one million gallons, from which water is conveyed to the cellar. When it is desired to use the presses named a section of hose is attached to the press, the water turned on, and the huge piston descends slowly, with tremendous power.

to twenty white men are employed the year round and from ten to fifteen Chinamen. In grape harvest several extra hands are engaged.

In the capacious vaults of this cellar all the vintage of '85 and '86 are still kept and a portion of that of previous years. No expense has been spared by the wealthy proprietor in making this a model cellar which, in its construction, architecture, finish and appointments, will rank with any one—if it does not excel all—in the State. The Captain is a genial host and heartily greets the visitor.

#### A MAGNIFICENT VIEW.

A few rods in the rear of the cellar and elevated above it, is situated a tank house, where 20,000 gallons of water are stored as it comes from the mountain springs. From the top of this building is obtained one of the finest views of the middle portion of the valley we have ever seen. The beautiful residence of Capt. Niebaum is located half a mile back at the foot of high wooded hills, appropriately named Inglenook.

#### Thos. Fawver's Cellar.

We found Thos. Fawver very busy picking grapes in his 84 acre vineyard. The crop on this place is very large of both white and black grapes. The vines are literally loaded down with fine fruit. Mr. Fawver has an excellent vineyard and gives it careful cultivation. Two or three months ago he built a wooden wine cellar in the midst of his vineyard, of a capacity of about 70,000 gallons. Twenty-two men were at work at the cellar and in vineyard at the time of our visit.

#### La Loma.

(The little hill) is the pretty name O. K. Drew has given to his place situated a short distance north of Yountville. Mr. Drew has a vineyard of 60 acres, 30 acres of which are planted to Zinfindels, the balance to mixed varieties. His wine cellar, built a year or two ago, has a capacity of 180,000 gallons. It is built into the hillside and makes a very fine building. Grapes from adjoining vineyards and from those at a distance are bought by the proprietor, who, last year, made 110,000 gallons of excellent wine. This was sold last Spring. Crushing commenced at the cellar two weeks ago. "I will buy in the neighborhood of 500 tons," said Mr. D. "and expect to crush 600 tons yet. We crush about 20 tons per day; employ ten men in the cellar. I had the best crop on my vines this year that I have had for two years."

#### Brun & Chaix.

A. Brun & Co., proprietors of the Nouveau Medoc wine cellar, at Oakville, and of a 115-acre vineyard on Howell mountain, were both found at their Oakville cellar. Mr. Chaix spends the most of his time on their Howell mountain property, on which is situated a large stone cellar, built last season. They have no vineyard in the valley, buying all the grapes they crush at their Oakville cellar. This cellar has a capacity of 200,000 gallons. The proprietors expect to make from 40,000 to 45,000 gallons of wine here [illegible]

Steam power is used to drive much of the machinery about the establishment, the engine being located in the distillery building, a few rods distant from the winery. There are two stills, each having a capacity of 610 gallons, and one copper still of 320 gallons. Next week the work of distilling singlings will be commenced, and next spring, brandy making.

#### Inglenook.

We were fortunate in finding, at his large, substantial and handsome stone cellar, at Rutherford, Captain G. Niebaum. Without doubt this cellar excells all others in the county in architectural beauty, in the completeness of its every arrangement and in its surroundings. The cellar was commenced four years ago and is not yet finished. As it will appear when completed our readers can form an excellent idea from the view of it we to-day present. The main building and the south wing were finished previous to last year, and the north wing was to have been completed by September 1st of this year, but cement could not be procured and the work is delayed. The walls of this wing are completed. The stone of which most of the building is constructed was obtained from adjacent hills; the very fine dressed brown stone trimmings from St. Helena. The ceilings of the lower floor, arched to give strength, are supported by numerous iron pillars. The floors, except through the storage vaults, are of concrete. The roof is of corrugated iron. The fermenting casks and presses rest on well framed supports of dressed and oiled timber, about four feet high.

#### WATER IN ABUNDANCE

is obtained from excellent springs in the hills, not far west of the cellar, which yield from 30,000 to 40,000 gallons of very fine water daily. Besides this there is a reservoir 10 by 400 feet, 8 feet deep, in which water from a creek is stored, though it is not used at this season of the year.

Throughout the cellar, from the crushing room to the storage vault, the greatest cleanliness is observed. Water, under much pressure, is conveyed to every part of the building and each night the concrete floors are sluiced down and cleansed of all impurities. "Cleanliness," said Capt. Niebaum, "is one to which the good wine cellar," [illegible] expenditure is given the [illegible]; not low but even temperature, the secret is cleanliness.

The grapes are elevated to the crusher, all decayed and imperfect grapes are removed and a fan blast drives away dust and impurities. Many labor saving appliances are seen on every hand. The motive power for driving the machinery is obtained from a 25-horse power engine situated in a building three or four rods east of the cellar.

"So far as my observation goes cellars, in general, have too little fermenting room." The fermenting rooms at this establishment are large and well-arranged. "This year, with us, white grapes ferment very well, but there is trouble with red grapes. To sum it all up, generally, the red grape lacks something—I know not what—owing to climatic conditions. Nature has played a trick on us this season. Some grapes ferment as poorly as in the season of 1885," said the Captain.

#### THE DISTILLERY.

In the distillery, situated in the engine house, from 3,000 to 4,000 gallons of brandy are made a year. A few feet distant is a convenient carpenter shop fitted up with machinery, driven by the engine heretofore mentioned. Mr. J. Armstong, who

this year. Crushing commenced September 6th. The Nouveau Medoc railroad—narrow gauge—connects this cellar with the railroad that runs up the valley and which passes by the cellar on the opposite side of the county road. Thus little work is necessary to ship wine to distant points.

#### AT RUTHERFORD STATION.

At the large concrete cellar of Ewer & Atkinson, a few rods distant from the railroad station at Rutherford, Wm. Hamahan, foreman, crushing is going on as rapidly as possible. Forty tons of grapes are used each day. This cellar has a capacity of 180,000 gallons. The proprietors have 225 acres of bearing vineyards. This year they have purchased largely from other vineyards. Last year 170,000 gallons were made, but the output this year is expected to be less. Ten men are now employed in the cellar and about 40 in the vineyard. The season will last till the middle of November

#### To Kalon.

H. W. Crabb's well-earned reputation as a successful grape grower and wine maker is the result of careful study, untiring industry, unflagging perseverance. Crossing the railroad track at Oakville, the drive to his large winery, leads along a wide avenue, bordered on either side by English walnut trees, the fruit of which is now being gathered. Sweeping away to the north, on ground that gently slopes from the not far distant hills to the railroad—the eastern boundary of this estate—the vineyard, consisting of over 300 acres, forms one of the prettiest views to be found in the upper valley. Crushing commenced at the large cellars two weeks ago. From 60 to 70 men are employed. Large quantities of grapes are purchased from outside parties. The capacity of the four cellars on the premises amounts to 450,000 gallons. The vintage of last year and that of the year previous is still unsold.

#### A FINE SHOWING.

Mr. Crabb made an elaborate showing of his grapes and wine at the Mechanics' Fair. His entire place consists of 345 acres, that portion not planted to vines being set out to fruit and nut trees—walnuts and almonds. Besides the cellars mentioned there are on the place, a distillery, cooper shop, three barns, three dwelling houses and other buildings. To care for this extensive estate a large number of men are employed the year round. The season at this cellar will last for about six weeks or longer.

#### Sheriff Harris' Cellar.

On his fine farm, one mile east of Rutherford, near the banks of Conn creek, H. H. Harris has, this season built a stone wine cellar, in size 60x110 feet, two and one-half stories high; storage capacity about 200,000 gallons. This cellar is not yet finished. Carpenters are busy putting on the roof. Mr. Harris purchases a good many grapes, his vineyard not yielding all he desires to crush. D. Ro[illegible] foreman and eleven men are employed in the cellar. Crushing commenced on the 13th of September. Forty thousand gallons of wine have been made. Work will last four or six weeks longer.

#### GENIAL, HOSPITABLE

G. P. Adamson, whose place is a few rods distant from that of Sheriff Harris', has a very fine vineyard, consisting of 140 acres of choice vines. His cellar, built in '84, is of wood, 60x120 feet in size, and is sit-

EDITOR'S NOTE: On October 14, 1887, the *Napa Register* reported in a survey of the crush for the year, that A. Brun & Co. would use these grapes to commence brandy making in the spring of 1888.

*Napa Register*
October 14, 1887

The Vine

Its Yield in Napa Valley
This Year

Reports of Wine Making From
Various Cellars

A. Brun & Co., proprietors of the Nouveau Medoc Wine Cellar at Oakville, and of a 115-acre vineyard on Howell Mountain, were both found at their Oakville cellar. Mr. Chaix spends most of his time on their Howell Mountain property, on which is situated a large stone cellar, built last season. They have no vineyard in the valley, buying all the grapes they crush at their Oakville cellar. This cellar has a capacity of 200,000 gallons. The properties expect to make from 40,000 to 45,000 gallons of wine here...

Steam power is used to drive much of the machinery about the establishment, the engine being located in the distillery building, a few rods distant from the winery. There are two stills, each having a capacity of 610 gallons, and one copper still of 320 gallons. Next week the work of distilling singlings will be commenced, and next spring, brandy making.

WINE AND VINE NOTES.

Messrs. Bousquet and Christin of Napa city, are engaged in an industry that will prove of value to our wine men in as much as it enables them to buy up and utilize the argals and lees which many of our manufacturers have heretofore permitted to go to waste. These enterprising gentlemen are of the California Pacific Cream of Tartar Works, with headquarters at the Alta wine cellar, Napa city. They are in the market to pay the highest price for argals and lees, and our wine men will do well to communicate with them. See ad.

At Ward and Worrell's cellar on Madrona avenue we found W. C. Ward so busy that he had hardly time to talk to reporters. He had not, as yet, made an estimate of the amount of wine made. The grapes from the home vineyard he said would be all in in a couple of days, but there was still considerable out in the vineyards of Worrell, Pratt and others which they will make up. Mr Ward is one of the most successful winemakers of the valley, but he assured us that "eternal vigilance is the price of good wine" this year.

M Furstenfeld has bought an interest with Paul Bieber in the wine-making plant of the Beretta cellar on the Brewery road. They have made this year 8,000 gallons of wine from Bieber's hill vineyard. Besides this they have bought several small lots of choice wine, and now have their cellars full of really fine clarets and white wine. They will make considerable brandy.

In a call at Brun and Chaix's, Oakville, Mr. Chaix treated the Star man to a drink of 1880 claret, the first they made on the present site of their fine cellars. This claret was on exhibition at the Mechanics' Fair, and it goes without saying was "A. 1.". It isn't every day that seven year claret is handed out even to ye newspaper man.

The water drought is seriously inconveniencing many of our cellars. At Krug's water for the cellars is derived by means of a steam pump from the well. The distillery however is shut down. Beringer Bros. have to haul all their water, even the home well having given out.

J. H. Norton at his cellar near Bello station, is in the midst of the vintage work. He finds his crop shorter than he expected, owing to deficiency in juice. Has had trouble in fermentation, but by careful work got his wine all through in good shape.

We understand that second crop grapes are selling for as much as first crop, as they are in demand both as aids to fermentation and to make up deficiency in quantity.

Rollo M. Wheeler reports the biggest rush over, though it will take two weeks yet to wind up. He has made so far about [illegible] gallons.

At [illegible] cellar Mr. Pellet has now got 150,000 gallons of wine through in fine condition.

*St. Helena Star*
October 28, 1887

Wine and Vine Notes

In a call at Brun & Chaix's Oakville, Mr. Chaix treated the *Star* man to a drink of 1880 claret, the first they made on the present site of their fine cellars. This claret was on exhibition at the Mechanics Fair, and it goes without saying was "A.1." It isn't every day that seven year claret is handed out to 'ye newspaper man.

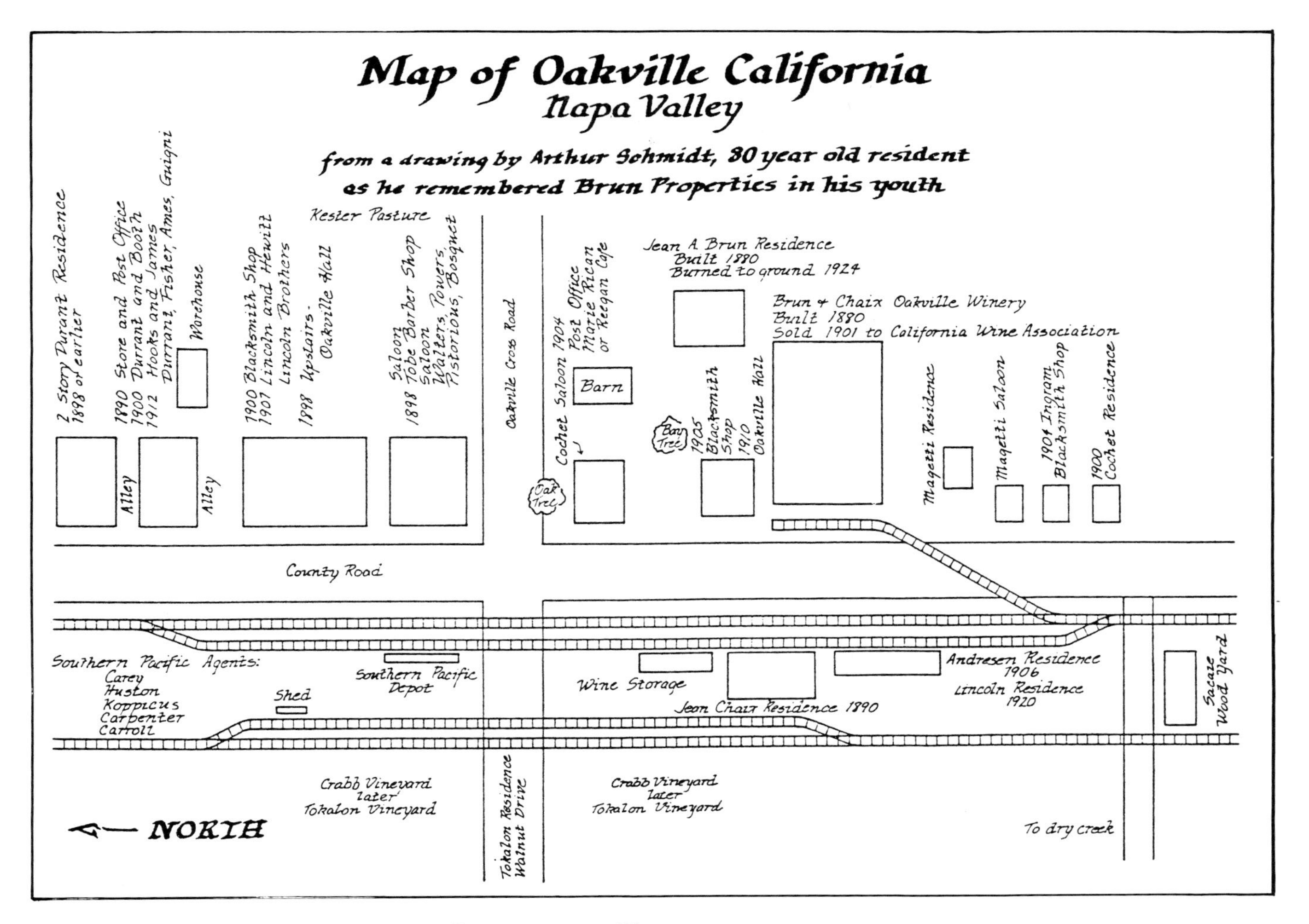


# Oakville Remembered

1890 - 1920

This map of Oakville was drawn from memory by Arthur Schmidt, a lifelong Oakville resident, in his 80s, in April 1986.

The original Brun & Chaix Oakville winery was built on the southeast corner of St. Helena Highway (Old County Road) and Oakville Crossroad. Part of the 1890 addition exists today, but its facade is hidden by the Inglenook additions built in the mid-1980s. Arthur Schmidt believes there may have been another small winery to the rear that could have been the first Brun & Chaix winery that was established in 1877.

Jean Brun built his family house nearby on a site north by northeast of the winery. In 1924, a Louis Bartolucci owned a house and a small winery in Oakville which were probably the house and winery built by Jean Brun circa 1880. Both of those buildings burned in a big fire in Oakville in 1924.

Jean Chaix built his house across the highway and railroad tracks from Jean Brun's house in Oakville. The Chaix house is still in excellent condition in 1989.

In 1887 the Brun & Chaix narrow-gauge railroad was mentioned in the *San Francisco Merchant* as operating from the winery to the main railway station. It is believed that the so-called "Nouveau Medoc Railroad" ran for a mile or two. However, Arthur Schmidt contends that it was a narrow-gauge spur track which transported the wine from the warehouses across the highway to the main railway station, a distance of approximately 1,500 feet. Sometime later, Schmidt says, the Southern Pacific built a siding which went directly into the Brun & Chaix winery.

Arthur Schmidt's map and his memories do give some idea of life in Oakville during the several decades that ended in 1920. Schmidt was still doing most of his own vineyard work in 1986.

SAN FRANCISCO MERCHANT

## NAPA VINEYARDS.

### Reports of the Yield and Wine Making.

Throughout this county grape growers are working hard, early and late, in order to harvest as soon as possible this season's yield—abundant in some vineyards, two-thirds of an average yield in others—but all requiring to be gathered so speedily as may be, while wine men are just as busy at every cellar. According to the estimates of close observers this season's crop in this valley will fall short about thirty per cent. Some vineyards are turning out better than expected earlier in the season. There is a general complaint regarding fermentation, which progresses very slowly, owing, possibly, to an excess of sugar—for grapes are very rich in saccharine matter this fall. Many vineyardists have difficulty in securing help—more than in any previous year. It is almost impossible to get Chinamen. White men are very independent. Wages both in vineyard and cellar are generally one dollar per day and board.

A representative of the *Register* visited several of the wine cellars at Yountville, Oakville and Rutherford this week and found the work of grape crushing progressing rapidly.

AT G. GROEZINGER'S

Well-known brick cellar crushing commenced about the first of September and will be continued for six weeks or more. The capacity of this cellar is about 750,000 gallons. The amount of wine to be made this season will vary with circumstances. "Our crop is turning out a great deal better than we expected and from our vineyard of 600 acres (150 acres of which are not bearing this year) we expect to make about as much as we did last year," said D. E. Greninger, who has had charge of the cellar for nearly three years. "We've about one thousand tons to pick yet. We have bought from 600 to 700 tons so far and will probably buy more. Expect to make from 300,000 to 500,000 gallons of wine. Prices range from $10 to $15 per ton." Over forty men are employed on this place—in cellar and in vineyard. Help is unreliable. Many hands will work for a day or two and then resume their tramps again. Mr. Groezinger has planted largely of resistant stock, grafted upon which are the finest varieties of wine grapes.

"We stem all our grapes before we crush them," said the foreman, "thinking this the better plan. Have two hand crushers and crush about 80 tons of grapes per day." Three hydraulic presses, which can be run up to a pressure of 100,000 pounds to the square inch, are used to press the grapes. One and a half miles back of the cellar is a reservoir containing one million gallons, from which water is conveyed to the cellar. When it is desired to use the presses named a section of the hose is attached to the press, the water turned on, and the huge piston descends slowly, with tremendous power. Steam power is used to drive much of the machinery about the establishment, the engine being located in the distillery building, out doubt this cellar excells all others in the county in architectural beauty, in the completeness of its every arrangement and in its surroundings. The cellar was commenced four years ago and is not yet finished. As it will appear when completed our readers can form an excellent idea from the view of it we to-day present. The main building and the south wing were finished previous to last year and the north wing was to have been completed by September 1st of this year, but cement could not be procured and the work is delayed. The walls of this wing are completed. The stone of which most of the building is constructed was obtained from adjacent hills; the very fine dressed brown stone trimmings from St. Helena. The ceilings of the lower floor, arched to give strength, are supported by numerous iron pillars. The floors, except through the storage vaults, are of concrete. The roof is of corrugated iron. The fermenting casks and presses well framed supports of dressed and oiled timber, about four feet high. water in abundance is obtained from excellent springs in the hills, not far west of the cellar, which yield from 30,000 to 40,000 gallons of very fine water daily. Besides this there is a reservior 100 by 400 feet deep, in which water from a creek is stored, though it is not used at this season of the year.

Throughout the cellar from the crushing room to the storage vault the greatest cleanliness is observed. Water, under much pressure, is conveyed to every part of the building and each night the concrete floors are sluiced down and cleansed of all impurities. "A good wine cellar," said Capt. Neibaum, "is one in whidh the temperature is even the year round; not low but even. The great secret is cleanliness:

As the grapes are elevated to the crusher all decayed and imperfect grapes are removed and a fan blast takes away dust and impurities. Many labor saving appliances are seen on every hand. The motive power for driving the machinery is obtained from a 25-horse power engine situated in a building three or four rods east of the cellar.

"So far as my observation goes cellars, in general, have too little fermenting room." The fermenting rooms at this establishment are large and well-arranged. "This year, with us, white grapes ferment very well, but there is trouble with red grapes. To sum it all up, generally, the red grape lacks something—I know not what—owing to climatic conditions. Nature has played a trick on us this season. Some grapes ferment as poorly as in the season of 1885," said the Captain.

In the distillery, situated in the engine house, from 3,000 to 4,000 gallons of brandy are made a year. A few feet distant is a convenient carpenter shop fitted up with machinery, driven by the engine heretofore mentioned. Mr. J. Armstrong, who has been with Capt. Niebaum, on sea and land, for 22 years, is cellar foreman, filling the position formerly held by Capt. H. W. McIntyre.

Capt. Niebaum has 150 acres of bearing vineyard. He buys very few grapes. With appointments, will rank with any one—if it does not excel all—in the State. The Captain is a genial host and heartily greets the visitor.

A few rods in the rear of the cellar and elevated above it, is situated a tank house where 20,000 gallons of water are stored as it comes from the mountain springs. From the top of this building is obtained one of the finest views of the middle portion of the valley we have ever seen. The beautiful residence of Capt. Niebaum is located half a mile back at the foot of high wooded hills, appropriately named Inglenook.

THOS. FAWVER'S CELLAR.

We found Thos. Fawver very busy picking grapes in his 85 acre vineyard. The crop on this place is very large of both white and black grapes. The vines are literally loaded down with fine fruit. Mr. Fawver has an excellent vineyard and gives it careful cultivation. Two or three months ago he built a wooden wine cellar in the midst of his vineyard, of a capacity of about 70,000 gallons. Twenty-two men were at work at the cellar and in the vineyard at the time of our visit.

LA LOMITA.

(The little hill) is the pretty name G. K. Drew has given to his place situated a short distance north of Yountville. Mr. Drew has a vineyard of 40 acres, 30 acres of which are planted to Zinfandels, the balance to mixed varieties. His wine cellar, built a year or two ago, has a capacity of 140,000 gallons. It is built into the hillside and makes a very fine building. Grapes from adjoining vineyards and from those at a distance are bought by the proprietor, who, last year, made 110,000 gallons of excellent wine. This was sold last Spring. Crushing commenced at this cellar two weeks ago. "I will buy in the neighbourhood of 500 tons," said Mr. D. "and expect to crush 600 tons yet. We crush about 20 tons per day; employ ten men in the cellar. I had the best crop on my vines this year that I have had for two years."

BRUN & CHAIX.

A. Brun & Co., proprietors of the Nouveau Medoc wine cellar, at Oakville, and of a 115-acre vineyard on Howell mountain, were both found at their Oakville cellar. Mr. Chaix spends the most of his time on their Howell mountain property, on which is situated a large stone cellar, built last season. They have no vineyard in the valley, buying all the grapes they crush at their Oakville cellar. This cellar has a capacity of 200,000 gallons. The proprietors expect to make from 40,000 to 45,000 gallons of wine here this year. Crushing commenced September 6th. The Nouveau Medoc railroad—narrow gauge— connects this cellar with the railroad that runs up the valley and which passes by the cellar on the opposite side of the county road. Thus little work is necessary to ship wine to distant points

AT RUTHERFORD STATION.

At the large concrete cellars of Ewer & Atkinson a few rods distant from the railroad station at Rutherford, Wm. Hamahan, foreman, crushing is going on as rapidly as

*San Francisco Merchant*
October 29, 1887

## Napa Vineyards
### Reports of the Yield and Wine Making

A. Brun & Co., proprietors of the Nouveau Medoc wine cellar, at Oakville, and of a 115-acre vineyard on Howell Mountain, were both found at their Oakville cellar. Mr. Chaix spends the most of his time on their Howell Mountain property, on which is situated a large stone cellar, built last season. They have no vineyard in the valley, buying all grapes they crush at their Oakville cellar. This cellar has a capacity of 200,000 gallons. The proprietors expect to make from 40,000 to 45,000 gallons of wine here this year. Crushing commenced September 6th. The Nouveau Medoc railroad—narrow-gauge—connects this cellar with the railroad that runs up the valley and which passes by the cellar on the opposite side of the county road. Thus little work is necessary to ship wine to distant points.

# TWENTY-SEVEN MEDALS.

## THATS WHAT CALIFORNIA [WINES WON AT PARIS.

### Complete List of American Exhibitors Who were successful, and the Prizes they Won—A Grand Showing.

From the Commissioner-General of the United States at the Paris Exposition, we have received a report of the awards of the jury in class 73—Fermented Drinks. It will be observed that the list includes no grand prize for California wines, notwithstanding the cable dispatch received during the fore part of the month reported that one had been given to Charles A. Wetmore. However, the Superior jury has got to pass upon these awards, and it is possible that California wines may yet receive the highest compliment that can be paid by the French people. At any rate the wine men of this State have occasion to greatly rejoice over the fact th their wines, in a world's contest, won four gold medals, eleven silver medals, twelve bronze medals and honorable mention in seven cases. Following is a complete list of the awards to American exhibitors of fermented drinks:

GRAND PRIZE.

Bergner & Engel Brewing Co., malt liquors.

GOLD MEDAL.

Beadleston & Woerz, 291 W. 10th street New York, lager beer, ale and porter.

California State Viticultural Commission, Experimental cellar,"San Francisco, Cal., five cases assorted wines.

Chauché, A. G., Livermore, Alameda, Co., Cal., wine.

Claret (sic) Migliavacca, Napa, Cal.

Kunz, Joseph, New York, beer.

Montgomery Brewery Co., beer.

Osborn, John Son & Co., New York and Montreal, "Antediluvian" rye whisky.

Wetmore, Chas. A., Livermore, Alameda Co., Cal., table wines.

SILVER MEDAL.

Beck, Adolph, San Francisco, Cal., wines.

Beringer Bros., St. Helena, Napa, Co., Cal., wines and brandies.

De Turk, I., Santa Rosa, Sonoma, Cal., our cases assorted wines.

Greenebaum, Alfred & Co., San Francisco, Cal., wine.

Hagner, Henry, Cedar Knoll Vineyards, Napa Co., Cal., brandy.

Haraszthy, Arpad & Co., San Francisco, Cal., wines.

Hooper, Geo. F., Sobre Vista Vineyard, Sonoma, Cal., wines.

Kohler & Frohling, San Francisco, Cal.

Monticello Wine Co., Charlotteville, Va., wines.

Napa Valley Wine Co., San Francisco Cal., wines.

New Urbana Wine Co., Hammondsport, N. Y., wines.

Pleasant Valley Wine Co., Reims, Steuben Co., N. Y., wines.

Schilling, C. & Co., San Francisco, Cal., wines.

Stone Hill Wine Co., Herman, Mo., wines.

Wineberger, Mrs. J. C., St. Helena, Cal., wines.

BRONZE MEDAL.

Adamson, Rutherford, Napa Co., Cal., wines.

Ardonin, H., Paris (*sic*).

American Wine Co., St. Louis Mo., wines.

Brun, . & Co., Nouveau Médoc, Oakville, Napa Co., Cal., wines.

Crabb, H. W., Oakville, Napa Co., Cal.

Craig, W. O., Sonoma, Cal., wine.

De Turk, I., Santa Rosa, Sonoma, Cal., brandy.

Edge Hill Wine Co, St. Helena, Cal., brandy.

Gundlach, J. & Co., San Francisco, Cal., wines.

Krug, Chas., St Helena, Cal., wines.

Matthews, J., Lisbon Winery, Napa, Cal., wines.

Nouveau Clos Vougeot Vineyard, St. Helena, Napa Co., Cal., wines.

Purity Wine Co., San Francisco, Cal., white and red wines. Electric Process.

Russow, Adolph, Proffits P. O., Va., wines.

Ryckman, G. F., Brocton Wine Co., Brocton, N. Y., champagne.

HONORABLE MENTION.

Ben Lomond Wine Co., Santa Cruz, Cal., white wines.

Edge Hill Wine Co., St. Helena, Cal., wines.

Ewer & Atkinson, Rutherford, Napa Co., Cal., wines.

Florida Wine Co., Clay Springs, Florida, orange wine.

Gast Wine Co., St. Louis, Mo., wines.

Grossman, H., Napa (*sic*)

Nouveau Clos Vougeot Vineyard, St. Helena, Napa Co., Cal., spirits.

Pearson, Alex. M., Vineland, N. J., burgundy and ironclad.

Schram, Jacob, St. Helena, Cal., wines

EDITOR'S NOTE: On October 22, 1889, the *San Francisco Merchant and Viticulturist* published the honors won in world competition at the Paris show of 1889. A. Brun & Co., Nouveau Medoc placed with a bronze medal.

*San Francisco Merchant and Viticulturist*
October 22, 1889

Twenty-Seven Medals

That's What California Wines
Won at Paris

Complete List of American Exhibitors
Who Were Successful, and the
Prizes They Won—
A Grand Showing

From the Commissioner-General of the United States at the Paris Exposition, we have received a report of the awards of the jury in class 73—Fermented Drinks. It will be observed that the list includes no grand prize for California wines, notwithstanding the cable dispatch received during the fore part of the month reported that one had been given to Charles A. Wetmore. However, the Superior jury has got to pass upon these awards, and it is possible that California wines may yet receive the highest compliment that can be paid by the French people. At any rate the wine men of this state have occasion to greatly rejoice over the fact that their wines, in a world's contest, won four gold medals, eleven silver medals, twelve bronze medals and honorable mention in seven cases.

*St. Helena Star*
March 2, 1894

**Death of J. A. Brun.**

Saturday morning, about 10 o'clock, the sufferings of J. A. Brun, the prominent wine maker and dealer of Oakville, came to an end in death, his illness having lasted for many months, during which time he came near reaching the other shore several times.

Jean Adolph Brun was born in France, July 25, 1845 and was therefore in his 49th year when removed from this earth. His home was made in his native country until 1872, during which time he had a varied experience, devoting considerable attention to wine, cider and oil making. In 1872 he left France, locating in Montreal, Canada, where he remained fourteen months, being engaged in the manufacture of photographic materials. He then went to England and after a month's sojourn sailed for Australia. Here he engaged in the same business, continuing in it for eight months. In September 1874 he came to California and shortly after reaching the State located in Napa county, finding employment as a laborer and afterwards as a wine-maker in several cellars. In 1879 he formed a partnership with John Chaix, locating at Oakville where they started on a small scale their present large business. In 1880 he was united in marriage to Miss Emma Mermond, of San Francisco. Mr. Brun gave close attention to business, making several trips to Eastern cities where the firm has built up a large wine trade. He was a liberal and honest business man and had many friends among the people of Napa county. About a year ago Mr. Brun was stricken down with illness, his liver becoming seriously diseased. He had the best of medical attention but of no avail. He gradually but steadily failed and when dropsy was added to chronic disease of the liver nothing could be done to save his life.

Deceased leaves a widow and six children,—Elise, Delphine, Jeannette, Louis, Julia and Jean Adolph, to mourn his loss. He was a member of St. Helena lodge, No. 167, I. O. O. F., and his funeral took place Monday at 11 o'clock under the auspices of that society. Services at the house were conducted by Rev. James Mitchell and at the grave by the Odd Fellows. The pall bearers were J. J. McIntyre, C. P. Adamson, B. Del Foch, L. Debanne, F. Sclarmni and J. Magetta. A large number of friends followed the remains to their last resting place.

EDITOR'S NOTE: In March of 1894 the long illness of Jean Brun took its final toll. His obituary, published in the *St. Helena Star,* March 2, 1894, was a tribute to this prominent citizen of the valley.

*St. Helena Star*
March 2, 1894

Death of J.A. Brun

Saturday morning, about 10 o'clock, the sufferings of J.A. Brun, the prominent wine maker and dealer of Oakville, came to an end in death, his illness having lasted for many months, during which time he came near reaching the others above several times.

Jean Adolphe Brun was born in France, July 25, 1845 and was therefore in his 49th year when removed from this earth. His home was made in his native country until 1872, during which time he had a varied experience, devoting considerable attention to wine, cider and oil making. In 1872 he left France, locating in Montreal, Canada, where he remained fourteen months, being engaged in the manufacture of photographic materials. He then went to England and after a month's sojourn sailed to Australia. Here he engaged in the same business, continuing in it for eight months. In September 1874 he came to California and shortly after reaching the state located in Napa county, finding employment as a laborer and afterwards as a wine-maker in several cellars. In 1877 he formed a partnership with Jean Chaix, locating at Oakville where they started on a small scale their present large business. In 1880 he was united in marriage to Miss Emma Mermoud of San Francisco. Mr. Brun gave close attention to business, making several trips to eastern cities where the firm has built up a large wine trade. He was a liberal and honest businessman and had many friends among the people of Napa county. About a year ago Mr. Brun was stricken down with illness, his liver becoming seriously diseased. He had the best of medical attention but of no avail. He gradually but steadily failed and when dropsy was added to chronic disease of the liver nothing could be done to save his life.

Deceased leaves a widow and six children—Elise, Delphine, Jeannette, Louis, Julie and Jean Adolphe to mourn his loss. He was a member of St. Helena Lodge, No. 167, I.O.O.F., and his funeral took place Monday at 11 o'clock under the auspices of that society. Services at the house were conducted by Rev. James Mitchell and at the grave by the Odd Fellows. The pallbearers were J.J. McIntyre, C.P. Adamson, B. Del Foch, L. Debanna, F. Sclaroni and J. Magetia. A large number of friends followed the remains to their last resting place.

# LETTER FROM EMMA BRUN ON THE DEATH OF HER HUSBAND

TO HIS MOTHER IN FRANCE, MAY 2, 1894

Oakville, le 2 Mai 1894

Ma chère belle-mère

Je voudrais
bien être auprès de vous
pour que nous puissons
partager nos grands
chagrins et nos troubles,
pauvre bonne mère, ayez
pitiée de moi, songez-a
ma double résponsabilité
d'une jeune famille a
guider et élever, la charge
des propriétés et des dettes
je ne sais comment je
vais m'én sortir, malgré

que Monsieur Chaix fait bien
tout ce quil peut pour le
mieux, mais tout cela ne
ramene pas notre pauvre
Adolphe, qui a tant souffert
pendant la langue maladie
il disait souvent qu'ai-je
donc fait, pour que Dieu
me fasse tant souffrir
et maintenant c'est mon
tour pauvre mère de
souffrir dans ce bas monde
pauvre ami qui aurait
voulu voir grandir ses
chers enfants, une perte
irreparable, pauvre enfants

O, Dieu pourvu que mes
enfants tourne tous bien,
vous faites une grande perte
aussi, mais vous avez de
bons enfants autour de vous
et moi je n'ai pas un seul
parent ici avec moi et tout
depends de moi, enfin je
tâche de faire pour le mieux.
Le pauvre est mort sans
connaissance, il est parti
comme une chandelle, je
ne m'attendais pas a ce
qu'il nous quitte si vite
malgré les souffrances, il
avait beaucoup de courage
O! que la vie est amer

surtout quand l'on a perdu son
meilleur ami, il y a des
moments que je suis bien
décourager, et je demande
à Dieu de me donner des
forces    Je n'ai reçu
aucune lettre de votre
frere Augustin de Paris.
Ecrivez moi souvent et
soignez bien votre bonne
chère mère

Tout a vous avec amitiés
et baisers de toute la
famille, et croyez votre
toute devouée bruce
Emma Brun

EDITOR'S NOTE: Translation of Emma Brun's letter to her mother-in-law, Marie Delphine Delavaud Brun, May 2, 1894, following the death of Emma's husband, Jean Adolphe Brun. Mme. Marie Brun's address in 1894 was: Aux Villettes, Par Naillat, Creuse, France.

My dear mother-in-law, Oakville, 2 May 1894

I would very much like to be with you in order to share our great sorrows and our troubles, poor dear mother; have pity on me. Think of my double responsibility of having a young family to guide and raise, and of the burden of the properties. I do not know how I will come out of all of this, though Monsieur Chaix does all that he can for the best. It does not bring back our poor Adolphe, who suffered so much during his long illness. He often said, "What did I do, for God to let me suffer so much," and now it is my turn, poor mother, to suffer in this world. Our poor dear friend who would have liked to see his beloved children growing has suffered an irreparable loss and so have our unfortunate children.

Oh, God, please provide that all my children will turn out well. You also suffer a great loss, but you have good adult children with you. I myself have not a single adult relative here with me, and everything depends on me. However, I try to do all for the best.

The poor man died while he was unconscious. He went out like a candle. I was not expecting him to depart this life so quickly; in spite of his suffering, he had much courage.

Oh, life is bitter, especially when one has lost his best friend. There are times when I am discouraged, and I am asking God to give me strength. I have not received any letter from your brother Augustin from Paris.

Write to me often, and take good care, our good dear mother. All the best to you, with love and kisses from all the family, your devoted daughter-in-law.

Emma Brun

EDITOR'S NOTE: The premature death in 1894 of Jean Adolphe Brun at age 49 was a great shock to his wife and children. The momentum of his successful career as a vintner in the Napa Valley came to an abrupt halt. His family would have to seek entirely new directions for their lives.

# Brun Family of Oakville
# Napa County, California

Jean Adolphe and Emma Mermoud Brun had been married only fourteen years at the time of his death in 1894. They were married in 1880 in San Francisco.

| | | |
|---|---|---|
| Father: | *Jean Adolphe Brun | 1845-1894 |
| Mother: | *Emma Mermoud Brun | 1860-1945 |
| Children: | | |
| | Elise Brun Thibodeaux | November 1881-1973 |
| | *Delphine Adrienne Brun | January 1883-1968 |
| | *Jeannette Brun Hewitt | April 1884-1970 |
| | *Louis Sylvain Brun | September 1885-1965 |
| | *Julie Pauline Brun | October 1888-1978 |
| | Jean Adolphe Brun | October 1892-1975 |

*Interred in the Brun plot in the St. Helena Cemetery on Spring Street.

Additionally, Ruth Finnell Brun 1889-1979 (Mrs. Louis Brun) and Ruth Ellis Brun West 1919-1966 (daughter of Ruth and Louis Brun) are interred in the Brun plot, St. Helena Cemetery.

Records show the Brun family plot was purchased from the St. Helena Cemetery Association in 1894 by Emma Brun. Information from the Cemetery office states the plot is covered by "endowment care," which provides upkeep and maintenance. The endowment is administered by Wells Fargo Bank in St. Helena, California, and is said to be substantial.

*St. Helena Cemetery, St. Helena, California, 1986.*

*Brun Plot, St. Helena Cemetery, July 1, 1986.*

*The Brun & Chaix Winery on Howell Mountain was constructed in 1886 by two young Frenchmen, Jean Adolphe Brun and Jean Chaix. Restoration of the three story stone cellar was completed in 1986 by Woltner & Company of Bordeaux, France. It is interesting to note that in 100 years French ownership had come full circle. The Brun & Chaix Winery is once again in French hands. Photograph by William Garnett, 1988.*

*Entryway of the stone cellar at ground level where barreled wine was stored for shipment by Brun & Chaix to Oakville for bottling and casing. Photograph by William Garnett, 1988.*

*Detail of doorway to the Brun & Chaix stone cellar showing keystone arch and the excellent stone masonry of the building. Photograph by William Garnett, 1988.*

EDITOR'S NOTE: In 1901 the Brun & Chaix properties in the Napa Valley were sold by Jean Brun's widow and Jean Chaix to a consortium named The California Wine Association. Information is not available regarding how long that association owned those properties, but the files of the California Wine Institute list the owners of the Brun & Chaix Howell Mountain vineyard and winery from 1936 on as follows:

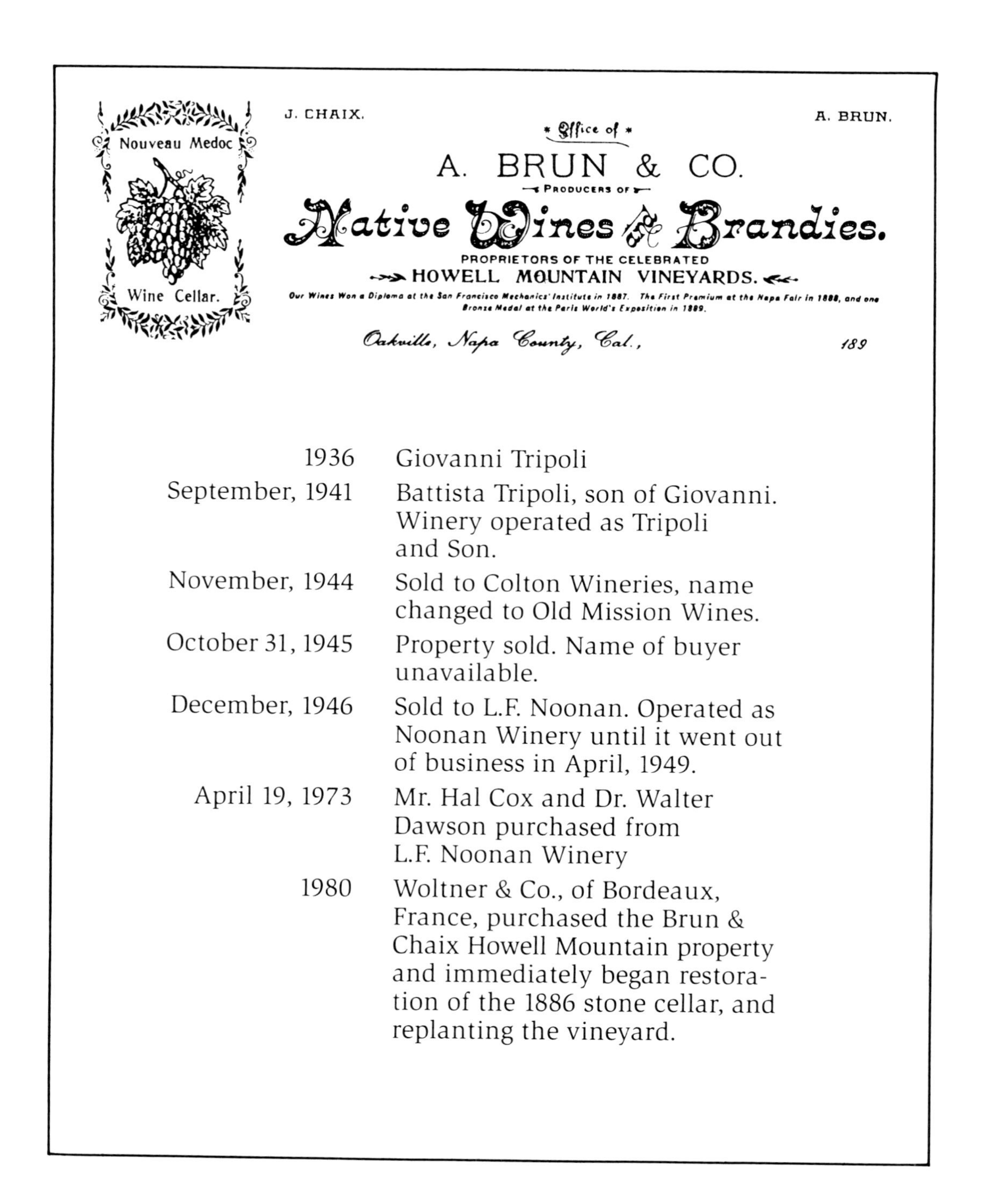


| | |
|---|---|
| 1936 | Giovanni Tripoli |
| September, 1941 | Battista Tripoli, son of Giovanni. Winery operated as Tripoli and Son. |
| November, 1944 | Sold to Colton Wineries, name changed to Old Mission Wines. |
| October 31, 1945 | Property sold. Name of buyer unavailable. |
| December, 1946 | Sold to L.F. Noonan. Operated as Noonan Winery until it went out of business in April, 1949. |
| April 19, 1973 | Mr. Hal Cox and Dr. Walter Dawson purchased from L.F. Noonan Winery |
| 1980 | Woltner & Co., of Bordeaux, France, purchased the Brun & Chaix Howell Mountain property and immediately began restoration of the 1886 stone cellar, and replanting the vineyard. |

*Howell Mountain Wine Cellar, built by Brun & Chaix in 1886, as seen in 1946 after it was purchased by L.F. Noonan.*

# DIRECTORY

OF THE

# GRAPE GROWERS, WINE MAKERS AND DISTILLERS

OF

# CALIFORNIA,

AND OF THE

## PRINCIPAL GRAPE GROWERS AND WINE MAKERS OF THE EASTERN STATES.

---

PUBLISHED BY THE

BOARD OF STATE VITICULTURAL COMMISSIONERS OF CALIFORNIA

SACRAMENTO:
STATE OFFICE, : : : : : A. J. JOHNSTON, SUPT. STATE PRINTING.
1891

Editor's Note: *The Directory of the Grape Growers, Wine Makers and Distillers of California, and of the Principal Grape Growers and Wine Makers of the Eastern States,* offered in its 1891 edition the following information on the Brun & Chaix operation.

## Napa County
## Name of Owner, Post Office and Name of Vineyard

| **Brun & Chaix** | **Oakville** |
| --- | --- |
| Total Acres in Grapes<br>210 | Total Acres in Bearing<br>210 |
| Acres in Wine Grapes<br>210 | Wine Maker<br>Yes |
| Product in 1890<br>1,000 Tons | Varieties<br>Zinfandel, Riesling, Mataro, S. Vert Burgundy |

THE

# VINEYARDS IN NAPA COUNTY;

BEING

THE REPORT OF E. C. PRIBER, COMMISSIONER FOR THE NAPA DISTRICT,

TO THE

BOARD OF STATE VITICULTURAL COMMISSIONERS OF CALIFORNIA.

---

PUBLISHED BY THE BOARD OF STATE VITICULTURAL COMMISSIONERS.

SACRAMENTO:
STATE OFFICE, : : : : : A. J. JOHNSTON, SUPT. STATE PRINTING.
1893.

## YOUNTVILLE DISTRICT
1893

*John Benson, Oakville.*—Total, 35 acres; in bearing, 30 acres; will replant 5 acres; infested by phylloxera, 10 acres, all to be uprooted; planted to Riparia, 25 acres, which is grafted to Semillon, Mondeuse, Cabernet Franc, and all succeed about alike; soil loam, bordering on adobe; vineyard low lying; European varieties most resistant, Zinfandel and Burger; vineyard replanted as vines become diseased; crop, 50 tons; cooperage, 90,000 gallons, of which 5,000 is oak and 85,000 redwood.

*W. P. Bolz, Oakville.*—Total, 15 acres; in bearing, 12 acres; all will be dug up; soil gravelly loam; vineyard upland; all European varieties succumb alike; crop, 35 tons.

*W. T. Bradley, Oakville.*—Total, 25 acres; all in bearing; infested by phylloxera, 12 acres, of which 4 acres are good for only one crop more; soil gravelly loam; vineyard low lying; European varieties all succumb alike; crop, 43 tons.

*B. Bradshaw, Oakville.*—Total, 5 acres; in bearing, 4 acres; infested by phylloxera, 4 acres, of which 2 acres are good for only one crop more; soil gravelly; vineyard upland; exposure northwest; European varieties all succumb alike; crop, 8 tons.
Vineyard will be gone in two years.

*George Brainard, Oakville.*—Total, 50 acres; in bearing, 48 acres; infested by phylloxera, 5 acres, of which 2 acres are good for only one crop more; vineyard low lying; all European varieties succumb alike; crop, 14 tons.

*Brun & Chaix, Oakville.*—Total, 115 acres; in bearing, 113 acres; will plant 15 or 20 acres; soil loam; vineyard low lying and mountain; exposure south; crop, 350 tons; cooperage, 300,000 gallons at Howell Mountain and 150,000 in valley at Oakville, mostly redwood.
One vineyard and cellar is on Howell Mountain. Have escaped phylloxera so far, but expect it before long.

*Duncan Campbell, Oakville.*—Total, 10 acres; in bearing, 6 acres; infested by phylloxera, 5 acres, of which 2 acres are good for only one crop more; soil loam; vineyard upland; exposure east; all European varieties succumb alike; crop, 12 tons.
Vineyard going fast.

*Thomas Dwyer, Oakville.*—Total, 10 acres; all in bearing; infested by phylloxera, 2 acres, of which 1 acre is good for only one crop more; soil loam; vineyard low lying; crop, 6 tons.

*H. W. Crabb, Oakville.*—Total, 120 acres; in bearing, 90 acres; infested by phylloxera, 20 acres; planted to resistants, 100 acres, of which 70 are Riparia and 30 Lenoir, and all of which are doing well; soil loam; vineyard low lying; exposure south and east; Tokay has proved most resistant; vines dug out as soon as diseased; crop, 100 tons; cooperage, 650,000 gallons, all of which is redwood.
This is one of the several vineyards in this vicinity that were very flourishing four years ago, but have rapidly decayed. The destruction was surprisingly rapid and very discouraging. Mr. Crabb is planting out resistants year by year, to a considerable extent, both Lenoir and Riparia, the former on the high drier soil, the latter on the lower, stiffer land. Success seems to attend the growth of resistants. Experience in this vicinity shows plainly that resistants (cuttings or rooted vines) should be planted early in the season, especially if the season should prove to be a dry one. In two or three years more definite views can be given as to bearing of resistants.

Editor's Note: In regard to the report on the opposite page, it should be noted that 1893 was the year Jean Brun became seriously ill, and the dreaded phylloxera was wreaking havoc in the Valley vineyards. However, the Brun & Chaix Howell Mountain property had escaped that vineyard disease up to this point.

*Vineyards in Napa County*

*Report of E.C. Priber, Commissioner for the Napa District*

*To the Board of State Viticultural Commissioners of California*

Sacramento:
1893

Yountville District
1893

*Brun & Chaix, Oakville* – Total 115 acres; in bearing, 113 acres will plant 15 or 20 acres; soil loam; vineyard low lying and mountain, exposure south; crop 350 tons; cooperage, 300,000 gallons at Howell Mountain and 150,000 in valley at Oakville, mostly redwood.

One vineyard and cellar is on Howell Mountain. Have escaped phylloxera so far, but expect it before long.

*St. Helena Star*, April 27, 1900

**EVENTS OF THE WEEK.**

BUY your lumber from Jeffreys.

ORANGES 15 cts. doz. at Mooney's.

Don't fail to take in the N. S. G. W. show May 1st.

THREE pounds of corn beef for 25 cents cash at Sutter's.

FOR a good smoke get your cigars and tobacco from Morris.

The steamer Zinfandel will leave Napa next week as follows: Monday, 4 P. M.; Wednesday, 5 P. M.; Friday, 6 P. M.

TEN-POUND can of home rendered lard for $1.10 at Sutter's.

THREE pounds of mutton stew for 25 cents cash at Sutter's.

The Native sons will present an excellent performance in Turner hall May 1st. Don't fail to see it.

EARLY Rose and Burbank seed potatoes at W. D. Mooney's.

Services will be held in the Presbyterian church next Sunday evening at 7:30 o'clock. All are invited to attend.

BUY your spring vegetables from Morris. Received fresh daily.

THE Pearl Steam Laundry is a busy place still we welcome visitors.

Judge W. H. Taft, one of the new Philippine commissioners, and E. Goodman were schoolmates in Cincinnati, Ohio.

NOW is the time to paper your house. See Stouter for samples and prices.

CHOICEST seasonable fruits always on hand at Morris. Your needs supplied.

"Fortune favors the brave." It is also favorable to those who purify their blood at this season by taking Hood's Sarsaparilla.

WHEN building buy your lumber, brick, lime and cement from Jeffreys.

FINE line of razors and pocket cutlery at W. D. Mooney's, Carver block.

The W. A. Mackinder Co. advertises an auction sale of cooperage at the old Ink place near Zinfandel station Saturday, May 5th. Read ad for particu-

Brun & Chaix have just had a lithographic picture of their establishments made for distribution in all the eastern cities, the object being to advertise their wines and thereby increase their already extensive trade. The picture is done in seven colors. In the background is their fine Howell mountain vineyard, the cellar and other buildings, while in the foreground is the large shipping cellars at Oakville, the residences of Mrs. Brun and Mr. Chaix, the office and other buildings. The photographs from which this picture was made were taken two years ago and since that time several proofs were submitted to the firm and important changes made. The lithograph is a work of art, 28x30 inches in size, and when framed will present a very attractive appearance and be a splendid advertisement.

"No family can afford to be without One Minute Cough Cure. It will stop a cough and cure a cold quicker than any other medicine," writes C. W. Williams, Sterling Run, Pa. It cures croup, bronchitis and all throat and lung troubles and prevents consumption. Pleasant and harmless. Smith's Pharmacy.

CONTRARY to the announcement made a few weeks ago, that I would remain in St. Helena, I will remain but a few days longer. Those indebted to me will call and settle with me as soon as possible. I also offer for sale furniture and household effects.

C. R. SABIN.

E. Goodman was called to San Francisco Monday by the serious illness of his mother, Mrs. A. Goodman. Before he reached her bedside she had breathed her last. Deceased was 71 years old and for years had suffered with asthma.

J. I. Carson, prothonotary, Washington, Pa., says, "I have found Kodol Dyspepsia Cure an excellent remedy in case of stomach trouble, and have derived great benefit from its use." It digests what you eat and can not fail to cure. Smith's Pharmacy.

FOR grain and feed of all kinds see Dockery & Hansen at their mill on Railroad avenue. Barley ground to order. Wood for sale. Price reasonable. Telephone 34.

DENTISTRY—None but firstclass, up-to-date in every particular, at lowest prices. Dr. Davis, Oak avenue, 4th door above M. E. church, St. Helena.

Nathan Lauter and the Levy brothers will open a store at Cape Nome as soon as they send goods to that place.

Editor's Note: For several years before he died in 1894, Jean Brun had wanted a colored lithograph to use as a sales aid for his products. In 1900 it was printed. The *St. Helena Star* of April 27, 1900, carried the following story.

*St. Helena Star*
April 27, 1900

Events of the Week

Brun & Chaix have just had a lithographic picture of their establishment made for distribution in all eastern cities, the object being to advertise their wines and thereby increase their already extensive trade. The picture is done in seven colors. In the background is their fine Howell Mountain vineyard, the cellar and other buildings, while in the foreground are the large shipping cellars at Oakville, the residences of Mrs. Brun and Mr. Chaix, the office and other buildings. The photographs from which this picture was made were taken several years ago, and since that time several proofs were submitted to the firm and important changes made. The lithograph is a work of art, 26 x 30 inches in size, and when framed will present a very attractive appearance and be a splendid advertisement.

*Napa Daily Journal,* January 15, 1901

# NAPA DAILY JOURNAL.

TUESDAY, JAN. 15, 1901

A man who gets into the habit of never making mistakes is altogether too near perfect for this world.

SENATOR GEO. F. HOAR has been unanimously renominated for United States Senator by the Republican members of the Massachusetts Legislature. Mr. Hoar has been a member of the Senate since March, 1877.

A. E. Glase shot and killed William Trewella, in San Francisco Monday afternoon. Glase and Trewella were partners and conducted the Windsor Hotel, corner of Fifth and Market streets. The murder is said to have been the culmination of family and business troubles.

In the list of Napa county employes of the Legislature published last week the JOURNAL credited P. H. Hurley and Charles Metcalf to the Assembly. Assemblyman Webber informs us that both Hurley and Metcalf are attaches of the Senate, and that their appointments are not chargeable to him.

Now that the Senate has abolished the army canteen, let them go one step further, aye, two steps—abolish the officers' club and the buffets adjoining the halls of the House of Representatives and Senate. These latter are doubtless responsible for much bad legislation and neglect of duty. "What is sauce for the goose is sauce for the gander;" that is, it ought to be.—*S. F. Star.*

## A BIG WINE DEAL.

### The Brun & Chaix Corporation Sell Out to a New Syndicate.

John Chaix and Mrs. A. Brun, who recently incorporated their wine business, have sold all the stock in their company to a new wine syndicate organized in San Francisco, consisting of the California Wine Association, Lachman & Jacobi, C. Schilling & Co., The Italian-Swiss Colony, I. W. Hellman (President of the Nevada Bank), and Antone Borel, the banker and Swiss Consul.

The property owned by the Brun & Chaix Corporation consists of the vineyard on Howell mountain and the large winery at Oakville. The consideration for the transfer is said to have been $250,000 cash.

The syndicate has engaged Mr. Chaix to manage the business for a term of years, and shipments will be made from Oakville direct to the large Eastern cities. The firm does a large trade in New Orleans and New York, their shipments aggregating one million gallons per year.

### Personal.

Wm. Overdick is on the sick list.

Dr. E. Haun is able to be out again.

Charles Johnson is recovering from an attack of la grippe.

Geo. Berry was among the arrivals on Monday evening's train.

Congressman-elect F. L. Coombs was in town Monday.

F. B. Mackinder of St. Helena made a business trip to Napa Monday.

Senator Corlett returned to Sacramento Sunday evening.

L. H. Boggs of Lakeport was a passenger on Monday evening's up train.

Mrs. Haitshn of Portland is the guest of Mr. and Mrs. Wms. Smith.

Miss Francis of Calistoga returned home Monday morning after a short visit in Napa.

Misses Smith, Murphy and Holden of San Francisco were guests of Dr. and Mrs. Stice over Sunday.

Gen. A. W. Barrett of Los Angeles came in on Monday evening's train to visit Dr. Gardner.

### Superior Court.

MONDAY, January 14.

Estate of Patience K Brown, petition for probate of will, continued to Jan. 21.

Estate of S E Holden, petition for probate of will granted.

Estate of Zino Zorgo, petition for letters continued to Jan. 21.

Estate of J O Langley, final acconnt

*Napa Daily Journal*
January 15, 1901

A Big Wine Deal
The Brun & Chaix Corporation
Sell Out to a New
Syndicate

Jean Chaix and Mrs. A. Brun, who recently incorporated their wine business, have sold all the stock in their company to a new wine syndicate organized in San Francisco, consisting of the California Wine Association, Lachman & Jacobi, D. Schilling & Co., The Italian-Swiss Colony, I.W. Hellman (President of the Nevada Bank) and Antoine Borel, the banker and Swiss Consul.

The property owned by the Brun & Chaix Corporation consists of the vineyard on Howell Mountain and the large winery at Oakville. The consideration for the transfer is said to have been $250,000 cash.

The syndicate has engaged Mr. Chaix to manage the business for a term of years, and shipments will be made from Oakville direct to the large Eastern cities. The firm does a large trade in New Orleans and New York, their shipments aggregating one million gallons per year.

*St. Helena Star*
September 25, 1903

**Doings at Oakville.**

Miss Robson recently purchased the Brun property at Oakville, including the Cochet saloon, the former residence of Mrs. Brun and the office building formerly occupied by Brun & Chaix. The old saloon is now a restaurant and is being conducted by a Mr. Arnold. Parties are also conducting a boarding-house in Mrs. Brun's old home. Murphy & Starr, the contractors, are at work constructing two buildings on the same property for Miss Robson. One is a cottage of five rooms and the other is a building 24x40, with shed 14x40, to be used as a blacksmith shop by George Ingram. The new cottage will also be occupied by Mr. Ingram.

At the Brun & Chaix cellar many improvements have been recently made. These include an addition 95x165 feet in size. This is used as a fermenting room and adjacent are the crushers, hydraulic presses and other conveniences. A good deal of wine is being made this year. A large force of coopers are kept busy making tanks and barrels and shipments of wine are constantly being made.

The little village of Oakville is very prosperous just now, about fifty men finding employment in that neighborhood.

Thomas Williams sold the Benson crop of grapes last year and has also sold this season's crop. Mr. Williams is one of those genial men it is a pleasure to meet and he makes the visitor feel welcome. One of his prides is a complete electric plant in the cellar which is run by water power and which lights up the place splendidly. A curiosity in the shape of a stump in which were imbedded nearly 2000 acorns was shown us. Many of the acorns have dropped out now but there is the stump to show for itself. A visit to Mr. Williams is one of the pleasant features of a trip about the valley.

Editor's Note: In 1903 the *St. Helena Star* published an article on September 25, which told of the sale of Mrs. Brun's family home and the Brun property in Oakville.

*St. Helena Star*
September 25, 1903

Doings at Oakville

Miss Robson recently purchased the Brun property at Oakville, including the Cochet saloon, the former residence of Mrs. Brun, and the office building formerly occupied by Brun & Chaix. The old saloon is now a restaurant and is being conducted by a Mr. Arnold. Parties are also conducting a boarding-house in Mrs. Brun's old home. Murphy & Starr, the contractors, are at work constructing two buildings on the same property for Miss Robson. One is a cottage of five rooms and the other is a building 24 x 40, with shed 14 x 40, to be used as a blacksmith shop by George Ingram. The new cottage will also be occupied by Ingram.

At the Brun & Chaix cellar many improvements have been recently made. These include an addition 95 x 165 feet in size. This is used as a fermenting room and adjacent are the crushers, hydraulic presses and other conveniences. A good deal of wine is being made this year. A large force of coopers are kept busy making tanks and barrels and shipments of wine are constantly being made.

The little village of Oakville is very prosperous just now, about fifty men finding employment in that neighborhood.

October 30, 1904

Pacific Wine & Spirit Review

## WINE AWARDS 1904

# CALIFORNIA WINES WIN WORLD-WIDE FAME.

THE wines and brandies of California made a splendid record at the Louisiana Purchase Exposition in competition with the products of all the rest of the wine-producing world, and one that will tend to more rapidly bring them to the notice of those people of the United States, who are stubborn in their belief that good wines cannot be produced in this country, and who drink "by the label." The proud record to the credit of California viniculture is four grand prizes, sixteen gold medals, twelve silver and five bronze medals. Naturally there are some heart burnings and there will, we understand, be some protests that may increase the number of prizes in this class to some extent. It is stated that the magnificent Golden Wine Temple is to be given a grand prize for the reason that it is the most classic and artistic exhibit in the building. Herewith is the roster of honor:

GRAND PRIZES.

California Commission ........................Wine
Dresel & Co., Sonoma ........................Wines
W. S. Keyes & Son, Howell Mountain, Napa Co......Wines
Paul Masson Champagne Co., San Jose ............Wines

GOLD MEDALS.

Long Syrup Refining Co., San Francisco............
..........Crystalized Fruits and Maraschino Cherries
California Wine Association, San Francisco .........Wines
Chauche & Bon, San Francisco ..................Wines
A. Finke's Widow, San Francisco ................Wines
Gundlach, Bundschu Wine Co., San Francisco......Wines
Italian-Swiss Co., San Francisco ................Wines
Mt. Diablo Wine Co., San Francisco ..............Wines
Napa and Sonoma Wine Co., San Francisco........Wines
A. Repsold & Co., San Francisco ..............Brandies
Wetmore, Bowen Co., San Francisco ............Wines
P. C. Rossi, San Francisco ..................Vermouth
Rosenblatt Co., San Francisco ...........Apricot Brandy
H. Jevne, Los Angeles ........................Wines
Sierra Madre Vintage Co., Los Angeles............Wines
H. J. Woollacott, Los Angeles ....................Wines
California Winery, Sacramento ...................Wines
Barton Estate, Limited, Fresno ...................Wines

SILVER MEDALS.

E. Martinoni, San Francisco ...............Vermouth
E. G. Lyons & Raas Co., San Francisco ..........Brandies
California Wine and Brandy Co., San Francisco.....Wines
French-American Wine Co., San Francisco.........Wines
Lachman & Jacobi, San Francisco ................Wines
C. Schilling & Co., San Francisco ...............Wines
Los Angeles Brewing Co., Los Angeles......Malt and Beer
Italian Vineyard Co., Los Angeles ...............Wines
Southern California Wine Co., Los Angeles.........Wines
Citrus Products Co., San Diego.....Fruit and Lemon Juice
Cook's Springs Mineral Water Co., Sacramento......
County .........................Mineral Water
Pure Water Co., Berkeley ....................Waters
Dr. H. N. Cross, Livermore ..................Wines
Brun & Chaix, Oakville ......................Wines }
El Quito Olive and Vine Farm, San Jose ............Wines
Pacific Congress Springs, San Jose.........Mineral Water
Golden West Soda Works, Santa Clara County......
.............................Mineral Water

BRONZE MEDALS.

Wm. Hoelscher & Co., San Francisco ..............Wines
C. M. Mann Co., San Francisco ..................Wines
Schlessinger & Bender, San Francisco............Wines
Ed. Germain Wine Co., Los Angeles ..............Wines
P. K. D. Kingsburg, San Bernardino ..........Lemon Juice
El Dorado Brewing Co., Stockton ................Beer
J. C. Mazel, Loomis .........................Wines
John S. Fouts, Colusa ................Mineral Water
Castle Rock Mineral Springs Co., Castella...Mineral Water
John Swett & Son, Martinez ...............Grape Juice
Mihalovich-Fletcher Co., Los Gatos...............Fruits
Martin & Correglino, Clayton ....................Wines
Alhambra Mineral Water Co., Contra Costa County....
.............................Mineral Water

The last mention of Brun & Chaix, found in Napa County newspapers, was in a short article which appeared in the *St. Helena Star,* November 15, 1912.

*St. Helena Star*
November 15, 1912

The wine business, in this part of California at least, was exceptionally good during October. The California Wine Association shipped thirty thousand barrels from Winehaven, 20,000 by water and 10,000 by rail. In Napa Valley, Brun & Chaix, Inc.; G. de La Tour, Beringer Brothers, F. Salmina & Co. and other shippers tell of heavy shipments.

Editor's Note: Portrait of the Chaix family a few years after Jean Chaix died. Mrs. Jean Chaix, center front, is holding hands with her youngest child, Theresa. Daughter Adele is at right of front row. Regrettably, I am not able to identify the others. My mother, together with my grandmother, sister, brother and I, occasionally called on the Chaix family at their Bush Street residence in San Francisco during the 1920s. Mrs. Chaix, Adele and Tessie were the ones we usually saw. The friendship that developed between the Brun and Chaix families in the Napa Valley continued to flourish for many years after both families moved to San Francisco.

*The Jean Chaix house, shown on this page, is also seen in the Brun & Chaix Nouveau Medoc Vineyard and Wine Cellars lithograph that appears in the first few pages of this book. Note how the palm trees have grown since 1900.*

EDITOR'S NOTE: The Jean Chaix family house, Oakville, Napa Valley, is located on the southwest corner of the Oakville Crossroad and State Highway 29. Photographs above were taken in 1988 by William A. Hewitt. The Oakville residence of Jean A. Brun was completely destroyed by fire in 1924. No old photographs are available.

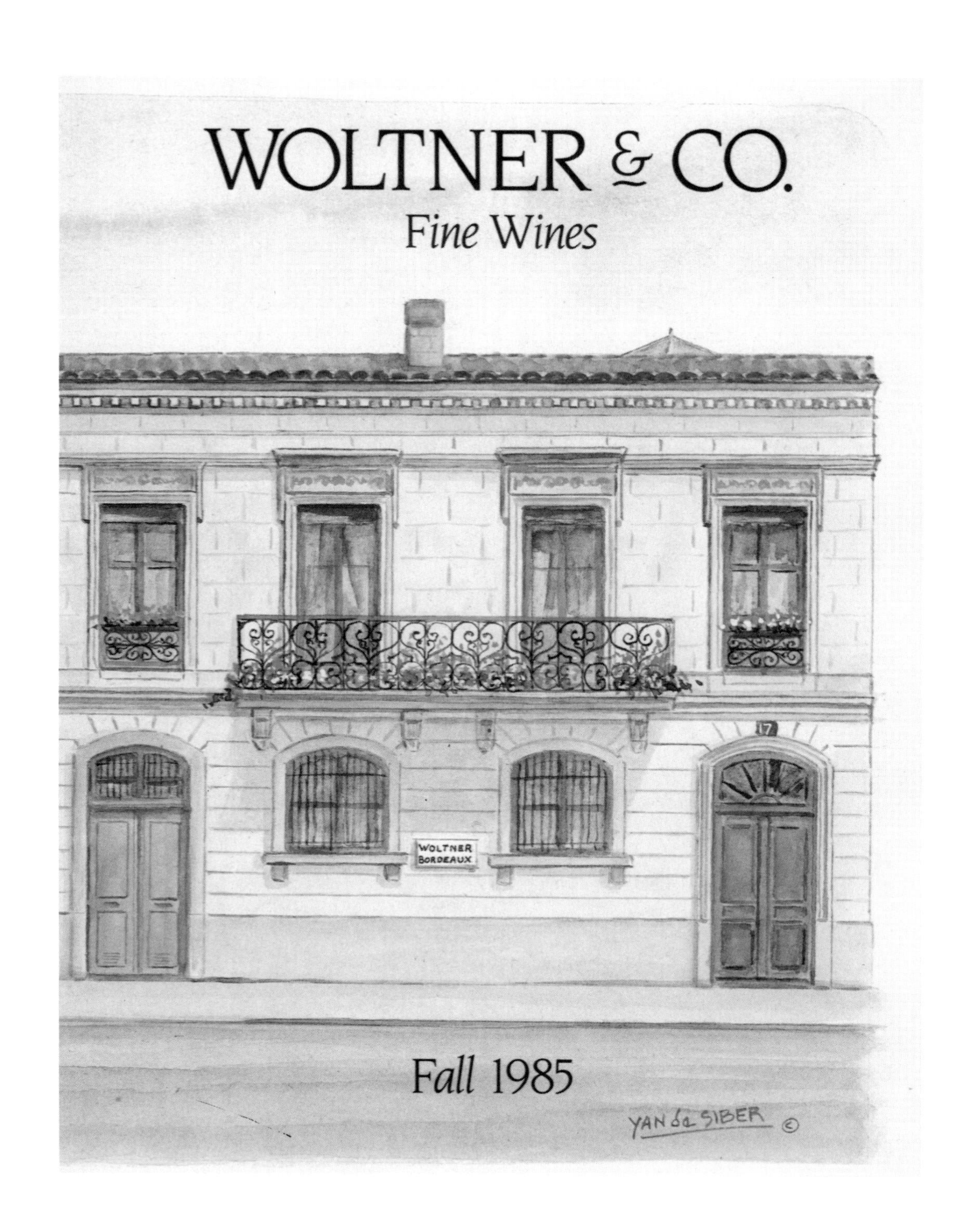


EDITOR'S NOTE: In 1980, Woltner & Co., of Bordeaux, France, purchased the original Brun & Chaix Howell Mountain property, which had been dormant for many years. The property was sold to Woltner & Co. by John Hasso, a resident of the Napa Valley. Mr. Hasso did not operate the property as a vineyard and winery, but had bought the property some years earlier as a land investment.

M. and Mme. Francis DeWavrin-Woltner restored the three-story stone winery, built by Brun & Chaix in 1886, and replanted many acres of the Brun & Chaix Howell Mountain Vineyard with Chardonnay vines. The above cover of the Woltner brochure, and the following pages from it, were issued by Woltner & Co. in the fall of 1985.

# A BRIEF HISTORY OF WOLTNER & CO.—1985

Woltner & Co. traces his history back to 1897 when Frédéric Woltner began his first wine company.

Woltner emigrated to France in the late 1800's. He worked for many years for the négociant firm of Schroeder & de Constans before founding his own company, F. WOLTNER, with offices in Bordeaux and Paris.

In 1919 Woltner bought Chateau La Mission Haut Brion, and later acquired the neighboring Chateau La Tour Haut Brion. Chateau Laville Haut Brion, the white vineyard of the Domaines Woltner, was created in the 1920's when Woltner replanted a section of the La Mission Haut Brion vineyard.

In the 1920's Frédéric Woltner's sons, Henri and Fernand, joined the family company. Henri worked chiefly at La Mission Haut Brion, while Fernand concentrated on the trade company, which was renamed WOLTNER FRÈRES.

After the death of the Woltner brothers in the 1970's, ownership of the Chateau passed to their families. Fernand's daughter Françoise and her husband Francis DeWavrin became the administrators. At the same time, Mme. DeWavrin-Woltner took control of the Woltner Frères firm, which was subsequently renamed SOCIÉTÉ WOLTNER. Family differences among the several partners involved in Chateau La Mission Haut Brion led to the sale of that estate in 1983.

After several visits to California, the DeWavrin-Woltners decided to expand their interest in the world of wine to include the United States. In 1980 they founded WOLTNER & CO. in partnership with René Rondeau. The American offices of Woltner & Co. have grown rapidly in the last five years, and are a logical extension of the venerable Bordeaux firm of Société Woltner.

Because of our longstanding contacts in Bordeaux, as well as our direct link with Société Woltner, Woltner & Co. is in a unique position to secure some of the finest wines in the area.

## NEWS FROM THE VINEYARD—1985

Chateau Woltner has just completed its first harvest and crush. Ninety-nine years after it was built, the old "Nouveau Medoc" cellar in the Napa Valley has been revived. This magnificent estate is situated on a plateau on Howell Mountain, between 1600 and 1800 feet in altitude. The microclimate is unique and varies according to the situation of each block of vines. Heat waves are unknown on this property because the vineyard benefits from cooling afternoon breezes.

The vineyard originally had been established by two young Frenchmen, Brun & Chaix in 1880. In 1886 they completed the construction of the three-story stone cellar which is focal point of the newly revived vineyard. The building is dug into the hillside, which means that the lower level is completely buried on three sides as well as shielded by two upper floors. That, combined with the thick stone walls, results in natural air conditioning which maintains the cellar temperature at a constant 60 degrees. The wines produced here by Brun & Chaix were famous worldwide. After years of success, the cellar was forced to close at Prohibition.

Francis and Françoise DeWavrin-Woltner bought this magnificent 181 acre property in late 1980, recognizing the great potential of the soils and the setting. They began clearing the land and replanting the vineyard, with the able assistance of Gary McConnell. Since the sale in 1983 of their Bordeaux estate, Chateau La Mission Haut Brion, the DeWavrin-Woltners have dedicated themselves completely to creating a California estate of equal caliber. To date, 55 acres of Chardonnay have been planted, and the old cellar is being restored to its former splendor.

The acreage planted is fantastic for Chardonnay. Each block has its own unique character, due to the amazing variety of microclimates on this hill. The 35 tons of grapes harvested this year are being barrel fermented in seven different lots, which will allow the evolution of each block to be carefully followed.

This is only the first phase of a project which will take 20 years. Approximately 2,000 cases are expected from the 1985 production.

Ninety-nine years after this noble estate was created it has gone full circle. Originally founded by two young men from the Bordeaux region, it has been revived by today's generation of Bordelais and once again the heady aroma of fermenting wine fills the ancient cellars.

*In the early 1980s, Francis DeWavrin, head of Woltner & Co., restored the winery on Howell Mountain built by Brun & Chaix in 1886. He is shown here in 1988 after his newly-acquired winery was in production.*

*Stone cellar built in 1886 by Brun & Chaix on Howell Mountain. William A. Hewitt (right) visits with Ted Lemon, cellarmaster for new owners, Woltner & Co., June 1986.*

# Wine Journal

## HOWELL MOUNTAIN

BY GERALD ASHER

Ten years ago, when meaty Zinfandels were setting the standard by which all red wines of California were judged, the most intense of them, if not the most substantial, were being made from grapes grown in a tangle of nineteenth-century vines on ridges and in shallow saddles at the top of Howell Mountain, a long-extinct volcano to the east of Napa Valley.

For the sneaker-clad help in wineshops around the nation, Howell Mountain Zinfandel was the focus of a cult, and their strategically influential enthusiasm made Howell Mountain Zinfandel part of that period's wine lore. When popular interest had shifted to less demanding wines there were still those for whom Howell Mountain and Zinfandel remained as inseparable as Pommard and Pinot Noir or Pauillac and Cabernet Sauvignon. Many Howell Mountain growers themselves cared so passionately about the partnership of Zinfandel and their thin, volcanic soil that new vineyards, as they were cleared, and old ones, as they were replanted, continued to be dedicated to this traditional California variety. As such growers explain their decision to stay with Zinfandel when Cabernet Sauvignon, now the consumer's favorite, would bring them double the revenues for the same risk and effort, they seem to reveal a barely conscious, and almost religious, sense of obligation to the mountain and its past rather than concern for the wine market and their own future.

Howell Mountain was defined as an American Viticultural Area at the beginning of 1984, yet it is among the oldest wine regions of the state. It stands among the most distinguished, too, a Howell Mountain Zinfandel having taken the Grand Prize at the Paris Exposition in 1900. Vines first had been planted there in the 1870s and were rapidly extended once the

*"The Wine Journal," by Gerald Asher (*Gourmet, *March 1988) spotlights Howell Mountain Wines and references Brun & Chaix cellars on page 2.*

quality of fruit was recognized by wineries on the Napa Valley floor. Among the earliest to establish vineyards at Howell Mountain were two Frenchmen, Jean Adolph Brun and Jean Chaix, whose Nouveau Médoc winery at Oakville was already one of the most successful in California. Brun and Chaix built a smaller, separate winery on the mountain to handle part of the crop they grew there. Charles Krug, one of Napa Valley's pioneer wineries, had vines on the mountain, too.

But probably the most eminent of the mountain's growers were William Keyes, son of an early commandant of the San Francisco Presidio (himself a winegrower), founder of the Liparita Winery and producer of the Zinfandel acclaimed in Paris; and Frederick Hess, a Swiss who built, with stone quarried from the mountain itself, the winery still in use at La Jota.

Few visitors to Napa Valley bother to drive up to the mountain's social hub at Angwin. The small community is dominated by the Seventh-Day Adventist college, and the five steep miles of Deer Park Road that separate it from St. Helena could be a hundred, so much does the landscape and atmosphere change. Though Howell Mountain wineries are hidden in woods along the side roads, a preliminary phone call (essential in any case because none of them are open to casual visitors) will establish locations and directions. They have no tasting rooms, no conducted tours, and no T-shirts. But a visit to any one of them is worth the small trouble involved. Apart from the secluded and rustic charm of the mountain, in contrast with the increasingly polished sophistication of the valley below, to visit vineyards that had been lost to brush and forest for decades following Prohibition and to see revived the old La Jota winery, for instance, or the original Brun & Chaix cellars restored by the former owners of Château La Mission-Haut-Brion in Bordeaux, is to be in the presence of Rip Van Winkle himself, stretching and blinking in the sun.

Howell Mountain's name had been used prominently on wine labels at the time of its early glory as well as in recent years, but almost always it appeared in conjunction with a Napa Valley appellation. When it was defined as a separate Viticultural Area it also remained an official subsection of Napa Valley, allowing growers within its boundaries the privileged option of using either appellation independently of the other. The double definition also allows Napa Valley wineries to buy Howell Mountain grapes to boost their blends without affecting their claim to a Napa Valley appellation.

Only four hundred acres of the Viticultural Area are presently planted with vines compared with six or seven hundred at the turn of the century. But though Howell Mountain's newly official limits, following the fourteen-hundred-foot contour, enclose more than fourteen thousand acres, it is unlikely that even a thousand of them will be planted to vines. Apart from the certain outcry if many more trees are removed—most vineyards recently planted merely restored what had been lost seventy years ago, but those who live on the mountain had become used to its sylvan isolation from the valley below—much of the mountain summit is inhospitable to vines. Exposure to sun on the mountaintop, an undulating plateau rather than a peak, is not universally favorable. Nutritionally deficient soils restrict yields even as they help concentrate flavor. The mountain has water problems. Scarcity in some of the old established vineyards is countered by occasional excess in newly cleared sites where shallow dips of soil over impervious rock create unexpectedly swampy conditions. These and other pockets also harbor freezing air on spring nights, often destroying tender buds and the year's crop with them. ("Vines on the mountain are usually pretty straggly," admits Tom Clark, who manages the Stout and the Park-Muscatine vineyards as well as cultivating a couple of acres of his own. "But then even weeds have difficulty surviving up here.")

As elsewhere in California, there are difficulties that seem quaint but aren't. Deer and rabbits raid the vineyards constantly, and a bear of gargantuan appetite forsakes his normal diet of domestic chickens at harvest time for the satisfaction of munching on the ripest, sweetest grapes. (Well, he doesn't exactly forsake the chickens. It would be more accurate to say he allows himself a change of menu from *poulet* tartare to *poulet* Véronique.)

Lee Stewart's old Souverain winery, now occupied by Burgess, produced outstanding wines from grapes grown both above and below the mountain's fourteen-hundred-foot contour line, whereas part of a vineyard recently planted on formerly uncultivated land high on the south summit suffers from strong winds and occasional fog. But though the contour might therefore seem to have been chosen as a boundary arbitrarily, no one denies that the mountaintop has a climate distinct from that of the valley below. Day temperatures there during the growing season are as much as ten degrees lower than those in the valley, protecting vines from the heat stress that typically weakens acidity. The warmer night temperatures, on the other hand, allow vines on the mountain to reach a temperature of fifty-five degrees, at which photosynthesis can occur, almost as soon as the sun is up, especially because the fog that creeps up the valley from San Francisco Bay each night leaves most of the mountain's summit untouched. If lack of stress allows the grapes to retain their refreshing acid zest, those longer hours of moderately warm sunshine provide the wines' strength and body.

Given the conditions in which mountain growers work, Michael Beatty, who farms fifty acres of vineyard on what was once the Domingos Ranch—Lee Stewart's source of Zinfandel in the sixties—is amused at Napa Valley growers' latest concern to limit the vigor and yield of their vines. "They need only have come up here," he suggested, "and they'd have had nothing more to worry about."

When cultivation is so trying and both yields and fiscal return so low, what drives the Howell Mountain growers? They would answer such a question only indirectly by talking of the extraordinary grapes produced on the mountain, and of the impressive wines that can be made from them. The combination of nutritional stress and the warm, even temperature in the growing season ensures tight bunches and small perfect berries with intense flavor. On the south side of the mountaintop, where Keyes and Hess had their vines and where the renewed Liparita and La Jota wineries are today, that flavor comes through as particularly spicy. However, on the north side, where Bob and Susan Brakesman have their Summit Lake Vineyards, and the Lamborn family has a few acres of Zinfandel, the red wines have intense fruitiness. All Howell Mountain reds, in any case and without exception, are terse and austerely muscular. They seem to be unavoidably tannic, perhaps because of their ratio of skin to juice. Paul Draper, winemaker at Ridge, says: "We had to adjust our winemaking to accommodate these grapes, and, even so, red wines from Howell Mountain can be so intense when young they seem unbalanced." Ridge buys from more than one vineyard but is best known for its association with the historic Park-Muscatine Vineyard, where Petite Sirah and Carignan vines are interspersed with Zinfandel to maintain a traditional field blend. (When I tried to understand, even to ascertain the proportions, Doris Muscatine, one of the owners, waved the question

*Continued on page* 92

*Continued from page 46*

away. "It was planted nearly a century ago by an old man who liked to mix a bit of this and a bit of that. We've just left it that way," she said.)

But in addition to these two varieties long used to support Zinfandel in California, there is now an important acreage of Cabernet Sauvignon on Howell Mountain, and recent plantings of Cabernet Franc and Merlot will soon be yielding their first crops. Dan Duckhorn, who every year receives Howell Mountain Cabernet Sauvignon from both Frank Stout's and Michael Beatty's vineyards, says he is considering bottling Cabernet Sauvignon under a Howell Mountain appellation once his own Cabernet Franc and Merlot vines planted on the mountain are bearing. At present, he says, the Cabernet Sauvignon he makes from Howell Mountain grapes tends to be overwhelming if bottled on its own, but it serves admirably to give backbone to others from the valley. He hopes that the introduction of a proportion of his other varieties from the mountain will let him offer an approachable Cabernet Sauvignon while maintaining its Howell Mountain character.

Randy Dunn, formerly the winemaker at Caymus and known for his own rather direct character, does not seem to find Howell Mountain Cabernet Sauvignon grapes particularly intractable. He swept to the forefront of California producers with a first release of his 1979 Howell Mountain Cabernet Sauvignon, and the succeeding releases made from grapes of his own and his neighbors' vines have kept him there securely—reverentially supported, of course, by the group who had spread the word on Howell Mountain in the first place. Indeed, it is the sneaker-clad insiders' ardor for Dunn's Cabernet Sauvignon that has led to a Howell Mountain cult revival. At present, only he and La Jota offer Howell Mountain Cabernet Sauvignon so labeled. Of the two, Dunn's wines are fuller, fuzzier, and *relatively* easier to enjoy—I am told he lets his grapes hang a little late on the vines to concentrate the sugar before picking. La Jota's more deeply colored Cabernet Sauvignons are less compromising. Their precise, etched style makes demands on the drinker, but it sums up effectively what everyone tries to articulate when talking of Howell Mountain and its wines. There is an important distinction shared by the Cabernet Sauvignons of both producers, however. Instead of the eucalyptus, cassis, even herbal aromas of those Napa Valley Cabernet Sauvignons laying claim to intensity, these wines from Howell Mountain are unmistakably, and irresistibly, violet scented.

Howell Mountain Zinfandels, though more widely available (I was even offered one in Tokyo recently), can be as formidable as the Cabernet Sauvignons. They are not to be confused with huggable Zinfandels from Amador County, or jolly Zinfandels from Dry Creek or anywhere else. Most have the force of a substantial Châteauneuf-du-Pape and can, on occasion, be quite as challenging. Because most of those available are young, they are more easily approached, and more readily enjoyed, if decanted an hour or two before drinking. Splashing them without ceremony into a carafe or jug encourages them to open up splendidly. In addition to Ridge, other Howell Mountain Zinfandels on the market include those from Lamborn Family Vineyards, La Jota, and Summit Lake Vineyards.

It is possible that the mountain's reputation for intense red wines will be matched by another for assertive whites. A vineyard of Sauvignon Blanc was installed as part of the program to revive the old Liparita Winery: We shall see the result in a first release still a year or two away. A small block of Semillon vines was recently planted. At La Jota, the Smiths have put in a few rows of Viognier, the Rhone valley grape used exclusively for Château Grillet, rarest of French white wines. If the 1986 sample I tasted from barrel lives up to its promise, the wine will be as flatteringly aromatic in California as it is in Condrieu.

We shall not have to wait to see the first results of new Chardonnay vineyards on the mountain, however. At Summit Lake, Bob and Susan Brakesman have been producing a few cases each year since 1984. Francis and Françoise DeWavrin crushed their first Chardonnay grapes at Château Woltner, once the Brun & Chaix winery, in 1985. Paul Draper of Ridge Vineyards crushed his first Howell Mountain Chardonnay grapes in 1987. Though these wines are neither ready nor numerous enough to be used as a basis for reliable predictions, they are clearly of generous scale and show a bony assertiveness, which suggests they will at least match the firm structure characteristic of Howell Mountain reds.

The DeWavrins are staking everything on their Chardonnay, making a complete break with the family's past at Château La Mission-Haut-Brion, where they had produced one of the finest red wines in the world. They recognize, however, that success on Howell Mountain will depend on quality high enough and style distinctive enough to justify prices that will make their difficult project economically feasible. So the fifty-five acres of former Brun & Chaix vineyards already replanted are divided into lots that follow carefully the microclimates of specific exposures. Through separate barrel fermentation and bottling over a series of vintages, the character both imposed and revealed by each section of vines should yield information that will be invaluable not only to the DeWavrins but to all who grow grapes and make wine on the mountain.

How do the traditional growers feel about the attention now directed at new varieties, particularly at previously unmentionable whites? Do they think it will change the general perception of Howell Mountain? Some are optimistic and even encouraged by the arrival of well financed proprietors ready to promote their wines in a way that could benefit the appellation as a whole. If Robert and Michael Lamborn's recent circular to their winery's customers is anything to go by, others are less sanguine. "We are glad we don't grow or make anything but Zinfandel," they declared defiantly. "The world is already too confusing." ◆

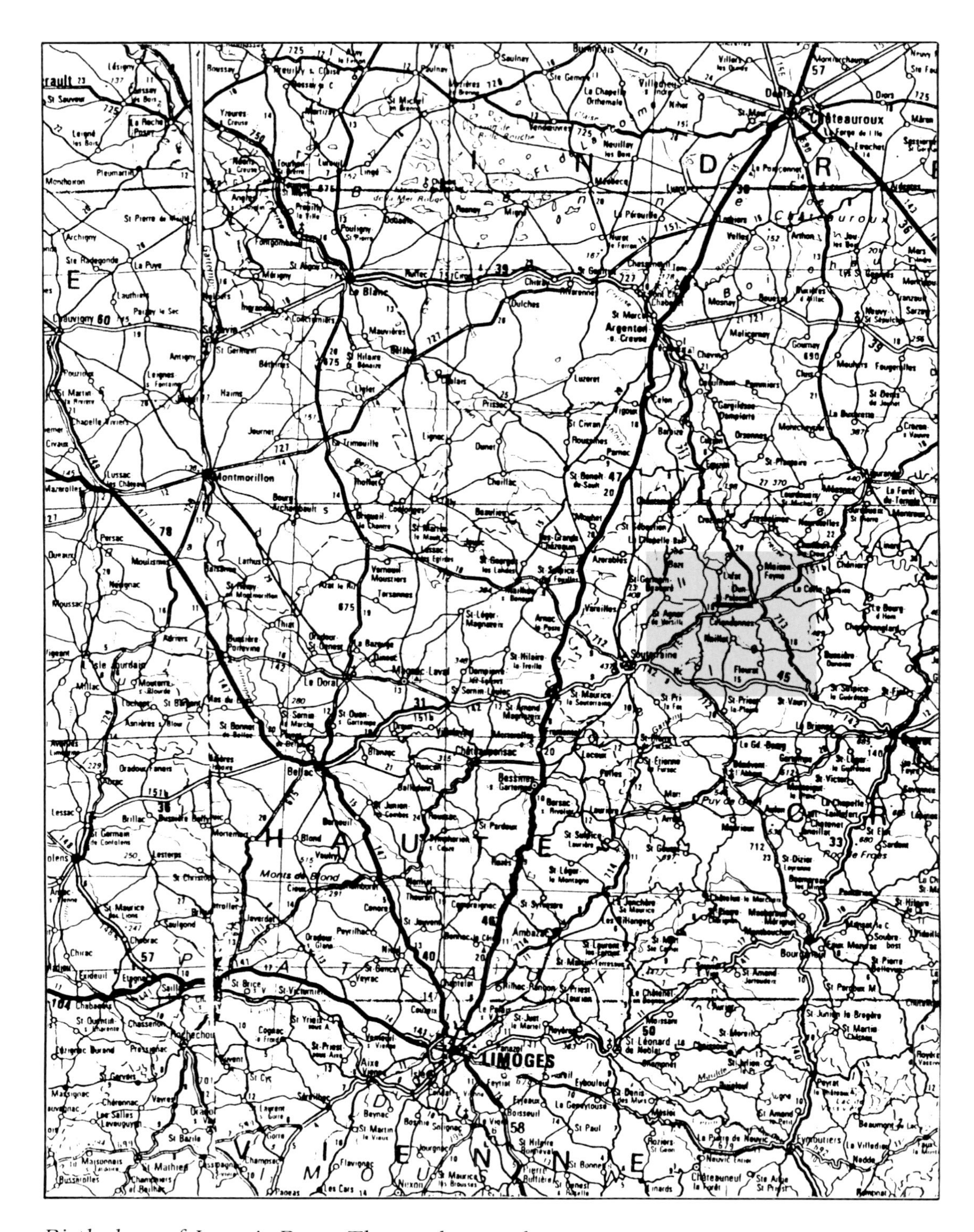


*Birthplace of Jean A. Brun. The road map above by Michelin (printed circa 1980) shows the location of the birthplace of Jean Adolphe Brun in the Village of Les Villettes, Parish of Naillat, County of Dun Le Palestel, Department of Creuse. One family in the village still had the name of Brun in July 1986. Agriculture remains the main activity of the village. Cognac is 100 miles to the west, and Bordeaux is 150 miles southwest.*

# CURRICULUM VITAE

## Jean Adolphe Brun 1845 - 1894

The following documents assembled in 1986-1987 record some of the early activities of Jean Adolphe Brun. These records indicate that his parents resided in the Parish of Naillat, County of Dun Le Palestel, Department of Creuse, France, in 1804. This was an agricultural area in the Bordeaux-Medoc region of France.

Jean Adolphe Brun was born in the Village of Les Villettes at 4:00 A.M., July 25, 1845.

EDITOR'S NOTE: The following pages offer photocopies of original French certificates, together with contemporary translations of their old-style administrative French.

Brun Jean
et
Delavaud
Marie Delphine

21

L'an mil huit cent trente et le vingt quatre du mois de [illegible]
à dix heures du matin en la chambre de la mairie, par devant nous
[illegible] maire, officier de l'état civil de la commune de [illegible]
[illegible] département de la Creuse sont comparu Jean [illegible]
[illegible] cultivateur âgé de vingt sept ans [illegible] en cette commune [illegible]
[illegible] fils [illegible] de [illegible] Brun [illegible]
cinquante quatre ans ici présent et consentant et de [illegible]
[illegible] décédée en cette commune le huit novembre mil huit cent onze
[illegible] avec son père au village des [illegible] en cette commune d'une part
Marie Delphine Delavaud âgée de vingt deux ans [illegible]
[illegible] le vingt neuf avril mil huit cent neuf fille [illegible]
de [illegible] Delavaud propriétaire et marchand [illegible] âgé de [illegible]
[illegible] et de dame [illegible] âgée de cinquante [illegible]
demeurant avec ses père et mère [illegible] de la commune de [illegible]
d'autre part. Lesquels nous ont requis de procéder à la célébration [illegible]
[illegible]
à la loi en cette commune les dix sept et vingt quatre du mois de
[illegible] et en celle [illegible] les mêmes jours et mois [illegible]
opposition ne nous ayant été signifiée faisant droit à leur réquisition
après avoir donné lecture de toutes les pièces et du chapitre six du titre du
Code civil intitulé du mariage, avons demandé au futur époux et à la future
épouse s'ils veulent se prendre pour mari et pour femme, chacun
ayant répondu séparément et affirmativement déclarons au nom de la
loi que Jean Brun et Marie Delphine Delavaud sont unis par
mariage en présence de [illegible] Brun [illegible] Pradeau [illegible]
[illegible] âgé de quarante [illegible]
[illegible] demeurant [illegible] au dit village des [illegible]
[illegible] de Jean [illegible] âgé de [illegible]
[illegible] âgé de vingt deux ans [illegible]
[illegible] de la commune de [illegible] Lesquels [illegible]
[illegible] après que lecture [illegible]
[illegible] qui a déclaré ne savoir signer [illegible]

Virchon Delavaud Catty Pradeau Brun
[illegible] Caillaud Brun
[illegible]

[illegible] le 31 [illegible] 1831 [illegible]

*Marriage Certificate:*
*Jean Adolphe Brun and Marie Delphine Delavaud*
*May 24, 1831*

Editor's Note: Document on the opposite page is the Marriage Certificate of the parents of Jean Adolphe Brun, founder of Nouveau Medoc Wineries, Napa Valley, California. Translation follows:

In the year 1831, on the 24th day of the month of May, at 10 o'clock in the morning, in the townhall in the presence of Augustin Lemoyne, Mayor, and the registration officer of the Parish of Naillat, County of Dun, Department of Creuse, there appeared Jean Brun, a landowner and farmer, age twenty-seven, born in this parish, the son of Silvain Brun, a farmer, who is too aged at fifty-four years to be present here today but is consenting, and of the deceased Anne Pradeau who died in this parish on the thirtieth of November in the year of 1811, who lived with his father in the Village of Les Villettes in this parish, on the one side; and Marie Delphine Delavaud, age twenty-two years, born in the Parish of Fleurat on the twenty-ninth of April 1809, the older daughter of Monsieur Valerie Delavaud, owner and blacksmith-toolmaker, age fifty-two years, and of Mme. Marie Ursule Viachon, age fifty-three years, living with her father and mother in the principal village of the Parish of Fleurat, on the other side.

These persons have requested us to proceed to the celebration of their projected marriage of which the bans have been published according to the law in this parish on the seventeenth and the twenty-fourth days of April in this Parish of Fleurat. Since no opposition has been signified to us, we are acceding to their request in accordance with Chapter Six of the Civil Code related to marriage. We have asked the future husband and the future spouse whether they want to take each other for husband and wife (each has answered separately and positively) so we declare, in accordance with the law, that Jean Brun and Marie Delphine Delavaud are united in marriage in the presence, on the side of the wife, of Louis Pradeau, farmer, age (————) years; and of Jean Brun, his parent, also a farmer, age (——) years, each living in the Village of Les Villettes; and on the side of the spouse of Jean, M. Caillaud, her parent, aged (——————) years, living in the principal village of the Parish of Fleurat. These, husband and wife, fathers and mother and witnesses, after the reading of the current certificate, have signed with us, but the wife has declared she does not know how to sign.

Brun Jean
adolphe

N° N° 21

L'an mil huit cent quarante-cinq, et le vingt sept du mois de Juillet
à Dix heures du matin par-devant nous Limoges François Philippe
Maire Officier de l'état civil de la commune de [illegible] canton
de Dun, département de la Creuse, est comparu le S. Brun Jean
cultivateur, âgé de quarante [illegible] ans, demeurant au village des Villettes [illegible]
Le quel nous a présenté un enfant du sexe masculin né le vingt cinq juillet à
sept heures du matin aux Villettes fils de lui
Déclarant et de [illegible] Delphine Lavaud son épouse
et auquel il a déclaré donner les prénoms de Jean Adolphe
lesdites déclaration et présentation faites en présence des sieurs Michel Lavaud propriétaire
[illegible] de la commune de [illegible] et Sylvain Brun,
cultivateur, demeurant audit village des Villettes, tous deux âgés de
trente huit ans,
et, lecture faite du présent acte aux déclarants et témoins, ils ont signé avec nous [illegible]
Sylvain Brun qui a déclaré ne savoir.

Brun Delavaud Limoges
Maire

*Document No. 21*
*Birth Certificate*
*Jean Adolphe Brun*

Document No. 21
Birth Certificate
Jean Adolphe Brun
Born July 25, 1845

Brun, Jean Adolphe

In the year 1845, on the twenty-seventh of the month of July, at ten o'clock in the morning, in our presence, Lemoigne Francois Philippe, Mayor and the Registration Officer of the Parish of Naillat, County of Dun, Department of Creuse, there appeared Jean Brun, farmer, age forty-two years, living in the Village of Les Villettes in this parish, who has presented to us a child of male sex born on the twenty-fifth of July at four o'clock in the morning in Les Villettes, his own son, registered by himself, and the son of Marie Delphine Delavaud, his wife, and to whom he has declared to give the name Jean Adolphe. The registration and presentation has been done in presence of Messrs. Michel Delavaud, and M. Grivain, farmer, living in the Village Les Villettes, both age thirty-eight years, and the reading of this current certificate has been done in the presence of the declarants and witnesses, and they signed it with us.

# Historical Notes Related to Jean Adolphe Brun's Military Service to France During the Franco-Prussian War

Editor's Note: In 1870 France declared war on Prussia. Able-bodied Frenchmen answered the call to arms. Jean Adolphe Brun (twenty-five years old at the time) joined the French army and served in the 19th Regiment of Infantry as a Soldier First Class. His service was for two years, to the conclusion of the war. Jean A. Brun's Captain (of the 4th Company) as Chief of the Battalion, stated on Brun's discharge that he "served with honor and fidelity under the colors, and with good behavior." This statement was signed by the Commanding Officer at Lyon on March 1, 1872. The following excerpt is from a book written by Professor Gordon A. Craig, of Stanford University. It is offered here as background information on the Franco-Prussian War.

**The Franco-Prussian War, January 1870-January 1871**—In his memoirs Bismarck claims that he had always believed "that a Franco-German war must take place before the construction of a united Germany could be realized." If he had in fact believed this—and one cannot always trust the veracity of Bismarck's recollections—he was proved right even before the firing began, for the first result of the French declaration was the decision of the South German states to throw their lot in with Prussia and to send troops against France.

Thanks to this and to superior efficiency in mobilization, the German armies at the outset of the war outnumbered the French nearly two to one. They also had the advantage of a better supply system, which provided the troops with the means to fight, which was not always true on the French side, as well as a superior staff system, and a high command whose war plan had long been in readiness and was now put into effect with speed and efficiency. Napoleon, in the last week before the fighting began, improvised a plan for diversionary amphibious operations in the Baltic and an offensive of massed armies against southern Germany. Before the widely dispersed French reserves could be concentrated for any such operations, however, the Prussians rammed their way through the Lorraine gap and, after some hard-fought battles in which they suffered greater casualties than the French, got between Paris and the two main French armies, those of Marshals Bazaine and MacMahon. Bazaine was forced back eastward and bottled up in the fortress of Metz. When MacMahon's army, which had now been joined by the emperor, tried to come to his aid, it was surrounded at Sedan on the Belgian frontier and hammered by artillery fire until it surrendered.

The news that Napoleon III and over 100,000 troops were in Prussian hands brought the imperial regime crashing to the ground. In Paris a republican regime was organized with General Trochu as president; and, under the leadership of Léon Gambetta (1838-1882), who made his way from Paris to the provinces by balloon, new armies were raised along the Loire and an attempt was made to prosecute the war. These raw levies fought valiantly throughout the autumn and early winter months, but the heart of their resistance was broken when Bazaine surrendered his still very substantial forces at Metz in October. When Paris, besieged since September, finally capitulated in January— after every scrap of food in the city, including the animals in the zoo and the rats in the garrets, had been eaten, and the trees in the Champs Élysées and the Bois de Boulogne had been cut down for fuel—the armies in the provinces gave up too.

Before peace could be concluded, the Germans insisted that France be represented by a government that could speak for the whole nation; and, in February 1871, elections were held for a National Assembly which then elected Adolphe Thiers as chief of the executive power and authorized him to negotiate with the enemy. Thiers discovered that the Germans were in no mood for bargaining. He was forced to agree to the payment within three years of a war indemnity of five billion francs and to accept a Germany army of occupation until the sum was paid. In addition, his country had to cede to the victor all of Alsace and most of Lorraine with their potentially rich deposits of iron ore and their flourishing textile industry. Thiers' diplomatic skill was able to ameliorate these terms in some details—he saved the fortress of Belfort for France—but the Treaty of Frankfurt of May 1871 was, even so, a heavy burden on France and one whose memory was to plague the peace of Europe for two generations.

**Gordon A. Craig**    **Stanford University**

8e DIVISION MILITAIRE.

PLACE de Lyon

(1) 19e Régiment provisoire d'Infie

# CERTIFICAT DE BONNE CONDUITE.

Nous soussignés, Membres composant le Conseil d'administration du (1) 19e Régiment provisoire d'Infanterie

Certifions que le sieur (2) Brun Jean Adolphe Soldat de 1re Classe

né le Vingt cinq Juillet 1841 à Maillat

canton de Dun département de la Creuse

cheveux et sourcils Châtains yeux Bleus front Large

nez Long bouche Moyenne menton Rond

visage Ovale marques particulières

taille d'un mètre 720 millimètres, a tenu une bonne conduite pendant le temps qu'il est resté sous les drapeaux, et qu'il a constamment servi avec honneur et fidélité.

La présente attestation est donnée sur la proposition du Capitaine commandant la (3) 1re Compagnie et du Chef de (4) 1er Bataillon auxquels appartient le sieur Brun Jean Adolphe après examen du registre de punitions en ce qui le concerne.

Certifions en outre (5) 1° Qu'il n'a aucune infirmité apparente ou cachée qui puisse l'empêcher de reprendre du Service

2° Qu'il n'est pas marié

Fait à Lyon, le 1er Mars 1872.

Les Membres du Conseil d'administration :

Le Major, Le Trésorier, Le Capne d'habt, Le Capitaine, Le Chef de Bon, Le Lieut Colonel, Le Colonel Président

Vu :

*Le Sous-Intendant militaire,*

Approuvé par nous :

*Le Général,*

6e Corps d'Armée 2me Don d'Infanterie — Le Général de Brigade — 1re Brigade

(1) Désignation du corps.

(2) Nom, prénoms et grade du militaire.

(3) La compagnie, l'escadron ou la batterie.

(4) De bataillon ou d'escadron.

(5) 1° Qu'il n'a aucune infirmité apparente ou cachée, qui puisse l'empêcher de reprendre du service, *ou bien* qu'il a (*indiquer le genre d'infirmité*); 2° Qu'il n'est pas marié, *ou* qu'il est veuf sans enfants, *ou bien* qu'il est marié ou veuf avec enfants.

N° 211. Modèle 1838. — NANCY et PARIS, Berger-Levrault et Cie.

*French Army Certificate of Good Conduct for Jean Adolphe Brun, March 1, 1872.*

8th Military Division — 19th Regiment Infantry (provisional)

Lyon

Certificate of Good Conduct

The undersigned members of the Council of Administration for the 19th Regiment Infantry

Certify that:

The said BRUN, Jean Adolphe, Soldier 1st Class, was born 25 July 1841 at Naillat, County of Dun, department of Creuse. Hair and eyebrows, brown; eyes, blue; forehead, wide; nose, long; mouth, medium; chin, round; face, oval; marks, none; height, 1 meter + 720 mm (5 ft. 7¾ inches). His conduct was good during the time he served under the colors, and he served with honor and fidelity.

This statement prepared at the request of the Captain commanding the 1st Company and the Chief of the Battalion, after examination of the Registre de Punitions (defaulters' book) concerning said BRUN, Jean Adolphe.

Further certified: he does not have any infirmities or handicaps that could disqualify him from further military service, and he is not married.

So constituted at Lyon the 1st March 1872.

The Members of the Council of Administration

(12 signatures)

Witness:

The Junior Officer

Quartermaster General's Office

(signature)

Approved,

The General,

(signature)

ERRATA: The Certificate of Good Conduct incorrectly states that Jean Adolphe Brun was born in 1841. His Certificate of Birth states that he was born July 25, 1845. The latter date is correct.

Brun Jean

No 11

L'an mil huit cent quatre-vingt-quatre, et le quatorzième jour du mois d'avril à deux heures du soir, par-devant nous Louis François Alfred Merlière Maire Officier de l'état civil de la commune de Naillat, canton de Dun-le-Palleteau département de la Creuse, sont comparus les sieurs Valery Lavaugautier cultivateur âgé de quarante-un ans voisin du décédé demeurant au village des Villettes, et Tissier Louis tailleur de pierre, âgé de trente-trois ans, gendre du décédé demeurant au village du Mandement, tous deux en cette commune lesquels nous ont déclaré que Brun Jean, époux de Jeanne Delphine Delavaud né à Naillat âgé de quatre-vingts ans, profession de cultivateur, domicilié audit village des Villettes, fils de feu Silvain Brun et de feue Anne Pradeau est décédé audit village des Villettes le treize du présent mois, à midi ~~heure du~~ ainsi que nous nous en sommes assuré, en nous transportant au domicile du décédé. Et, lecture faite du présent acte, (*) les comparants ont signé avec nous

[illegible] Lavaugautier Alf Merlière

Death Certificate: Jean Brun (father of Jean Adolphe Brun)
Died April 13, 1884 (age 80)

Brun, Jean

In the year 1884, on the 14th day of the month of April at two o'clock in the afternoon in our presence, Louis Francois Alfred Merliere, Mayor and the Registration Officer of the parish of Naillat, County of Dun Le Palleteau, department of Creuse, have appeared Messrs. Valery Lavaugautier, farmer, age forty-one years, neighbour of the decedent living in the village Les Villettes, and Louis Tissier, hewer, age thirty-three, son-in-law of the decedent, living in the village of Mandement, both in this parish, who have declared to us that Jean Brun, husband of Marie Delphine Delavaud, born in Naillat, age eighty years, who was a farmer living in the village Les Villettes, son of deceased Silvain Brun and of deceased Anne Pradeau, died in the village Les Villettes on the 13th day of the current month at midday, as we assured ourselves by going to the domicile of the deceased.

And reading the current certificate, the declarants have signed with us.

Delavaud
Marie Delphine

N° 26

L'an mil neuf cent trois, et le vingt du mois d'octobre à deux heures du soir par-devant nous Barange Ernest maire Officier de l'état civil de la commune de Naillat canton de Dun le Palleteau, département de la Creuse, sont comparus [illegible] lesquels nous ont déclaré que Delavaud Marie Delphine, veuve de Jean Brun née à Fleurat âgée de quatre vingt quatorze ans profession de cultivatrice, domiciliée aux Villettes en cette commune, fille de feu Delavaud Valery et de feue Marie Ursule Viachon est décédée à [illegible] Villettes le dix neuf du présent mois, à neuf heure du soir ainsi que nous nous en sommes assuré, en nous transportant au domicile de la décédée

Et, lecture faite du présent acte, [illegible]

Brun    Brun    Barange

Death Certificate: Marie Delphine Delavaud (mother of Jean Adolphe Brun)
Died October 19, 1903 (age 94)

Delavaud, Marie Delphine

In the year 1903, on the 20th of October at two o'clock in the afternoon, in our presence, Ernest Barange, Mayor and Registration Officer of the parish of Naillat, County of Dun Le Palleteau, department of Creuse, have appeared the Messrs. J. Brun, farmer, age forty-seven years, nephew of the decedent, and F. Brun, farmer, age sixty years, son of the decedent, living separately in Les Villettes in this parish, who have declared to us that Marie Delphine Delavaud, widow of Jean Brun, born in Fleurat, age of ninety-four years, occupation of farmer's wife, living in Les Villettes in this parish, daughter of deceased Valery Delavaud and of deceased Marie Ursule Viachon, died in this locality, Les Villettes, on the 19th of the current month at nine o'clock in the evening, as we assured ourselves by going to the domicile of the decedent.

And reading the current certificate, the declarants have signed with us, Mayor.

CALIFORNIA STATE CENSUS OF JUNE 18, 1880 SHOWS A LISTING FOR JEAN BRUN.

No. 3
No. 70

Note B.—All persons will be included in the Enumeration who were living on the 1st day of June, 1880. No others will. Children BORN SINCE June 1, 1880, will be OMITTED. Members of Families who have DIED SINCE June 1, 1880, will be INCLUDED.

Note C.—Questions Nos. 13, 14, 22 and 23 are not to be asked in respect to persons under 10 years of age.

1.—Inhabitants in [illegible], in the County of Napa, State of Cal, enumerated by me on the 18th day of June, 1880.

[illegible], Enumerator.

| Name | Color/Sex | Age | Relationship | Occupation | Place of Birth | Father's Place of Birth |
|---|---|---|---|---|---|---|
| [illegible] | W | [illegible] | aunt | [illegible] | [illegible] | [illegible] |
| [illegible] | W | [illegible] | aunt | [illegible] | Cal | " |
| [illegible] | W | [illegible] | [illegible] | [illegible] | [illegible] | [illegible] |
| [illegible] | W | [illegible] | " | [illegible] | [illegible] | " |
| Rossi Joseph | W | [illegible] | [illegible] | [illegible] | " | " |
| [illegible] | W | [illegible] | [illegible] | [illegible] | " | " |
| [illegible] | W | [illegible] | " | [illegible] | Cal | " |
| Donaldson James | W | [illegible] | [illegible] | [illegible] | N.Y. | N.Y. |
| [illegible] | W | [illegible] | wife | Keeps house | " | " |
| [illegible] Ellen | W | [illegible] | [illegible] | [illegible] | [illegible] | " |
| [illegible] | W | [illegible] | aunt | [illegible] | Iowa | " |
| Johnson George | W | [illegible] | [illegible] | [illegible] | Mo | Mo |
| [illegible] | W | [illegible] | wife | [illegible] | " | " |
| [illegible] Thomas | W | [illegible] | [illegible] | Laborer | " | [illegible] |
| [illegible] | W | [illegible] | wife | Keeps house | Iowa | U.S. |
| Edward | W | [illegible] | [illegible] | [illegible] | Mo | Mo |
| William | W | [illegible] | son | [illegible] | [illegible] | [illegible] |
| John | W | [illegible] | son | [illegible] | Cal | " |
| Tilden | W | [illegible] | son | [illegible] | [illegible] | [illegible] |
| Robert | W | [illegible] | son | [illegible] | " | " |
| [illegible] | W | 39 | [illegible] | Laborer | [illegible] | [illegible] |
| [illegible] Michael | W | 23 | [illegible] | Laborer | [illegible] | [illegible] |
| [illegible] Richard | W | 43 | [illegible] | Laborer | Canada | Canada |
| [illegible] | W | 33 | [illegible] | Saloon keeper | Penn | Penn |
| Benicia | W | 27 | wife | Keeps house | Iowa | Iowa |
| [illegible] | W | [illegible] | aunt | [illegible] | Cal | Mo |
| Harry J. | W | 8 | son | [illegible] | " | Iowa |
| [illegible] | W | 6 | son | [illegible] | " | " |
| Augustine | W | 4 | son | [illegible] | " | " |
| [illegible] | W | 1 | aunt | [illegible] | " | " |
| Brun Adolph | M | 39 | | Winemaker | France | France |
| [illegible] John | W | 22 | [illegible] | [illegible] | " | " |
| [illegible] | W | 31 | [illegible] | Cook | [illegible] | [illegible] |
| [illegible] | W | 54 | [illegible] | Laborer | France | France |
| [illegible] James | W | 40 | [illegible] | Farmer | Ohio | Ireland |
| [illegible] | W | 44 | wife | Keeps house | Tenn | U.S. |
| [illegible] Sarah | W | 23 | aunt | [illegible] | Mo | [illegible] |

TWELFTH CENSUS OF THE UNITED STATES.

SCHEDULE No. 1—POPULATION.

State California
County Napa
Township or other division of county: Yount Township Rutherford precinct
Name of Institution: x
Name of incorporated city, town, or village, within the above named division: x
Ward of city: x
Supervisor's District No. 2
Enumeration District No. 97
Enumerated by me on the 4th day of June, 1900, Chas. A. Davis, Enumerator.

| Dwelling | Family | Name | Relation | Color | Sex | Birth month | Birth year | Age | Marital status | Years married | Mother of how many children | Number living | Place of birth | Father's birthplace | Mother's birthplace | Year of immigration | Years in U.S. | Naturalization | Occupation | Months not employed | Attended school (months) | Can read | Can write | Can speak English | Owned or rented | Owned free or mortgaged | Farm or house |
|---|---|---|---|---|---|---|---|---|---|---|---|---|---|---|---|---|---|---|---|---|---|---|---|---|---|---|---|
| | | Naomi A. | Wife | W | F | Nov | 1870 | 29 | M | 7 | 3 | 1 | California | Illinois | Missouri | | | | | | | yes | yes | yes | | | |
| | | Phillis L. | Daughter | W | F | Sept | 1894 | 5 | S | | | | California | California | California | | | | | | | | | | | | |
| | | Georgia B. | Daughter | W | F | May | 1899 | 1 | S | | | | California | California | California | | | | | | | | | | | | |
| 49 | 49 | Pictorious, John | Head | W | M | Nov | 1865 | 34 | S | | | | Germany | Germany | Germany | 1884 | 16 | Na | Saloon keeper | 0 | | yes | yes | yes | R | | H |
| 50 | 50 | Grant, George | Head | W | M | Dec | 1866 | 33 | S | | | | Scotland | Scotland | Scotland | 1888 | 12 | Na | Barber | 0 | | yes | yes | yes | R | | H |
| 51 | 51 | Brun, Emma | Head | W | F | Sept | 1860 | 39 | Wd | | 6 | 6 | California | Switzerland | Switzerland | | | | Wine Dealer | 0 | | yes | yes | yes | O | F | H |
| | | Elise L. | Daughter | W | F | Nov | 1881 | 18 | S | | | | California | France | California | | | | | | | yes | yes | yes | | | |
| | | Delphine A. | Daughter | W | F | Jan | 1883 | 17 | S | | | | California | France | California | | | | | | | yes | yes | yes | | | |
| | | Jeannette A. | Daughter | W | F | Apr | 1884 | 16 | S | | | | California | France | California | | | | At school | | 9 | yes | yes | yes | | | |
| | | Louis S. | Son | W | M | Sept | 1885 | 14 | S | | | | California | France | California | | | | at school | | 9 | yes | yes | yes | | | |
| | | Julie P. | Daughter | W | F | Oct | 1888 | 11 | S | | | | California | France | California | | | | At school | | 9 | yes | yes | yes | | | |
| | | Jeanne S. | Son | W | M | Oct | 1892 | 7 | S | | | | California | France | California | | | | | | | | | | | | |
| 52 | 52 | Tong, Sing | Head | Ch | M | Dec | 1849 | 50 | S | | | | China | China | China | 1875 | 25 | Al | Farm laborer | 4 | | No | No | yes | R | | H |
| 53 | 53 | Wyatt, Harty | Head | W | M | Mar | 1870 | 30 | S | | | | California | Tennessee | California | | | | Saloon keeper | 0 | | yes | yes | yes | O | F | H |
| | | Follmer, Julius W. | Servant | W | M | Nov | 1870 | 29 | S | | | | Germany | Germany | Germany | 1885 | 15 | Al | Bar tender | 0 | | yes | yes | yes | | | |
| 54 | 54 | Jock, Harriey | Head | Ch | M | Apr | 1839 | 61 | M | 40 | | | China | China | China | 1870 | 30 | | Day laborer | 0 | | No | No | yes | R | | H |

Twelfth Census of the United States of June 4, 1900, shows a listing for Emma Brun and children.

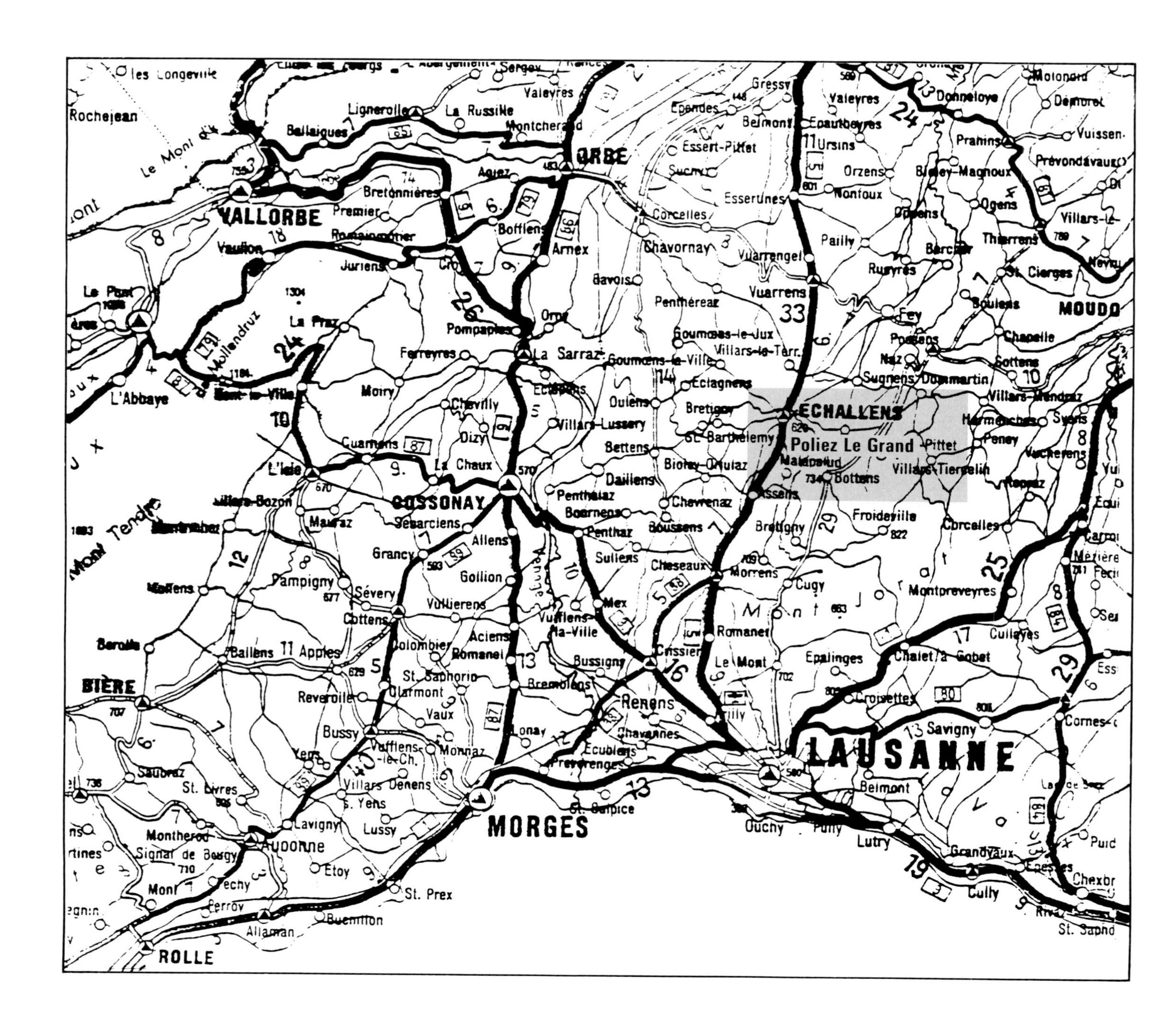


Editor's Note: Louis Mermoud, the father of Emma Mermoud Brun, was born in Poliez Le Grand, Vaud, Switzerland, a few kilometers south of Echallens, and to the north of Lausanne. Louis Mermoud emigrated from Switzerland to San Francisco in 1849.

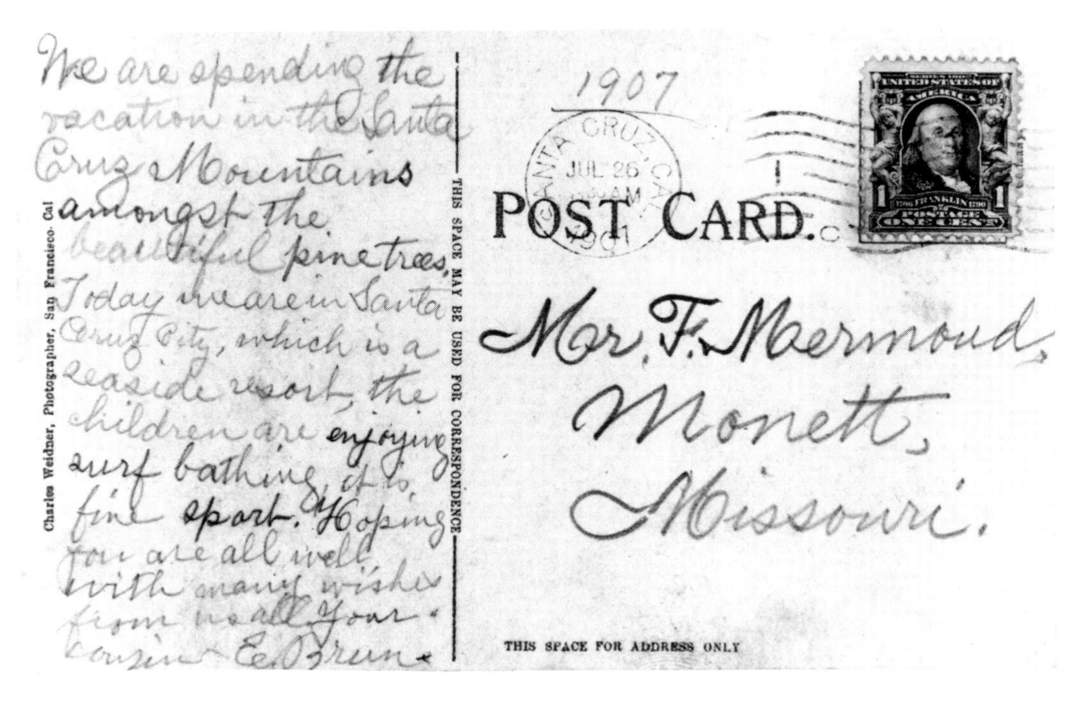
Charles Weidner, Photographer, San Francisco, Cal

We are spending the vacation in the Santa Cruz Mountains amongst the beautiful pine trees. Today we are in Santa Cruz City, which is a seaside resort, the children are enjoying surf bathing, it is fine sport. Hoping you are all well with many wishes from us all Your cousin E. Brun

THIS SPACE MAY BE USED FOR CORRESPONDENCE

1907

SANTA CRUZ, CAL. JUL 26 AM 1907

POST CARD.

Mr. F. Mermoud,
Monett,
Missouri.

THIS SPACE FOR ADDRESS ONLY

Postcard written by Emma Mermoud Brun in 1907 on vacation in Santa Cruz, California, to her cousin, Jules Francois Mermoud III in Monett, Missouri.

San Francisco, le 20 Juillet, 1915.

Ma chère Anna,

Je voudrais tant recevoir
de vos nouvelles, ainsi que de ~~tout~~ les parents
aux Villettes et au Mendement. J'attendais
toujours une lettre de quelqu'un de labas,
mais rien dutout; enfin j'ai conclus que
probablement, vous avez égaré notre dernière
adresse. Si je n'ai pas écrit avant ceci
nous pensions bien souvent à vous tous.
et surtout depuis la guerre avons nous
penser à vous tous, le temps se passe si
vite, ici, que l'on ne peut realisé, qu'il y
bien longtemps que nous n'avons point
eu de vos nouvelles, d'aucun des parents.
Je vous prie bien, ma chère Anna de
bien vouloir nous donner des nouvelles
du pays, que nous soyons un peu au
courant ce qu'il se passe labas, si loin
de se pays. Comment vont Emile et

*Letter from Emma Brun, San Francisco, to her niece, Anna Guillon, in France, July 20, 1915.*

J'aime souvent pensér des temps de
notre séjour aux Villettes, je trouvais le
paysage si beau, et nous en parlons bien
souvent, l'ont n'oublie pas des longs voyage,
ainsi, et nous étions tous bien heureux
de connaitre la grand-mère. J'éspère
que ma lettre vous trouve tous en bonne
santé et tranquil, car vous êtes, je crois
bien loin du lieu de bataille. Y a-t-il
aucun des parents de la famille Brun
qui ont été appellé au service de la
France, donnez nous un détail de tout
nous prions toujours pour la paix.
Toute la famille ici se porte bien,
Dieu merci; nous attendons la visite
d'Élise et sa famille dans quelques
semaines, elle n'a toujours qu'un enfants,
il a donze ans, il y aura trois ans que
je ne lés ai pas vu. Jeannette a deux
enfants, deux garçons, l'ainé a trois
ans, le bébé à un ans. Delphine
Louis et Julie ne sont pas marié,
mais, alors, Adolphe est marié

il y a environ deux ans et demi, ils ont
une mignonne petite fille de quinze
mois. Les affaires dans ce pays
marche trés lentement, la Guerre en
Europe fait du tort aux monde entier,
personne n'est content de savoir le
désacord des Pays et la destruction des
Pays; il faut espérer que la fin sera
bientôt. Ecrivez nous bientot et pour
que ayons de vos nouvelles que nous
attendont avec impatience.
Nos bons souvenirs et amitiés de toute
notre famille a tous et tout les parent.

Votre tante qui pense à vous

Emma Brun.

Adresse 4724 - Seventeenth Street,
San Francisco,
California.

N. B. J'adresse cette lettre a nom de fille
car je ne sais pas votre nom de mariée.

San Francisco, July 20, 1915

My dear Anna,

I would like so much to receive news from you, as well as from all relatives in Les Villettes and in Le Mandement. I am always waiting for a letter from someone there, but nothing arrives. I have concluded that you have lost our address. Quite frequently we think of all of you, and since the war started we have thought of you even more often.

Time is passing by so quickly here that one cannot realize that much time has passed since we have had news of any of our relatives. I beg you, dear Anna, give us news of France so we can be more conversant with what is happening there. We are so far from our home country.

I often like to think of the time of our stay in Les Villettes, where I found the countryside so beautiful, and we speak of it often. One does not forget such long journeys, and we were all very happy to get to know grandmother. I hope that my letter finds you in good health and feeling tranquil because, I believe, you are far away from the battlefields. Are there any relatives of the Brun family who have been called up to the military service of France? Please give me details. We always pray for peace.

All the family here is keeping well, thanks to God. We are waiting for a visit by Elise and her family in a few weeks. She still has only one child. He is twelve years old, and it has been three years since I have seen them. Jeannette has two children, two sons. The elder is three years old, and the baby is one year old. Delphine, Louis, and Julie are not married, but Adolphe has been married for about two years and has a nice little girl of fifteen months.

Business in this country is going very slowly. The war in Europe is harming the whole world. Nobody is satisfied with the discord between countries and the destruction of countries. One must hope the end of the war will be soon.

Write us soon so we will have news of you. We await it with impatience.

With pleasant memories and kind regards from all of our family to all of our relatives and friends.

Your aunt who thinks of you,

Emma Brun

N.B. I address this letter to your maiden name, for I do not know your spouse's name.

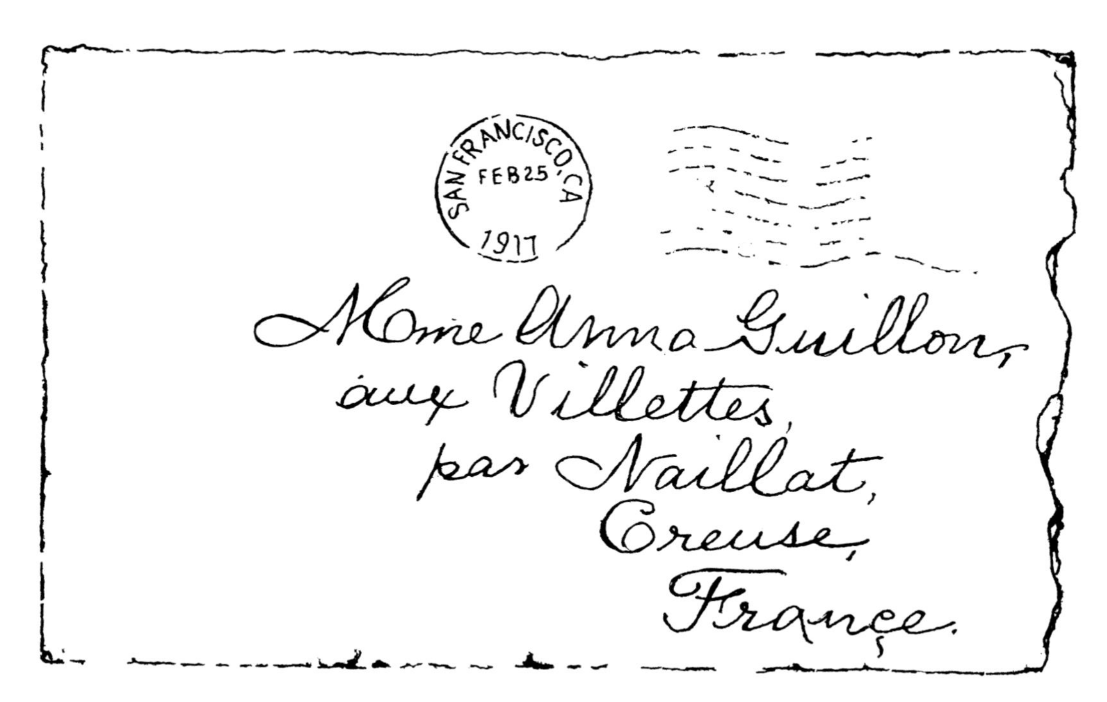
SAN FRANCISCO, CA
FEB 25
1917

Mme Anna Guillon,
aux Villettes,
par Naillat,
Creuse,
France.

*Envelope and letter from Emma Brun to her niece, Anna Guillon, in France, February 25, 1917.*

San Francisco, le 25 ver -17-

Ma chère Anna

Aujourd'hui je suis avec vous je ne voulais remèttre de vous écrire, car il y a deja longtemps je pensais repondre votre lettre, qui m'à fait plaisir d'apprendre ce qu'il se passe aux Villettes, et je suis contente de vous donner de nos nouvelles. Je vous dirai que nous avons été bien bien peiné d'apprendre la mort de la pauvre tante Mietta et surtout par une si terrible maladie, nous avons été très surprise, car vous n'aviez nea dis de sa maladie dans votre première lettre, sa nous a fait bien de la peine aussi la mort d'Emile, la guerre d'aujourd'hui et bien terrible, Nous avons bien de la peine par sa femme et ses enfants.

2/

votre mari est-il toujours auprès de vous, j'éspère qu'il n'à pas été appelles au front, nous prions que la fin de cette affreuse guerre arrive bientôt. Je vois par votre lettre que vous avez une bien interressante petite famille. Vous m'aviez envoyé l'adresse d'Amédée, je lui avait écris environ un an, et j'ai reçu une reponse de lui, il y a une semaine, mais il n'a pas écrit grand chose. Lorsque vous écrirez, je vous prie de me donner des nouvelles de ce qu'il se passe aux Villettes, j'aurais bien voulu écrire quelques lignes a tante Victoire, veuillez me donner son adresse. Avec qui demeure-t-elle la veuve du defunt Emile, était-elle une fille née aux Villettes.

Ma chère Anna, les parents de votre mari vivent-ils?

3.

Je pense quil y a bien des changement aux pays depuis notre visites labas; j'éspere que vous êtes tous en bonne santé, vous avez tous bien besoin de votre santé et un grand courage.

Votre cousine Jeannette et l'heureuse mère une mignonne petite fille, elle a huit mois, maintenant elle a deux petits garçons et la petite Adrienne, toute sa famille se porte bien, et tous vos cousines et cousins sont aussi en bonne santé, ainsi que moi-meme je me porte très bien. Nous avons eu un hiver très froid, et pas beaucoup de pluie. Les affaires marche doucement, et les vivres sont très chers, tout a beaucoup augement en prix, pensez donc les pommes de terre

4.

que se vendaient un sou la livre, c'est maintenant cinq sou la livre. Lorsque je parle de pomme de terre je pense toujours au bonnes pomme de terre des Villettes, et les bons légumes que votre bonne mère avait dans les jardins, ils étaitent bons.

Je vais terminer ma lettre, car il commence a faire nuit, et je veux mettre cette lettre a la poste de suite. Ne manquez pas d'écrire aussitôt que vous aurez un moment de libre car nous seront si heureux d'apprendre de vos nouvelles. Nos amitiés, a vous et votre famille, et tous les parents et le bonjour aux amies.

Votre tante
Emma Brun

San Francisco
February 25, 1917

My dear Anna,

Today I am with you. I have not wanted to delay writing to you, but for a long time, I have been trying to answer your letter which pleased me. Now that I know what is happening in Les Villettes, I am happy to give you news of me. I can say that we were very distressed to learn of the death of poor dear Aunt Miette. Because she had such a terrible disease we were very amazed that you had not said anything of her disease in your first letter. This has distressed us, as has the death of Emile. The war today is terrible. We are deeply in sorrow for his wife and his children. Is your husband still with you? I hope he was not called up to the front. We pray for the end of this dreadful war, and want it to come to an end soon.

I see from your letter that you have a very interesting little family. You sent me the address of Amedee. I wrote to him about a year ago, and I received an answer from him one week ago, but he did not write much When you write again I beg you to give me news of what is happening in Les Villettes. I would have liked to write a few lines to Aunt Victoire. Will you give me her address? With whom is she living, as the widow of deceased Emile. Was she born in Les Villettes? My dear Anna, are your husband's parents still alive?

I think there are many changes in the village since our visit there. I hope that you are all in good health. You all need your health and great courage.

Your cousin Jeannette is the happy mother of a nice little girl, Adrienne She is eight months old and has two brothers. All of Jeannette's family is well, and all our cousins are also in good health and I am very well. We had a very cold winter and little rain. The business is going slowly and food is very expensive. Everything has greatly increased in price. Just think potatoes which were selling for one cent per pound are now at five cents When I speak of potatoes I always think of the good potatoes in Les Villettes, and of the good vegetables our Mother had in the gardens. They were so good.

I will now finish my letter because it is beginning to be night and I want to put this letter into the mail immediately. Please write to me as soon as you have free time. We will be so happy to have news from you.

Our affectionate regards to you and your family, and to all our relatives and to our friends.

Your aunt,

Emma Brun

Dombasle, Dec-1-18,

My dear children —

Well, Louis old kid, I was sure surprised when I heard you were in line for the big leap and much more so when I heard it was done so soon. Believe me I am glad to hear that you had enough courage to do it, but I can imagine how weak at the knees you were. It sure must be tough to keep your footing while the big ceremony is going on, but after that its smooth sailing. I missed all that you know, but I am just as well off as every thing is going on fine and dandy in my little family. — Before I go any further I want to bestow upon you my sincere blessings & my best wishes for a happy married life.

Believe me, I am mighty happy to hear that I have such a good little girl and that everyone loves Jeanne. There is no one in the world more anxious than I to come home, so that I can see her and love her that way I want to. Believe me if anything should happen to her while I am away, there will be no such happy home coming for me as I have been picturing since the war has stopped. At one time before the war ended, I used to try and picture myself going home, but just about then some Boche would drop one near and bing would go my dream & after that I would be scared to dream any more.

Well on March 28th at 4 P.M. we left Green Burnie Md. - and on 29th at 9 A.M. arrived at New Jersey depot - from there we boarded a ferry & were headed up to Hoboken, while on the ferry we had another physical examination. The ferry landed us next to the transport docks & from there we were marched on to the George Washington. We left port Mar. 31st at 9 P.M. We sure had wonderful trip, as we only had two rough days & will you believe me I wasn't sick at all. Of course it was a terribly monotonous trip as for days we hardly made any headway. They had a little target practice and on about the 11th day out the siren gave five blood curdling shrieks (sub alarm) & they started shooting at what they thought was a sub, but instead it was a porpoise and he was splashed all over the ocean. The Navy took all kinds of precautions to get us safely across. There were six transports in convoy & 1 cruiser leading. On the 11th day, four chasers joined us & early on the 12th five more cruisers came up - and that night four of our boats & five chasers left us & on morning of 13th we arrived at Brest, France. At 5 P.M. we landed & then we were marched five miles to the barracks - Can you imagine us hiking five miles with a full pack & rifle, after being 14 days, on a boat? Wow! not unless you tried it. On April 20th we harnessed up and walked back to depot, where we were loaded

*Letter from Jean Adolphe Brun, written in France, to his brother and sisters in San Francisco. December 1, 1918.*

on to the regulation French cars & eventually arrived at Nevers. (4 days) The we hiked about 4 miles & when we arrived there we looked all over for barracks but none were in sight and it didn't take long for us to figure things out, after awhile we had our pup tents and were ready to turn in, luckily it was not cold, so I really enjoyed the 2 days stay. On the 26th we embarked for St. Sulpice, a town near Bordeaux (10 miles) There we remained about five weeks doing a little of everything. From here we returned to Nevers, this time we had barracks to sleep in. From Nevers, two boys and

myself were sent to St. Nazaire to bring back 2 Mack 5½ ton hydraulic dump trucks. We made the trip in five days & believe me some trip. We went through Nantes, Tours, Bourges, & a lot of smaller towns. In a short time we got our 31 trucks - all Macks. They are one of the best trucks here, best 5½ ton anyway. They sure stand up fine. Also the Giant tire stands up way better than the Dual. We stayed in Nevers until Aug 6th, hauling a little of every thing, but especially rock. All along different roads used by the U.S.A. as the army intended keeping up the roads they used.

On Aug 6th we loaded our belongings & started for Chateau Thierry front. The first night we stopped near Grim & the second in Fontainebleau Forest, (largest forest in France) & on the third in La Ferte & arrived in Chateau Thierry next morning & in afternoon we made camp near Mezy staying until next afternoon, when four of us with our trucks went to Neeles, beyond Fere en Tardenois where we hauled rocks for roads to the front, which was 6 miles away. There we were not bothered by guns, but the planes came over & there I got my first lesson in diving for dug outs & believe me, it came kind of natural. When I heard the whistle of the first one I didn't

bother to look where it landed, but headed for my room, but as I was a stranger in the village, I got lost, so I couldn't help seeing the show & when I saw the hole he made big enough to bury two Mack trucks, Wow that got my goat. Soon we were hauling things nearer the front & shortly after the boys drove the boche out of Fisme & over the Vesle. I had occasion to drive into Fisme. Every house in town ruined, as I was going up the main street, I heard a loud report & when I looked, I saw one of the walls near by going to pieces, well I just spoke a word of encouragement to my truck & you should

have seen her whiz one off & we
didn't stop until we were out
of town. Soon after that we
camped up near to the front,
& then you should have heard
the shells come close. Some of the
towns we had to go through, we
often had to wait outside until
they finished shelling, then
beat it through.
About the last of Aug. the
Americans turned the front
over to the French, so we moved
toward the St. Mihiel front, to
a town where we stayed on
reserve for a week.
On our way we passed Epernay
& Chalons Sur Marne. From
St. Mihiel front we came over

to the Argonne front on the Verdun
sector, our first camp was in the
woods near Parois where we
stayed a few days, then moved
to woods near Clermont, here
we worked right near the front
all the time, & Oh! boy! talk about
dodging shells it was an every
day occurance, and a few planes
thrown in. Just before the
Americans started their big
drive, we were hauling rock &
lumber into a little town less
than a mile from the front
Fritz used to chase us out
nearly every night. The big
drive started Sept 26th at
about 11 P.M. & if could have
heard the barrage, you would

December 1, 1918

My dear children,

Well, Louis old kid, I was sure surprised when I heard you were in line for the big leap, and much more so when I heard it was done so soon. And believe me I am glad to hear that you had enough courage to do it, but I can imagine how weak at the knees you were.

It sure must be tough to keep your footing while the big ceremony is going on, but after that it is smooth sailing. I missed all that, you know, but I am just as well off as everything is going on fine and dandy in my little family.

Before I go any further I want to bestow upon you my sincere blessings and my best wishes for a happy married life. Believe me, I am mighty happy to hear that I have such a good little girl and that everyone loves Jeanne. There is no one in the world more anxious than I to come home, so that I can see her and love her the way I want to. Believe me, if anything should happen to her while I am away, there will be no such happy homecoming for this one as I have been picturing since the war has stopped. At one time before the war ended I used to try and picture myself going home, but just about then some Boche would drop one near, and bing would go my dream, and after that I would be scared to dream any more.

Well, on March 28th at 4 P.M., we left Green Burnie, MD, and on the 29th at 9 A.M. arrived at New Jersey depot. From there we boarded a ferry and were headed up to Hoboken. While on the ferry we had another physical examination. The ferry landed us next to the transport docks, and from there we were marched onto the *George Washington*. We left port on March 31st at 9 P.M. We sure had a wonderful trip, as we only had two rough days and, will you believe me, I wasn't sick at all. Of course, it was a terribly monotonous trip, as for days we hardly made any headway. They had a little target practice, and on about the 11th day out the siren give five bloodcurdling shrieks (sub alarm) and they started shooting at what they thought was a sub. But instead it was a porpoise and he was splashed all over the ocean.

The Navy took all kinds of precautions to get us safely across. There were six transports in convoy, and one cruiser leading. On the 11th day four sub chasers joined us and, early on the 12th, five more cruisers came up and that night four of our boats, and five chasers, left us and on the morning of the 13th we arrived at Brest, France.

At 5 P.M. we landed and then we marched five miles to the barracks. Can you imagine us hiking five miles with a full pack and rifle, after being 14 days on a boat? Wow! Not unless you tried it. On April 20th we harnessed up and walked back to depot, where we were loaded onto the regulation French cars and eventually arrived at Levers (4 days). Then we hiked about 4 miles and, when we arrived there, we looked all over for barracks but none were in sight and it didn't take long for us to figure things out. After awhile we had our pup tents up and were ready to turn in. Luckily, it was not cold, so I really enjoyed the 2-day stay.

On the 26th we embarked for St. Sulpice, a town near Bordeaux (10 miles). There we remained about five weeks, doing a little of everything. From here we returned to Levers. This time we had barracks to sleep in. From Levers, two boys and myself were sent to St. Lazaire to bring back 2 Mack 5½ ton hydraulic dump trucks. We made the trip in five days and believe me, it was some trip. We went through Lantes, Tours, Bourges, and a lot of smaller towns. In a short time we got our 31 trucks, all Macks. They are one of the best trucks here, best 5-ton anyway. They sure stand up fine. Also, the giant tire stands up better than the Dual.

We stayed in Levers until Aug. 6th, hauling a little of everything, but especially rock. All along different roads used by the U.S.A., as the army intended keeping up the roads they used.

On August 6th we loaded our belongings and started for the Chateau Thierry front. The first night we stopped near Grim, and the second in Fontainebleau Forest (largest forest in France), and on the third in La Ferte and arrived in Chateau Thierry next morning. In the afternoon we made Camp Mezy, staying until next afternoon when four of us with our trucks went to Lesles, beyond Fer en Tardenius, where we hauled rocks for roads to the front, which was 6 miles away. There we were not bothered by guns, but the planes came over and there I got my first lesson in diving for dugouts and, believe me, it came kind of natural.

When I heard the whistle of the first bomb I didn't bother to look where it landed but headed for my room, but as I was a stranger in the village I got lost, so I couldn't help seeing the show and when I saw the hole he made big enough to bury two Mack trucks, WOW! that got my goat. Soon we were hauling things nearer the front, and shortly after the boys drove the Boche out of Fisme and over the Lesle.

I had occasion to drive into Fisme. Every house in town was ruined, and as I was going up the main street I heard a loud report and, when I looked, I saw one of the walls nearby going to pieces. Well, I just spoke a word of encouragement to my truck and you should have seen her whizz me off, we didn't stop until we were out of town.

Soon after that we camped up near the front and then you should have heard the shells come close. Near some of the towns we had to go through we often had to wait outside until they finished shelling, then beat it through.

About the last of August the Americans turned this front over to the French, so we moved towards the St. Mihiel front, to a town where we stayed on reserve for a week. On our way we passed Eperney and Chalons sur Marne. From the St. Mihiel front we came over to the Argonne front on the Verdun sector. Our first camp was in the woods near Parois, where we stayed for a few days. Then we moved to woods near Clarmont. Here we worked right near the front all the time and, oh boy, talk about dodging shells. It was an everyday occurrence, and a few planes thrown in.

Just before the Americans started their big drive we were hauling rock and lumber into a little town less than a mile from the front. Fritz used to chase us out nearly every night. The big drive started Sept. 26th at about 11 P.M., and if you could have heard the barrage, you would..........

(LAST PAGES OF ORIGINAL LETTER ARE MISSING)

Oilfields California
Le 30 Janvier 1921.

Mon Cher Cousin.

Depuis que j'etai
là en France i vous voir
je pensé de vous écrire
tout le temps mais comm
je ne peu pas écrire en
français moi même il a
fallu que j'attend jusqu
que je rencontre quelqu'u
pour l'écrire pour moi.
j'ai reçue votre carte
postal et j'étais tres heureu
de vous savoir tous en bonn

*Letter from Jean Adolphe Brun in California, to his cousin in France, January 30, 1921.*

santé et que vous pensiez à moi.
Je travail dans les huiles de pétrol à peu près 300 kilometres de chez moi San Francisco et j'étais à la maison rien que une fois pendant six mois.
Je ne jamais oublirais du bon traitement et bon temps que vous m'avez donné pendant que j'étais là chez vous et je desire que vous me r'appellerez à mes amis et ~~especially~~ surtout aux deux ~~Tantes~~ Tantes.
Avant que je suis partie de la France une petite cousine m'a écrite une lettre de Dun Le Palteau la ville où j'ai pris le train, alors c'étais impossible pour moi la répondre mais je voudrais bien lui écrire maintenant si je ~~s~~avais qui c'était et puis si j'avais son adresse
C'est drôle comme le peuples est different ici est là vous dite que vous voudriez venir dans ce pays

et moi je voudrais être bien
là si je n'étais pas marié
je voudrais vivre là en
France, le peuple là à
l'air d'être plus content
et satisfait qu'ici.
maintenant ici depuis la
guerre il y a beaucoup de
monde sans travail et
au lieu de venir mieux
çà va pire et les ~~gages~~ guages
s'abaissent mais bientôt
j'espère d'aller en Mexique
à travailler au même metier
je finie ma lettre en attendant
vos bonnes nouvelles.
~~avec~~ mes amitiés à vous tous
de ma part. votre Cousin.

Jean Adolphe LeBrun

Oilfields, California

January the 30th, 1921

My dear Cousin,

Since I was in France visiting you I frequently have thought of writing you. But since I cannot write in French, I had to wait till I met someone to translate it for me. I received your postcard and I was very happy to know you all are in good health and that you have been thinking of me.

I am working in the oil fields about 300 kilometers away from our house in San Francisco, and I have been home only once in six months. I'll never forget the good treatment and the good time you gave me while I was at your house and I hope that you will remember me to my friends and also to my two aunts.

Before I left France, a second cousin wrote me a letter from Dun Le Palteau, the town where I took the train. At that point it was impossible for me to answer, but I would like to write her now, if I could know her name and if I could have her address. It's amazing how different people are between here and there. You say you would like to come to this country and I would very much like to be in France. If I was not married I would like to live there in France. The people there seem to be happier and more satisfied than here.

Since the war there are many unemployed people here and, instead of becoming better off, it is turning worse and wages are decreasing. But soon I hope to go to Mexico for work in the same profession, in the oil fields.

I now finish my letter awaiting your news. With my kindest regards to all of you, from me,

Your cousin,

Jean Adolphe Brun

*Envelope of letter from Emma Brun in San Francisco, to her niece, Anna Guillon, in France, November 7, 1923.*

San Francisco Nov-7-1923

Ma chère niece, Anna,
J'écrie pour vous faire
part que mon avocat a écrit
au Notaire de Naillat pour mettre
notre propriété aux Villettes en vente
Ce quil me decide de prendre
se pas, c'est que j'ai reçu une
lettre de M. André Pradeaux de
Paris, en disant quil aimerait
bien acheter ce quil reste de
la vielle maison. J'ai perdu
son adresse, alors je vous
ecris a vous.
Je vous prié d'en faire part

2/
aux reste des parants.
Notre frère Adolphe a bien
souvent parlé de vous, lors
son retour de France. Il a
beaucoup joui de son petit
séjour aux Villettes. Il
noubliera jamais vos bontés.
Il y a un an quil est en
Perse - Asia. Il travail
pour une grande compagnie
de petrole Anglo-Perse. Il
éspere y rester encore deux ans.
Louis est marié, et ils ont deux
gantil petites filles. Une a

3/
quatre ans et l'autre a deux
ans. Delphine et Julie sont
toujours celebataires. La
petite famille de Jeannette
grandi. L'ainné a onze
ans et demi, le cadet a neuf
ans et la petite fille Adrienne
a sept ans. Élise vas
toujours bien ainsi que sa
famille. Son fils a vingt ans.
Ma chère Anna nous serions
bien heureux d'aprendre de
vos nouvelles. Combien de
parents il y a t'il de reste?

4/
Bien le bonjour aux parents
et aux amis.
Je vous embrasse de tout
cœur,
Votre tante
Emma Brun
4124-17th St
San Francisco,
California.
U.S.A.
U.S

*Letter from Emma Brun in San Francisco, to her niece, Anna Guillon, in France November 7, 1923.*

Mrs. Anna Brun Guillon
Les Villettes, Creuse, France
by Naillat

San Francisco, November 7, 1923

My dear niece Anna,

I write to tell you that my lawyer has written to the Notary Public for selling my property in Les Villettes. The reason for my deciding to make this step is that I have received a letter from Mr. Andre Pradeau, from Paris, saying that he would like to buy from me what is remaining from the old house but I have lost his address so that is why I am writing to you.

I am asking you to give it to his relatives. Our son Adolphe has been telling us much about you since he returned from France. He appreciated very much his short stay in Les Villettes. He will never forget your kindness. During the past year he has been in Persia. He works for a big oil company, Anglo-Persian. He hopes to stay there two more years. Louis is married and they have two nice little girls. One is four years old and the other one is two years old. Delphine and Julie are still spinsters. The small family of Jeannette is growing. The oldest son is eleven and a half years old. The second is nine years old, and the little girl Adrienne is seven years old. Elise is well and so is her family. Her son is twenty years old.

My dear Anna, we would be very happy to hear your news. How many relatives are remaining?

Kind regards to our relatives and friends.

I embrace you with all my heart.

Your aunt,

Emma Brun

San Francisco - le 3 Janvier - 1924

Ma chere Anna

Votre lettre nous a fait grand plaisir - nous étions si contente d'aprandre de vos nouvelles. Je me hate de repondre pour vous dire que si vous voulez la maison paternelle que vous pouvez l'avoir pour les frais de reparations. Et pour les terrains - vous pouvez vous arranger entre vous et les autres parents, et garder cela dedans la famille.

Votre tante qui pense souvent a vous et qui vous aime toujours.

Emma Brun
4724 - 17th St
San Francisco
California

*Letter from Emma Brun to her niece, Anna Guillon, in France, January 3, 1924.*

San Francisco

January 3, 1924

My dear Anna,

Your letter pleased us very much. We were so happy to learn of your news. I hurry to answer and to tell you that if you want the paternal house you can have it for the repair costs.

As for grounds, you can arrange it between yourself and the other relatives to keep them in the family.

I would like to arrange it for you not to pay anything, but you might pay the cost for the Notary Public so it will be yours.

I hope that all this will be arranged in a friendly manner. Let me know what you think of it.

The family is joining me to wish you a good and happy New Year, and also to the whole family and to all our relatives.

Your aunt who thinks often of you
and always loves you,

Emma Brun

*Portrait of Emma Brun, taken in 1935, that she presented to her daughter, Jeannette.*

# BRUN FAMILY PHOTOGRAPHS

*Jean Adolphe Brun, 1845-1894.*

*Emma Mermoud Brun, 1860-1945.*

*Louis Mermoud, Born in Poliez Le Grand, Vaud, Switzerland; Emigrated to California 1849; Married Suzette Muelmeister of Switzerland.*

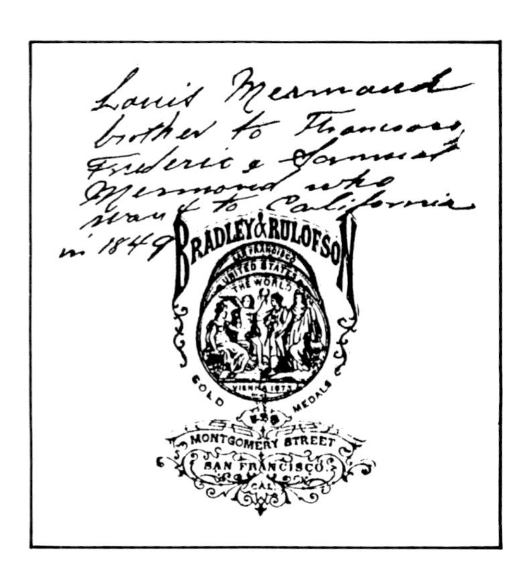


*Handwritten note on back of photograph states, "Louis Mermoud, brother to Francois, Frederic, and Samuel Mermoud who went to California in 1849."*

*Mrs. Louis Mermoud, Emma Mermoud Brun's mother. Her maiden name was Suzette Muelmeister.*

*Emma Mermoud and her father, Louis Mermoud, San Francisco, circa 1870.*

*This house was built by Emma Mermoud Brun's grandfather, Jules Francois Mermoud, in Poliez Le Grand (near Lausanne), Canton of Vaud, Switzerland. Inset: Emma Mermoud Brun's grandfather, Jules Francois Mermoud, born in the village of Poliez Le Grand.*

*Jean Adolphe Brun and his bride, Emma Mermoud Brun, early 1880s, Napa Valley.*

*Four of the six children of Jean and Emma Brun: Delphine, Louis, Elise and Jeannette, Napa Valley, California, circa 1887.*

*Oakville Primary School, Napa County, California, 1891.*
*The students' names were listed on the back of the original photograph, but no effort was made to fit the names to their faces.*

*James Walters, George Smith, Wirt Walters, Joseph Smith, Louis Brun, Jesse Fisher, Andrew Hansen, James Walters, Daisy Roberts, Ethel Liteman, Lizzie Davis, Miss L. Bell, Elise Brun, Louie Walters, Fred Smith, Cecelia Dwyre, Pearl Luney, Cyetta Hansen, Susie Davis, Katie Fisher, Ethel McQuaid, Cyetta McQuaid, Delphine Brun, Jeannette Brun, Louis Hansen, Dixie Walters*

EDITOR'S NOTE: I have been able to identify the four family members among the students: Uncle Louis Brun is in front, fifth from the left, holding his hat; Aunt Elise Brun (Thibodeaux) is in middle row, left of center, in front of teacher wearing black dress; my mother, Jeannette Brun (Hewitt) is second girl from right; Aunt Delphine Brun is third girl from right.

Following her graduation from the Oakville primary school, Jeannette Brun received her high school education at the Ursuline Academy in St. Helena, six miles north of Oakville. Since the distance between Oakville and St. Helena was too great for a daily commute by horse and buggy, Mother attended Ursuline as a boarding student.

*Jean and Emma Brun's children in 1891 (from left): Jeannette, 7; Elise, 10; Julie, 3; Delphine, 8; Louis, 6. Young Jean Adolphe is not in this picture as he was less than 2 years old and consequently did not make the 15-mile trip from Oakville to the photographer's studio in the town of Napa.*

*Jeannette Brun, early 1900s.*

*Jeannette Brun, early 1900s.*

*This is the only available photograph of Jean Adolphe Brun's widow, Emma Brun, together with her six young adult children, in the early 1900s, San Francisco. Back row (from left): Louis, Elise, Emma Mermoud Brun, Adolphe. Front row (from left): Jeannette, Julie, Delphine.*

*From left, Jeannette Brun, a friend, and Delphine prepare flowers for their sister Elise's wedding. Jeannette was maid of honor when Elise married Pages Thibodeaux of Chicago, February 3, 1902, in Oakville, California.*

*St. Helena Star*
February 1, 1902

The culmination of a pretty and interesting romance will be the marriage on Monday, February 3, of Miss Elise Brun, of Oakville, and Mr. Pages J. Thibodeaux, of Chicago. The bride-to-be is the eldest daughter of Mrs. E. Brun, and is a beautiful and attractive lady possessed of many rare accomplishments, which have been enhanced by recent extensive traveling with her family throughout the East and in Europe. It was while traveling that she met Mr. Thibodeaux and the friendship thus formed quickly, ripened into love, and the wedding day has now been set. The marriage will take place at Mrs. Brun's Oakville villa next Monday at high noon.

*San Francisco Chronicle*
February 4, 1902

The wedding of Pages Joseph Thibodeaux of Chicago and Miss Elise Brun took place at the home of Mrs. Emma Brun at Oakville, Napa County, on Monday afternoon. The officiating clergyman was the Rev. W. Powell of St. Helena. The ceremony took place under an artistically constructed floral canopy. The bride wore a white organdy dress trimmed with lace and ribbons and a bridal veil crowned with fresh orange blossoms. Miss Jeannette Brun acted as maid of honor and Louis Brun as best man. The following were present: Mrs. Emma Brun, Mr. and Mrs. J. Chaix, Mr. and Mrs. P. A. Bergerot of San Francisco, Miss Jeannette Brun, Miss Delphine Brun, the Rev. W. Powell, Miss Margaret Powell, Mr. and Mrs. M. Kemper, Miss Cyetta McQuaid, Miss Julie Brun, Louis Brun, Miss Henriette Laroste, Adolph Brun, Mr. and Mrs. J. Sehallagne, Miss Elise Chaix, Jean Chaix Jr., Adolph Chaix, Miss Mabel Taylor.

The bridal couple left the same night for their honeymoon, which will be spent partly in Southern California and partly in New Orleans, during the Mardi Gras festival. They will thence proceed to Chicago, the home of the groom.

*Napa Valley and San Francisco newspapers carried articles on the marriage of Elise Brun to Pages Thibodeaux, February 3, 1902, at the Brun residence in Oakville, California.*

*St. Helena Star*
February 3, 1902

**Pretty Oakville Wedding.**

A very pretty wedding took place last Monday, February 3rd at the home of Mrs. Emma Brun, at Oakville.

The contracting parties were Miss Elise Brun, one of the beauties of Napa valley, eldest daughter of Mrs. Brun and Pages Joseph Thibodeaux, a well known business man of Chicago, who belongs to one of the oldest and best known French families of New Orleans, Louisiana.

The nuptial knot was tied at high noon by Rev. W. R. Powell, of St. Helena, beneath an artistically constructed canopy and bower made of smilax, ferns and palm-leaves entwined with beautiful cut-flowers.

The bride was the recipient of many costly presents from relatives and numerous friends.

After the ceremony was performed, the guests were invited to partake of a delicious luncheon spread in the parlors. None but the immediate relatives and most intimate friends were present.

Among those in attendance were Mrs. Emma Brun; J. Chaix, who gave the bride away; Mrs. J. Chaix; Mr. and Mrs. P. A. Bergerot, of San Francisco; Mr. and Mrs. M. Kemper, of Vallejo; Mr. and Mrs. Jean Schablaque; Miss Cyetta McQuaid; Misses Jeanette Brun, Leonie Lacoste, Delphine Brun, Elise Chaix, Henriette Lacoste, Julie Brun, Mabel Taylor, Margaret Powell, Masters Louis Brun, Jean Chaix Jr., Adolphe Brun Adolphe Chaix, Rev. W. R. Powell.

The bride and groom left in the evening for San Francisco. On arriving at Vallejo, they were given a royal ovation. All the locomotives on the wharf, the pier bell, the steamer and flour mills joyously tooted and rang them a happy good-bye.

Mr. and Mrs. Thibodeaux will proceed to Southern California where they will spend a few days; they will thence depart for New Orleans to attend the Mardi Gras Carnival and will then go to Chicago, which will be their home.

*Jeannette Brun, sitting on the step, and Delphine Brun, in back seat of a surrey, Oakville, Napa Valley, California, 1901.*

*Elise Brun Thibodeaux and her son, Pages, Chicago, circa 1904.*

*Pages and Elise Thibodeaux with their son, Pages Jr. (rear row), Salt Lake City, November 19, 1915. Inset: Pages Thibodeaux Jr., Chicago, circa 1912.*

*Delphine Brun (third from left, front row), at Military Ball of the California Greys, in the main ballroom of the Fairmont Hotel, San Francisco, circa 1903. The room still looks almost exactly the same in 1989.*

*Red Cross volunteers accompany U.S. sailors on an excursion by train from Mill Valley to the top of Mount Tamalpias, 1916. Julie Brun at far right.*

*Red Cross volunteers at the canteen in the Ferry Building during World War I, San Francisco, 1916. Julie Brun, standing, second from left, and Delphine Brun, sitting, second from right.*

*Jack Brun (Jean Adolphe Brun) returning from active duty in France, World War I. He is standing against the middle area of the railing, with his face partly hidden, holding his cap above his head with his right hand. The sun is shining on his light-colored jacket. Inset: "Jack" Brun, 1918.*

*Jeannette Brun Hewitt and her son, Edward, San Francisco, 1912.*

*Edward T. Hewitt Sr. with his son Ed, 1913.*

*Edward Thomas Hewitt Sr., circa 1910. Photograph by: Howland Studio, San Francisco.*

*Ed, Bill and Adrienne Hewitt at Aunt Mary's house, Mill Valley, Marin County, California, circa 1920.*

*Louis Brun (right) and a friend, with a very early pickup truck, circa 1922. Inset: Louis Brun, circa 1918.*

*Jeannette Brun Hewitt, San Francisco, 1920s.*

*Delphine Brun, San Francisco, 1920s.*

*Julie Brun, Yosemite National Park, late 1920s.*

*Louis S. Brun, San Francisco, mid-1920s.*

*Jean Adolphe Brun, 1920s.*

*Elise Brun Thibodeaux, Chicago, 1930s.*

*Emma Mermoud Brun, right, and three of her children, Delphine, Julie, Adolphe, 1920s.*

*Emma Brun, back row, center; Julie Brun is in middle row, left side. Yosemite National Park, California, circa 1915.*

*Deets, Ed and Bill Hewitt, with Aunt Elise Brun Thibodeaux, circa 1920.*

*Elise and Pages Thibodeaux, while living in the Drake Towers, Chicago, early 1930s.*

*Elise Brun Thibodeaux, Yosemite National Park, 1930s.*

*Emma Mermoud Brun and her daughter, Elise Brun Thibodeaux, San Francisco, mid-1930s.*

*Elise Brun Thibodeaux, Chicago.*

*Deets Hewitt, right, with her cousin, Jeanne Brun (those are bows, not hats), circa 1923.*

*Front to rear: Deets, Bill and Ed Hewitt, Cousin Mary Hobart, Josephine Finnell, Uncle Louis Brun, in the Muir Woods Redwood Grove, Marin County, California, circa 1918.*

*Left to right: Bill Hewitt, Cousins Sue and Ruth Brun, Deets and Ed Hewitt, Ocean Beach, San Francisco. Windmill in background was built to pump water to the lakes in Golden Gate Park.*

*Bill and Ed Hewitt with Uncle Louis Brun, Crissy Field, San Francisco Presidio, early 1920s. This was the day that Ed and Bill flew for the first time in an airplane. They sat side-by-side in the same seat of this two-place open cockpit Jenny. The short flight took them from Crissy Field across the Golden Gate and back for five dollars.*

*Ed and Bill Hewitt, with Cliff Longfellow at bat, Larkspur, Marin County, during a summer vacation.*

*Left to right: Edward Hewitt, Ruth Brun, Louis Brun, Suzanne, Ruthie, Bill and Deets Hewitt (wire-haired terrier is "Nancy"), observing a ship that had run aground in a storm, Ocean Beach, San Francisco.*

*Louis Brun, Sue Brun, unidentified, Ruth Brun, unidentified, Deets, Bill and Ed Hewitt, Marin County, early 1920s.*

*Cousin Emma Jeanne Brun, San Francisco, early 1920s.*

*Adrienne (Deets) Hewitt, Cousin Ruth Brun, Bill Hewitt, Cousin Suzanne Brun, and "Nancy," the Brun's wire-haired terrier, San Francisco, late 1920s.*

*Ed Hewitt with Cousin Ruth Brun on his shoulders, Uncle Louis Brun and his daughter, Sue, San Francisco, late 1920s.*

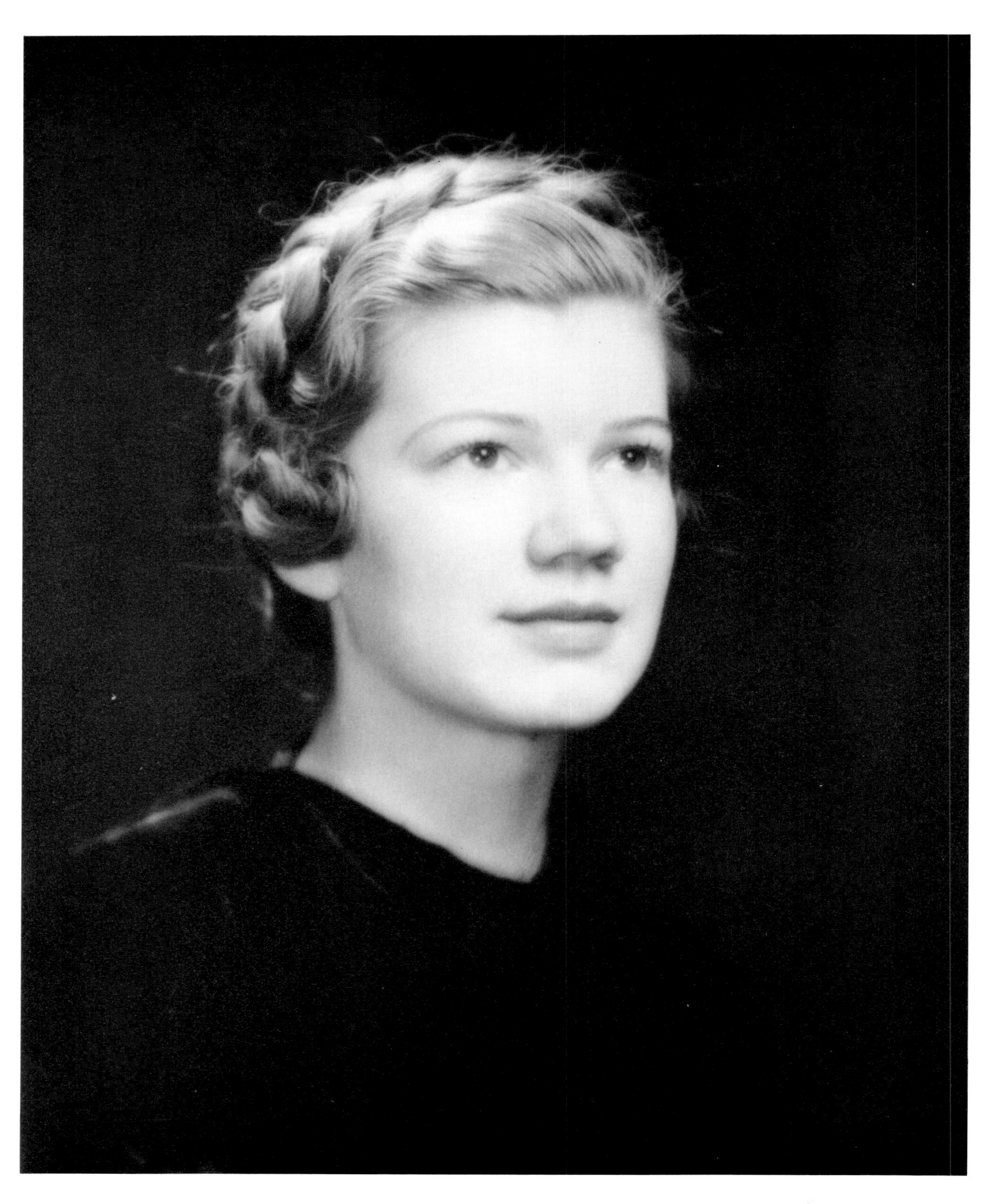

*Adrienne Hewitt, circa 1938. Photograph taken while Deets was a student at Lake Forest College, Illinois.*

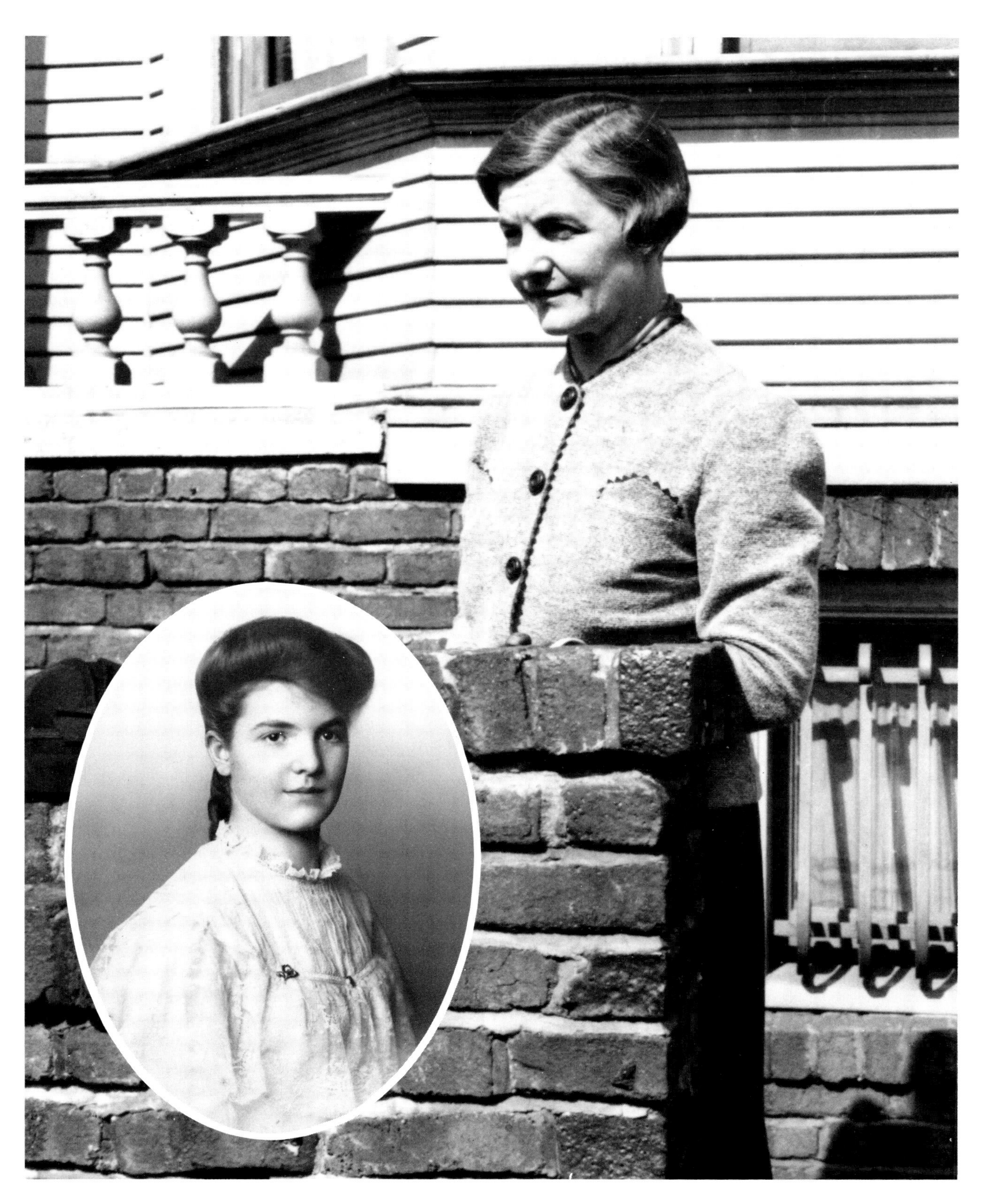

*Julie Brun, San Francisco, mid-1930s. Inset: Julie Brun, San Francisco, circa 1912.*

*Cousin Pages Thibodeaux Jr., and his wife, Dorothy, with their son Page on the Chicago shore of Lake Michigan, circa 1927.*

*Pages Thibodeaux Jr., Elise's son, Chicago, circa 1940.*

*Ed Hewitt gives away the bride, his sister, Adrienne, November 7, 1940, San Francisco.*

*Bride and groom, Deets and Don Gordon, November 7, 1940, San Francisco. Deets is wearing her mother's wedding dress.*

*Left to right: Bill Hewitt, Cousin Pages Thibodeaux, Cousin John McLeod, Uncle Bill Hewitt, Uncle Louis Brun, Ed Hewitt, at Deets' wedding reception, November 7, 1940, San Francisco.*

*Part of the family at Adrienne Hewitt Gordon's wedding reception, November 7, 1940, San Francisco.*

*1 - Louis Brun, 2 - Josephine Finnell, 3 - Suzanne Brun, 4 - Julie Brun, 5 -Viola "Cooks" Koster, 6 - Ruth Brun, 7 - Emma Mermoud Brun, 8 - Ed Hewitt, 9 - Delphine Brun, 10 - Mrs. Steve Garin (Steve took the picture), 11 - Elise Brun Thibodeaux, 12 - Jeannette Brun Hewitt, 13 - Pages Thibodeaux Jr., 14 -Ruth Finnell Brun.*

*Emma Mermoud Brun, with her great-grandsons, Marshall Gordon and Steve Benton, October 1942.*

*Emma Mermoud Brun, San Francisco, circa 1943.*

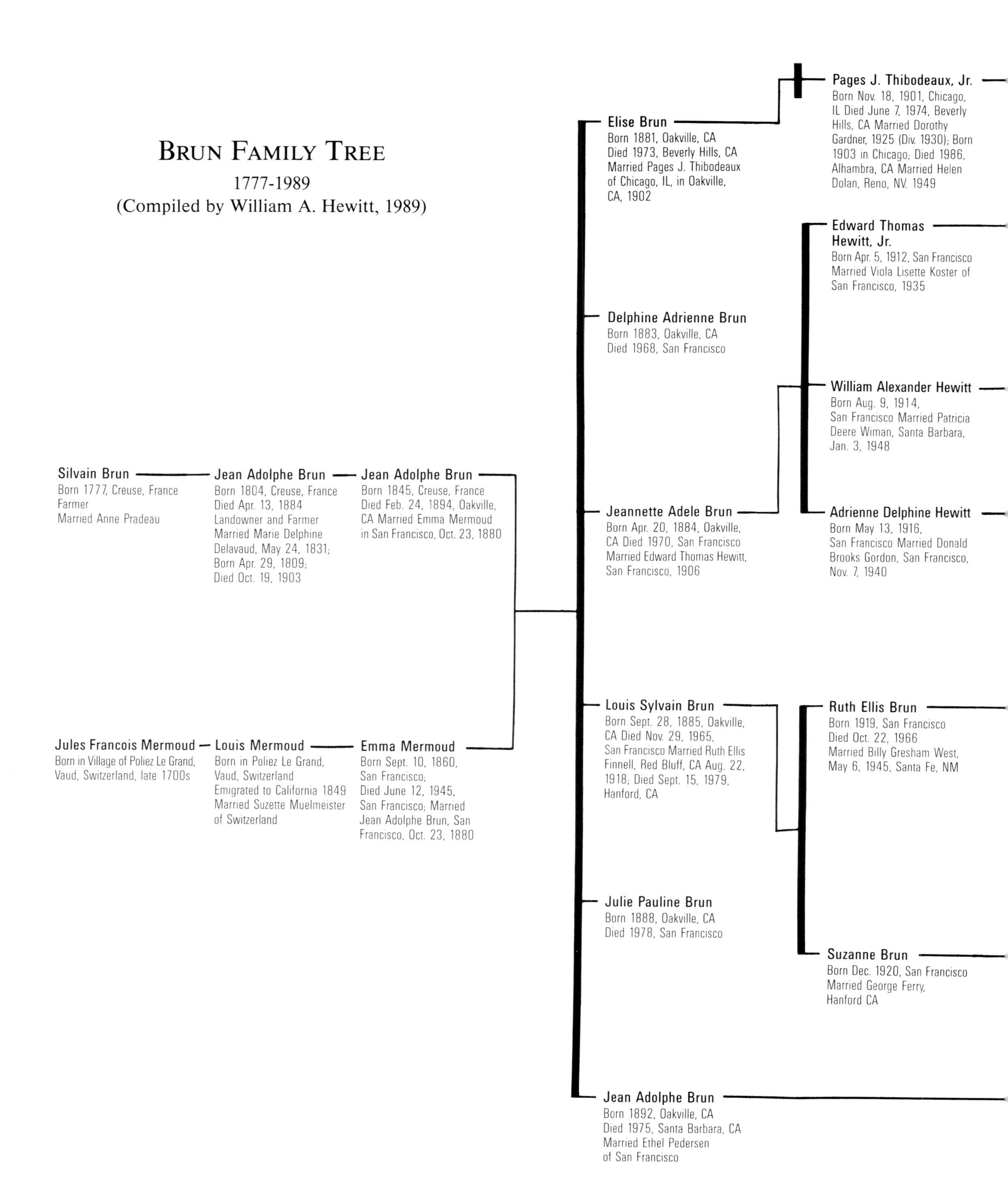

BRUN FAMILY TREE
1777-1989
(Compiled by William A. Hewitt, 1989)
Silvain Brun
Born 1777, Creuse, France
Farmer
Married Anne Pradeau
Jean Adolphe Brun
Born 1804, Creuse, France
Died Apr. 13, 1884
Landowner and Farmer
Married Marie Delphine Delavaud, May 24, 1831; Born Apr. 29, 1809; Died Oct. 19, 1903
Jean Adolphe Brun
Born 1845, Creuse, France
Died Feb. 24, 1894, Oakville, CA Married Emma Mermoud in San Francisco, Oct. 23, 1880
Jules Francois Mermoud
Born in Village of Poliez Le Grand, Vaud, Switzerland, late 1700s
Louis Mermoud
Born in Poliez Le Grand, Vaud, Switzerland
Emigrated to California 1849
Married Suzette Muelmeister of Switzerland
Emma Mermoud
Born Sept. 10, 1860, San Francisco; Died June 12, 1945, San Francisco; Married Jean Adolphe Brun, San Francisco, Oct. 23, 1880
Elise Brun
Born 1881, Oakville, CA
Died 1973, Beverly Hills, CA
Married Pages J. Thibodeaux of Chicago, IL, in Oakville, CA, 1902
Delphine Adrienne Brun
Born 1883, Oakville, CA
Died 1968, San Francisco
Jeannette Adele Brun
Born Apr. 20, 1884, Oakville, CA Died 1970, San Francisco
Married Edward Thomas Hewitt, San Francisco, 1906
Louis Sylvain Brun
Born Sept. 28, 1885, Oakville, CA Died Nov. 29, 1965, San Francisco Married Ruth Ellis Finnell, Red Bluff, CA Aug. 22, 1918; Died Sept. 15, 1979, Hanford, CA
Julie Pauline Brun
Born 1888, Oakville, CA
Died 1978, San Francisco
Jean Adolphe Brun
Born 1892, Oakville, CA
Died 1975, Santa Barbara, CA
Married Ethel Pedersen of San Francisco
Pages J. Thibodeaux, Jr.
Born Nov. 18, 1901, Chicago, IL Died June 7, 1974, Beverly Hills, CA Married Dorothy Gardner, 1925 (Div. 1930); Born 1903 in Chicago; Died 1986, Alhambra, CA Married Helen Dolan, Reno, NV. 1949
Edward Thomas Hewitt, Jr.
Born Apr. 5, 1912, San Francisco
Married Viola Lisette Koster of San Francisco, 1935
William Alexander Hewitt
Born Aug. 9, 1914, San Francisco Married Patricia Deere Wiman, Santa Barbara, Jan. 3, 1948
Adrienne Delphine Hewitt
Born May 13, 1916, San Francisco Married Donald Brooks Gordon, San Francisco, Nov. 7, 1940
Ruth Ellis Brun
Born 1919, San Francisco
Died Oct. 22, 1966
Married Billy Gresham West, May 6, 1945, Santa Fe, NM
Suzanne Brun
Born Dec. 1920, San Francisco
Married George Ferry, Hanford CA

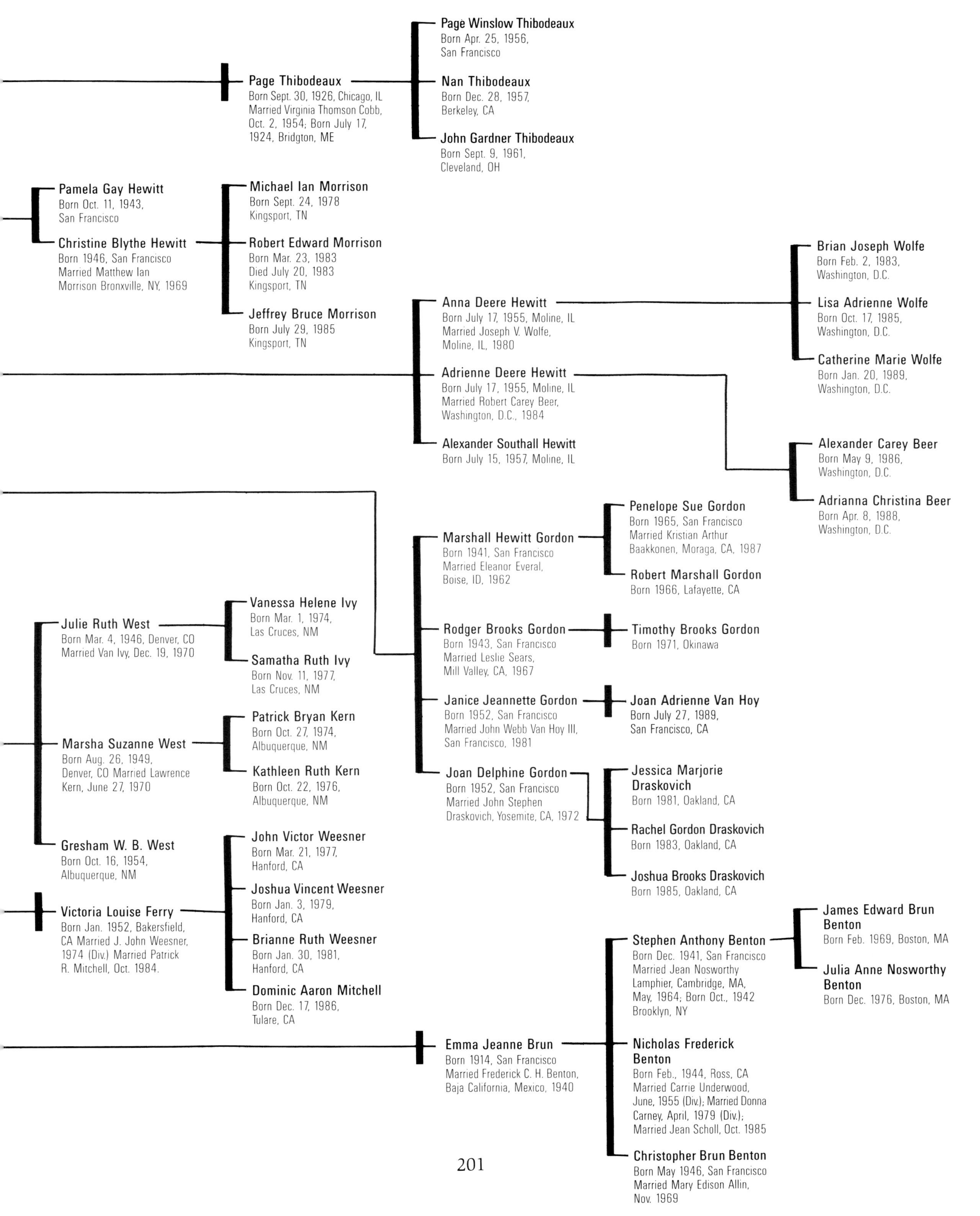

Page Winslow Thibodeaux
Born Apr. 25, 1956, San Francisco
Page Thibodeaux
Born Sept. 30, 1926, Chicago, IL Married Virginia Thomson Cobb, Oct. 2, 1954; Born July 17, 1924, Bridgton, ME
Nan Thibodeaux
Born Dec. 28, 1957, Berkeley, CA
John Gardner Thibodeaux
Born Sept. 9, 1961, Cleveland, OH
Pamela Gay Hewitt
Born Oct. 11, 1943, San Francisco
Michael Ian Morrison
Born Sept. 24, 1978 Kingsport, TN
Christine Blythe Hewitt
Born 1946, San Francisco Married Matthew Ian Morrison Bronxville, NY, 1969
Robert Edward Morrison
Born Mar. 23, 1983 Died July 20, 1983 Kingsport, TN
Brian Joseph Wolfe
Born Feb. 2, 1983, Washington, D.C.
Anna Deere Hewitt
Born July 17, 1955, Moline, IL Married Joseph V. Wolfe, Moline, IL, 1980
Jeffrey Bruce Morrison
Born July 29, 1985 Kingsport, TN
Lisa Adrienne Wolfe
Born Oct. 17, 1985, Washington, D.C.
Catherine Marie Wolfe
Born Jan. 20, 1989, Washington, D.C.
Adrienne Deere Hewitt
Born July 17, 1955, Moline, IL Married Robert Carey Beer, Washington, D.C., 1984
Alexander Southall Hewitt
Born July 15, 1957, Moline, IL
Alexander Carey Beer
Born May 9, 1986, Washington, D.C.
Adrianna Christina Beer
Born Apr. 8, 1988, Washington, D.C.
Penelope Sue Gordon
Born 1965, San Francisco Married Kristian Arthur Baakkonen, Moraga, CA, 1987
Marshall Hewitt Gordon
Born 1941, San Francisco Married Eleanor Everal, Boise, ID, 1962
Robert Marshall Gordon
Born 1966, Lafayette, CA
Vanessa Helene Ivy
Born Mar. 1, 1974, Las Cruces, NM
Julie Ruth West
Born Mar. 4, 1946, Denver, CO Married Van Ivy, Dec. 19, 1970
Rodger Brooks Gordon
Born 1943, San Francisco Married Leslie Sears, Mill Valley, CA, 1967
Timothy Brooks Gordon
Born 1971, Okinawa
Samatha Ruth Ivy
Born Nov. 11, 1977, Las Cruces, NM
Janice Jeannette Gordon
Born 1952, San Francisco Married John Webb Van Hoy III, San Francisco, 1981
Joan Adrienne Van Hoy
Born July 27, 1989, San Francisco, CA
Patrick Bryan Kern
Born Oct. 27, 1974, Albuquerque, NM
Marsha Suzanne West
Born Aug. 26, 1949, Denver, CO Married Lawrence Kern, June 27, 1970
Kathleen Ruth Kern
Born Oct. 22, 1976, Albuquerque, NM
Joan Delphine Gordon
Born 1952, San Francisco Married John Stephen Draskovich, Yosemite, CA, 1972
Jessica Marjorie Draskovich
Born 1981, Oakland, CA
Rachel Gordon Draskovich
Born 1983, Oakland, CA
John Victor Weesner
Born Mar. 21, 1977, Hanford, CA
Gresham W. B. West
Born Oct. 16, 1954, Albuquerque, NM
Joshua Brooks Draskovich
Born 1985, Oakland, CA
Joshua Vincent Weesner
Born Jan. 3, 1979, Hanford, CA
Victoria Louise Ferry
Born Jan. 1952, Bakersfield, CA Married J. John Weesner, 1974 (Div.) Married Patrick R. Mitchell, Oct. 1984.
James Edward Brun Benton
Born Feb. 1969, Boston, MA
Brianne Ruth Weesner
Born Jan. 30, 1981, Hanford, CA
Stephen Anthony Benton
Born Dec. 1941, San Francisco Married Jean Nosworthy Lamphier, Cambridge, MA, May, 1964; Born Oct., 1942 Brooklyn, NY
Julia Anne Nosworthy Benton
Born Dec. 1976, Boston, MA
Dominic Aaron Mitchell
Born Dec. 17, 1986, Tulare, CA
Emma Jeanne Brun
Born 1914, San Francisco Married Frederick C. H. Benton, Baja California, Mexico, 1940
Nicholas Frederick Benton
Born Feb., 1944, Ross, CA Married Carrie Underwood, June, 1955 (Div.); Married Donna Carney, April, 1979 (Div.); Married Jean Scholl, Oct. 1985
Christopher Brun Benton
Born May 1946, San Francisco Married Mary Edison Allin, Nov. 1969

BOOK II

# HEWITT FAMILY
# SAN FRANCISCO · FROM 1882

*A wood framed tintype photograph of Edward Thomas Jones, taken in Ironbridge, England, in 1861. He was the father of Mary Rebecca Jones who eventually married William A. Hewitt.*

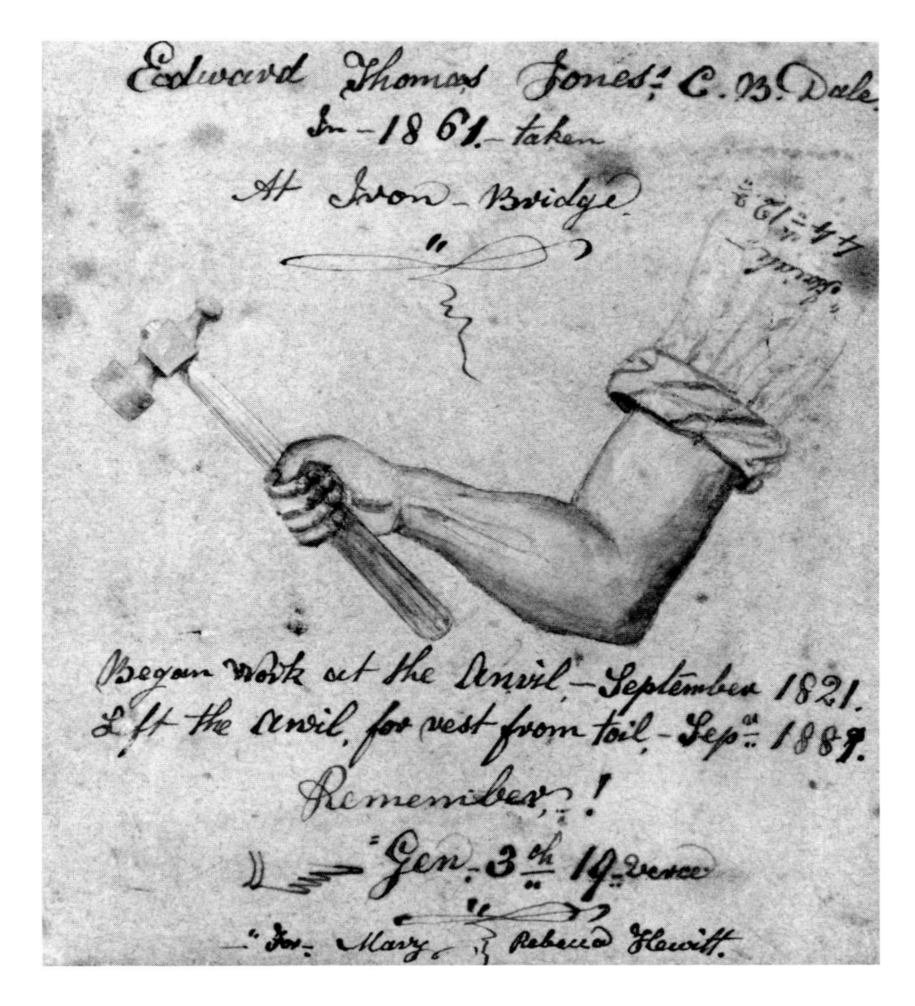


*Photograph of a watercolor and ink drawing by Edward Thomas Jones. It is attached to the back of the frame of the 1861 tintype photograph of him on the opposite page, and commemorates his* Work at the Anvil 1821-1881. *Mr. Jones presented this tintype and drawing to his daughter, Mary Rebecca Jones Hewitt, just before she and her husband and their six children left England to make their residence in San Francisco in 1883.*

*Front Side*

*Back of Front Side*

*Back Side*

Editor's Note: In 1865 Edward Thomas Jones fashioned a circular metal picture frame to hold a record of his immediate family. In pen and ink he wrote his words after attaching cutouts for his pictorial. Clear glass was placed over the items that faced both the front and back of the frame.

In 1988 the frame was opened for conservational care, and an additional message inside was seen for the first time in 123 years. In a small, beautiful hand Jones told that the surviving members of his family were living in London.

Front Side

Below drawing of family group:
1 Det. 3-20
Refers to Deuteronomy, Chapter 3, Verse 20

Inner circle of handwritten inscription, from the top: 1 Father, 2 Mother, 3 Ann, 4 John, 5 Edward, 6 Rebecca, 7 James, 8 Jonathan, represent all of my family.

Second circle:
Ezek. 18-4 "All souls are mine, saith the Lord, the soul of the Father, Mother, Son and Daughter; Time how short, Eternity how long."

Third Circle:
Acts 17-26 "God hath made of one blood all nations of men for to dwell upon all the face of the earth."

Heb. 2-9 "Jesus tasted death for all, every man."

Back of Front Side

Handwritten message that was concealed in the frame between front and back items from 1865 until 1988:
"Edw'd. Thomas and Mary Ann Jones of Coalbrookdale in Shropshire...in May 1865...and their children...four are living in London and 2 in Heaven."

Back Side

Handwritten note at top:
Edw'd. Thos. Jones
C.B.D.

At bottom: 2 Pet. 3 Ch. 16th Verse
"...wrest, as they do also the other scriptures, unto their own destruction."

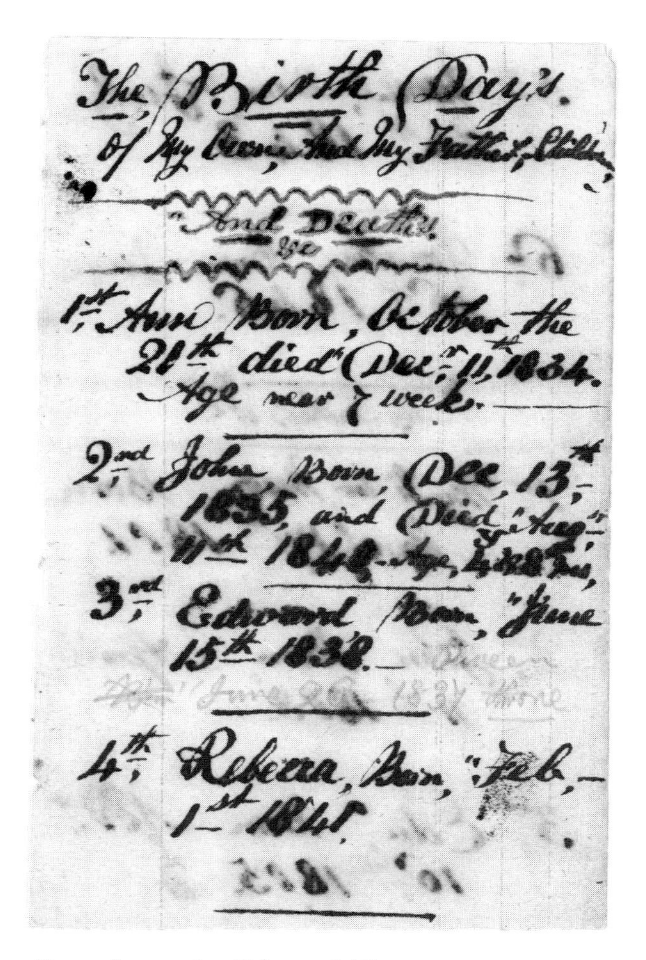
The Birth Day's.

And Deaths

1st Ann Born, October the
21th died Dec 11th 1834.
Age near 7 week.

2nd John Born, Dec 13th
1835, and Died Aug
11th 1840

3rd Edward Born June
15th 1838.

4th Rebecca, Born Feb
1st 1841

*Page from the Edward Thomas Jones Family Bible, Coalbrookdale, England, 1834.*

The Birth Days of My Own (Edward Thomas Jones), and My Father and Children.

And Deaths

1st Ann, Born October the 21st died December 11, 1834.
Age near 7 weeks.

2nd John, Born Dec. 13, 1835 and died August 11, 1840.
Age 4 years 8 months.

3rd Edward, Born June 15, 1838
EDITOR'S NOTE: Edward T. Jones was our great-uncle who later lived in San Francisco until he died in 1928, at age 90. Two photographs of him are in this book.

4th Rebecca, Born Feb. 1, 1841
EDITOR'S NOTE: Rebecca was our grandmother. Several photographs of her are in this book.

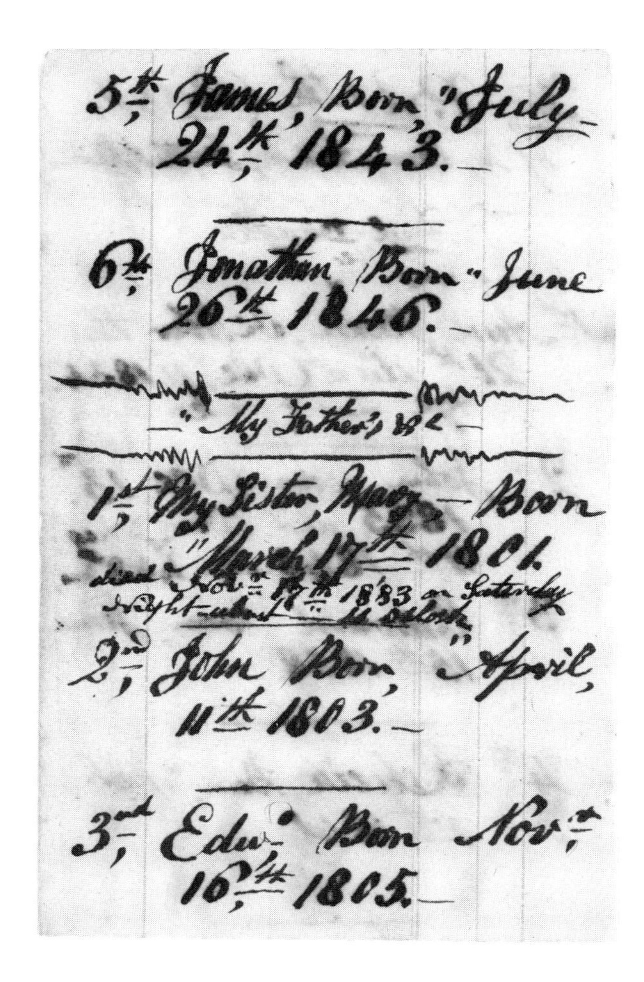

5th James, Born "July 24th 1843. —

6th Jonathan Born "June 26th 1846. —

"My Father's &c —

1st My Sister, Mary — Born "March 17th 1801.
died Nov. 17th 1883 on Saturday
Night — about 11 o'clock

2nd John Born "April 11th 1803. —

3rd Edw. Born Nov. 16th 1805. —

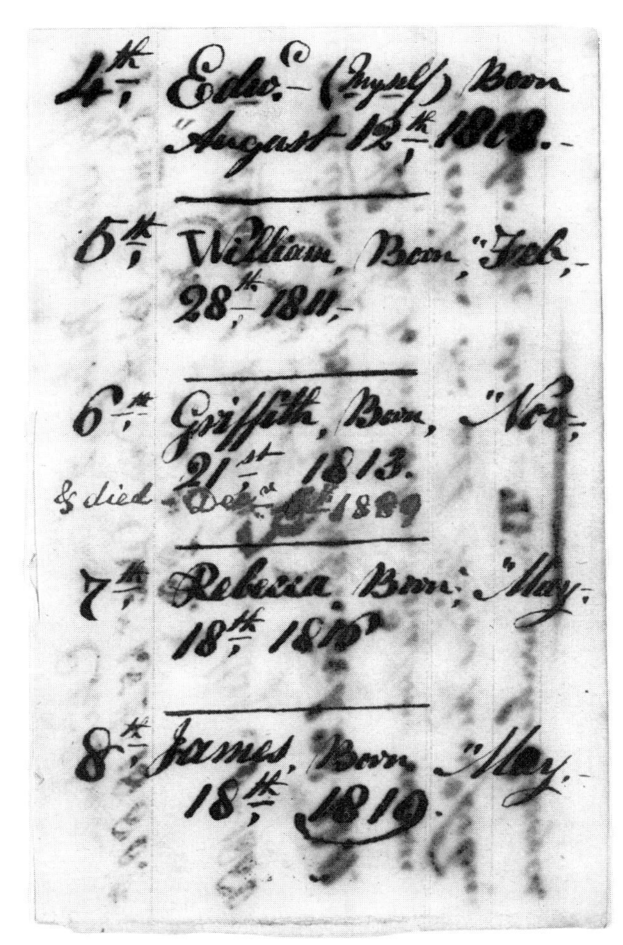

4th Edw. (myself) Born "August 12th 1808. —

5th William, Born, "Feb. 28th 1811. —

6th Griffith, Born, "Nov. 21st 1813.
& died Dec. 5th 1889

7th Rebecca Born "May 18th 1816

8th James Born "May 18th 1819.

*More entries from the Jones Family Bible.*

5th James, Born July 24, 1843

6th Jonathan, Born June 26, 1846

1st My sister Mary—Born March 17, 1801 died Nov. 17, 1883 on Saturday night about 11 o'clock.

2nd John, Born April 11, 1803

3rd Edw. Born Nov. 16, 1805 (died in France)

4th Edw. (myself) Born August 12, 1808 (EDITOR'S NOTE: Great-grandfather of W. A. Hewitt, editor of this book.)

5th William, Born Feb. 28, 1811

6th Griffith, Born Nov. 21, 1813 and died Dec. 5, 1889

7th Rebecca, Born May 18, 1816 (EDITOR'S NOTE: Our great-grandfather's sister, after whom our grandmother was named)

8th James, Born May 18, 1810

Rebecca's Confinement of her
5th Child (a Boy) Octo. 1874.
" She was over one week in August
1874.) " She Came over again
with her Boy (Arthur) Saturday
September 4th returned on
Saturday: Sep 18th 1875.
(Fare to London from Dub. — 12s.)

Rebecca's Confinement of her
6th Child — on Wednesday — 15th
of February — 1877 — had
3 Boys & 3 Girls — Children in No.
the same now as her Mother
who had 4 Boys & 2 Girls

Rebecca and her Dear Boy
Edwd. Came over from Limerick
400 Miles — on Thursday — July
22 — 1869 & returned on Monday
September 6th Booked from Wellington
to Dublin, — fare 9s — at 1 o'clock on
Monday — from Dublin to Limerick
12 or 12s — arrived ½ past 11 on Tuesday
night. — Confinement at
Greenock in Scotland of A Son
on Sunday August 7th 1870.

×Rebecca, her Husband & 2 Children
again Came to see us. July, 6th
returned on 15th 1871.
Rebecca & William with
3 Children Came over
on May 31st 1873
William Returned June
9th) Rebecca & Children
July 8th —

*More entries from the Jones Family Bible.*

Text of handwritten notes on opposite page from the Jones Family Bible:

Rebecca's confinement of her 5th child a boy October 1874. (Editor's Note: The boy was Arthur. Her first child, Catherine, born in 1865, died in infancy. Consequently, Rebecca's 5th child was Arthur.) She came over again with her Boy, Arthur, Saturday, September 4th. Returned on Saturday, Sep. 18th 1875. Fare to London from Dale—£12.11—Rebecca's confinement of her 6th child on Wednesday 15th of February 1877,—had 3 Boys and 3 Girls,—children in number the same now as her Mother who had 4 Boys and 2 Girls. (Editor's Note: Daughter Daisy was yet to be born in February 1881. Although my father, Edward Thomas Hewitt was English by heredity, he was born in Belfast, Ireland; and his brother, William Alexander Hewitt, was born in Greenoch, Scotland. The notes listed above describe visits from Ireland and Scotland by Rebecca Jones Hewitt and her first two sons to her parents' residence in Coalbrookdale, England.)

Rebecca (Mary Rebecca Jones Hewitt) and her dear boy Edw. (Editor's Note: Edward was my father who was then one year and 5 months old.) came over from Limmerick—400 miles—on Thursday, July 22, 1869 and returned ______ ? ______ September 6th booked from Walington to Dublin, fare £9 at 1 o'clock, on Monday—from Dublin to Limmerick £12 on 12 am—arrived ______ ? ______ ______ ? ______ on Tuesday night.—Confinement at Greenoch in Scotland of A Son on Sunday, August 7th, 1870. (Editor's Note: He was my Uncle Bill.)

Rebecca, her husband & 2 children again came to see us, July 6th—returned on 15th 1871.

Rebecca and William (her husband) with 3 children came over (the third child was Mary, born on September 26, 1872) on May 31st 1873. William returned June 9th—and Rebecca and children on July 8th.

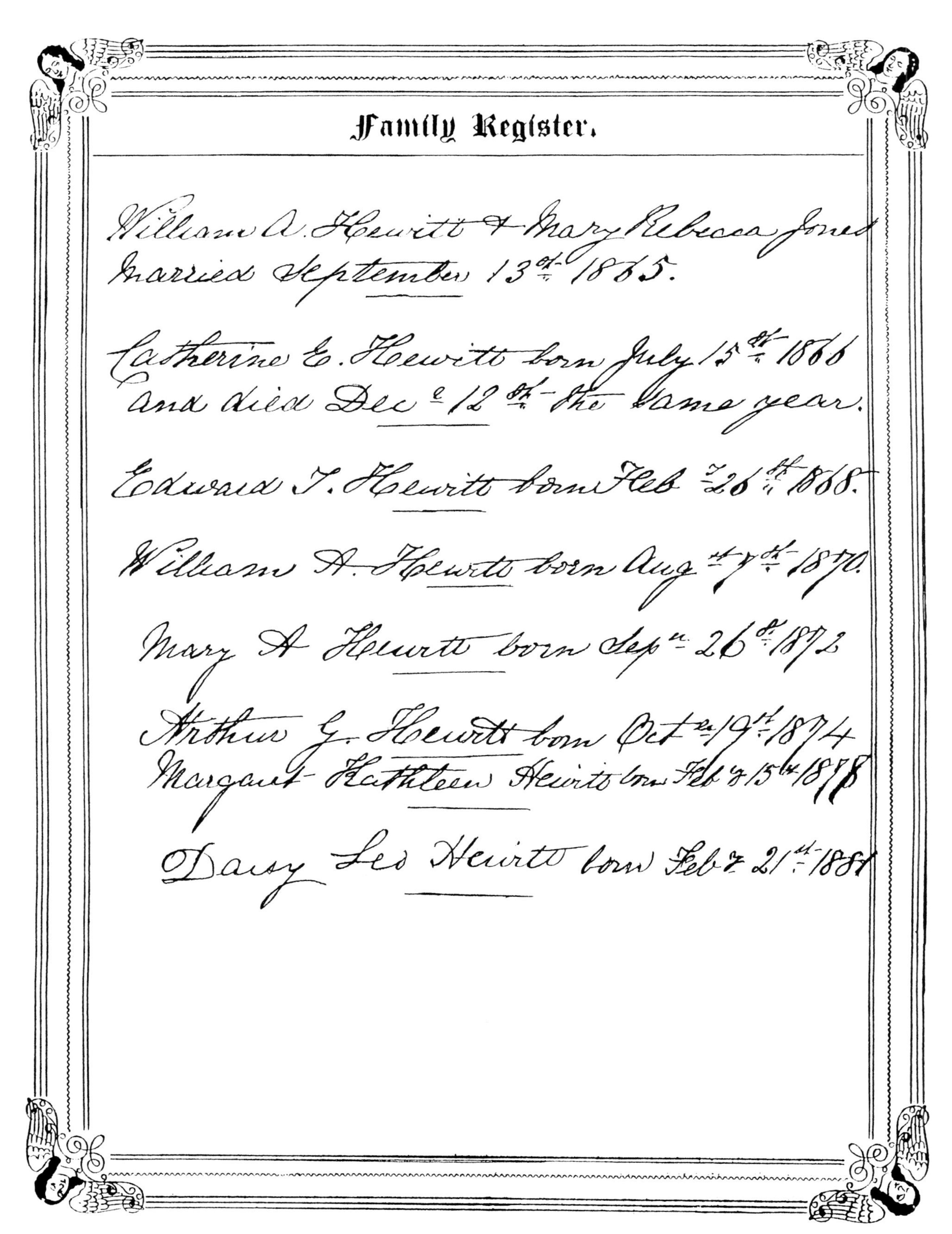
Family Register.

William A. Hewitt & Mary Rebecca Jones
married September 13th 1865.

Catherine E. Hewitt born July 15th 1866
and died Decr 12th the same year.

Edward T. Hewitt born Feby 26th 1868.

William A. Hewitt born Augst 7th 1870.

Mary A Hewitt born Sepr 26th 1872

Arthur G. Hewitt born Octr 19th 1874
Margaret Kathleen Hewitt born Feby 15th 1878

Daisy Leo Hewitt born Feby 21st 1881

*Leaf from Family Bible Register of Hewitt Family.*

HI BILL
OUR PATERNAL GRANDMOTHER'S FAMILY HOME WAS — AND MAY STILL BE — IN COALBROOKDALE, NEAR IRONBRIDGE. AM STILL HOPING TO VISIT THERE AGAIN ONE DAY — ALL THE BEST
ED

Section **10**

Sunday, April 20, 1975

The New York Times

The birthplace of the Industrial Revolution: "Time, that infallible cosmetician, has given an extraordinary, melancholy charm" to the 6-square-mile Ironbridge Museum in Shropshire. A classic grace attends machinery and the first iron bridge.

EDITOR'S NOTE: The following *New York Times* article, dated April 20, 1975, on the history of Ironbridge, England, was sent to the editor of this book by his brother, Ed Hewitt. Ed's handwritten note at the top of the article refers to our grandmother, Mary Rebecca Jones Hewitt who was born in the Ironbridge area. Her father, Edward Thomas Jones was a Welshman. (See a reproduction of the 1861 tintype photograph of him on the first page of Book II of this volume.)

# *Britain's Ironbridge: Where the World Was Irrevocably Changed*

**By EDMUND MORRIS**

THERE is a small brick chamber in the depths of rural Shropshire, England, where one of the most momentous revolutions in history was forged. Here, one winter's morning early in 1709, a dour Quaker piled ore and limestone on a bed of incandescent coke, blew air through the mass with waterwheel bellows, and, 16 hours later, tapped off a trickle of pure iron.

With this experiment Abraham Darby proved that it was no longer necessary to decimate hundreds of acres of trees to fuel a single blast furnace. By perfecting the use of "coak'd" coal—a purified, smokeless distillate of England's most abundant natural resource—he at one stroke made the production of iron easy and cheap. That first trickle became a stream, and then a flood that seethed and hissed out of the furnaces of Shropshire for almost two centuries. Thus was born the Industrial Revolution, and the world was irrevocably changed.

Today Abraham Darby's furnace stands cool and empty, the nucleus of England's newest and biggest open-air monument—the Ironbridge Gorge Museum, 10 miles southeast of Shrewsbury, about an hour's drive from Stratford. Chosen as the most outstanding tourist development in Britain when it opened in 1973, the museum already embraces six square miles of astonishingly beautiful ruins and is expanding all the time.

---

*EDMUND MORRIS is a freelance writer who lives in New York.*

"Beautiful" may seem an incongruous adjective to apply to an industrial landscape, but time, that infallible cosmetician, has given the whole place an extraordinary, melancholy charm. Wild flowers poke through rails that have long since borne their last puffing billy; rabbits hop out of abandoned coal tunnels; fat blackberries sprout from the graves of forgotten ironmasters, men with names like Solomon Flint, Ebenezer Armitage and Samuel Spittle.

All, however, is not ruin and decay. The Museum Trust has excavated and restored an intricate complex of buildings, canals, bridges, machinery, mines and railways. The whistle and thump of century-old steam engines, the whir of pottery wheels, the hiss of gas lamps and creak of vintage printing presses make a lively contrast with relics that have been left to sleep undisturbed. This is a museum that works as well as preserves. As such, it is probably the world's foremost example of the new science of industrial archeology: Restoration work is expected to continue for the rest of this century.

The most rewarding way to tour the museum is to explore it chronologically, starting at Abraham Darby's 17th-century furnace in Coalbrookdale, and working one's way down the gorge, via Thomas Pritchard's 18th-century iron bridge, to the stupendous 19th-century steam engines on Blists Hill. This way you can follow, in microcosm, the whole saga of Shropshire's revolution, from birth through zenith and decline. Be warned this two-mile stroll will take all day, allowing for a pie and a pint halfway in some riverside pub.

Coalbrookdale is, as its name indicates, a stream running through a valley richly seamed with coal. Abraham Darby, arriving here in 1708, did not have to look far for fuel or hydraulic power. Neither was there any shortage of raw material: Where the valley was not solid coal, it was solid ironstone. So, combining the four medieval elements of earth, water, air and fire, Darby set to work and ushered in a new industrial age. His descendants, Abraham Darby 2d, 3d and 4th, went on to develop engineering wonders that would have bewildered the old man, who died in 1717.

The Old Blast Furnace, as it is now known, stands in the middle of the valley, against a vast background of red-brick viaducts, cottages, mansions and mills as impressive, in its way, as the Roman Forum. Children—and nimble adults—delight in crawling through the tunnel whence old Abraham used to rake off his slag. You can stand upright in the skylit interior. Here, in this clean cool space, with its neat floor of pink pebbles, is where it all began: the machinery, the railways, the ships, the skyscrapers, the whole roaring, banging, slamming, smoky world we, for good or ill, now inhabit.

Out of this crucible poured a dazzling stream of technological innovations, including the world's first iron rails (1767), the world's first iron bridge (1779), the world's first iron boat (1787) and the world's first steam locomotive (1802). The valley attracted a new breed of engineers, including such geniuses as James Watt, Matthew Boulton, William Jessop, John MacAdam and Thomas Telford. By the middle of the 19th century Coalbrookdale was reverberating to the beat of hundreds of steam engines and formed the pulsating heart of an industrial landscape that covered most of the West Midlands.

"One would be inclined to believe," wrote the Victorian traveler Elihu Burritt, "on seeing the black forests of chimneys smoking over large towns and villages, as well as the flayed spaces in between, that all the coal and iron in the district must be used in it. . . . The furnaces, foundries and manufactories seem almost countless, and the vastness of their products infinite. Narrow canals, filled with water as black as the long sharp boats it floats, cross each other here and there in the thick of the furnaces and twist out into the green lands in different directions. . . . Railways, crossing the canals and their creeping locomotion, dash off with vast loads to London and other great centers of consumption."

By the end of the 19th century the valley's natural resources were worked out. One by one its mines and furnaces lapsed into darkness and silence. Now only one commercial foundry operates in Coalbrookdale, the "flayed spaces" are grassed over, and the water runs clean again.

Some of the minor products of the Darbys and their interrelated clan, the Reynolds, are on display in the Great Warehouse (1835): iron stoves, iron furniture, iron lampposts, iron dogs, pots, screens and plaques, pig iron, cast iron, wrought iron—iron, iron, iron, iron. Even the amateur eye can see why Coalbrookdale iron was so famous: It has a pure cool glow like pewter, a look of immense, satiny strength. At the Great Exhibition of 1851, Abraham Darby's casting of the figure of Andromeda was compared to the silver sculpture of Benvenuto Cellini.

By far the most beautiful example of Coalbrookdale ironwork is the lacy 100-foot structure that crosses the Severn Gorge about half a mile downstream. Known only as the Iron Bridge (considering it was the world's first, the simplicity of the name seems appropriate), it was designed by Thomas Pritchard of Shrewsbury and cast, in the Old Blast Furnace, by Abraham Darby 3d. A graceful arch of four parallel ribs, supporting a gently inclined roadway between massive masonry abutments, it is a perfect combination of strength and delicacy. Wedges and sockets, tenons and mortises recall that its builders, although working with iron, still thought in terms of carpentry. Moss has softened the sharp silhouette in places, and four-horse carriages are no longer allowed to rumble over, but the Iron Bridge is still open to pedestrians and forms a dramatic centerpiece to the whole Gorge Museum.

An idea of how revolutionary a prefabricated bridge seemed in its day can be gained from reading advertisements put out by nervous subscribers to the project in May, 1776, *after* Pritchard's initial plans had been approved. "Persons willing to undertake to build a bridge—of stone, brick or timber" were urgently requested to submit alternative designs. But none were forthcoming, and in July, 1779, the first great pair of ribs was swung into place. Before completion of the bridge late the following year Abraham Darby had supplied 378 tons of iron for it, a proportion greater than any subsequent engineer has found necessary. The imponderables of a new technology doubtless made Darby err on the side of caution, and he was rewarded by his bridge's triumphant survival of the Great Flood of 1795, which wrecked every other structure on the Severn. "Neither huge logs of timber nor parts of houses which came with such mighty force made any impression upon it," marvelled a contemporary newspaper. Illustrators from all over the world came to paint the bridge, and their pictures invariably show admiring groups of tourists.

So great was the flow of visitors in the late 18th century that in 1784 the Darby family built a special hostelry, the Tontine Hotel, opposite the north abutment. It is now a rather seedy commercial pub, but its Georgian facade is still an imposing feature of the little town of Ironbridge. Seen from the south bank, the town presents a charmingly vertiginous aspect: row upon row of cottages, each teetering at a different angle, seem to have crept higgledy-piggledy over the rim of the gorge and commenced an inexorable slide down into the Severn.

The third main unit of Ironbridge Gorge Museum is Blists Hill, a 42-acre woodland estate about a mile downriver. There, amid the yawning ruins of blast furnaces that look for all the world like the gates of hell, is a restoration of traditional Shropshire industries—ironworking, coal-mining and pottery—and the transport systems that moved the resultant products about.

If you allot a couple of hours to Coalbrookdale, an hour to lunch and a couple more to Ironbridge, you will probably arrive at Blists Hill in the late afternoon. This is about the right time, since lowering light adds an appropriate touch of gothic mystery to the place. One explores, as the English say, on Shank's pony, dodging weaving swallows and clambering over great wheels and cogs half-buried in thick grass. An oval gravel path connects the main points of interest, and it takes about an hour and a half to wander around.

The path begins at David and Sampson, two Brobdingnagian beam-blowing engines (1851), which used to blast the furnaces of nearby Priorslee. Their steam chests, separated by an enormous flywheel, are incongruously capped with Grecian pediments, and age has tinted the whole mass of iron a delicate blue-green.

Moving up the hill past an ironworking field (where a puddling furnace, rolling mill and foundry are being restored to working order), one hears the stentorian snorts of a steam engine. It comes from the pithead of Blists Hill Mine, which in the 18th century used to supply coal, ironstone and fireclay to adjoining furnaces and tileworks. The obliging young man who steams the engine for visitors shows how miners were hauled up and down the shaft in dangling wooden cages. The demonstration is curiously hynotic. A brass level is coaxed into place; the engine, lovingly restored as a vintage car, vibrates and groans; vials of green oil bob merrily; the engineer sweats; pistons heave; a weighted marker begins to record the descent of an imaginary crew.

Next to the pithead engine house there is a clay workshop, where Roy Evans demonstrates the rather splattery art of wheel-thrown pottery. Every inch of floor, wall and ceiling seems to have been daubed with flying flecks, but there is no daubery about the symmetrical blue earthenware he offers for sale.

Another old trade being revived nearby is that of job printing, in a shop that is an authentic piece of Victorian England. Here a shirtsleeved printer, working by gaslight as the evening draws in, shows how visiting cards, handbills and catalogues used to be typeset and printed to order. His early 19th-century press, surmounted by a Columbian eagle, was designed and built in the United States.

Walking across the brow of Blists Hill to the Shropshire Canal, one passes a surrealistic jumble of industrial bric-a-brac: four-foot bellows with rotten leather lungs, piles of split purple slate, rusting boilers sonorous with frogs. The canal towpath leads south to the Hay Inclined Plane (1793). This excavation has been described as "the most spectacular surviving monument of the tug-boat canal system." Gazing down its dizzy descent into the Severn Gorge, one marvels afresh at the ingenuity of man in the face of topographical obstacles.

The Incline is nothing more nor less than a gigantic double railroad rolling down the thickly wooded hillside. Its rails, which emerge from the waters of the Shropshire Canal like sunbathing eels, plunge steeply into Coalport Basin, 207 feet below. Dripping barges laden with china and coal used to be winched up and down these parallel rails on trolleys. When the descending barge weighed more than its ascending partner, the Incline was self-operating. It worked perfectly for 100 years, carrying its last load in 1894. Today the remains of the upper steam engine can still be seen, and visitors with strong heels may jog their way all the way down to Coalport.

Here there is an even stranger excavation: the Tar Tunnel (1787), a 1,000-foot horizontal shaft that drives straight into the black depths of Blists Hill. Originally the tunnel was intended to be an access route to the coal mine, but its walls sweated so much natural bitumen that digging came to a sticky end. This "tar" continued to flow in such quantities that it was collected and sold at the rate of 1,000 gallons a week. The tunnel's seepage gradually diminished over the years, and in the end it was boarded up and forgotten. Only recently was it rediscovered and opened to the public. One enters it, in typically eccentric British fashion, through the cellar of the Coalport village store. The first 300 yards of tunnel, which open out occasionally into miniature underground lakes of tar, can be explored without mishap. But don't wear your Gucci loafers.

Ironbridge Gorge offers many other curious relics of the Industrial Revolution. Restorations currently under way include an operating blast furnace, with waterwheel bellows; a nailer's shop and forge, with a live-in blacksmith; a narrow-gauge railway to transport visitors from one site to another and a ceramics museum in the famous chinaworks of Coalport. Mere listing, however, does not do justice to the weird fascination of the area as a whole. This quiet cradle of a revolution whose thunders still deafen us must, like all truly significant ruins, be seen to be believed. The strange thing is that one drives away remembering, not the pounding of pistons, but the chirrup of starlings in the chimney of Abraham Darby's ancient furnace.

# If You Go . . .

. . . to Ironbridge Gorge Museum, you'll find it 140 miles northwest of London on the Telford limb of the M6 Motorway. (Ironbridge is actually part of Telford New Town, and the Museum is well signposted.) A more leisurely and historically interesting route is to follow Thomas Telford's old London-Holyhead toll road, now called the A5, which winds through the bleak "Black Country" west of Birmingham before penetrating the exquisite farming lands of Shropshire. Incidentally, a section of Telford's roadway has been excavated on Blists Hill, together with a restored toll house.

The museum is open every day of the year except Christmas (Tar Tunnel is open on weekends only). General admission: 75 cents for adults, 35 cents for children 16 and under. Guided tours are available to groups only, and advance notice is required. Parking is plentiful and free. There is an official Information Center on the south abutment of the Iron Bridge, which offers an excellent series of illustrated guides to the various sites. The Shop in the Square sells books on industrial archeology, transport history and ceramics as well as maps, prints and reproductions of Coalport china and decorative iron castings.

The best book of local history is Barrie Trinder's massive "The Industrial Revolution in Shropshire" (Phillimore, $14.50). The same author has written a much shorter work entitled "The Darbys of Coalbrookdale" (soft cover, $2.50), which makes excellent, nontechnical reading. The Shell Guide "Shropshire," by Michael Moulder (Faber, $7) is a good local guide.

Accommodations are available in Ironbridge at the riverside Valley Hotel (about $12 a night), but baths are few and far between. If you prefer private ablutions, try the Feathers Hotel in Ludlow or the Prince Rupert in Shrewsbury (both about $26 to $31 double). These two beautiful towns are within easy driving distance of Ironbridge. Bridgnorth, a delightful, little-known hill town a few miles downriver, has one of the densest concentrations of fishing pubs in England. You could stay at the Falcon Inn ($17 to $19 double), but don't expect too much in the way of plumbing.

The British Tourist Authority, 680 Fifth Avenue, has a supply of Ironbridge Gorge Museum brochures.—E.M.

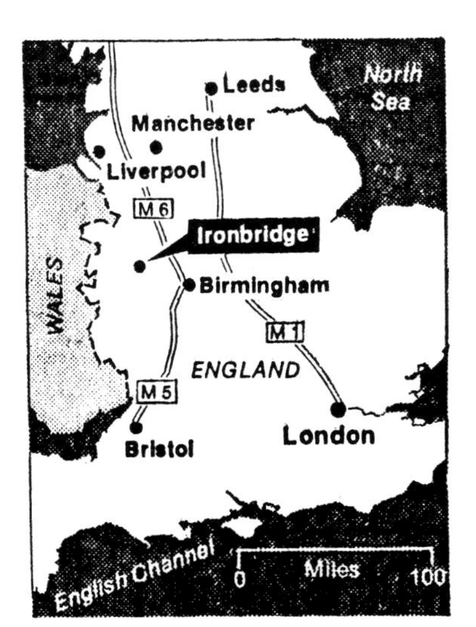

British Tourist Authority

"That first trickle became a stream, and then a flood that seethed and hissed out of the furnaces of Shropshire for almost two centuries." Below, Abraham Darby and an apprentice marvel at the discovery that iron can be smelted with coal. Above, the Coalport chinaworks.

Culver Pictures

# Hewitt Family Moves to San Francisco In 1883

| | Born | Died | Age On Arrival In San Francisco | Age at Death |
|---|---|---|---|---|
| William A. Hewitt | 1838 | 1910 | 45 Years | 72 Years |
| Mary Rebecca Jones (Married William A. Hewitt September 13, 1865) | 1844 | 1904 | 39 Years | 60 Years |
| Their children were: | | | | |
| Catherine E. Hewitt | July 15, 1866 | Dec. 12, 1866 | | 5 Months |
| Edward T. Hewitt | Feb. 26, 1868 | Nov. 3, 1933 | 15 Years | 65 Years |
| William A. Hewitt | Aug. 7, 1870 | Aug. 1, 1950 | 13 Years | 80 Years |
| Mary Hewitt | Sept. 26, 1872 | Aug. 12, 1925 | 10 Years | 52 Years |
| Arthur G. Hewitt | Oct. 19, 1874 | 1912 | 9 Years | 38 Years |
| Margaret Hewitt (McLeod) | Feb. 15, 1877 | 1946 | 6 Years | 69 Years |
| Daisy Hewitt (Hobart) | Feb. 21, 1881 | 1964 | 2 Years | 83 Years |

Editor's Note: My grandfather, William A. Hewitt, traveled from England to San Francisco in 1882. After a few weeks in California, he returned to England. In 1883 he traveled again to San Francisco, this time with his wife and six children, to establish their permanent residence there.

*Grave marker of Mary Ann Jones, mother of Mary Rebecca Jones Hewitt.*

M. R. Hewitt's Mothers
Grave & Tabletts &c
April 18th 1880

*Handwritten note on back of photograph of grave marker of Mary Ann Jones.*

IN
MEMORY
OF
MARY ANN JONES
WIFE OF
EDWARD THOMAS JONES
OF
COALBROOKDALE
WHO DEPARTED THIS LIFE
APRIL 18, 1876
AGED 71 YEARS

DIED IN FAITH
LOOKING UNTO JESUS

1865 Marriage Solemnized at the Holy Trinity Church in the Parish of Coalbrookdale, Co. Salop

| No. | When Married. | Name and Surname. | Age. | Condition. | Rank or Profession. | Residence at the Time of Marriage. | Father's Name and Surname. | Rank or Profession of Father. |
|---|---|---|---|---|---|---|---|---|
| 71 | September 13 | William Alexander Hewitt | Full | Bachelor | Iron Founder | St. Pauls, Deptford | William Hewitt | Iron Founder |
| | | Mary Rebecca Jones | Full | Spinster | — | Coalbrookdale | Edward Thomas Jones | Smith |

Married in the above Church according to the Rites and Ceremonies of the Established Church

By me John Hayes

…riage was solemnized between us, William A. Hewitt, Mary Rebecca Jones

In the presence of us, Edward Thomas Jones, Samuel Ward Hilton

…bove is a true Copy of the Marriage Register of the Holy Trinity Church, Coalbrookdale aforesaid.

…xtracted this thirteenth Day of September in the Year of our Lord One Thousand Eight Hundred and sixty five

By me, John Hayes

Shaw & Sons, Law Publishers, Fetter-lane.

ONE PENNY

*Marriage certificate of William A. Hewitt and Mary Rebecca Jones Hewitt, 1865.*

J 600

13

Uimh.

ÉIRE IRELAND

Foirm A

Form A

Deimhniú breithe ar na h-éisiúint de bhun na hAchta um Chlárú Breitheanna agus Básanna 1863 go 1972.

**BIRTH CERTIFICATE issued in pursuance of Births and Deaths Registration Acts 1863 to 1972**

Breith a Cláraíodh i gCeantar / Birth Registered in the District of Ballymacarrett — i gCeantar an Chláraitheora Maoirseachta do / in the Superintendent Registrar's District of Belfast — i gContae / in the County of Down

| Uimh. No. (1) | Dáta agus Ionad Breithe / Date and Place of Birth (2) | Ainm (má tugadh) / Name (if any) (3) | Gnéas / Sex (4) | Ainm Sloinne agus Ionad Chónaithe an Athar / Name and Surname and Dwelling Place of Father (5) | Ainm agus Sloinne na Máthar agus a Sloinne roimh phósadh di / Name and Surname and Maiden Surname of Mother (6) | Céim nó Gairm Bheatha an Athar / Rank or Profession of Father (7) | Síniú, Cáilíocht agus Ionad Chónaithe an Fhaisnéiseora / Signature, Qualification and Residence of Informant (8) | An Dáta a Cláraíodh / When Registered (9) | Síniú an Chláraitheora / Signature of Registrar (10) | Ainm Baiste, má tugadh é tar éis Chlárú na Breithe, agus an Dáta / Baptismal Name, if added after Registration of Birth, and Date (11) |
|---|---|---|---|---|---|---|---|---|---|---|
| 218 | Twenty Sixth February 1868 Woodstock Place Ballymacarrett | Edward | Male | William Hewitt Woodstock place Ballymacarrett | Mary Rebecca Hewitt Iníon / Formerly Jones | Mechanic | William Hewitt Father Woodstock Place Ballymacarrett | Eighteenth March 1868 | James Murray Cláraitheoir / Registrar | |

Deimhnitear gur fíor Chóip i seo de thaifead atá i gClár-leabhar na mBreitheanna in Oifig an Ard-Chláraitheora i mBaile Átha Cliath.
Certified to be a true copy taken from the Certified Copies of Births in Oifig an Ard-Chláraitheora, Dublin.

Arna Thabhairt faoi Shéala Oifige an Ard-Chláraitheora / Given under the Seal of Oifig an Ard-Chláraitheora an / this Twenty Ninth lá so de / day of July 1988

Is é Bliain na Breithe sa Chóip deimhnithe thuas ná / The Year of Birth shown in the above Certified Copy is
Míle / One Thousand Eight gCéad / Hundred and Sixty Eight

Ath-Scríofa / Copied ....

Scrúdaithe / Examined ....

Is cion trom é an teastas seo a athrú nó é a úsáid tar éis a athraithe.

TO ALTER THIS DOCUMENT OR TO UTTER IT SO ALTERED IS A SERIOUS OFFENCE

*Birth certificate of Edward Thomas Hewitt, 1868. Note that he was born in the district of Belfast, County Down, Ireland.*

1861 – 1965

**Extract of an entry in a REGISTER of BIRTHS** 073468

*Registration of Births, Deaths and Marriages (Scotland) Act 1965*

| No. | 1. Name and surname | 2. When and where born | 3. Sex | 4. Name, surname, and rank or profession of father, Name, and maiden surname of mother, Date and place of marriage | 5. Signature and qualification of informant, and residence, if out of the house in which the birth occurred | 6. When and where registered and signature of registrar |
|---|---|---|---|---|---|---|
| 530 | William Alexander Hewitt | 1870 August Seventh 1h Pm Lyle's Land Hillend Greenock | M | Wm Alexander Hewitt Ironfounder (Journ[illegible]) Mary Rebecca Hewitt M. S. Jones 1865 Sept 14 Coalbrookdale Shropshire [illegible] | [illegible] Hewitt Father Present | 1870 August 23 At Greenock James Slator Registrar |

The above particulars are extracted from a Register of Births for the East Parish of Greenock in the County of Renfrew

Given under the Seal of the General Register Office, New Register House, Edinburgh, on 15th November 1988.

The above particulars incorporate any subsequent corrections or amendments to the original entry made with the authority of the Registrar General.

This extract is valid only if it has been authenticated by the seal of the General Register Office. If the particulars in the relevant entry in the statutory register have been reproduced by photography, xerography or some other similar process the seal must have been impressed after the reproduction has been made. The General Register Office will authenticate only those reproductions which have been produced by that office.

**Warning**

It is an offence under section 53(3) of the Registration of Births, Deaths and Marriages (Scotland) Act 1965 for any person to pass as genuine any copy or reproduction of this extract which has not been made by the General Register Office and authenticated by the Seal of that Office.

Any person who falsifies or forges any of the particulars on this extract or knowingly uses, gives or sends as genuine any false or forged extract is liable to prosecution under section 53(1) of the said Act.

*Birth certificate of William Alexander Hewitt, 1870. Note that Uncle Bill was born in Greenoch, Scotland.*

**CERTIFIED COPY OF AN ENTRY OF BIRTH**

GIVEN AT THE GENERAL REGISTER OFFICE SOMERSET HOUSE LONDON.

Statutory fee for this certificate is 3s. 9d. Where a search is necessary to find the entry, a search fee is payable in addition.

*Application Number* 951175

REGISTRATION DISTRICT GREENWICH

1881 BIRTH in the Sub-district of St Paul Deptford in the Counties of Kent and Surrey

| No. | 1 When and where born | 2 Name, if any | 3 Sex | 4 Name, and surname of father | 5 Name, surname, and maiden surname of mother | 6 Occupation of father | 7 Signature, description, and residence of informant | 8 When registered | 9 Signature of registrar | 10* Name entered after registration |
|---|---|---|---|---|---|---|---|---|---|---|
| 37 | Twentyfirst February 1881 25 Abinger Terrace | Daisy Leo | Girl | William Alexander Hewitt | Mary Rebecca Hewitt formerly Jones | Iron Moulder | Mary Rebecca Hewitt Mother 25 Abinger Terrace Deptford | Fourth April 1881 | W.T. Hunt Jr. Registrar | ——— |

CERTIFIED to be a true copy of an entry in the certified copy of a Register of Births in the District above mentioned.

Given at the GENERAL REGISTER OFFICE, SOMERSET HOUSE, LONDON, under the Seal of the said Office, the 26th day of October 1961.

*See note overleaf.

BC 285789

This certificate is issued in pursuance of the Births and Deaths Registration Act, 1953 (1 & 2 Eliz. 2, c. 20).
Section 34 provides that any certified copy of an entry purporting to be sealed or stamped with the seal of the General Register Office shall be received as evidence of the birth or death to which it relates without any further or other proof of the entry, and no certified copy purporting to be given in the said Office shall be of any force or effect unless it is sealed or stamped as aforesaid.
CAUTION.—Any person who (1) falsifies any of the particulars on this certificate, or (2) uses a falsified certificate as true, knowing it to be false, is liable to prosecution.

*Birth certificate of Daisy Leo Hewitt, 1881. Note that Aunt Daisy was born in Greenwich, England. Aunt Margaret, Aunt Mary and Uncle Arthur were also born in England.*

*Master William A. Hewitt, Deptford, England, 1872.*

Editor's Note: Although the photograph above appears to be of a little girl, it is of my Uncle Bill. Apparently it was a British custom to have little boys wear dresses.

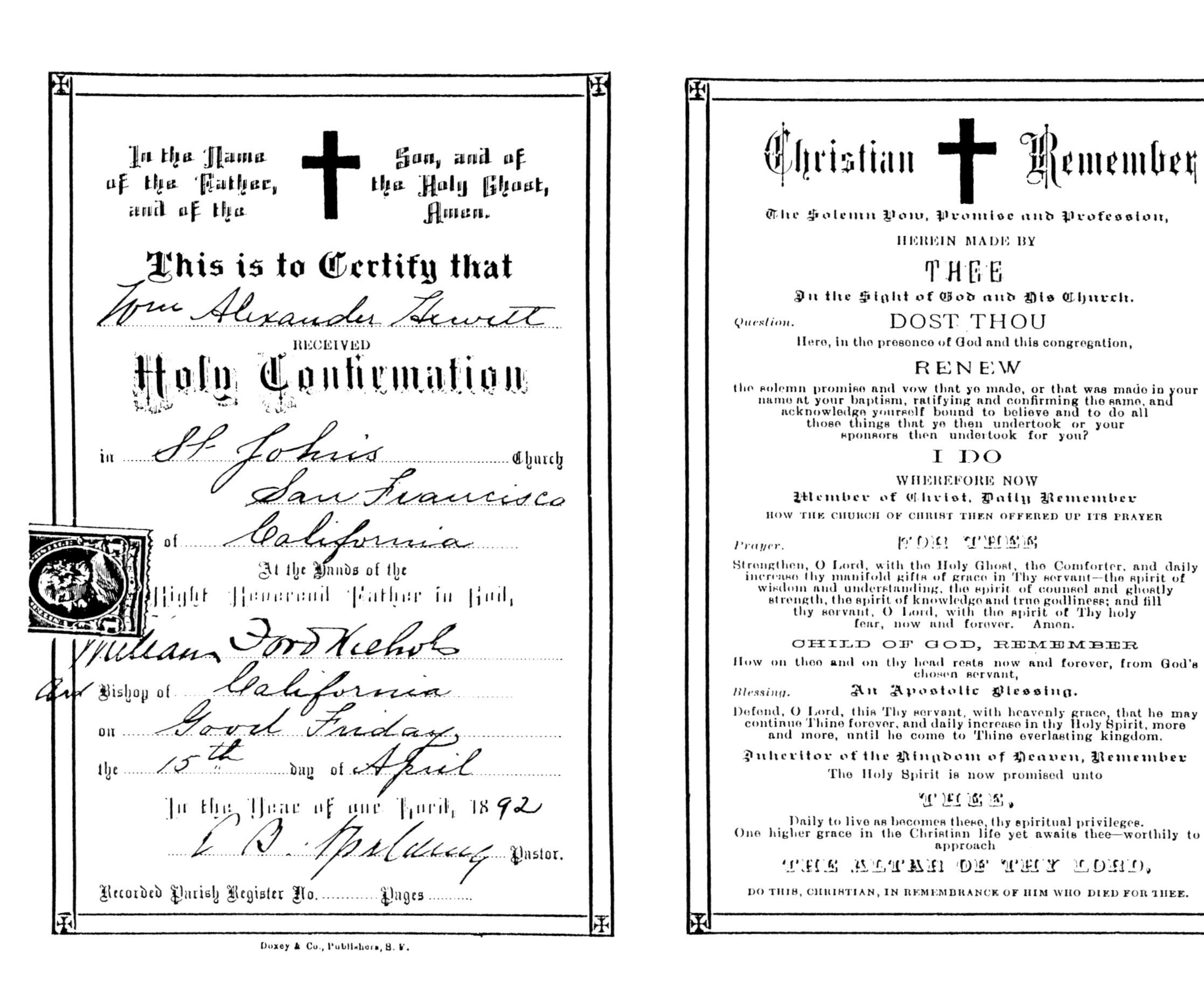

In the Name of the Father, and of the Son, and of the Holy Ghost, Amen.

**This is to Certify that**

Wm Alexander Hewitt

RECEIVED

**Holy Confirmation**

in St. John's Church San Francisco

of California

At the Hands of the Right Reverend Father in God,

William Ford Nichols

Asst Bishop of California

on Good Friday

the 15th day of April

In the Year of our Lord, 1892

C. B. [illegible] Pastor.

Recorded Parish Register No. ........ Pages ........

Doxey & Co., Publishers, S. F.

**Christian Remember**

The Solemn Vow, Promise and Profession,

HEREIN MADE BY

THEE

In the Sight of God and His Church.

*Question.* DOST THOU

Here, in the presence of God and this congregation,

RENEW

the solemn promise and vow that ye made, or that was made in your name at your baptism, ratifying and confirming the same, and acknowledge yourself bound to believe and to do all those things that ye then undertook or your sponsors then undertook for you?

I DO

WHEREFORE NOW

Member of Christ, Daily Remember

HOW THE CHURCH OF CHRIST THEN OFFERED UP ITS PRAYER

*Prayer.* FOR THEE

Strengthen, O Lord, with the Holy Ghost, the Comforter, and daily increase thy manifold gifts of grace in Thy servant—the spirit of wisdom and understanding, the spirit of counsel and ghostly strength, the spirit of knowledge and true godliness; and fill thy servant, O Lord, with the spirit of Thy holy fear, now and forever. Amen.

CHILD OF GOD, REMEMBER

How on thee and on thy head rests now and forever, from God's chosen servant,

*Blessing.* An Apostolic Blessing.

Defend, O Lord, this Thy servant, with heavenly grace, that he may continue Thine forever, and daily increase in thy Holy Spirit, more and more, until he come to Thine everlasting kingdom.

Inheritor of the Kingdom of Heaven, Remember

The Holy Spirit is now promised unto

THEE,

Daily to live as becomes these, thy spiritual privileges. One higher grace in the Christian life yet awaits thee—worthily to approach

THE ALTAR OF THY LORD,

DO THIS, CHRISTIAN, IN REMEMBRANCE OF HIM WHO DIED FOR THEE.

*Confirmation Certificate of William A. Hewitt, age 22, San Francisco, 1892.*

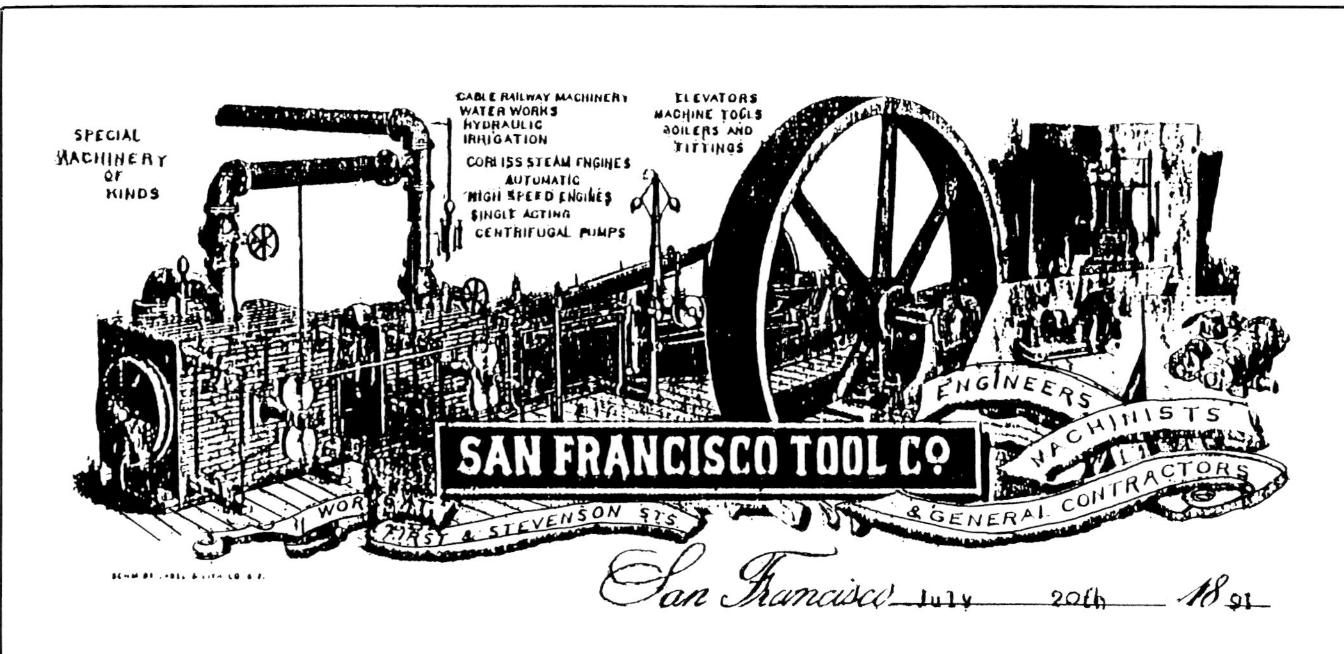


To whom it may concern:-

This is to certify that William Hewitt has been in our employ for four and one-half years learning the pattern making trade.

During his term of service with us we found him competent, and trustworthy and we are pleased to recommend him to any one having need of his services.

Yours truly,

San Francisco Tool Co.

by Chas C Moore

Sec'y.

*Letter of recommendation for William Hewitt from San Francisco Tool Company, signed by Charles C. Moore, indicates that Uncle Bill, at age 21 in 1891, had completed four and one-half years "learning the pattern making trade."*

**EXTRACT FROM 1900 CENSUS** **Person No.:** ____

State CA County or Parish SF Township/Ward/Beat SF Street CAPP

Extracted by: AF Date of Enumeration 4 JUNE 1900 Microfilm reel No. CA 103

| Enumeration district | House No. | Sheet | Line | Names | Relationship to head of house | Color | Sex | Month and year of birth | Age | Marital status | Years married | Mother of how many children | No. of these children living | Person's birthplace | Father's birthplace | Mother's birthplace | Year of Immigration | No. of years in U.S. | Naturalized | Occupation |
|---|---|---|---|---|---|---|---|---|---|---|---|---|---|---|---|---|---|---|---|---|
| 113 | 69 | 4 | 11 | HEWITT, WILLIAM | HEAD | W | M | OCT 1836 | 63 | M | 32 | | | IRELAND | ENGLAND | ENGLAND | 1882 | 18 | NA | MANAGER MACHINE WAREHOUSE |
| | | | | MARY R. | WIFE | W | F | FEB 1848 | 52 | M | 32 | 7 | 6 | ENG | ENG | ENG | 1883 | 17 | | |
| | | | | EDWARDT | SON | W | M | FEB 1869 | 31 | S | | | | IRE | IRE | ENG | 1888 | 17 | NA | TEACHER AT SCHOOL |
| | | | | MARY A | DAU | W | F | SEP 1873 | 26 | S | | | | ENG | IRE | ENG | 1883 | 17 | | |
| | | | | ARTHUR G | SON | W | M | OCT 1875 | 24 | S | | | | ENG | IRE | ENG | 1883 | 17 | — | CASHIER NEWSPAPER |
| | | | | MARGARET K | DAU | W | F | FEB 1878 | 22 | S | | | | ENG | IRE | ENG | 1883 | 17 | | |
| | | | | DAISY BL | DAU | W | F | FEB 1881 | 19 | S | | | | ENG | IRE | ENG | 1883 | 17 | | AT SCHOOL |



EDITOR'S NOTE: The above extract from the San Francisco Census of the year 1900 was provided by the California Historical Society, from state records in Sacramento. It is assumed that the original census documents were burned in the great San Francisco fire of 1906. The listing shows that our grandparents, William and Mary R. Hewitt, were then living in their house on Capp Street with five of their six children. Their son, William, was then living elsewhere in San Francisco.

The above document also includes information verifying the fact that my grandfather, William Hewitt and my father, Edward Hewitt, were both born in Ireland. The parents of my grandfather were both born in England.

My grandmother, Mary Rebecca, and her parents, were all born in England, as were my aunts, Mary, Margaret and Daisy, and my Uncle Arthur. Uncle Bill (William), not listed above, was born in Scotland.

*During the early 1900's, Edward T. Hewitt was a strong advocate of vocational schools for young men. He believed that such schools were more effective than apprenticeship in the shops. He summed up his thoughts on this subject as follows:*

"Having had the opportunity to observe closely the results of apprenticeship in the shops, and of training in the special schools, I feel confident in saying that the school method has, in most cases, the advantage. We have letters on hand from employers, parents, and graduates which prove our statements. Of course, there are some boys whom no amount of schooling could improve, just as there are boys in the shops whom no amount of adverse circumstances could hold down. In its broader meaning, the school gives the greatest good to the largest number."

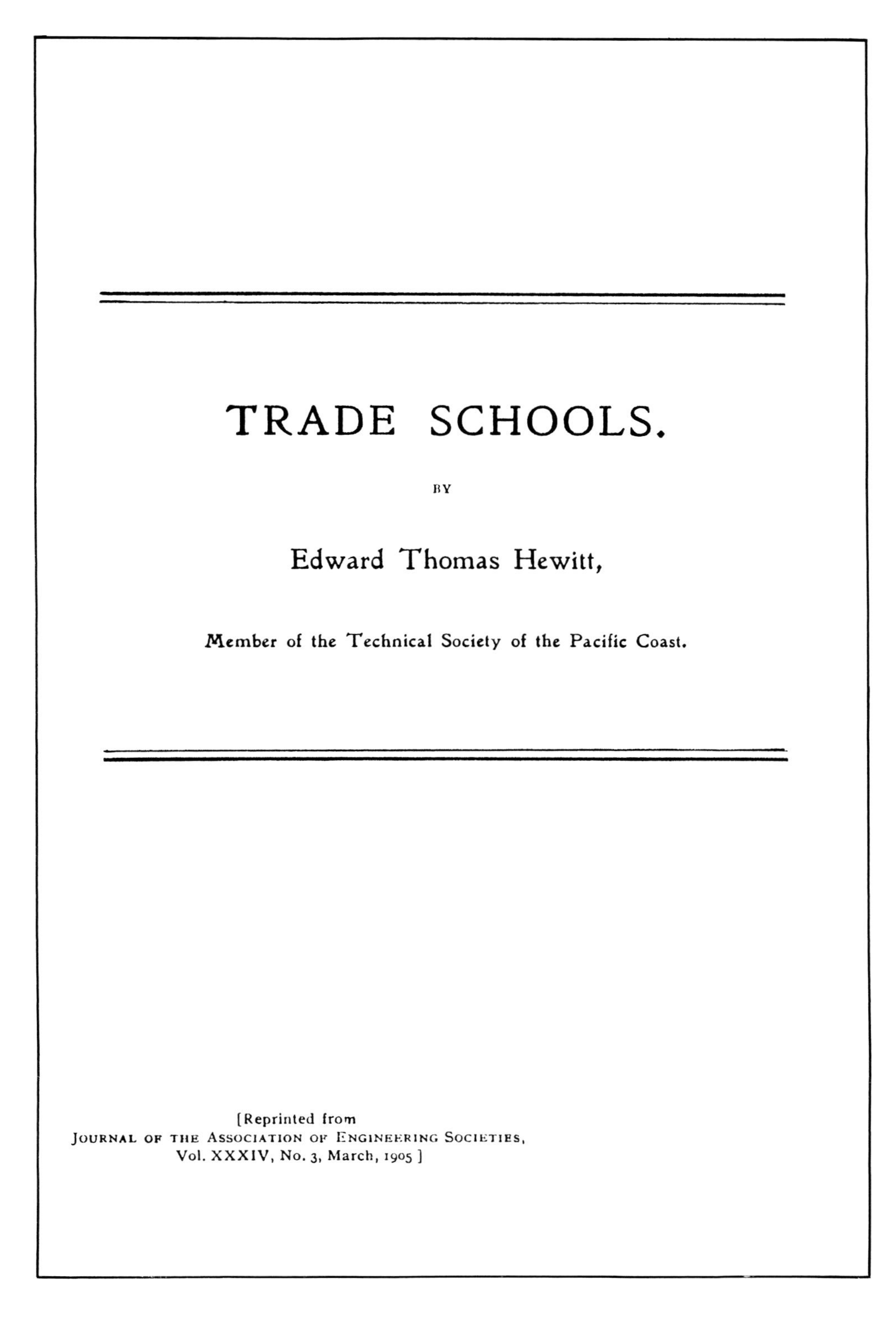

# TRADE SCHOOLS.

BY

Edward Thomas Hewitt,

*Member of the Technical Society of the Pacific Coast.*

[Reprinted from
JOURNAL OF THE ASSOCIATION OF ENGINEERING SOCIETIES,
Vol. XXXIV, No. 3, March, 1905.]

EDITOR'S NOTE: The following 15-page treatise on trade schools was written by Edward Thomas Hewitt, member of the Technical Society of the Pacific Coast. He was then 36 years old. Hewitt presented this paper at the Society's Autumnal Meeting on December 2, 1904. It was an excellent statement of his ideas on basic education.

## TRADE SCHOOLS.

By Edward Thomas Hewitt, Member of the Technical Society of the Pacific Coast.

[A paper read before the Autumnal Meeting of the Society, December 2, 1904.*]

What is the necessity for such schools, what are they accomplishing, what possibilities have they for future development, what is their present status? The subject is one so broad and deep, that it affects the whole social structure. The stability of a nation depends largely upon the welfare of its people, upon their fitness for the many pursuits of life, requiring constant and serious consideration. Recognizing this to be the case, the utmost attention is given to the education of the youth of our country. The public school system will always maintain its proper position. The trade school is coming prominently to the fore, and is an influential factor in the preparation of young men and women to be successful in their life-work.

There are two great problems that open out before everyone: First, how to get a living, and second, how to get the most meaning out of life. Often the first overshadows the second, until the latter has become, to many, a half-forgotten dream. It has been a source of great pleasure and benefit to me, in the past, to have been associated with men who had learned their trades under the old system in this and other countries, and I can testify to the fact that they were thorough workmen.

Conditions have changed a great deal since those men first started out on their life-work. Sometimes in the past it had been maintained that the shop was the best school in which to learn a trade, and that the sooner a boy entered the shop as an apprentice, after acquiring the rudiments of a common-school education, the better it was for him. That may be true, where a boy's only desire is to become and remain just an ordinary workman. There are, of course, some exceptions to this rule. The general prosperity of the present time permits the parent to give his children a better education than was formerly obtainable. The trade school of to-day aids materially in the accomplishing of this purpose. The graduates are demonstrating to employers their superiority, acquired through proper training for their chosen lines of work. After the boy has graduated from this school, obtained employment, become familiar

* Manuscript received February 13, 1905.—Secretary, Ass'n of Eng. Socs.

with shop methods, his education proves its real value. The results have been very encouraging to all concerned.

The general tendency nowadays is toward obtaining an education before looking for regular employment. This means a more effective power for work. I have frequently seen young men make great sacrifices, in order that they might be enabled to continue at school. The future years will prove the wisdom of their present application to study. We find the sons of professional men, mechanics, farmers, miners, business men and of manufacturers, in short, men representing many classes of society, earnestly working side by side in trade schools, this class of school being just what they wanted. To many, ordinary school life had been somewhat distasteful. Boys of fourteen years of age pass through a period of physical transition, their bodies and minds are growing and developing rapidly; hence the great care that is necessary at this time, as their whole life is shaped by the course that is taken by them then. Of the children who enter the grammar schools a very small percentage reach the university.

As a basis for this discussion, allow me to submit some statistics on school attendance. The school census of this city and county, for the year 1901, stated that there were 105,512 children under 18 years of age. Of the 82,173 children between the ages of 5 and 17 years, 48,517 are reported as having attended school at some time during the year. The average daily attendance was 34,771. The number of children, between the ages of 5 and 17 years, attending private schools during the year was 10,586. The number of children of school age, who have not attended school at any time during the year, was 20,634. The report states that while the school age in our own State extends over eleven years, from the sixth to the seventeenth year of life, very few pupils attend school for that length of time. The average child has a little more than 6 years' schooling. San Francisco ranks well with other cities of this country in school attendance.

The efficiency of the secondary school has been greatly increased through the introduction of manual training and industrial work. Boys having a natural aptitude for mechanics are now desirous of entering these trade schools, as they give them a better opportunity for developing their talents and for finding out for themselves what particular line of work they are best suited to follow. In former years boys did not have this opportunity. A large majority of the graduates of grammar schools entered for employment at almost anything they could find to do, having no definite plan in view. If they chose a trade, they possibly attended a night school. Many a boy has gone through life totally unfitted for any particular calling. Restrictions as to the number of apprentices still further placed him in a precarious position.

Young men must obtain some kind of employment, employers cannot conduct their many enterprises without the aid of skilled help.

While the author fully recognizes much good in the old apprenticeship system, it is evidently inadequate under present conditions. Business is conducted by employers for profit, and it costs something to teach the apprentice his trade, so the boy often loses a great deal of time doing rough work. If he shows an aptitude, he may possibly be given some small job on which to try his skill. If he spoils it, some time may elapse before he is given another opportunity. As a rule, in the average shop, he has to shift for himself.

Cheap help proves to be the most expensive in the long run.

It may not please some educators to have to consider the utilitarian phase of education. But then, every head of a household cannot afford to send his children into the higher schools, unless he sees future possibilities which warrant his doing so. Therefore, the schools must adapt themselves to his wants, and reserve the university courses for those who are better able to take them. The trade school here finds its place, proving its worth, which is now universally recognized.

The old order changeth, gradually giving place for the new. August Belmont, the man who financed the stupendous Subway undertaking in New York City, in commenting on the opening of the Subway, recently remarked philosophically to a friend: "That I am pleased that the Subway is at last completed, goes without saying. But, the longer I live, the more keenly I feel that, whatever is good enough for us to-day, is not good enough for us to-morrow. The Subway is only the beginning of great things in its line."

Now I will endeavor to sum up briefly the various avenues of employment that are open to the young man. Graduating from the grammar school, he may, if so inclined, enter some large iron works to learn a trade, and attend a night school to study arithmetic, mechanical drawing, physics, geometry, science, etc. If the boy is of the right sort, he will stick to his work and studies, thus qualifying for advancement. Very often it happens that he has nobody to direct his efforts for mental improvement. Employers have no special interest in his welfare, and there may be no suitable night school available to attend.

Some of the representative firms of this country, feeling the need for more high-grade workmen than could be obtained in the old way, decided that it was imperative to give closer attention to the care and training of the young men in their employ. This has been productive of very good results. The young men, in turn, appreciate the efforts in their behalf, and are as proud of their shops as any university graduate is of his Alma Mater. The Baldwin Locomotive Works, Brown and Sharpe Manufacturing Company, the Westinghouse Electric and Manufacturing Company, are notable instances of firms which are solving the apprenticeship question. Each of the aforementioned firms has an experienced man who has complete supervision of the apprentices. He examines them in the first instance to see if they come properly prepared, and upon their preparation depends the group in which they may be placed, of which there are three. First-class apprentices comprise boys who have had a good common-school education and who are not over 17 years of age. Second-class apprentices are boys who have had an advanced grammar or high-school training and who are not over 18 years of age. There is also a special course of instruction for young men over 21 years of age who are graduates of colleges or technical schools.

The director of apprentices sees that each apprentice receives a full and sufficient training in his particular work, and also directs the studies, choosing the particular school which they are to attend. He stands as guardian for them in many respects while they are in the city, as many are from other parts of the country.

The director is really a school principal in these large works. His efforts promote system and efficiency, and these are what his employers want. In reality, this is an ideal type of trade school. It is the outgrowth of the urgent necessity for high-grade work. This particular apprenticeship system at present is limited to a few noted manufacturing companies. It is practically putting the school in the shop. This, no doubt, would please our old friend, Professor Sweet.

It is hardly possible for smaller companies to follow the example set by these firms. Trade schools must fill the gap. They are now giving to young people a thorough and systematic training in a very large number of industrial pursuits. In the future it will be the graduates of these schools, who, after a riper experience, will naturally assume the leading positions in the industrial world. I would like to add that the schools of San Francisco are amply able to give our youth the training they require.

If a young man intends to study law, medicine or theology, the regular high school, giving the classical course, is preferable.

If he has a business career in view, the commercial school will help him. To become a successful farmer, a course in a school of agriculture is to the purpose. If he desires to become a professional engineer, in some one of the many branches of the art, a college preparatory course in a mechanic arts school will give him the necessary preliminary training. The young man who wishes to learn a trade, and also to obtain a good education, would do well to spend four years in a school of industrial arts. It will be time well spent. These schools are enabled to offer good inducements, having an excellent equipment, efficient instructors and practically free tuition. The school day is of longer duration than in the common schools. Thus it is possible to accomplish a great amount of work during the term.

Educators, philanthropists, statesmen, men of affairs, have given their time and money to further the advancement of industrial education. Mistakes have been made in the past, as in all new and important undertakings, but they are gradually being remedied. Industrial education has passed the experimental stage. The splendid schools, now open to students in this and other countries, testify to the universal need of them. To speak of some of our local institutions, I might mention the Wilmerding School of Industrial Arts, founded by J. C. Wilmerding; the California School of Mechanical Arts, founded by James Lick; Coggswell Polytechnic College, founded by the late Dr. Coggswell; Polytechnic High School; Drawing Department of the Humboldt Evening School; the California Polytechnic School, a secondary school of agriculture. The foregoing are secondary schools.

For those who desire to study for a professional life, the University of California and Stanford University are amply prepared.

Passing through the many different departments of a large modern school devoted to the training of young men in the mechanic arts, the question arises in our mind, What would our youth do if such schools did not exist? Observe them carefully, see how engrossed they are with their work. They have learned the secret of being happy through occupation. Greater interest is taken in mathematics and science, for the students now see their application. The knowledge of free-hand drawing enables them to make quick, serviceable sketches. The study of mechanics, including the strength of materials, helps them in machine design. Boiler and engine tests are conducted under the most favorable conditions. In the school devoted to the building trades, everything is considered that is necessary in the construction of a complete building. Agricultural schools will enable the future farmer to manage his farm to better advantage. The field of industrial chemistry is now offering abundant opportunities.*

Such an earnest desire is shown by the students, that the noon hour is utilized by many for work, as they do not want to lose a minute. Discipline is maintained not by severity or strictness, but by leaving the students on their honor to conduct themselves in a proper manner. The greatest punishment we can inflict is to compel a student to remain out of his class. Much interest is taken by them in athletics, music, debating, etc. The experiments in the laboratory, work in the shop, studies in the class room, track athletics, social pleasures, are taken up with enthusiasm. Under such influences, a splendid type of man is produced.

Having had the opportunity to observe closely the results of apprenticeship in the shops, and of training in the special schools, I feel confident in saying that the school method has, in most cases, the advantage. We have letters on hand from employers, parents and graduates which prove our statements. Of course, there are some boys whom no amount of schooling could improve, just as there are boys in the shops whom no amount of adverse circumstances could hold down. In its broader meaning, the school gives the greatest good to the largest number. Applications for entrance next July are already on file in many of these special schools.

The Wilmerding School of Industrial Arts for boys was founded by Mr. J. Chute Wilmerding, $400,000 being left to establish and maintain a school to teach boys trades, fitting them to make a living with their hands, with some study and plenty of work. The school is open to any earnest, industrious boy who wants to learn one of the building trades. Any boy who has completed the grammar-school course is eligible for admission. It is intended to give something more than the mere equivalent of a workshop apprenticeship. Its graduates must have a fair command of the English language. They must know enough of mathematics, drawing and science to insure intelligent and progressive workmanship. But, with all these things, the student must acquire a thorough mastery of his trade. He must become a skillful, rapid and thorough workman. The trades taught are carpentry, architectural drawing, plumbing, cabinet making, electrical working, bricklaying, blacksmithing, wood carving, clay modeling. Four years is the course. The new brick buildings of this school, also an enlargement of the Lick School buildings (including the many branches of

---

* The girls, in addition to their academic work, are taught domestic science. The value of all this is apparent.

detail work involved), are being built by the students, and are attracting much favorable attention.

The California School of Mechanical Arts was founded by James Lick, and was endowed at a cost of $540,000. Its object is to educate boys and girls in the practical walks of life. The school is free of charge for tuition, and is open to any boy or girl of this State who has completed the eighth grade of the grammar school. The following trades and technical courses are given:

| Boys. | Girls. |
|---|---|
| *Forgework.* | *Industrial arts.* |
| Iron and brass molding. | Cookery. |
| Machine-shop practice. | Dressmaking. |
| Electrical construction. | Millinery. |
| Machine and ship drawing. | |
| Industrial chemistry. | |
| Polytechnic course. | |

The boys and girls are eligible for a technical college preparatory course. Four years are required for each trade. A full academic course is given in conjunction with the trade selected. A short term is devoted by each student to each of the foregoing trades, and is called the manual training or preliminary course. This covers the first two years. They are then re-classified, and the student may take up further studies, to prepare himself for the technical college or university course. Again, any student, who may not care to specialize in any of the courses given, may pursue a general elective course, made up by selection from the various subjects offered in the different departments of the school. This is called the polytechnic course. To avoid dissipation of effort on the part of the student, and to prevent him from taking up work for which he is unfitted, his progress must be approved by the instructor in charge of each department concerned.

A large number of students choose the trades courses. During their term of apprenticeship, the major part of their time is devoted to a practical study of their trade in all its forms; as large a variety of work as possible is given. Such studies as are necessary for efficient work in their trade are required, viz: mechanical drawing, strength of materials, mechanics, boiler and engine tests, mathematics. The class of work done is of an educational and practical nature. The instructors in charge are men who have had practical experience. I might mention that several castings have been made recently, each weighing 1800 pounds. Electric motors, steam pumps, machine tools, hoists, steam engines, an electric traveling crane of

2500 pounds capacity, and many special tools, have been made by the students in a workmanlike manner.

The Coggswell Polytechnic School, under its new principal, intends so to shape its policy as to include a course of mineralogy and assaying. In time a practical mining course will be adopted. Graduates of the eighth grade of the grammar schools are admitted.

The California Polytechnic School is a State institution, situated in San Luis Obispo. The purpose of this school is to furnish, to young people of both sexes, mental and manual training in the arts and sciences, including agriculture, mechanics, engineering, business methods, domestic economy, and such other branches as will fit the student for the non-professional walks of life. Its location is extremely favorable for its success.

The Drawing Department of the Humboldt Evening School of this city is doing a good work. Here may be seen 460 students spending their evenings, from 7.15 to 9.15. The course requires three years or more.

There are two classes in naval architecture.
One class in electrical engineering.
Two classes in architecture.
Six classes in mechanical engineering.

The last item is divided into the following special branches:
Two classes in special and automatic machinery.
Two classes in marine engineering.
One class in gas-engine construction.
One class in mining and mill work.

In addition to these there remain:
One class in geometry and trigonometry.
One class in algebra and advanced arithmetic.
One class in theoretical mechanics and electricity.

Lectures are given every Friday evening in each class by the class instructor, from 8.35 to 9.15. Semi-annually six lectures are given by professional technical men on the various branches given in the school. The instructors are men daily engaged in the branches they teach. The school has been established seven years. Its rapid growth and large attendance of students testify to the necessity for such a school and to the good work done by those in charge. Allow me to add that the social feature of so many earnest young men, meeting together every evening, is of incalculable benefit. Their minds are improved, daily work is raised in quality, employers are benefited. Many life-long friendships have their beginnings where such conditions exist.

TRADE SCHOOLS.

In the Polytechnic High School of our city, a very good course is given in mechanical drawing, woodwork, machine practice, wood carving, clay modeling, free-hand drawing. Many of the graduates are employed in our various shops.

Children in the public schools are now given elementary instruction in woodwork.

Throughout this country there are many schools that have been established in recent years, notably the New York Trade School, Pratt Institute, Worcester Polytechnic Institute, Drexel Institute of Philadelphia, Cooper Institute of New York, Armour Institute of Technology, Chicago. The reputable correspondence schools are assisting young men who would otherwise remain without any systematic training.

In the South, Booker T. Washington is trying to solve the negro question by education. He has established a school of trades at Tuskegee, Alabama, and, by encouraging thrift and industry, he expects to raise the standard of living for the colored man.

The Kamehameha Schools, in the Hawaiian Islands, were erected for the benefit of the native boys and girls. Instruction is given in the common English branches, manual training, sewing, tailoring, printing, practical agriculture, carpentry, forgework, machine work, painting and electrical work. This school was founded by Mrs. Chas. R. Bishop.

Every country needs skilled workers along many lines of industry. It is interesting to note that modern methods are invading the cities of the Orient. The Philippine School of Arts and Trades has been established in Manila, offering to the native young men an excellent opportunity to fit themselves for positions in industrial lines of work. The people of these islands have much latent mechanical skill, and the object of this school will be to develop this ability, guide it into modern channels, and foster a sentiment in favor of honest labor.

The Japanese recognized the benefits of industrial training long ago, and were quick to adopt it. In England and Scotland, many schools are doing excellent work. The idea is gaining in favor, in fact, it is becoming a necessity. Competition, in the markets of the world, with the United States and Continental Europe, is compelling new methods to be adopted.

In Germany, industrial chemistry has created new lines of manufactures and revolutionized old methods. Mr. Carnegie and Mr. Schwab, Sir Philip Magnus and many others have given much of their time, labor and means for the improvement of men, and methods of performing work.

At the laying of the cornerstone of the new building of the Hebrew Technical School for girls, now being erected in New York City, former President Grover Cleveland, in his address as presiding officer of the exercises, said: Public appropriations and private charity are mindful of men and women in poverty, sickness and distress; orphan boys and girls are compassionately cared for and sheltered, but it was an inspiration of genuine benevolence, which led to a different field of human endeavor, and to the establishment of an agency for good which goes farther than to furnish the objects of its care with food and raiment, and the things that perish with the using. Here, girls and boys, who would otherwise be shut out from opportunity for needed improvement, are to be taught remunerative occupations, and thus the thoughts and inclinations of these children will be so molded as to affect our citizenship and our country's weal for years to come."

Periods of prosperity and of depression will always recur, but the path of modern civilization will always have an upward trend.

We should feel proud to be citizens of this beautiful city by the Golden Gate, in this wonderfully productive State of California, where the sturdy pioneers paved the way for us. History proves that engineers have also had a prominent place in its development. The many gifts which nature has so bountifully bestowed afford opportunity for the employment of a very large number of people. One of the greatest forces in the civilization of the present generation is being manifested through the mechanic arts. The magnificent ships of war, steam and sailing vessels; the splendid machinery constructed for mining, milling, manufacturing and power plants; the handsome buildings that grace our city, testify to the great ability and skill of our engineers, architects and mechanics. The construction of the Panama Canal will require much machinery. Who can tell what position our Western cities will take when the canal is finished?

Classes of work are so diversified that specialization in the schools is necessary. To avoid dissipation of effort, and to obtain the best results, different schools are allotting to themselves certain spheres of influences.

The California School of Mechanical Arts intends to add to its curriculum, at some time in the future, such trades as belong to the field of mechanical and electrical engineering and marine architecture.

The Wilmerding School will confine itself to the building trades, the Coggswell College to the mining industry, and the California Polytechnic School to agriculture, etc.

The employer, the employe, the educator and the heads of households must consider this vital question of education. Professional men have always taken a personal interest. We would, therefore, especially invite our citizens and civic bodies to visit our many institutions and to see for themselves what is being done for the uplifting of the youth of our city, developing them in the fullest sense of the word, making them better men and women and teaching them to enjoy life as the Creator designed they should.

## DISCUSSION.

PROF. W. F. DURAND, of Stanford University.—How the training of our future mechanics is to be divided between the schools and shops, I cannot tell, but I believe that there will be room for both. Each has its mission, as there are certain things the trade school can do better than the shop, and others which the shop can do better than the schools. The two institutions ought to be combined. The trade school is of special value.

After all, life is something more than living—it consists in living and enjoying the good things of this world, and if the student can gain a little broader view of the world, or cultivate good taste in literature, becoming more of a man and getting more out of life, he is at the same time gaining something which will enable him to make a better use of life. The secret of instruction is development, and keenness of attention to things outside of himself. Very few are sensitive to a high degree, but when one is found in the hands of a good teacher, then the highest type of man is developed.

The schools are for the purpose of turning out a mechanic, a workman, while in the shop the output is to be a piece of machinery, etc., to be sold at a profit. Schools cannot do everything. The question of labor cannot be handled successfully in the trade schools. Each has its mission to perform, and, if we can only find the right combination, they can work together for one purpose.

As to the need of cultivating skilled labor as a necessity for maintaining our position in the industrial world, it has been proved over and over again, in the shop world, that repetition work saves both time and labor, and both have thus been enormously economized. The products of industry can be manufactured with vastly reduced cost if we will only find the right process of production. Our present processes are imperfect and admit of improvement, and the question is only to find out how to make the improvements so as to produce the items in the quickest and cheapest way. The trade school is simply one step in this general development of skilled labor. Whatever may be our future, as determined in the next 10 or 15 years, our progress will be, in a great degree, due to the good work which our trade schools are doing to-day.

PROF. C. B. WING.—Education is the development of a person; it is his capacity to see things, and to use what he sees for benefiting himself and the world at large. The desire for education is, primarily, the purpose of providing a livelihood, and a wish to make this world a better place in which to get a livelihood. We must not only teach a person's mind to see things, to reason, to express what he sees and to draw a conclusion from his observations, but he must also be able to apply his intellect to some practical purpose in the bettering of his condition and that of the world around him. Thus, the boy who is raised upon the farm has less opportunity for training his mind than the boy in the city; yet, placing them side by side, the boy from the farm has had his manual skill developed, and, at the same time, his mental capacity, and he is not only able to hold his own with the boy who has had intellectual training in the city, but can also use his hands.

When we merely teach persons to do things with their hands for the mere sake of doing it, without giving the necessary intellectual training as a basis, it is hard to meet, in the trade schools, the condition of competition existing in the shop. Any task set in the school is merely play and not work, and there is where the shop has to take the place of the trade school. In the shop, the boy knows that if he does not do his work well he will lose his apprenticeship, and the workman knows he will lose his job. Thus, the object of manual training is not only to learn the work itself, but also for the intellectual development of the student, and to enable him to see how he is going to solve the problem of his daily life.

MR. MARSDEN MANSON.—I have gone through the Lick and Wilmerding Schools and have seen the type of work they do, and I was impressed with the interest the pupils take in their work.

In the South Carolina Agricultural College, cotton is manufactured. Every grade of cotton is raised. It is ginned, cleaned, carded, spun, woven and put in the shop for use, so that every manipulation of the cotton, from the seed to the cloth, is gone through there. There are 600 pupils. The college shows the wide range these technical schools are taking.

MR. A. E. ROBERTS, Head of Drawing Department, Humboldt Evening School.—It is impossible to teach certain trades and certain lines of work in an ordinary trade school, and I believe that the proper system of technical education is where the workshop and the school are intimately related. A combination of practical work, in the daytime, with evening training, including algebra, trigonometry, science, etc., is the ideal system of education.

The trade school has its mission. Its mission is to go along with work to a certain extent, but to undertake to teach to any man a trade is attempting too much. The schools can go to a certain extent only. The principal value of the trade school is to give a young man a good academic training, with an insight into the trade he selects. He will then become a first-class mechanic, for he will understand the whys and wherefores of the different problems he meets in the shops.

I find the trade schools do not pay proper attention to the important question of time. A young man, going into a shop from a trade school, does not properly understand the value of time. The school overlooks the importance of practical work, and thus the force of its instruction is lost.

I am a friend of the trade schools, but they have their limits, and I do not believe in carrying them too far.

In order to have practical men carry on the work of instruction the professors should do practical work on the outside, as in that way they are enabled to keep in touch with the work.

I indorse what you say about the workshop method of instruction, but I add that academic work should go on in the evenings.

MR. ORION BROOKS.—At one time I was for several years engaged in manufacturing, and I then employed apprentices, not very largely, but enough to understand the needs of an apprentice. At that time, some twenty years ago, there were no regular apprentice laws.

The employer lacks the incentive to teach an apprentice. In order to make an intelligent workman, a man must be something more than a machine, and, in order to be that, he must have some instruction, which it seems can hardly be obtained in the workshop.

It is almost if not quite impossible to impress on the pupil in the trade school the seriousness of his work.

Without the trade schools we would be very likely to fall behind in the various industries. The difficulty lies in making the trade schools comply with trade conditions. The trend seems to be toward incorporating commercial trade customs in the trade schools, which is very encouraging, as it comes nearer, year by year, to the conditions found in the shops, and when such conditions shall be reached, we can turn out from our schools thorough workmen, who will be something more than machines, and who will find the doors of all shops open to them.

MR. G. W. DICKIE.—This is a very interesting paper and one that should command the attention of all technical men. I do not quite agree with Mr. Hewitt in regard to the trade schools taking the place of the apprentice system. The majority of tradesmen have been, and, I think, always will be, educated in the workshop. I noticed, however, four years ago, a tendency abroad to introduce a certain amount of technical work in the shops. I found this idea worked out and in operation in several of the large industrial institutions in England and in some places in Scotland. This I found especially the case in Berlin, where, in several large establishments, the apprentices had to spend two hours each day in the schoolroom attached to the works.

There is a large class of industries, which, from the nature of the operations, cannot be taught practically in any school. We could never expect to go to a trade school and get fitters, riveters, etc., for work in the shipyard—such work could never find a place in any school. Then, the commercial element is almost excluded from the trade training of the school; that is, the ability to do work in commercial competition with others forms no part of such teaching, and this is the most important part of trade education. One hard thing for a boy to learn is to be prompt at work when the whistle blows at seven o'clock, and to keep steadily doing effective work until the whistle blows at five o'clock in the evening, and thus acquire the ability to produce enough to enable his employer to keep him steadily employed, and give him the regular compensation for such work. The schools are not required to run a profitable business in order to keep open, and they thus fail to teach the most important thing that always confronts the tradesman; that is, that his production must be worth more in the market than the remuneration he expects to get for it.

I am quite interested in the subject, and I occasionally visit the trade schools, especially the evening schools for imparting technical knowledge to young men who are at work in the shops all day. They are doing a grand work, and they should receive support from all technical men. The day trade schools are also a great help, but we must not expect too much from them. I do not think that they can ever take the place of the regular system of apprenticeships in the shop. We have a large number of apprentices, about 600, but not many of them come to us from the trade schools.

## TRADE SCHOOLS.

THE AUTHOR.—The great benefits of trade and technical schools to humanity are now universally recognized. These schools are now receiving the best attention from thoroughly competent and trained teachers, men of broad education and practical experience. There are many excellent night schools in all of the large cities, their work being supplementary in character. The good work that is being done by the particular schools aforementioned is so self-evident that argument against them seems futile. Shops offering instruction to their employes are so few as hardly to be noticeable in comparison with the large number of places which demand only routine work, and where the men drift along and do not develop in the proper way. How much better workmen they would be if they had a good education! Employers, educators of the proper experience and heads of families should come together and plan for a definite policy of instruction for the youth of our land. How often it happens that they are pulling in opposite directions.

In the meanwhile, the boy does not know what course to pursue. If he does obtain some kind of employment, the chances are he is unsuited for it. Give a young man or woman an opportunity to start life properly, with some definite goal in view, enabling him or her to enjoy life in the fullest and broadest sense of the word.

*Edward T. Hewitt (third from left) was the teacher of this manual training class at the California School of Mechanical Arts, San Francisco, in the early 1900's.*

*Edward T. Hewitt, teacher, (fifth from left, wearing dark suit) in his shop class at the California School of Mechanical Arts, San Francisco circa 1905. He was 36 years old at that time.*

*Edward T. Hewitt, manual training teacher, wearing dark suit and bow tie, to the left of man on ladder, California School of Mechanical Arts, San Francisco, circa 1905.*

*Edward T. Hewitt in front of right-hand dark column, wearing a "Gates Ajar" collar and a four-in-hand tie, circa 1905.*

*California School of Mechanical Arts, front view of buildings.*

EDITOR'S NOTE: The following is a short history of the California School of Mechanical Arts, and the Lick Wilmerding School of which CSMA later became a part. All three of these schools were located in San Francisco.

The material presented in this historical sketch was written by a former Lick Wilmerding faculty member in 1983 based on information from the library of the California Historical Society.

The Lick-Wilmerding and Lux Schools were privately endowed, industrially-oriented high schools and junior colleges, designed, according to their first director, George Merrill, for the "training of the mind and hand in unison." Each of the donors, Miranda Lux, James Lick and Jillis Wilmerding, possessed similar ideas about the necessity of integrating the book knowledge of the public school system with what Lick called the "practical arts of life." These ideas manifested themselves in generous endowments which were used to found and sustain, with no tuition, three schools: The California School of Mechanical Arts, 1894; The Wilmerding School, 1900; and the Lux School, 1913.

When the CSMA (Lick) was formed, it was the only institution of its kind west of Chicago. Beseiged with applications from the start, the pressure was somewhat relieved when Wilmerding opened its doors in 1900. The two schools cooperated to develop supplemental programs, and as the machinery trades were already well-established at Lick, Wilmerding concentrated on the building trades. A few courses in sewing, cooking and artwork were offered for women, but in 1913, the Lux School took over the women's courses and developed a program specially designed to train young women in marketable skills that could support them until their marriage and help them later as "modern homemakers." Women interested in a college preparatory course could still attend Lick-Wilmerding. Each of the three schools maintained separate but sometimes overlapping, boards of trustees, curricula, teaching staffs and buildings, all superintended by one director. In 1915, Lick-Wilmerding commenced a policy whereby boys were enrolled concurrently in, and received diplomas from, both schools.

Miranda Wilmarth Lux, widow of wealthy cattle baron, Charles Lux, was a patron of the kindergarten movement and a long-time supporter of technical and trade schools. She stated in her will that the Lux endowment should be used for "the promotion of schools for manual training, industrial training and for teaching trades to young people of both sexes, in the State of California, and particularly in the City and County of San Francisco..."

Initially, the emphasis at Lux was upon an interdisciplinary education based on a "girl's natural interest in the home," but in the 1920's its method and direction began changing to fit the needs of modern women. By 1933, programs in playground directing, medical and dental assisting, pre-nursing and occupational therapy had been successfully instituted at Lux. So successfully, in fact, that Lux began phasing out its lower division, general education courses and expanding its growing curriculum of vocational junior college courses.

In 1934, the Lux School became the Lux Technical Institute and officially dropped its ninth grade. The course work was divided into the lower division (10th-12 grades), which offered a college preparatory course (in conjunction with Lick) and a general education course; and an upper division (junior college), which awarded associate of arts degrees in medical or dental assisting, pre-nursing, food preparation, merchandising and salesmanship, dressmaking, and millinary, arts and crafts and polytechnic.

In 1942, the Lux College dropped its high school division entirely and continued granting associate of arts degrees until 1953, when the trustees determined that the school and the curriculum were not meeting either commercial needs or student expectations. Following the 1953 graduation, the school closed and soon afterwards the Miranda Lux Foundation was formed. The foundation continues to support "pre-school through junior college programs in the fields of pre-vocational and vocational education and training in San Francisco."

James Lick, a wealthy but miserly entrepreneur, demonstrated his interest in boys' education by leaving his second largest charitable bequest to the forming of the Lick School. Jillis Wilmerding, a prosperous San Francisco merchant, donated $400,000 when he died in 1894 for the establishment and maintenance of the Wilmerding School of Industrial Arts.

In 1930, after over thirty years of complementary existence as technical and industrial high schools, the status of the Lick School was raised to the junior college level, while Wilmerding became an advanced trade school. The trustees also instituted a program of cooperative instruction, whereby students could integrate class time with actual work experience. The Lick Junior College awarded associate of arts degrees in major fields of industrial concern such as radio theory and practice; architecture and mechanical drafting; utility engineering; aeronautics and electronics. The Wilmerding School allowed boys to begin apprenticeships in mechanical trades without taking all of the math and science subjects required in the junior college technical courses. The two schools have continued to meet the needs of their students and are in full operation at the present time. They appear to maintain the educational vision of George Merrill in his hopes for the future of Lick, Wilmerding and Lux. (1915) "Our schools will not be all that they ought to be until the liberal education so freely offered is made liberal enough to include the useful and serviceable, in unison with the cultural, each reinforcing the other, and until a teacher is not a teacher who cannot make the cultural useful and the useful cultural. This is an ideal that may never be more than moderately and imperfectly approximated, but 'tis a consummation devoutly to be wished, and a realization of it is among the things that the Lick, Wilmerding and Lux endowments are trying to encourage in California."

CIRCULAR No. 8

# The California School of Mechanical Arts

FOUNDED BY

JAMES LICK

SAN FRANCISCO

MAY, 1904

EDITOR'S NOTE: The following pages are from a brochure on the California School of Mechanical Arts, dated 1904. They include the faculty roster which lists Edward T. Hewitt, the floor plan of the shop in which he taught, and an outline of the course taught by Hewitt.

# Faculty.

GEORGE A. MERRILL, B. S., PRINCIPAL,
*Instructor of Theoretical Mechanics.*

MISS AIDA M. BURNS,
*Recorder.*

## Academic Department.

MISS LAURA L. MANN, A. B., *English.*

MISS MARION ADAMS, A. B., *History and Government.*

JAMES H. WISE, B. S., *Mathematics.*

MISS L. B. BRIDGMAN, B. S., *Physics.*

HERBERT A. BURNS, B. S., *Chemistry.*

JOHN S. DREW, Ph. B., *German.*

MISS EDA MENZEL, *Freehand Drawing.*

WM. J. DREW, B. S., *Mechanical and Ship Drawing.*

MISS M. L. CRITTENDEN, *Sewing and Cookery.*

## Mechanical Departments.

EDWARD T. HEWITT, *Manual Training and Pattern-Making.*

CHARLES A. MCLERAN, *Assistant in General Woodwork.*

J. L. MATHIS, *Forgework.*

W. H. WOODMAN, *Machine Shop Practice.*

WILLIAM A. GILL, *Assistant Machinist.*

# OFFICERS OF INSTRUCTION.

GEORGE A. MERRILL, B. S., PRINCIPAL, *Theoretical Mechanics.*

[1] GEORGE B. MILLER, M. A., VICE-PRINCIPAL, *Mathematics.*

[1] MISS EMMA HEFTY, B. L., *English.*

[3,4] MISS MARION C. WHIPPLE, B. L., *English.*

[5] MISS LAURA L. MANN, A. B., *English.*

MISS MARION ADAMS, A. B., *History and Government.*

[6] JAMES H. WISE, B. S., *Mathematics.*

MISS L. B. BRIDGMAN, B. S., M. S., *Physics.*

[3] WILLIAM H. HOLLIS, B. S., *Chemistry.*

[6] HERBERT A. BURNS, B. S., *Chemistry.*

JOHN S. DREW, Ph. B., *German.*

MISS EDA MENZEL, *Freehand Drawing.*

WM. J. DREW, B. S., *Mechanical and Ship Drawing.*

MISS M. L. CRITTENDEN, *Sewing and Cookery.*

EDWARD T. HEWITT, *Manual Training & Pattern-Making.*

[1] FREDERICK W. LURMANN, *Assistant in General Woodwork.*

[3] CHARLES A. McLERAN, *Assistant in General Woodwork.*

J. L. MATHIS, *Forgework.*

[3] BERNARD LACOSTE, *Molding.*

W. H. WOODMAN, *Machine-Shop Practice.*

[2,4] OSCAR H. FIDDES, *Assistant Machinist.*

[6] WILLIAM A. GILL, *Assistant Machinist.*

MISS AIDA M. BURNS, *Recorder.*

[1] IRVING P. HENNING, *Engineer.*

[1] Resigned June 30, 1903.
[2] Absent on leave, 1903-4.
[3] Beginning July 1, 1903.
[4] Resigned Dec. 30, 1903.
[5] Beginning Jan. 1, 1904.
[6] During 1903-4.

10 THE CALIFORNIA SCHOOL OF MECHANICAL ARTS.

pipes placed around the window-sides of each room, fed from the engine exhaust and from the boiler in the shops.

The Shop Building is made up of a two-story portion, 200x40 feet, a one-story portion, 50x155 feet, and an ad-

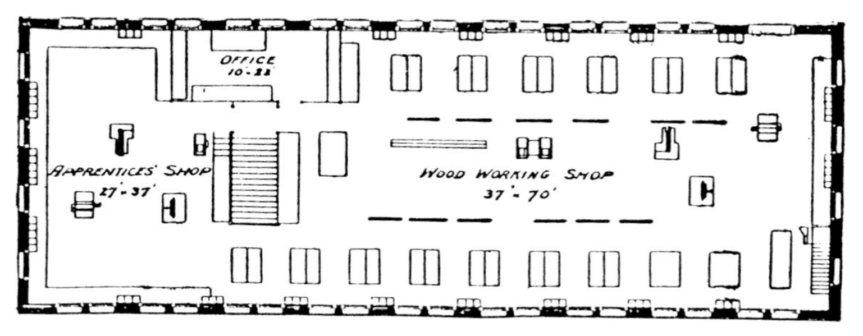


Fig. 5.—Second Floor, Shops.

ditional cupola shed—a structure, 10x13 feet, built entirely of iron. This building also is heated by steam.

A third building, 16.5x31 feet, surrounds the brass furnaces, core oven, and terra cotta kiln. This structure is of corrugated galvanized iron on wooden frame.

The new blacksmith-shop and foundry and the proposed shop for electrical construction, shown on the first-floor plan of the Shop Building, are part of a scheme of enlargement contemplated for both buildings.

## CONDITIONS OF ADMISSION.

The school is free of charge for tuition, and is open to any boy or girl of this State who has completed the eighth grade of the grammar schools.

Places for boys are apportioned among the different Counties according to population, as follows:—

| | | |
|---|---|---|
| 9 Alameda, | 1 El Dorado, | 1 Lassen, |
| 1 Alpine, | 3 Fresno, | 11 Los Angeles, |
| 1 Amador, | 1 Glenn, | 1 Madera, |
| 1 Butte, | 2 Humboldt, | 1 Marin, |
| 1 Calaveras, | 1 Inyo, | 1 Mariposa, |
| 1 Colusa, | 1 Kern, | 1 Mendocino, |
| 1 Contra Costa, | 1 Kings, | 1 Merced, |
| 1 Del Norte, | 1 Lake, | 1 Modoc, |

*Floor plan of the classroom where Edward T. Hewitt taught.*

In Mathematics and Science all apprentices take one or more of the following, as explained under each apprentice course:—

1. Theoretical mechanics.
2. Strength of materials, including laboratory practice and tests.
3. Determination of stresses in framed structures by graphical and analytical methods.
4. Heat calculations and phenomena of combustion, including a general study of transformations of energy; hydrostatics; laws of gases; computations for electrical transmission, etc.
5. Simple boiler and engine tests; dynamo tests.
6. Metallurgy of iron.
7. Bookkeeping and business forms.

All apprentices do one year's work in Industrial History, Commercial Geography, and the History and Government of the United States.

All apprentices are required to meet one hour per week, either in a body or in sections, for the purpose of discussing papers and reports submitted by individual members. The subjects of these reports are selected or assigned by the pupils themselves, as far as possible, and relate to manufacturing processes and devices, to topics from the history of art and industry, and to scientific subjects. Each report must be exhaustive, and is placed before the class as clearly as possible by means of printed abstracts and the stereopticon, the presentation to be followed by a thorough discussion.

## I.—Apprentice Course of Pattern-making.

EDWARD T. HEWITT, Instructor.

### TECHNICAL INSTRUCTION.

Continuous practice upon patterns for actual use in the foundry, including gear wheels, steam pumps, engines, hoists, propeller blades, dynamo frames, etc.; corework and sweep-work; model-making.

### SUPPLEMENTAL INSTRUCTION.

Study of advanced foundry work.
Methods of manufacturing, preserving and seasoning lumber.
Shop arrangement and management.
Woodworking machinery and mill methods.
Methods of storing and checking patterns.
Mechanical drawing.
Science and mathematics, 1, 2, 6, 7, page 25.

No. ...

# SPECIAL CERTIFICATE.

RECORDED SECONDARY

**State of California. County of** Los Angeles

**The County Board of Education** *of* Los Angeles *County hereby issues to* Edward Th. Hewitt, *in accordance with the provisions of Sections 1771 Subdivision 3, and 1772 Subdivision 2, of the Political Code, this*

**Special Certificate,**

*which entitles the holder to teach* Manual Training *in any Public School in* Los Angeles *County, and it shall remain valid for the term of Six Years from date, unless sooner revoked or suspended for cause.*

*The statements and representations on the back of this Certificate are hereby made a part of the same.*

*Office of County Board of Education,*

Los Angeles July 1, 1905.

Mark Keppel
Secretary, and County Superintendent of Schools.

A. A. Wheat.
President.

Frank A. Bouelle
G. W. Griffith
B. W. Reed

County Board of Education.

*Los Angeles County required only five signatures to issue this Special Certificate to Edward T. Hewitt in 1905, enabling him to teach manual training in any public school in Los Angeles County.*

*Edward Hewitt had an ongoing relationship with Los Angeles Polytechnic High School from 1900 until 1906, when he resigned his teaching position there, just before his marriage.*

**Los Angeles Polytechnic High School**
J. H. FRANCIS, PRINCIPAL
Los Angeles, California

July 9. 00

Dear Mr Hewitt:

I saw Co Supt Keppel on your certificate and think he wishes Prof Merrill's O.K. on your credentials filed with the Co Board.

You had best have O.K. of the manufacturing establishments for whom you have worked also.

Our bonds for equipment struck a legal tangle and we have been at sea for some time. We hope, however to get a limited appropriation soon and equip the bench room for Dept. Let me have your summer address. Very truly J H Francis

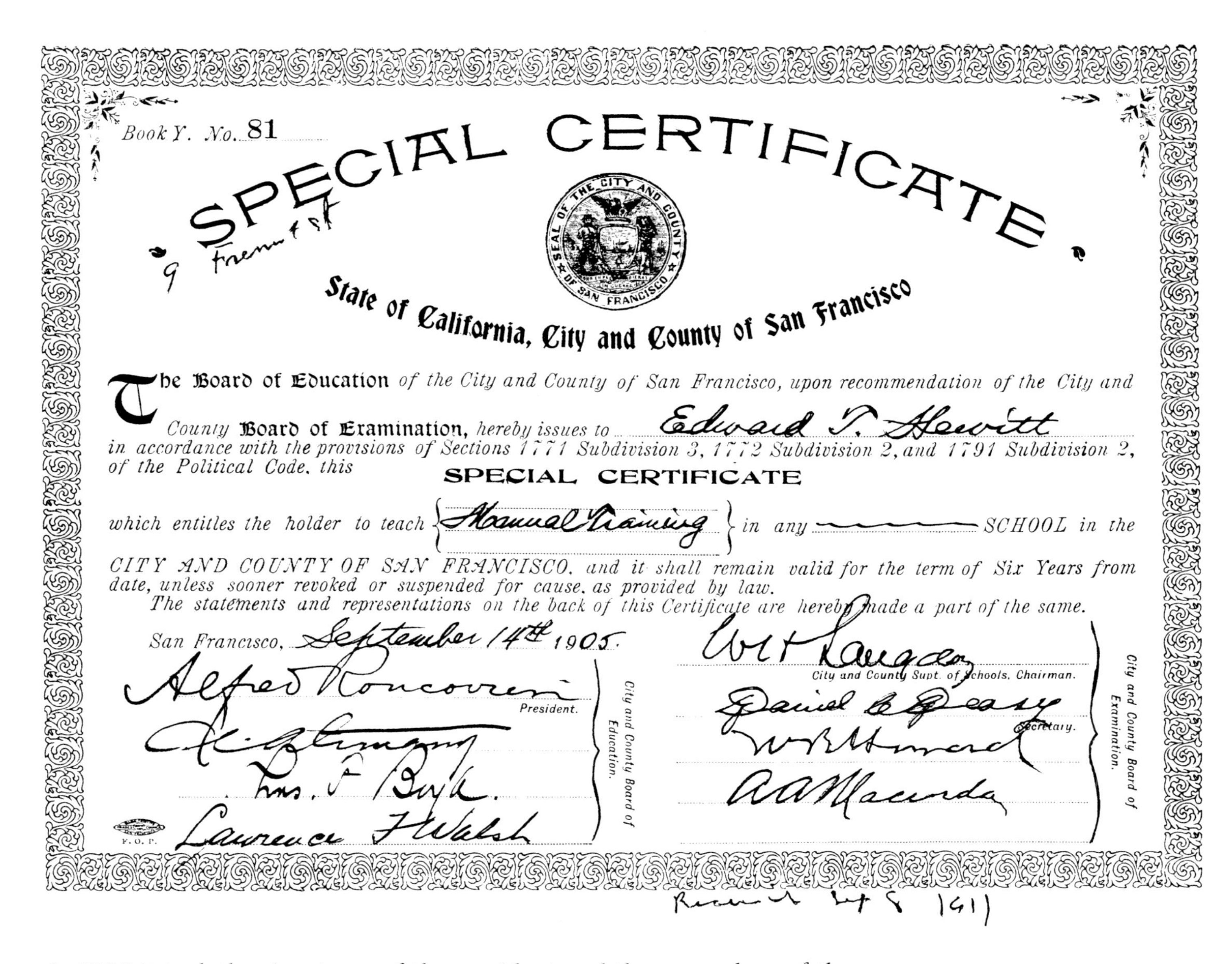
Book Y. No. 81

SPECIAL CERTIFICATE

9 Fremont St

State of California, City and County of San Francisco

The Board of Education of the City and County of San Francisco, upon recommendation of the City and County Board of Examination, hereby issues to Edward T. Hewitt in accordance with the provisions of Sections 1771 Subdivision 3, 1772 Subdivision 2, and 1791 Subdivision 2, of the Political Code, this

SPECIAL CERTIFICATE

which entitles the holder to teach Manual Training in any SCHOOL in the CITY AND COUNTY OF SAN FRANCISCO, and it shall remain valid for the term of Six Years from date, unless sooner revoked or suspended for cause, as provided by law.

The statements and representations on the back of this Certificate are hereby made a part of the same.

San Francisco, September 14th 1905.

Alfred Roncovieri, President.

Lawrence F. Walsh

City and County Board of Education.

W. H. Langdon, City and County Supt. of Schools, Chairman.

Daniel C. Deasy, Secretary.

City and County Board of Examination.

In 1905 it took the signatures of the president and three members of the San Francisco Board of Education, plus the signature of the chairman of the City and County Board of Examination, and three of its members, to issue this Special Certificate to Edward T. Hewitt. The certificate allowed him to teach manual training "in any school in the city and county of San Francisco."

# Earthquake And Fire Devastate San Francisco

At 5:13 in the morning of Wednesday, April 18, 1906, the earth beneath San Francisco began to heave. Pressures that had been accumulating along the San Andreas fault were suddenly released, and it took a full minute for the colossal forces to spend themselves. In that time many places on the west side of the rift were thrust 16 or more feet to the northwest.

The fires began immediately, caused by overturned stoves, fallen chimneys, exploding gas mains, and downed wires. Firemen responded to dozens of calls, and everywhere they went they made the same awful discovery: there was little or no pressure in the water mains. The earthquake had destroyed San Francisco's water system.

For three and a half days the fires burned out of control. Finally the authorities resorted to dynamiting streets full of buildings and pumping water from the San Francisco Bay to stop the conflagration. Amid the smoldering ruins of 522 city blocks, more than 200,000 San Franciscans were left refugees in their own city.

News of the unparalleled disaster horrified the country. In Chicago, George R. Lawrence made plans to get to San Francisco as soon as possible and make a photographic record of the devastated city. Three weeks later he was there, hard at work with his crew. It must have been terribly difficult to work amid the chaos of a shattered city, but in the end his efforts provided a remarkable series of photographs, the likes of which had never been seen before.

One of his pictures in particular caught the attention of the world. "San Francisco in Ruins" showed the entire city on a single print 48¾ inches long and 17½ inches wide. The gargantuan image was not an enlargement; it was a contact print made from a single piece of film. Even today it is difficult to imagine a camera capable of making such a photograph. But it isn't just the size of the equipment that seems astonishing. When the famous photograph was made, the camera was hanging from kites that were flying 2,000 feet above San Francisco Bay.

Drawings and text courtesy of the *Smithsonian.*

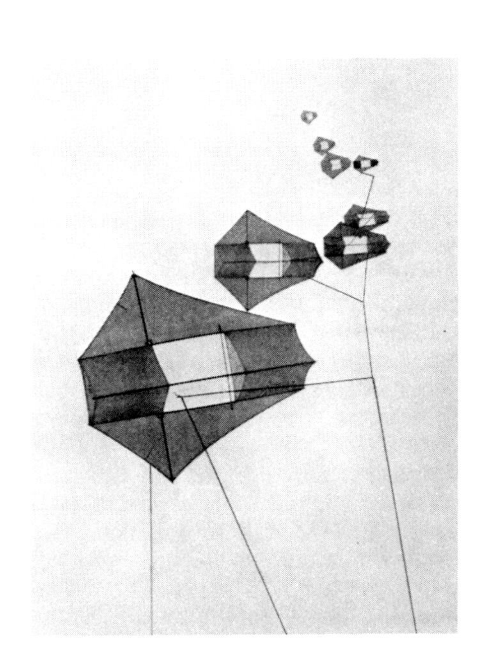

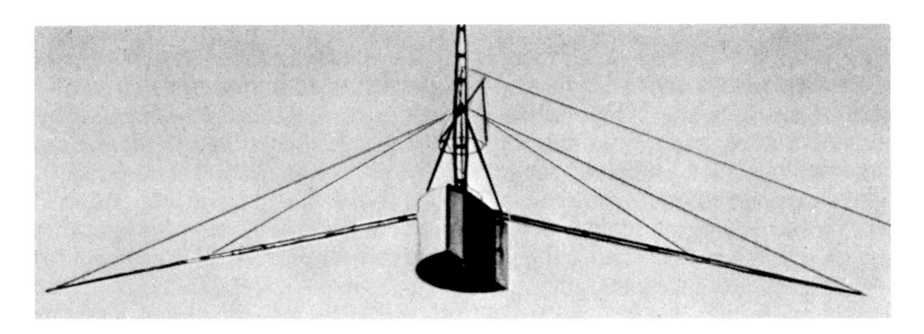

*Above, Lawrence's kite-born "airship" that carried his camera aloft to make early aerial photographs. It was stabilized by three poles with weighted cords hung from the ends. Left, kite train devised by George R. Lawrence to elevate his camera 900 feet to make the photograph of San Francisco that appears on the following pages.*

*San Francisco looked oddly tranquil just a few weeks after it was devastated by the great earthquake and fire of 1906. This photograph was made by George R. Lawrence of Chicago (see preceding page). As the first aerial photograph of San Francisco it dramatically illustrates how the city was built on a peninsula, surrounded on three sides by water. San Francisco Bay sweeps across the foreground up to the shores of the Marin County hills, upper right. Beyond the Golden Gate between San Francisco and Marin County, one catches a glimpse of the Pacific Ocean. The foregoing information and photographs, related to the 1906 earthquake and fire, were provided by the Smithsonian Institution.*

EDITOR'S NOTE: In order to stop the raging fire storm started by the San Francisco earthquake, city engineers started dynamiting buildings to form a firebreak in the path of the spreading fires. This photograph taken by Edward T. Hewitt shows the International Order of Odd Fellows building just after the first charge of dynamite was set off. This scene is on Market Street looking west from Fourth Street, April 20, 1906.

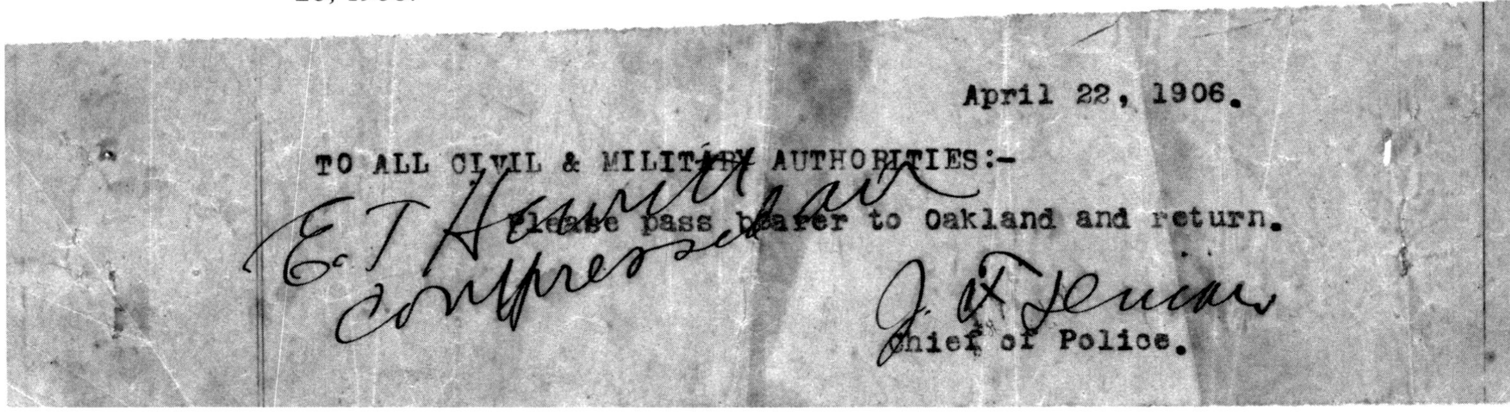

April 22, 1906.

TO ALL CIVIL & MILITARY AUTHORITIES:-

E. T. Hewitt compressed air

Please pass bearer to Oakland and return.

J. F. Dinan

Chief of Police.

*Pass given to Edward T. Hewitt by the chief of police of San Francisco, to allow Hewitt to cross San Francisco Bay to Oakland two days after the earthquake and fire of 1906.*

Courtesy California Historical Society, San Francisco.

*San Francisco residents watch homes and businesses burn following the earthquake.*

Courtesy California Historical Society, San Francisco.

*The downtown commercial district is hit by the firestorm which caused building after building to burst into flame.*

Courtesy California Historical Society, San Francisco.

*The great fire in San Francisco on April 18, 1906. General view of downtown business district from Telegraph Hill, looking south.*

Courtesy California Historical Society, San Francisco.

*Market Street, April 18, 1906, downtown business district burning.*

Courtesy California Historical Society, San Francisco.

*The San Francisco fire was an awesome sight.*

Courtesy California Historical Society, San Francisco.

*Downtown San Francisco burning, corner of Third and Mission Streets.*

EDITOR'S NOTE: In a special supplement to the *San Francisco Examiner,* June 10, 1906, William Randolph Hearst printed this double-page photograph showing a birdseye view of San Francisco two months after the earthquake and fire. The photograph was taken from the top of the wrecked city hall dome. The dome is shown in the inset on opposite page.

*After the great earthquake and fire all household cooking was done in makeshift stoves outdoors on the sidewalks.*

*Spectators view damage caused by earthquake and fire, April 1906. This photograph by Edward Hewitt is looking down California Street toward the Bay. Spire of Ferry Building is in center. Sausalito hills are across Golden Gate at left.*

*From 1890-1906, Edward T. Hewitt lived with his parents at 619 Capp Street, in the Mission District of San Francisco. This photograph pictures the 600 block of Capp Street immediately following the earthquake and fire of 1906. Because of gas main damage and potential danger of more fires, no one was allowed to cook indoors at home. Consequently the residents improvised, either lugging their big old cast iron stoves out to the street, or by building make-do cooking structures of brick or stone rubble in front of their houses. The third little clump of bricks on the right is very likely the Hewitt's outdoor kitchen.*

*The fire was stopped at 18th Street and the Hewitts lived on Capp Street between 21st and 22nd Streets.*

LOS ANGELES POLYTECHNIC HIGH SCHOOL

J. H. FRANCIS, PRINCIPAL

LOS ANGELES, CALIFORNIA.

Sept. 17, 1906

Mr. E. T. Hewitt,

503 Monadnock Bldg.,

San Francisco, Cal.

Dear Mr. Hewitt:

I have presented your resignation to Supt. Moore.

Please allow me to express appreciation at this time of the energy, effort, thought, and heart you put into your work with us last year. It was unusually arduous and taxing and the responsibility resting upon you was great. You shirked neither responsibility nor work, but gave your best efforts to its success.

I shall give your message to teachers, pupils and the Board of Education and can assure you now of the best wishes of us all for your success and happiness.

Very truly,

J H Francis

Principal.

Note

Mr Francis letter to Ed. T. Hewitt after leaving L. A. P. H. S.
1906

*Edward T. Hewitt resigned his teaching position at the Los Angeles Polytechnic High School shortly before his marriage to Jeannette Brun, of San Francisco, in September 1906. During that same year he and his brother, William A. Hewitt, started the Hewitt Machinery Company in San Francisco.*

Mrs. Emma Brun

requests the honour of

presence at the marriage of her daughter

Jeannette Adele

to

Mr. Edward Thomas Hewitt

on Saturday evening, the fifteenth of September

at eight o'clock

St. John's Episcopal Church

San Francisco

*Invitation by Mrs. Emma Brun to the marriage of her daughter, Jeannette Adele, to Mr. Edward Thomas Hewitt in 1906...as it appeared before the guest's name was filled in.*

H — 1743

**MARRIAGE LICENSE**

AND CERTIFICATE

Edward Thomas Hewitt

—AND

Jeannette Adele Brun

Sept-15-1906

Filed for Record at Request of

this Louis C. Danford day

of OCT 11 1906 A.D. 190

at min. past

o'clock M., and recorded on Book

4 New series of Marriage Certificates

on page 377 Records of San Francisco County.

County Recorder.

By Deputy Recorder.

BROWN & POWER INC.

*1906 was a hectic year in San Francisco. The devastating earthquake and fire on April 18 left 3,000 persons dead, and 250,000 homeless. Five months later, on September 15, Edward Hewitt married Jeannette Brun in St. John's Episcopal Church in San Francisco.*

EDITOR'S NOTE: Readers who are seeking accurate dates will observe that although October 11, 1906 is stamped on the cover of the Hewitt-Brun Marriage License, the handwritten information on the face of the license indicates it was issued on "this 11th day of September of 1906."

The handwritten date on the cover, which reads Sept. 15th 1906, was the date of the wedding, which is officially recorded on the face of the license. However the handwritten date on the cover seems to be correcting the stamped date of issue.

During the research we have done for this book, we have learned that dates shown on various records, such as birth and death certificates, military records, grave markers, historical publications, etc., sometimes don't jibe with each other. However, the inaccuracies are usually relatively small, and the information provided is generally helpful.

STATE OF CALIFORNIA

City and County of San Francisco

MARRIAGE LICENSE

These Presents are to authorize and license any Justice of the Supreme Court, Judge of the Superior Court, Judge of the Police Court, Justice of the Peace, Priest or Minister of the Gospel of any denomination to solemnize within said County the Marriage of Edward Thomas Hewitt aged 27 years and past, resident of City and County of San Francisco State of California and Jeannette Adele Brun aged 22 years and past, resident of City and County of San Francisco State of California, said parties being of sufficient age to be capable of contracting marriage.

In Witness Whereof, I have hereunto set my hand and affixed the Seal of the Superior Court of said County this 11th day of September A.D. 1906

H. T. Mulcrevy
County Clerk and ex-officio Clerk of the Superior Court in and for said City and County of San Francisco

State of California, City and County of San Francisco. } SS by G. L. Munson Deputy County Clerk

This Certifies That

Edward Thomas Hewitt and Jeannette Adele Brun the parties in the above license were joined in marriage by me on the 15th day of September A.D. 1906 in said City and County and State, that Wm. A. Hewitt a resident of San Francisco County of San Francisco State of California and Delphine Brun a resident of San Francisco County of San Francisco State of California were present as witnesses of said ceremony.

WITNESSES NAME Wm. A. Hewitt. No. Monadnock Building, Market STREET
NAME Delphine Brun No. 1219 O'Farrell STREET

In Witness Whereof, I have hereunto set my hand this 15th day of September A.D. 1906

Louis Childs Sanford. Rector of the Church of St John the Evangelist.

*The above marriage license was issued on September 11, 1906, in the city and county of San Francisco.*

*The lower part of the license certifies that on September 15, 1906, Edward Thomas Hewitt and Jeannette Adele Brun were joined in marriage and that William A. Hewitt and Delphine Adrienne Brun were present as witnesses at said ceremony. The certification also bears the signature of Louis C. Sanford, Rector, of the Church of St. John the Evangelist, an Episcopal church.*

EDITOR'S NOTE: Please note this marriage license shows my father's age as 27, although he was 38 years old at the time it was issued.

120 Julian Ave
San Francisco
Sept 14. 1906.

Dear Mr. Hewitt:

I inclose your marriage license which has been too long undelivered. I hoped to bring it to the house & so held it the longer, but now, as I shall be going East on the 24th to be gone until the middle of November, I think I had better trust it to the mail.

Mrs. Sanford joins me in felicitations on your first anniversary which comes to-morrow. We are sure the year has been a very happy one both for you & Jeannette, & we send all good wishes to you both for the future. Please remember us kindly to Mrs Brun and the other members of the household

Very cordially yours

Louis C Sanford

EDITOR'S NOTE: Letter from Reverend L.C. Sanford, the Episcopal priest who performed the marriage ceremony for Edward T. Hewitt and Jeannette Adele Brun, September 15, 1906.

120 Julian Avenue
San Francisco
Sept. 14, 1906

Dear Mr. Hewitt,
I inclose your marriage license which has been too long undelivered. I hoped to bring it to the house and so held it the longer, but now, as I shall be going East on the 24th to be gone until the middle of November, I think I had better trust it to the mail.

Mrs. Sanford joins me in felicitations on your first anniversary which comes tomorrow. We are sure the year has been a very happy one both for you and Jeannette and we send all good wishes to you both for the future. Please remember us kindly to Mrs. Brun and the other members of the household.

Very Cordially Yours,

Louis C. Sanford

EDITOR'S NOTE: In the second paragraph of the above letter, the Reverend Mr. Sanford congratulates the young couple on the first anniversary of their marriage. This means he should have dated his letter September 14, 1907. Apparently he had 1906 on his mind.

*Bill and Ed Hewitt.*

*The house at 4718 Seventeenth Street, San Francisco, was built by Mr. and Mrs. Edward T. Hewitt in 1908. Each of their three children was born in this house: Edward Jr. in 1912; William in 1914; and Adrienne in 1916. Dr. Harry Robarts delivered the babies. Jeannette Hewitt's mother, Emma Brun, built the house next door at 4724 Seventeenth Street a year or two later. Jeannette Hewitt exercised considerable influence in the design of the house at 4718. It is in the style of Bernard Maybeck, a distinguished San Francisco architect in the early 1900s. Edward Hewitt, an experienced builder, was in charge of the construction of both houses. He personally compiled the specifications and made the drawings. Soon after the house was built, Jeannette Hewitt planted a small olive tree, as seen in the right background of the photograph. It was taller than the house in 1989.*

*Bill Hewitt placed the flag to celebrate a Fourth of July at 4724 Seventeenth Street, San Francisco, his grandmother's house. This house was built by Emma Brun, circa 1910.*

*During the years circa 1908-1928, the house in the photograph above, located at 32nd Avenue and El Camino del Mar, in the Sea Cliff District of San Francisco, was the residence of my uncle, William A. Hewitt, and my aunt, Dr. Sophie K. Hewitt. There were many family gatherings in their house, especially during the Christmas holidays. Since the William Hewitts were childless, they enjoyed being surrounded by the children of his brother, Edward, and sister, Daisy, as well as other family members. The editor has many happy memories of those gatherings, and also vividly recalls gathering on the lawn to watch the U.S. fleet sail through the Golden Gate in the early 1920s. Eventually the William Hewitt house on 32nd Avenue plus adjoining property became part of Miss Burke's School for Girls, with the Misses Burke residing in the former Hewitt house.*

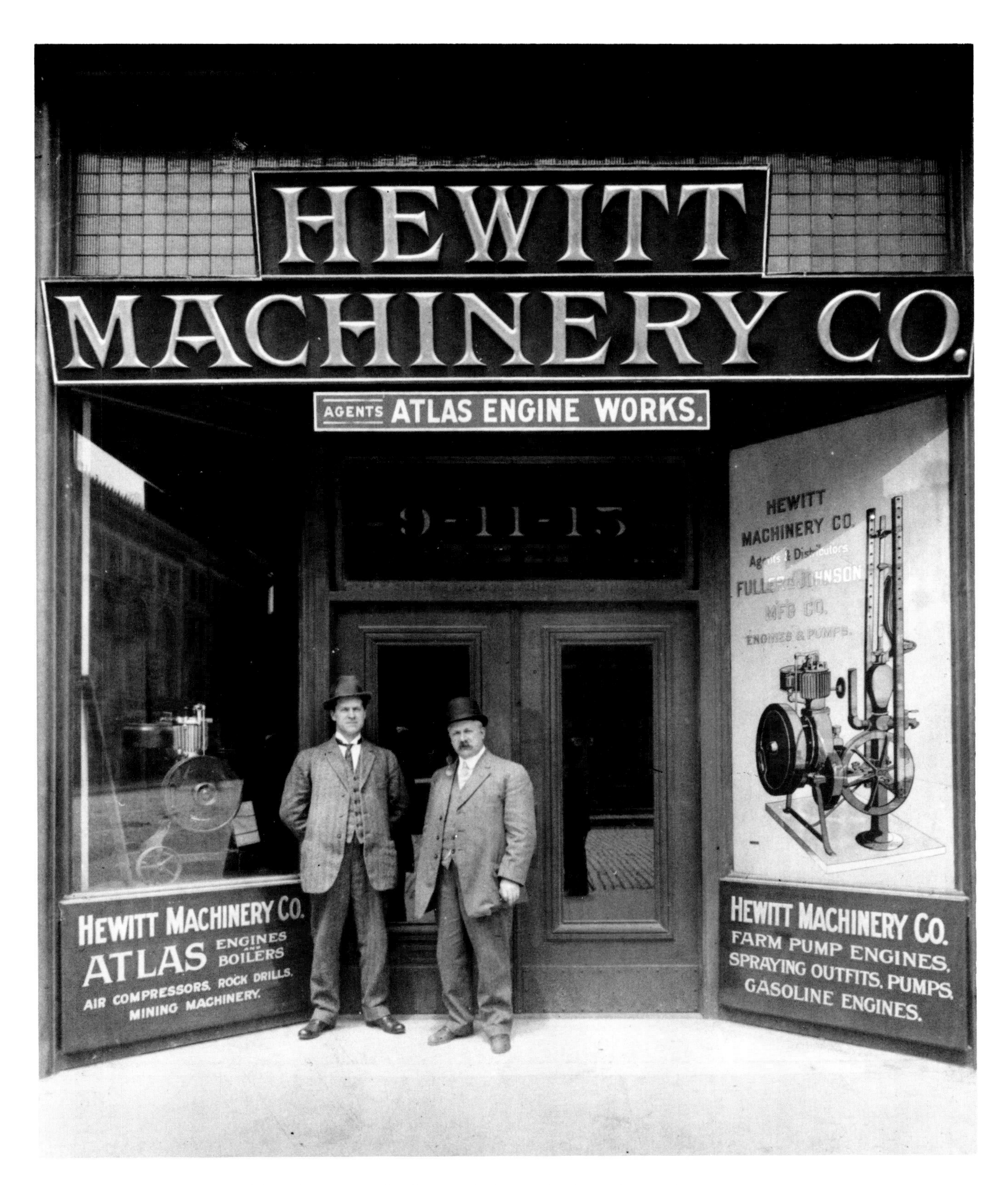


*Edward T. Hewitt and his brother, William A. Hewitt, San Francisco, circa 1907.*

1684-
ARTICLES OF INCORPORATION
48814
OF
THE HEWITT MACHINERY CO.
48814
*****************************
Dated, January ____, ,1907.
*****************************

FILED in the Office of the
SECRETARY OF STATE
the 14th day of
Jan A. D. 1907
C. F. Curry
SECRETARY OF STATE
By J. Hewitt
DEPUTY
Record Book 195 Page 123

ENDORSED,
Filed in the Office of the
County Clerk of the City and
County of San Francisco, State
of California, this 12
day of Jan A. D. 1907
H. I. MULCREVY, County Clerk
By L. J. Welch
Deputy Clerk

*Articles of Incorporation of the Hewitt Machinery Co. of San Francisco were dated January 12, 1907.*

ARTICLES OF INCORPORATION

of

THE HEWITT MACHINERY CO.

*****************************************************************

KNOW ALL MEN BY THESE PRESENTS:-

That we, the undersigned, have this day voluntarily associated ourselves together for the purpose of forming a corporation under the laws of the State of California;

AND WE HEREBY CERTIFY:-

First:- That the name of said corporation is

THE HEWITT MACHINERY CO.;

Second:- That the purposes for which it is formed are:-

To conduct a general machinery business; to buy, sell and manufacture machinery; to transact business on commission in handling all kinds of machinery; to hold real estate and to mortgage and sell the same; to borrow money; to establish agencies and branches of the business in all the states and territories of the United States, or in foreign countries; and to do everything of any kind or nature pertaining to, or beneficial to, the development of the machinery business in all shapes and forms;

Third:- That the place where its principal business is to be transacted shall be the City and County of San Francisco, State of California;

Fourth:- That the term for which it is to exist is fifty (50) years from and after the date of its incorporation;

Fifth:- That the number of its directors shall be five, and that the names and residences of those who are appointed

-1-

for the first year are:-

| NAMES. | RESIDENCES. |
|---|---|
| W. A. HEWITT, | San Francisco, California; |
| E. T. HEWITT, | San Francisco, California; |
| A. G. HEWITT, | San Francisco, California; |
| S. B. HEWITT, | San Francisco, California; |
| A. W. STAUFFER, | San Francisco, California; |

Sixth:- That the amount of the capital stock of this corporation shall be One Hundred Thousand ($100,000) Dollars, divided into One Thousand ( 1,000) Shares of the par value of One Hundred ($100) Dollars each;

Seventh:- That the amount of said capital stock which has been actually subscribed is Five Hundred ($500) Dollars, and the following are the names of the persons by whom the same has been subscribed, to wit:-

| NAMES OF SUBSCRIBERS. | NO. OF SHARES. | AMOUNT. |
|---|---|---|
| W. A. HEWITT, | 1 | $ 100.00 |
| E. T. HEWITT, | 1 | $ 100.00 |
| A. G. HEWITT, | 1 | $ 100.00 |
| S. B. HEWITT, | 1 | $ 100.00 |
| A. W. STAUFFER, | 1 | $ 100.00 |
| | 5 | $ 500.00 |

IN WITNESS WHEREOF, we havehereunto set our hands and seals this 10th day of January, 1907.

Wm. A. Hewitt. (SEAL)

Edward Thomas Hewitt (SEAL)

Arthur G. Hewitt (SEAL)

S. B. Hewitt (SEAL)

A. W. Stauffer (SEAL)

-2-

STATE OF CALIFORNIA, } ss.
City and County of San Francisco.

On this 10th day of January, 1907, before me, John H. Ware, a notary public in and for said City and County, residing therein, duly commissioned and sworn, personally appeared W. A. HEWITT, E. T. HEWITT, A. G. HEWITT, S. B. HEWITT and A. W. STAUFFER, known to me to be the persons whose names are subscribed to the within instrument, and each duly acknowledged to me that he executed the same.

IN WITNESS WHEREOF, I have hereunto set my hand and affixed my official seal at my office in the City and County of San Francisco, the day and year in this certificate first hereinabove written.

John H. Ware
Notary Public in and for the City and County of San Francisco, State of California.
307 Monadnock Building

Co. Clerk [illegible]

*STATE OF CALIFORNIA,* } *ss.*
*City and County of San Francisco*

*I,* H. I. Mulcrevy *County Clerk of the City and County of San Francisco, State of California,*

**Do hereby certify** *that the annexed is a full, true and correct Copy of the Original Articles of Incorporation of* The Hewitt Machinery Co.

*and of the whole thereof now remaining on file and of record in my office.*

**Witness** *my hand and official Seal this* 12th *day of* January *A. D. 1907*

H. I. Mulcrevy *County Clerk*

*By* L. J. Welch *Deputy Clerk*

F. F. CONNOR, 1st Ward
THOS. RICKARD, 2d Ward
F. FERRIER, 3d Ward
A. F. SCHAD, 4th Ward
E. L. FAVOR, 5th Ward
NELS OLSEN, 6th Ward
O. HOFF, 7th Ward

**BOARD OF TRUSTEES**

**TOWN OF BERKELEY**

THOS. RICKARD,
President

J. V. MENDENHALL,
Clerk

Phone Berkeley 1350

Berkeley, Calif., Feb. 26, 1907.

Mr. Edward T. Hewitt,
37 Sec nd Street,
San Francisco, Cal.

My dear Sir:-

I take pleasure in informing you that the Board of Education, at the meeting held on the 19th instant, instructed me to notify you of your appointment to act with Prof. Charles Derleth, Jr., as a committee to confer with Architect Louis Stone, who is at present working on plans for the proposed new High school building in Berkeley, and to examine the said plans critically and render an expert opinion particularly as to the strength of materials and such other points as may in your mind be considered important.

Very truly yours,
J. V. Mendenhall
Town Clerk.

EDITOR'S NOTE: Shortly after his marriage, Edward T. Hewitt was asked to serve on a building committee with architect Louis Stone, a prominent architect of the day, who was working on the proposed new high school building in Berkeley, California.

ALL AGREEMENTS CONTINGENT UPON STRIKES FIRES ACCIDENTS AND OTHER CAUSES BEYOND OUR CONTROL

Ed. T. Hewitt
San Francisco
9-11 Fremont St.

# CHAS. C. MOORE & CO. ENGINEERS

INCORPORATED

DESIGN AND
CONSTRUCTION OF
COMPLETE PLANTS
POWER LIGHTING
MINING
PUMPING

ADDRESS ALL CORRESPONDENCE TO THE COMPANY

PACIFIC COAST BRANCH
THE BABCOCK & WILCOX COMPANY
CHAS. C. MOORE, MANAGER
MANUFACTURERS OF
WATER TUBE STEAM BOILERS

99 FIRST STREET, COR. MISSION

BRANCH OFFICES

LOS ANGELES, 321 AMERICAN BANK BLDG
SEATTLE, MUTUAL LIFE BUILDING
SALT LAKE, 313 314 ATLAS BLOCK
NEW YORK, 1681 FULTON BUILDING
PORTLAND, 416 WELLS FARGO BLDG

REGISTERED CABLE ADDRESS "CHASMORE"
IN REPLY PLEASE STATE FOR ATTENTION OF

SAN FRANCISCO July 31,1911.

To Whom It May Concern:

For many years we have known Mr. Edward T. Hewitt, and are glad of the opportunity of speaking a good word for him as the occasion presents.

Mr.Hewitt has had a long and varied experience in a responsible capacity as a designer and constructor of machinery, and has been well trained in all the departments of a large iron works.

He was for many years associated with the California School of Mechanical Arts, San Francisco, successfully initiating a complete course of manual training, industrial and trades work etc., the same being recognized of great benefit to this City, the graduates of this institution have no trouble in finding positions when seeking employment; their training is also of great benefit when they enter the university.

Mr. Hewitt also successfully planned and inaugurated courses of manual training in the Department of Mechanic Arts at the Los Angeles Polytechnic High School, the same being both of great practical and educational value.

At the present time he is engaged in the engineering business with his brother. We take pleasure in recommending Mr. Hewitt to anyone requiring his particular services, as we know him to have ability, executive capacity, is well fitted for such duties, and is honest and trustworthy in all his dealings.

We hope he will receive your favorable consideration.

Yours very truly,

CHAS.C.MOORE & CO.ENGINEERS.

Elgin Stoddard

Vice President.

ES:L

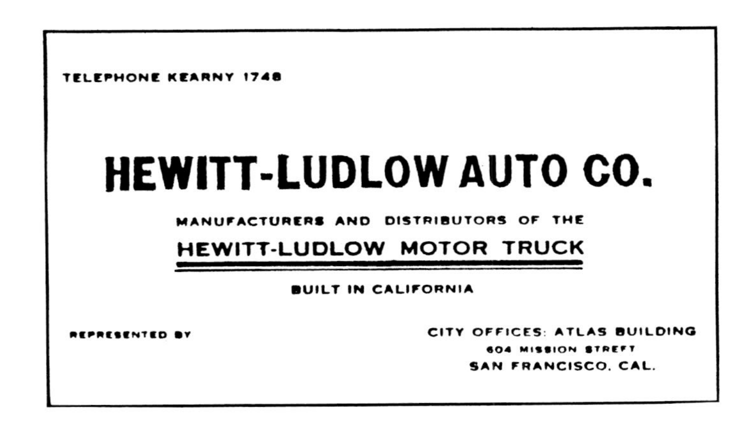
TELEPHONE KEARNY 1748

HEWITT-LUDLOW AUTO CO.

MANUFACTURERS AND DISTRIBUTORS OF THE
HEWITT-LUDLOW MOTOR TRUCK
BUILT IN CALIFORNIA

REPRESENTED BY

CITY OFFICES: ATLAS BUILDING
604 MISSION STREET
SAN FRANCISCO, CAL.

*Business card of the new Hewitt-Ludlow Auto Co., 1912.*

CAPITAL
$100,000.00
100,000 SHARES
$1.00 EACH

San Francisco, Cal., July 18th 1912 Number 21

This Certifies, that Ed. T. Hewitt 12000 Shares

is the owner of Twelve thousand Shares of the Capital Stock of

HEWITT-LUDLOW AUTO COMPANY

Transferable on the books of the Company by endorsement hereon and surrender of this Certificate

Ed. T. Hewitt SECRETARY.

INCORPORATED UNDER THE LAWS OF THE STATE OF CALIFORNIA JUNE 27, 1912

Wm. A. Hewitt PRESIDENT.

*An example of the certificate of shares of the capital stock issued by the Hewitt-Ludlow Auto Company, San Francisco.*

Editor's Note: In 1912 William Hewitt and his brother, Edward, changed the focus of their machinery business when they founded the Hewitt-Ludlow Auto Company to manufacture motor trucks.

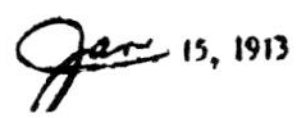 15, 1913 THE COMMERCIAL CAR JOURNAL 7

# Factory News, New Trucks and Changes

ROCKFORD MOTOR TRUCK COMPANY, Rockford, Ill., has been incorporated with $10,000 capital to manufacture and sell electric and gasoline motors.

WESTINGHOUSE ELECTRIC & MANUFACTURING COMPANY, Pittsburgh, Pa., is said to be bringing out an electric engine starter, patented by George Westinghouse.

MOTOR WAGON COMPANY, Detroit, Mich., is putting out a new 1000-lb. delivery wagon, which is equipped with a four-cylinder, four-cycle engine. It has a three-speed transmission, double side chain drive and solid tires.

FOUR TRACTION AUTO COMPANY, Mankato, Minn., has sold its stock, etc., to the Nevada Manufacturing Company, who will establish a factory for the manufacture of trucks at Nevada, Ia. The company has a capital stock of $200,000.

LEE & PORTER MANUFACTURING COMPANY, Buchanan, Mich., which had contemplated moving its plant to obtain better facilities, has decided to remain in its home city and build an addition to its plant, so as to greatly increase its output of motor car axles.

GARFORD COMPANY, of Elyria, Ohio, is building two additions to its plant, one being 60 x 100 ft., of reinforced concrete, and another being 56 x 280 ft., of the same construction. This is in line with the plans of Mr. Willys to greatly increase the output of the Garford factory.

THE FORD MOTOR COMPANY, Detroit, Mich., will discontinue the light delivery car which they have been making, as soon as the few delivery bodies they have on hand are sold, but it is understood that they are at work on a new light delivery car which will be ready in March next.

HEWITT-LUDLOW COMPANY, San Francisco, has been formed to manufacture Hewitt-Ludlow motor trucks. The company has extensive shop facilities in the Potrero district. It is also the purpose of the company to establish a service station in the downtown district for the accommodation of its patrons.

TOLEDO MOTOR TRUCK COMPANY has just moved into its new plant on Spencer Street. The concern has bought the land and buildings formerly occupied by the McCreery Engineering Company, and has joined the Bunting Brass and Bronze Company, the Rathburn-Jones Company and others in forming the South End colony of factories.

AMERICAN MOTOR TRAFFIC COMPANY, of Washington, D. C., has been organized to manufacture a heavy motor truck of the four wheel drive type. The officers of the company are E. S. Alvord, S. J. McFarren, 1st Vice-President and Manager; W. J. Moore, Second Vice-President; A. L. Kley, Secretary. Additional Directors, J. C. Moncaster and J. C. Menoher.

BROWN COMMERCIAL CAR COMPANY, of Peru, Ind., which was recently organized for the manufacture of 1500 lb. commercial trucks, has purchased the plant of the Otis Elevator Company. This modern plant includes, among other numerous buildings, a large gray iron foundry, 88 x 300 ft., equipped with power cranes and all modern factory appliances. To facilitate the rapidly growing business, a new company has been formed, known as the Peru Castings Machine Company, to operate this plant, and make and machine rough castings.

NEVADA MANUFACTURING COMPANY, Nevada, Ia., has purchased the patents, business and machinery of the Four Traction Auto Company, of Mankato, Minn., and will build commercial cars embodying the four-wheel drive idea, on an extensive scale. The capital of the company has been increased to $200,000, and further additions will be made to it to provide for the building of the trucks.

BUFFALO ELECTRIC VEHICLE COMPANY, Buffalo, N. Y., has acquired the plant and business of the Buffalo Motor Vehicle Service Company, which has a complete garage and service station at 178 W. Utica Street, Buffalo, N. Y. This acquisition provides the Buffalo Electric Vehicle Company with facilities for the garaging and care of electric commercial vehicles. The Buffalo company expects to put a complete line of electric commercial trucks on the market this year.

HEWITT—LUDLOW COMPANY, San Francisco, has been formed to manufacture Hewitt-Ludlow motor trucks. The company has extensive shop facilities in the Potrero district. It is also the purpose of the company to establish a service station in the downtown district for the accommodation of its patrons.

*The* Commercial Car Journal *printed one of the first notices on the formation of the Hewitt-Ludlow Motor Truck Company on January 15, 1913 (see bracketed paragraph reproduced above).*

The photographs and a drawing on the following seven pages are of models of Hewitt-Ludlow trucks, commissioned by William Hewitt, and made by Clive Jones of Edmonton, Alberta, Canada, on a scale of 1/32 inch.

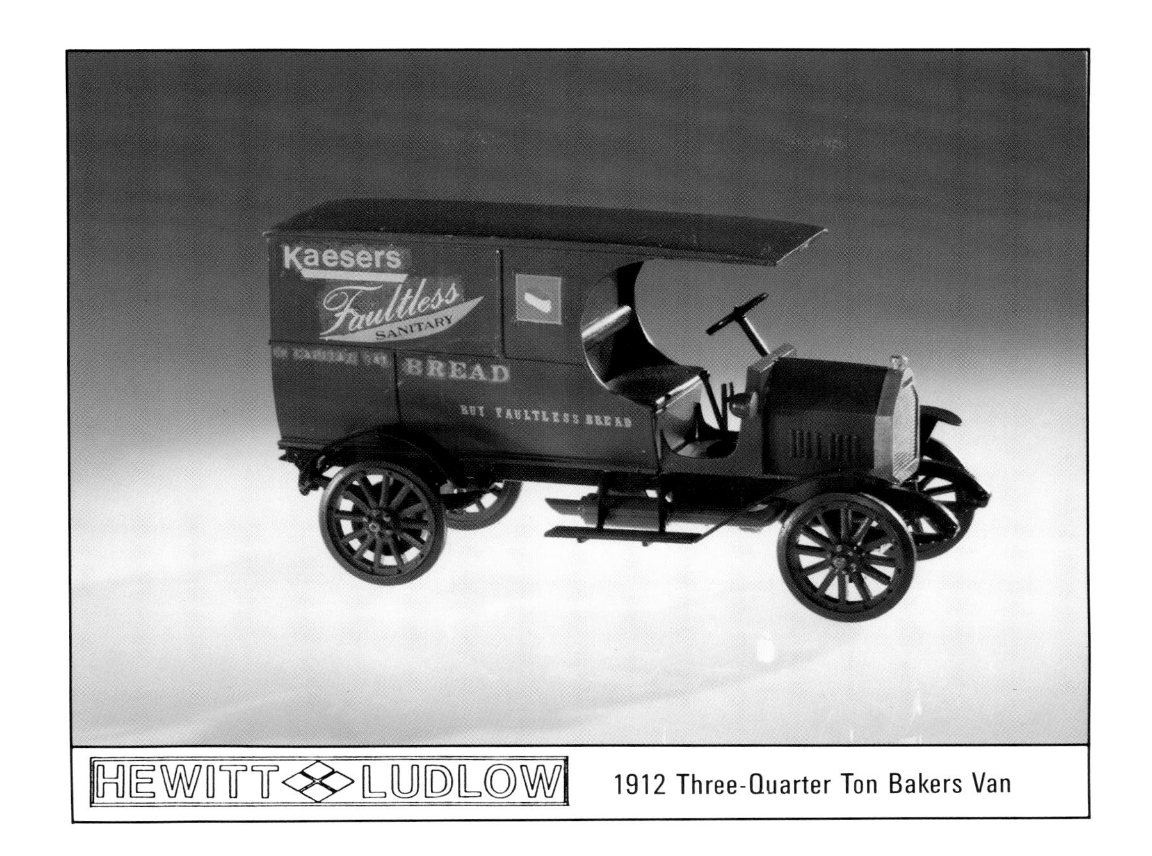


HEWITT LUDLOW 1912 Three-Quarter Ton Bakers Van

HEWITT LUDLOW 1914 One Ton Cordage Truck

HEWITT LUDLOW 1917 Two Ton Bakers Van

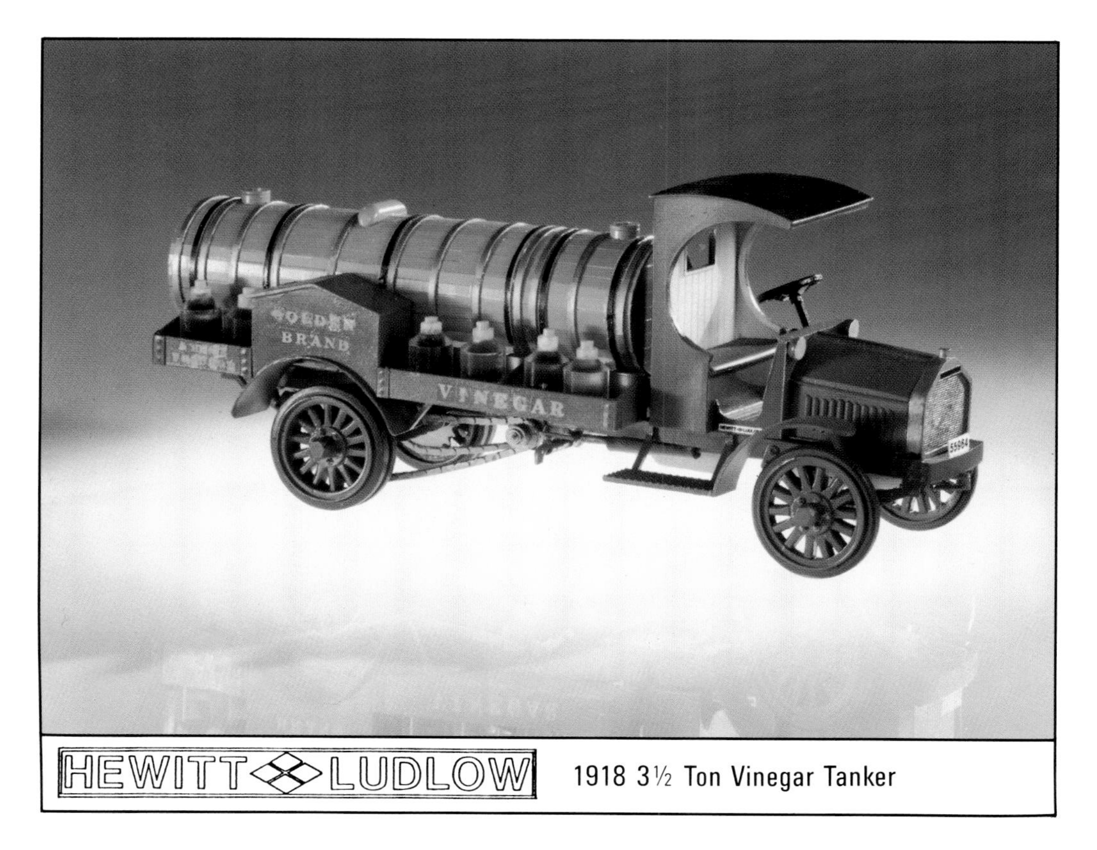


HEWITT LUDLOW 1918 3½ Ton Vinegar Tanker

HEWITT LUDLOW 1919 2½ Ton Sheriff's Van

HEWITT LUDLOW 1919 3½ Ton Stake Truck

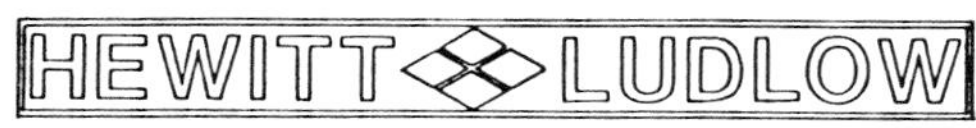


1919 3½ Ton Stake Truck

HEWITT LUDLOW 1919 3½ Ton Retail Service Gasoline Tanker

HEWITT LUDLOW 1915 One Ton Soft Drink Delivery Truck

HEWITT LUDLOW 1914 One Ton Vinters Truck

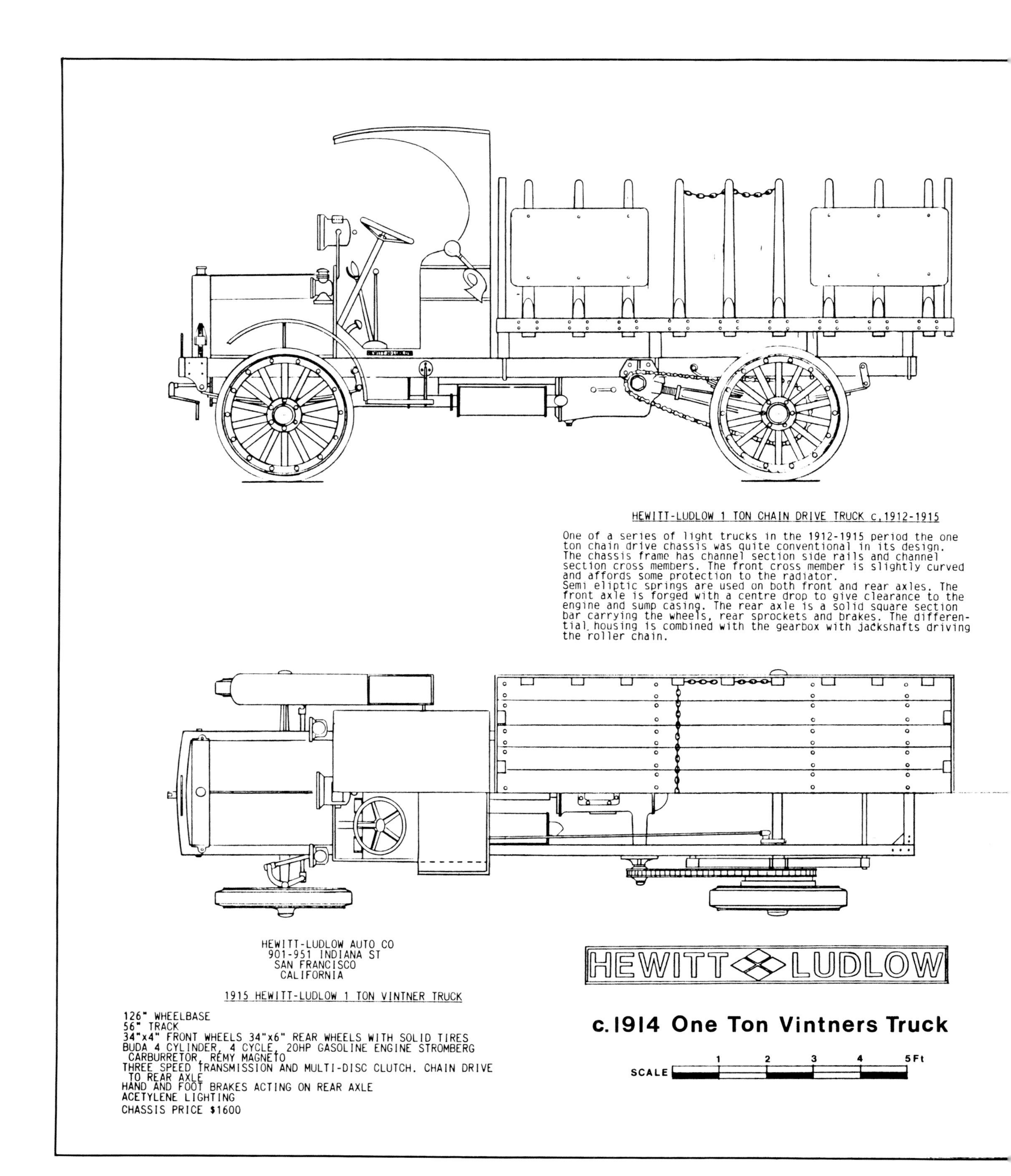

HEWITT-LUDLOW 1 TON CHAIN DRIVE TRUCK c.1912-1915
One of a series of light trucks in the 1912-1915 period the one ton chain drive chassis was quite conventional in its design. The chassis frame has channel section side rails and channel section cross members. The front cross member is slightly curved and affords some protection to the radiator.
Semi eliptic springs are used on both front and rear axles. The front axle is forged with a centre drop to give clearance to the engine and sump casing. The rear axle is a solid square section bar carrying the wheels, rear sprockets and brakes. The differential housing is combined with the gearbox with jackshafts driving the roller chain.
HEWITT-LUDLOW AUTO CO
901-951 INDIANA ST
SAN FRANCISCO
CALIFORNIA
1915 HEWITT-LUDLOW 1 TON VINTNER TRUCK
126" WHEELBASE
56" TRACK
34"x4" FRONT WHEELS 34"x6" REAR WHEELS WITH SOLID TIRES
BUDA 4 CYLINDER, 4 CYCLE, 20HP GASOLINE ENGINE STROMBERG CARBURRETOR, REMY MAGNETO
THREE SPEED TRANSMISSION AND MULTI-DISC CLUTCH. CHAIN DRIVE TO REAR AXLE
HAND AND FOOT BRAKES ACTING ON REAR AXLE
ACETYLENE LIGHTING
CHASSIS PRICE $1600
HEWITT LUDLOW
c.1914 One Ton Vintners Truck
SCALE
1
2
3
4
5Ft


*Mechanical drawing of 1914 Hewitt-Ludlow one ton vintners truck.*

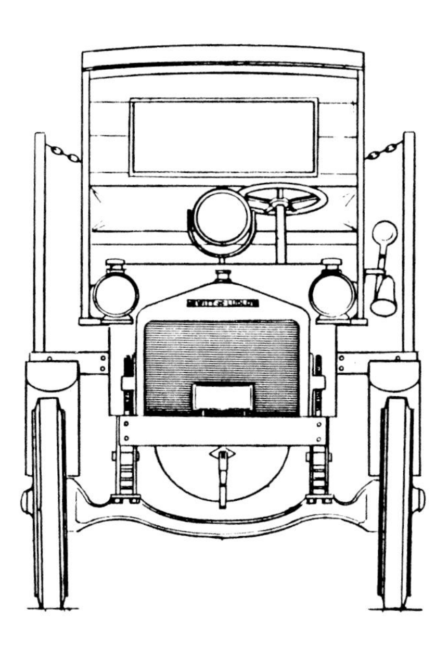


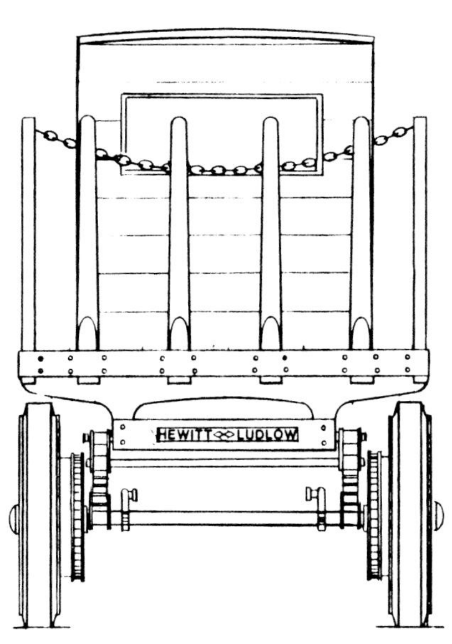


The solid rubber tires are molded onto steel bands which are then pressed onto the wooden wheels.
A four cylinder four cycle Buda engine of 18HP provides motive power. A leather lined cone clutch connects the engine to the three speed gear box and the vehicle attains a maximum speed of 15MPH.
The sheet brass radiator shock contains vertical spiral wound funnel tubes giving thermosyphon cooling to the engine.
The drivers position is on the left side. There is no windshield but the cab roof extends out over the firewall. The gear and hand brake levers are set in the cab centre. Acetylene lighting is provided and the large single firewall mounted light is manoeuverable from the drivers position.
The deck of the vintners truck is provided with stake pockets and stakes. Chains divide the deck into three areas and restrain cargo movement somewhat. Side boards fastened to the stakes carry the owners name, address, etc.

**42**

# Hewitt-Ludlow Auto Company

Hewitt-Ludlow Auto Company was organized June 27, 1912, in San Francisco, California by Edward T. Hewitt, William A. Hewitt and James Ludlow, to manufacture motor trucks. By 1917 they were producing seven different models ranging from 1½ to 5½ ton capacity. In the early days "chain drive" trucks were standard in the industry. A few years after the company was started, Hewitt-Ludlow produced the first trucks built in San Francisco to use "worm drive" which coupled engine power to the rear wheels by a direct drive shaft. This was a bold innovation.

The factory at 901-951 Indiana Street produced a basic chassis with engine, running gear, electric lights, storage battery, fenders, horn, seat and tool box. From this basic unit the customer could order any style body that suited his needs.

Over the years, the Hewitt brothers produced two makes of trucks. Hewitt-Ludlow made conventional units and later, Hewitt-Talbot made tractor-trailer units which featured a low-bed design which facilitated loading. Edward Hewitt did much innovative work in pioneering low-bed, semi and tandem trailers and specialized trailers such as the pole type. His use of the "fifth-wheel" concept made the Hewitt trailer a standard in the industry with "absolute tracking" of the trailer to the truck guaranteed. The value of his slogan, "The Hewitt trailer doubles the hauling capacity of your truck," was well known to the trade of the day.

After the sale of the Hewitt truck line to the Ralston Iron Works, the Hewitts continued building trailers up to 1930. On phasing out the trailer line, Edward T. Hewitt developed a line of mobile air compressors. These he mounted on Ford trucks which were well suited to hauling compressors which also used Ford engines. This simplified maintenance.

These large air compressors were ideally suited to road work and mining operations. The Hewitts also produced air compressors that were mounted on two-wheel trailers.

The Hewitt Machinery Company prospered until Edward T. Hewitt's untimely death in 1933. William A. Hewitt continued the operation for a few more years then retired from business.

156″ WHEELBASE
59″ TRACK
36″ X 5″ FRONT WHEEL 14-SPOKE WOOD WITH SOLID TIRES 36″ X 5″ REAR WHEEL
14-SPOKE WOOD WITH SOLID TIRES
BUDA HU 4-CYLINDER 4-CYCLE GASOLINE ENGINE 4.25″ BORE AND 5.5″ STROKE
38 HP AT 1200 RPM STROMBERG CARBURETOR DIXIE MAGNETO
MODINE SPIRAL FIN RADIATOR
WISCONSIN WORM AND WORMWHEEL SEMI-FLOATING REAR AXLE
ROSS WORM STEERING
6V LIGHTING SYSTEM
CHASSIS WEIGHT 7500 POUNDS

EDITOR'S NOTE: In 1917 Edward T. Hewitt submitted the design of a 2½ ton Hewitt-Ludlow truck to the U.S. Army. It was one of the few "worm drive" truck designs submitted in the Army's national competition (chain drive trucks were the standard of the day). It was the "worm drive" which placed him among the fifteen manufacturers nationwide which were chosen to participate in the "standard" lorrie design from which manufacturers would produce the tough, easy maintenance vehicles needed for the war effort. Edward Hewitt photographed and noted in ink on his entry: "A number built by us for U.S. Army in national competition, 2½ ton worm" on the file photograph printed above.

# AMERICAN LORRIES IN THE FIRST WORLD WAR

by Paul Berliet

When war was declared on 3 August 1914 the French army had, all in all, less than 150 lorries in its possession.

In November 1918, when the armistice was signed, there were more than 80,000 lorries and tractors on the French front alone. The French Heavy Road Vehicle Industry had of course performed wonders in increasing its production by 700 percent, but 55,000 American lorries had also been delivered, without which the war would have had a different ending.

APRIL 1917: The great American nation entered the conflict and threw itself into the preparation of an expeditionary force of 3 million men.

This called for a lot of improvisation since the U.S.A. hardly had an army at all to start with. The country had not seen a real war since the War Between the States and, unlike France, ran no risk of being invaded. Thus, nothing was ready: no heavy artillery, no air force and few lorries, in spite of the lessons provided by the Mexican campaign of 1916. At the time, no theory really existed about the use of motorised vehicles in wartime.

The army nevertheless began to send out impressively large invitations to tender for lorries with a payload up to six tons--120,000 of them! French and English shared their three years of wartime experience with their new allies. American industry, with its huge capacity for adapting to new situations, responded very quickly, and the production of "trucks" in 1917 exceeded 100,000 units.

The diversity of makes and models, however, soon created almost insurmountable maintenance problems. The MTC, who had wisely chosen only three makes (Cadillac, Dodge and Ford) as far as cars were concerned, had brought 23 different makes of light lorries to France, along with 21 makes of 3 ton lorries and six makes of 5/6 ton lorries, without mentioning the 34 different makes of trailers.

It is easy to imagine the headache such a mixed pool of vehicles must have been for the maintenance personnel, especially since everything was in English measurements and it was impossible to find even a replacement bolt where they were stationed.

Faced with this situation, our allies reacted very swiftly: in the early autumn of 1917, a group of engineers from the SAE (Society of Automotive Engineers), working for several different manufacturers, met in Washington to agree on a standard lorry which would comply with army specifications and which could be produced in large quantities by different companies. The project was carried through in record time and the first standard lorries carrying the "USA" badge came out in 1918.

Fifteen manufacturers were to participate in this project which involved not just one model but a full range of models from two to six tons, intended to meet at least 75 percent of the armies' needs.

In practice, only one model was actually produced, the type B with a payload of 5/6 tons, and even then less than 10,000 units were made, 8,000 of which reached France before the end of the hostilities. Although this model carried the "USA" badge on its front, the "boys" and the French soldiers soon renamed it "Liberty," and it was under this nickname that it was to go down in history.

Just for the record, it appears that the promoters of the standard lorry project had obtained an assurance that, once the war was over, the vehicles which had been built would not be shipped back to the United States. There was obviously the fear that their reappearance would create rather embarrassing after-sales problems among the various partners. It appears that this agreement was kept, since a "Liberty" is a very rare find in its country of origin.

In November 1918, the total number of lorries on French soil was about 80,000, nearly 60 percent of which had come from the far-off shores of America. It was these "trucks," more and more of which were used in battles as the war went on, which by the extraordinary mobility they provided in the transport of men, artillery and provisions, shifted the balance in the Allies' favor and away from the cumbersome German war machine which had to rely mainly on the railways for its transport.

In August 1914, the French army had gone to war with less than 150 lorries, and although the French industry managed, through herculean efforts, to bring out more than 35,000 lorries, it was the massive influx of American lorries which gave the French forces their remarkable mechanical mobility.

*EDITOR: SAH member Paul Berliet is the President of the Fondation de l'Automobile Marius Berliet, 39, avenue Esquirol, 69003 Lyon, France.*

*The above article, published in* Automotive History Review, *is related to Hewitt-Ludlow activities described on the previous page. It was made available by the Society of Automotive Historians.*

*One of the first advertising efforts by Hewitt-Ludlow Auto Co. was a group of photographs showing the product with a copy of the company's business card. This was printed on a single sheet and used as a promotional piece for the San Francisco market.*

*Interior view of Hewitt-Ludlow truck manufacturing plant on Indiana Street, San Francisco.*

*Exterior of Hewitt-Ludlow plant, circa 1915.*

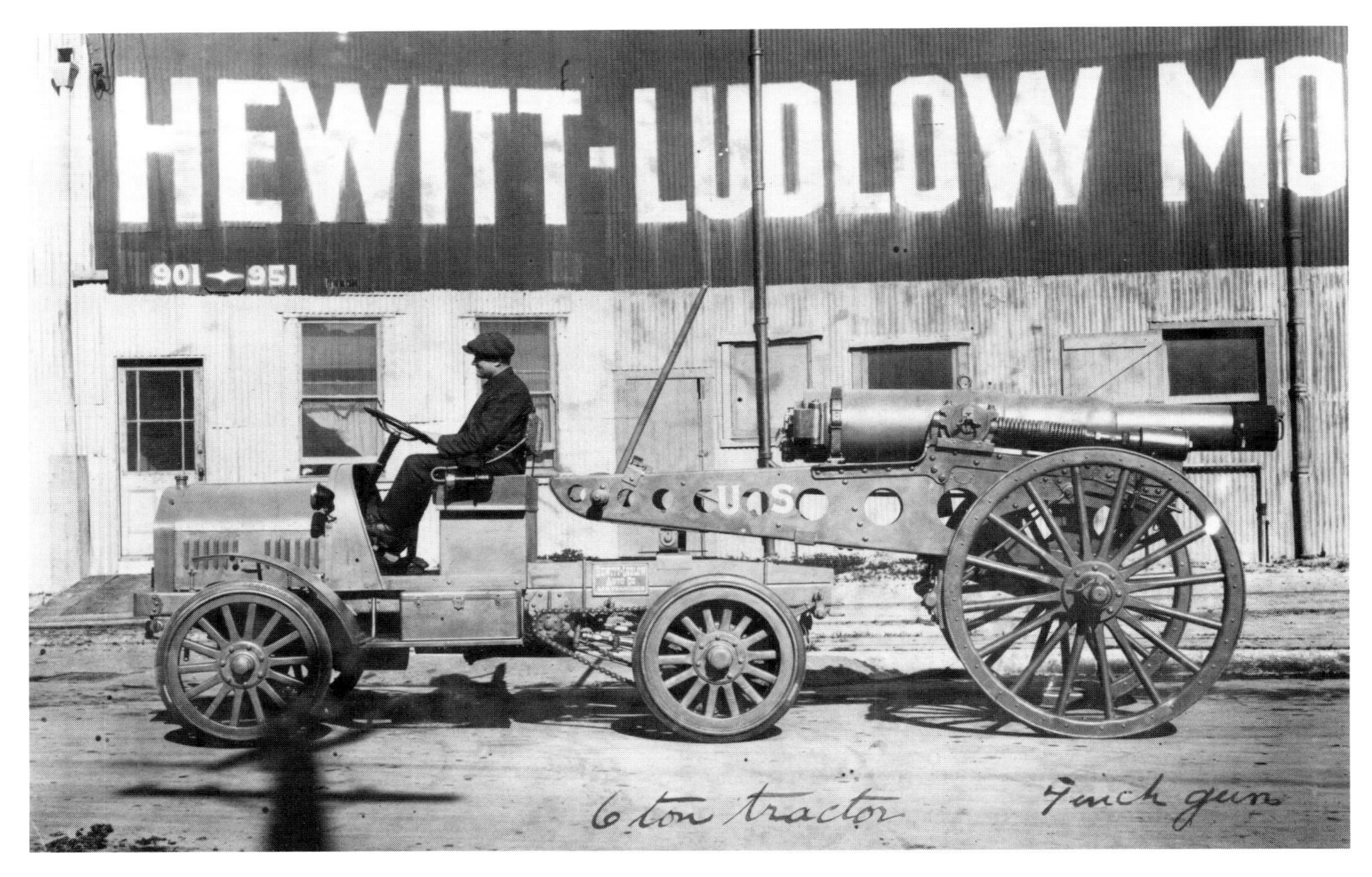


*A six ton "tractor" built by Hewitt-Ludlow during World War I, to pull a seven-inch U.S. Army gun.*

*Edward T. Hewitt in front of the manufacturing plant of Hewitt-Ludlow on Indiana Street, San Francisco, with trucks built for U.S. Army.*

*The two flareboard, worm drive trucks shown on this page were built for Anchor Packing Co., by Hewitt-Ludlow, for fast city delivery service. These trucks were forerunners of today's pickup trucks that can easily be loaded or unloaded from three sides. Additionally, the worm drive, that employs a differential to transfer power from the engine to the rear wheels, is much more efficient than the old style chain drive. It is smoother and ideally suited for the frequent stop and go driving that is characteristic in city deliveries. Hewitt-Ludlow produced the first worm drive trucks built in San Francisco. The handwritten note on the bottom photograph was inscribed by Edward Hewitt.*

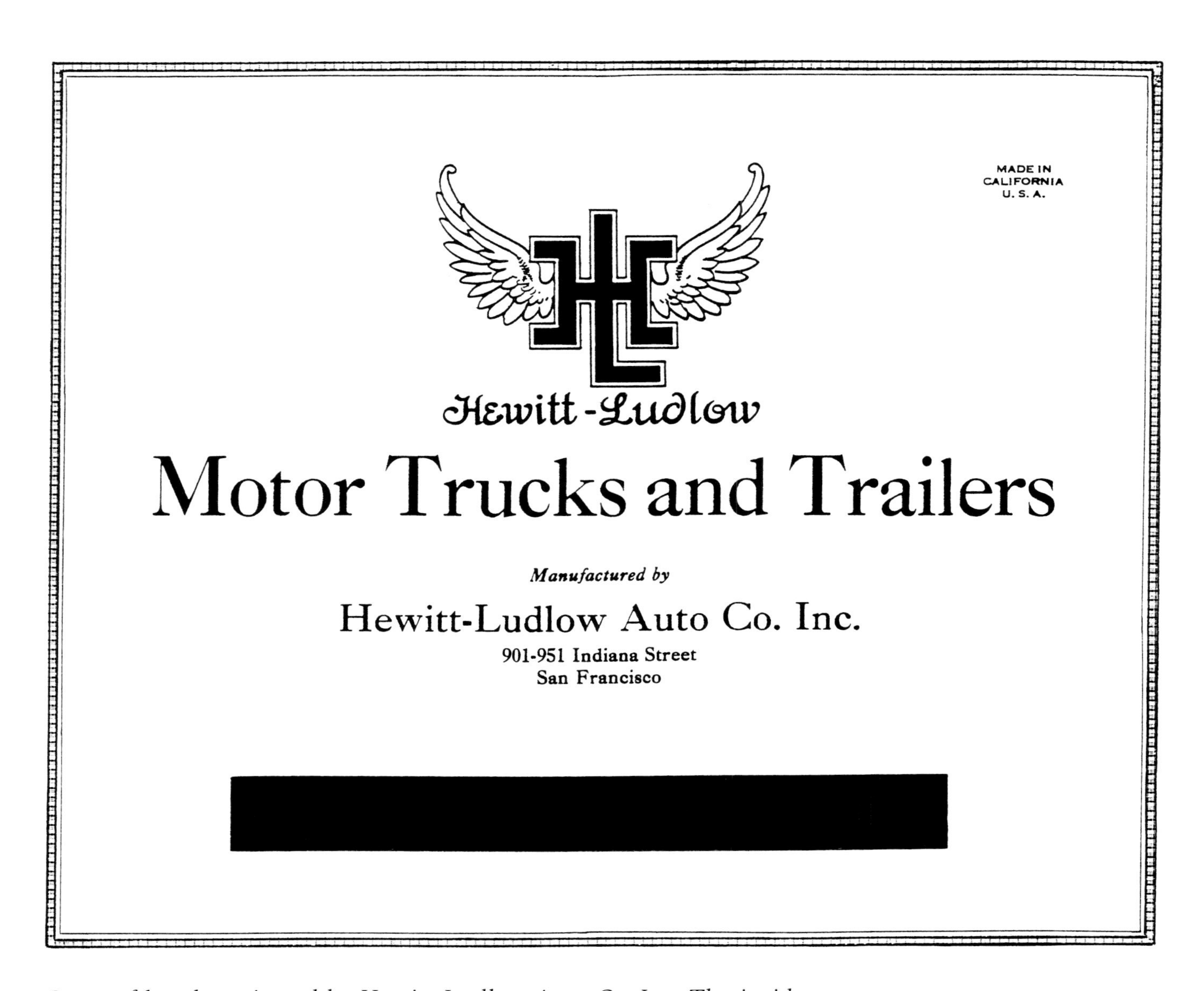

MADE IN
CALIFORNIA
U. S. A.
Hewitt-Ludlow
Motor Trucks and Trailers
Manufactured by
Hewitt-Ludlow Auto Co. Inc.
901-951 Indiana Street
San Francisco


*Cover of brochure issued by Hewitt-Ludlow Auto Co. Inc. The inside pages of the brochure follow on the next six pages.*

*Hewitt-Ludlow 2, 2½, and 3½ Ton Capacity Worm Drive and 3½ and 5 Ton Chain Units*

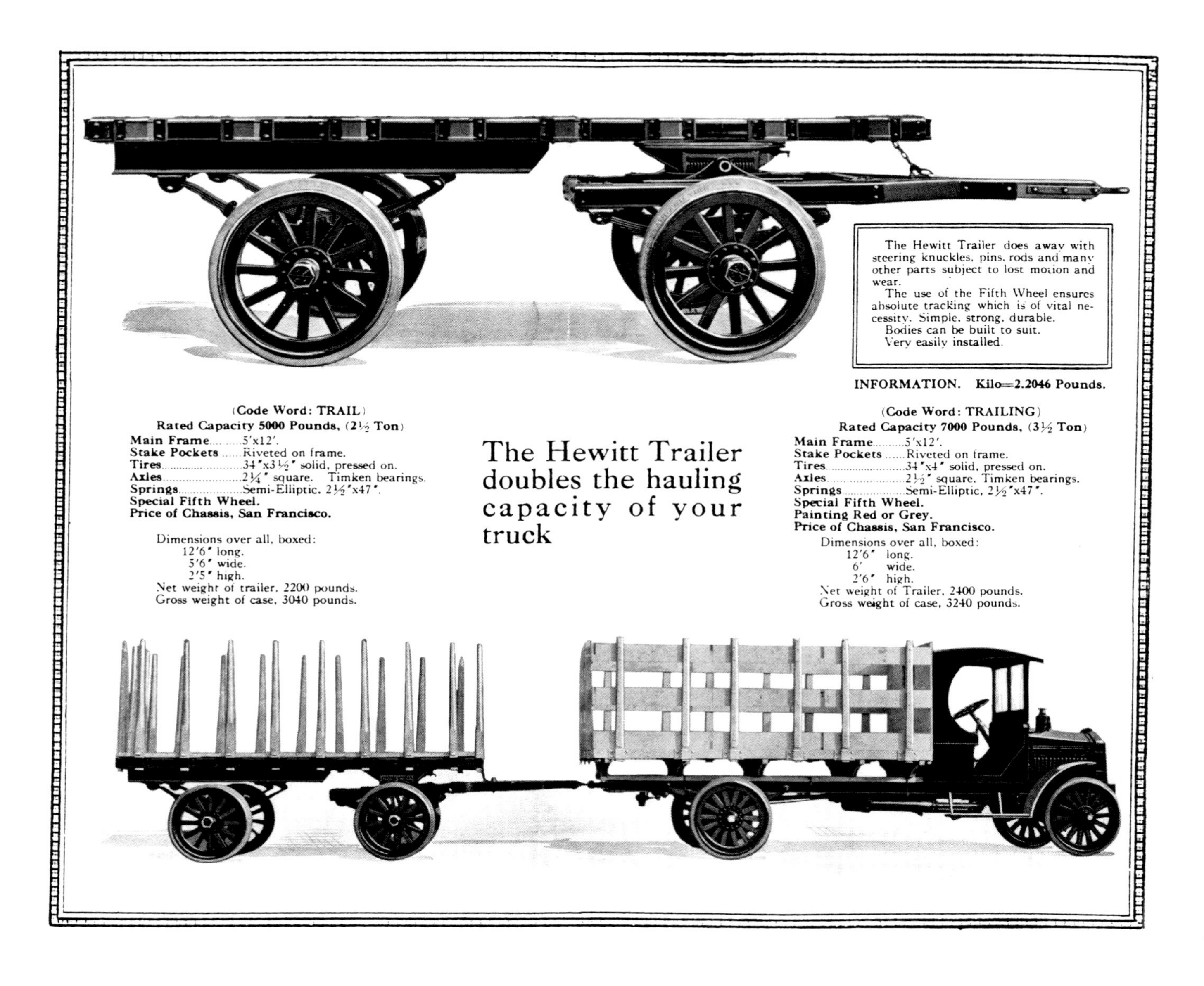
The Hewitt Trailer does away with steering knuckles, pins, rods and many other parts subject to lost motion and wear.
The use of the Fifth Wheel ensures absolute tracking which is of vital necessity. Simple, strong, durable.
Bodies can be built to suit.
Very easily installed.
INFORMATION. Kilo=2.2046 Pounds.
(Code Word: TRAIL)
Rated Capacity 5000 Pounds, (2½ Ton)
Main Frame........5'x12'.
Stake Pockets......Riveted on frame.
Tires........34"x3½" solid, pressed on.
Axles........2¼" square. Timken bearings.
Springs........Semi-Elliptic, 2½"x47".
Special Fifth Wheel.
Price of Chassis, San Francisco.
Dimensions over all, boxed:
12'6" long.
5'6" wide.
2'5" high.
Net weight of trailer, 2200 pounds.
Gross weight of case, 3040 pounds.
The Hewitt Trailer doubles the hauling capacity of your truck
(Code Word: TRAILING)
Rated Capacity 7000 Pounds, (3½ Ton)
Main Frame........5'x12'.
Stake Pockets......Riveted on frame.
Tires........34"x4" solid, pressed on.
Axles........2½" square. Timken bearings.
Springs........Semi-Elliptic, 2½"x47".
Special Fifth Wheel.
Painting Red or Grey.
Price of Chassis, San Francisco.
Dimensions over all, boxed:
12'6" long.
6' wide.
2'6" high.
Net weight of Trailer, 2400 pounds.
Gross weight of case, 3240 pounds.

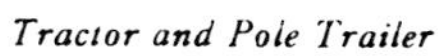
*Tractor and Pole Trailer*

*Hewitt-Ludlow 5-Ton Tractor complete with Semi-Trailer*

# Hewitt-Ludlow Motor Trucks

## SPECIFICATIONS

*SUBJECT TO CHANGE WITHOUT NOTICE*

Hewitt-Ludlow        Hewitt-Ludlow

(Code Word: FLIP)

**3½-TON WORM DRIVE**

**Load Capacity 7000 to 8000 Pounds**

**Motor**............Buda, heavy duty, four cylinder, 4¼"x-5½" HU, 3-point suspension type, fitted with force-feed oiling system.
**Horsepower**..........At 1200 revolutions, 38.
**Magneto**..........Dixie high tension, with Impulse Starter.
**Carburetor**..........Stromberg, 1¼".
**Radiator**..........Modine, spiral fin, straight full area tubes, heavy duty, cast tanks and side standards.
**Clutch**..........Multiple disc.
**Transmission**......Four speeds and reverse, selective type.
**Steering Gear**......Ross worm.
**Center Control**....Central, left-hand steer.
**Fuel Tank**..........Twenty-gallon capacity. Stewart Warner vacuum tank feed.
**Axles**..........**Front:** Drop forged "I" beam, chrome nickel knuckles, heat treated, fitted with standard taper roller bearings.
**Rear:** Wisconsin worm and gear drive, semi-floating, single piece housing, strongly ribbed, highest grade ball bearings.
**Joints**..........Universal joints and shafts.
**Muffler**..........Gemco, with cut-out.
**Springs**..........Chrome vanadium steel, spring eyes bronze bushed.
**Front:** 45" long, 3" wide.
**Rear:** 54" long, 3" wide.

**Frame**..........."I" beam section, hot riveted and strongly gusseted. All holes drilled.
**Wheels**..........Heavy artillery type, 14 spokes.
**Tires**..........36x5 front, 35x5 rear, dual; pressed-on type.
**Brakes**..........Both service and emergency in rear brake drums.
**Wheel Base**..........156".
**Tread**..........59".
**Loading Space**....Length, back of seat to end of frame, 12'.
**Equipment**..........Standard seat, lamps, horn, tool kit, steel tool box and oil can and lifting jack.
**Painting**..........Red or grey.
**Price**..........Chassis as specified, f. o. b. San Francisco, Cal.

**(Cab and Windshield extra)**

**SHIPPING INFORMATION**

Special boxing for export:
Dimensions, over all, boxed:
Length, 21' 0" boxed (estimated).
Width, 6' 6" " "
Height, 5' 6" " "
Net weight chassis, 7500 pounds (estimated).
Gross weight, 10,000 pounds (estimated).
Cubic feet, 750.

**(Code Word: FLIPPAGE)**

**3½-TON WORM-DRIVE, SPECIAL**

**Loading Capacity, 7000 lbs. to 8000 lbs.**

Where the 3½-ton truck is to be used under extremely heavy road conditions, such as in mountain work, or where the maximum motor power must be provided, we will furnish our 3½-ton standard motor truck, with all other specifications as shown in the previous column, but equipped with

**Motor**.......Buda heavy duty, slow speed, long stroke, fitted with force feed oiling system, four cylinders, 4½x6 three point suspension.
**Horsepower**..At 1000 revolutions per minute, 45.

Extra charge for this equipment over our standard 3½-ton.

EDITOR'S NOTE: To accommodate overseas customers, Hewitt-Ludlow printed specifications for boxing its various sizes of trucks for export.

(Code Word: FLOAT)

## 2-TON WORM DRIVE

**Load Capacity 4000 to 5000 Pounds**

**Motor**........Buda, heavy duty, four cylinder, 4⅛"x-5½", 3-point suspension.
**Horsepower**........30 at 1200 revolutions.
**Magneto**........Dixie high tension, with Impulse Starter.
**Carburetor**........Stromberg, 1¼".
**Radiator**........Modine, spiral fin, straight full area tubes. Heavy duty cast tanks and side standards.
**Clutch**........Multiple disc, dry plate, adjustable.
**Transmission**........Selective type, three speeds and reverse.
**Steering Gear**........Ross worm.
**Center Control**........Left-hand steer.
**Fuel Tank**........Twenty-gallon capacity. Stewart Warner vacuum feed.
**Axles**........**Front**: Drop forged "I" beam, chrome nickel knuckles, heat treated, fitted with standard taper roller bearings.
**Rear**: Wisconsin worm and gear drive, semi-floating, single piece, strongly ribbed housing, highest grade ball bearings.
**Muffler**........Gemco, with cut-out.
**Springs**........Chrome vanadium steel; spring eyes, bronze bushed.
**Front**: 39" long, 2½" wide.
**Rear**: 50" long, 2½" wide.
**Joints**........Universal joints and shafts.
**Frame**........"I" beam section, hot riveted and strongly gusseted. All rivet holes drilled.
**Wheels**........Heavy artillery type, 14 spokes.
**Tires**........36x4 front, 36x6 rear, pressed-on type.
**Brakes**........Service and emergency in rear brake drums.
**Wheel Base**........140".
**Tread**........58".
**Loading Space**........Length, back of seat to end of frame, 10' 6".
**Equipment**........Standard seat, lamps, horn, tool kit, steel tool box, oil can and lifting jack.
**Painting**........Red or grey.
**Price**........Chassis as specified, f. o. b. San Francisco, Cal.

**(Cab and Windshield extra)**

---

**SHIPPING INFORMATION**

Special boxing for export:
Dimensions, over all, boxed:
Length, 18' 0" boxed (estimated).
Width, 5' 9" " "
Height, 5' 0" " "
Net weight, chassis, 4800 pounds (estimated).
Gross weight, 6600 pounds (estimated).
Cubic feet, 485.

(Code Word: FLINCH)

## 2½-TON WORM DRIVE

**Load Capacity 5000 to 6000 Pounds**

**Motor**........Buda, heavy duty, four cylinder, 4¼"x-5½" HU, 3-point suspension type, fitted with force-feed oiling system.
**Horsepower**........At 1200 revolutions, 38.
**Magneto**........Dixie high tension, with Impulse Starter.
**Carburetor**........Stromberg, 1¼".
**Radiator**........Modine, spiral fin, straight full area tubes, heavy duty cast tanks and side standards.
**Clutch**........Multiple disc.
**Transmission**........Selective type, four speeds and reverse.
**Steering Gear**........Ross worm.
**Center Control**........Central; left-hand steer.
**Fuel Tank**........Twenty-gallon capacity. Stewart Warner vacuum feed.
**Axles**........**Front**: Drop forged, "I" beam, chrome nickel knuckles, heat treated, fitted with standard taper roller bearings.
**Rear**: Wisconsin worm and gear drive, semi-floating, single piece housing, strongly ribbed, highest grade ball bearings.
**Joints**........Universal joints and shafts.
**Muffler**........Gemco, with cut-out.
**Springs**........Chrome vanadium steel; spring eyes bronze bushed.
**Front**: 39" long, 2½" wide.
**Rear**: 50" long, 3" wide.
**Frame**........"I" beam section, hot riveted and strongly gusseted; all holes drilled.
**Wheels**........Heavy artillery type, 14 spokes.
**Tires**........36x4 front, 36x7 rear, pressed-on type.
**Brakes**........Service and emergency in rear brake drums.
**Wheel Base**........150".
**Tread**........58".
**Loading Space**........Length, back of seat to end of frame, 11' 9".
**Equipment**........Standard seat, lamps, horn, tool kit, steel tool box, oil can, and lifting jack.
**Painting**........Red or grey.
**Price**........Chassis as specified, f. o. b. San Francisco, Cal.

**(Cab and Windshield extra)**

---

**SHIPPING INFORMATION**

Special boxing for export:
Dimensions, over all, boxed:
Length, 19' 0" boxed (estimated).
Width, 6' 0" " "
Height, 5' 0" " "
Net weight chassis, 5500 pounds (estimated).
Gross weight, 8000 pounds (estimated).
Cubic feet, 600.

(Code Word: FLOCKLY)

## 5-TON CHAIN DRIVE

**Built Only on Order**

**Motor** ..... Buda, heavy duty, four cylinder, 4½"x6", slow speed, long stroke, fitted with force-feed oiling system, motor mounting, 3-point suspension.
**Horsepower** ..... At 1000 revolutions, 45.
**Magneto** ..... Dixie high tension, with Impulse Starter.
**Carburetor** ..... Stromberg, 1½".
**Radiator** ..... Modine, spiral fin, straight full area tubes, heavy cast tanks and sides.
**Clutch** ..... Multiple disc.
**Transmission** ..... Selective type, individual clutch, gears always in mesh with differential mounted in case.
**Steering Gear** ..... Ross worm.
**Center Control** ..... Central, left-hand steer.
**Fuel Tank** ..... Twenty-gallon capacity. Stewart Warner vacuum feed.
**Frame** ..... "I" beam section.
**Brakes** ..... Service brakes on jack-shafts. Emergency brakes on rear wheels.
**Drive** ..... Heavy double chain, 1¼x1¼x2, Baldwin.
**Joints** ..... Universal joints and shafts.
**Springs** ..... Chrome vanadium steel with bronze bushed eyes.
**Rear:** 60" long, 4" wide.
**Front:** 44" long, 3½" wide.
**Wheels** ..... Heavy duty artillery type, 14 spokes.
**Tires** ..... 36x6 front, 40x6 rear, dual; pressed-on type.
**Wheel Base** ..... 168".
**Tread** ..... 64".
**Axles** ..... **Front:** Drop forged "I" beam, chrome nickel knuckles, heat treated, fitted with standard taper roller bearings.
**Rear:** Solid axle of alloy steel, 2¾x4", with standard taper roller bearings.
**Muffler** ..... Gemco or Powell, with cut-out.
**Painting** ..... Red or grey.
**Equipment** ..... Seat, horn, oil lamps, steel tool box, tool kit.
**Price** ..... Chassis as specified, f. o. b. San Francisco, Cal.

**(Cab and Windshield extra)**

---

### SHIPPING INFORMATION

Special boxing for export:
Dimensions, over all, boxed:
Length, 21' 0" boxed (estimated).
Width, 6' 6" " "
Height, 6' 0" " "
Net weight chassis, 8000 pounds (estimated).
Gross weight, crated, 11,000 pounds (estimated).
Cubic feet, 820.

(Code Word: FLOG)

## 5-TON TRACTOR TRUCK

**Built only on Order**

**Load Capacity, with Semi-Trailer, 5 Tons**

**Motor** ..... Buda, heavy duty, four cylinder, 4¼"x5½" HU, 3-point suspension type, fitted with force-feed oiling system.
**Horsepower** ..... At 1200 revolutions, 38.
**Magneto** ..... Dixie high tension, with Impulse Starter.
**Carburetor** ..... Stromberg, 1¼".
**Radiator** ..... Modine, spiral fin, straight full area tubes, heavy cast tank and side standards.
**Clutch** ..... Multiple disc.
**Joints** ..... Universal joints and shafts.
**Transmission** ..... Selective type, individual clutch system, gears always in mesh.
**Drive** ..... Double chain from jack-shafts to rear axle.
**Axles** ..... **Front:** Heavy drop forged "I" beam section.
**Rear:** Heavy "I" beam dead axle.
**Steering Gear** ..... Ross worm.
**Center Control** ..... Central, left-hand steer.
**Fuel Tank** ..... Twenty-gallon capacity. Stewart Warner vacuum feed.
**Bearings** ..... Standard tapered roller.
**Frame** ..... Heavy special channel.
**Springs** ..... Chrome vanadium steel, eyes bronze bushed.
**Front:** 39" long, 2½" wide.
**Rear:** 50" long, 3" wide.
Rear cross springs also furnished for carrying overload.
**Wheels** ..... Heavy artillery type, 14 spokes.
**Tires** ..... 36x4 front, 36x4 rear, dual; pressed-on type.
**Brakes** ..... Service brakes mounted on jack-shafts. Emergency brakes on rear brake drums, all brakes equalized.
**Equipment** ..... Martin fifth wheel for attaching semi-trailer, towing connections, lamps, horn, tool kit, steel tool box and seat.
**Painting** ..... Red or grey.
**Price** ..... Truck Tractor chassis only, complete.

**(Cab and Windshield extra)**

**(Rear Semi-Trailer, chassis only, extra to order)**

---

### SHIPPING INFORMATION

Special boxing for export:
Net weight of Truck chassis, 5500 pounds.
Gross weight of Truck, boxed, 8000 pounds.
Net weight of Semi-Trailer chassis, 3500 pounds.
Gross weight of Semi-Trailer, boxed, 5000 pounds.

270 AUTOMOBILE TRADE JOURNAL.

# Hewitt-Ludlow Trucks Come in Three-Quarter to Five Tons Capacities

THE Hewitt-Ludlow Auto Co., San Francisco, Cal., is offering a line of trucks which are made in seven different capacities, the 3½ and 5-ton models being chain drive, while the lighter are worm drive. However, the 1½, 2 and 2½-ton models can be equipped with chain drive if desired. Buda 4-cylinder cast in block type engines are used in all of these trucks, the first two having 3½ x 5⅛ in., the next three in order 3¾ x 5½ in. and the last two 4¼ x 5½ in. Corresponding to the various size cylinders, the horsepowers are 25 at 1500 revolutions, 30 at 1200 revolutions and 35 at 1200 revolutions.

Lubrication in all is by splash and a positive plunger pump, having sight feed on the dash. Cooling is by the thermo-syphon system in the ¾ and 1-ton models and by centrifugal pump in the others. Honeycomb type of radiators are utilized and the fans are belt driven. Ignition is by the Remy dual magnetic system and storage battery. Stromberg carburetors with hot air attachments are used throughout the line. The control is left hand drive with center control, hand throttle and foot accelerator. In the ¾ and 1-ton sizes multiple disc, dry plate clutches are used, while in the remainder they are leather faced cone type. The selective type of transmission is incorporated in all models, having three speeds forward and one reverse. All springs are semi-elliptic. The first two, the ¾ and 1-ton models have front springs 2¼ in. wide and rear 2½ in. wide; the 1½, 2 and 2½-tonners, 2½ in. front and 3 in. rear, while the 3½ and 5-ton models are 3 in. wide, front and 3 in. rear. All of the front axles are heavy forged I-beam section, while the rear are of the semi-floating worm gear type except in the 3½ and 5-ton sizes, which are heavy drop forged rectangular section Wheel diameters are, corresponding respectively to truck capacities, 34 in., 34 in., 36 in., 36 in. and front 36 in., rear 40 in. All service brakes are of the external contracting type, while the emergencies are internal expanding. Tires are all solid and are, in order, 34 x 3 in. front, 34 x 4 in. rear; 34 x 3 in. front, 34 x 4 in. rear; 36 x 3½ in. front, 36 x 6 in. rear; 36 x 3½ in. front, 36 x 7 in. rear; 36 x 5 in. front and 40 x 5 in. dual rear. Wheelbases are respectively 120 in., 126 in., 126 in., 140 in., 144 in. and 156 in. Gasoline tanks all have 20 gal. capacity and equipment includes electric tail and side lights, storage battery, fenders, horn, seat and tool kit.

The price for the 1½-ton model is $2270, for the 2-2½-ton, $2250; for the 3½-ton worm drive $3350, and for the 5-ton chain, $4500. These prices are for chassis only and are f.o.b. San Francisco.

---

**Lumb Motor Truck & Tractor Co., Aurora,** Ill., has been formed to manufacture a 2-ton model, weighing only 5400 lb., equipped with a 37 hp. engine and Bosch ignition and lighting system.

**Hewitt-Ludlow's Five-Ton Chain-Drive Model Chassis.**
Has Buda four-cylinder in-block type engine, Stromberg carburetor and Remy dual-ignition system and sells for $4500, f.o.b. San Francisco.

*Hewitt-Ludlow also did some national advertising. This piece in the* Automobile Trade Journal, *July 1917, has shop foreman, "Chappie" Friend, in the driver's seat.*

## HEWITT-LUDLOW TRUCKS

Manufactured by

**HEWITT-LUDLOW AUTO CO., 901-951 Indiana St., San Francisco, Cal.**

S P E C I F I C A T I O N S

| | | | |
|---|---|---|---|
| **Model** | 1917 | 1917 | 1917 |
| **Capacity** | 2—2½ tons | 3½ tons | 3½ tons |
| **Drive** | Worm | Worm | Chain |
| **Chassis Price** | $2,550 | $3,350 | $3,000 |
| **Motor** | | | |
| **H. P.** (S.A.E.) | 22.5 | 30 | 30 |
| **H. P.** (Actual) | 30 at 1150 R.P.M. | 35 at 1150 R.P.M. | 35 at 1150 R.P.M. |
| **Cylinders** | 4 en bloc | 4 en bloc | 4 en bloc |
| **Bore** | 3¾″ | 4¼″ | 4¼″ |
| **Stroke** | 5½″ | 5½″ | 5½″ |
| **Wheel Base** | 140″ | 144″ and 156″ | 144″ and 156″ |
| **Tread Front** | 59″ | 69″ | 69″ |
| **Tread Rear** | 59″ | 69″ | 69″ |
| **Tires Front** | 36x4″ | 36x5″ | 36x5″ |
| **Tires Rear** | 36x7″ | 40x5″ dual | 40x5″ dual |
| **Frame** | 6″, 10½ lb. Channel | 6″, 13 lb. Channel | 6″, 13 lb. Channel |
| **Front Axle** | I-beam Sheldon Type | I-beam Liggett Type | I-beam Liggett Type |
| **Rear Axle** | Hewitt-Ludlow Worm Semi-floating | Semi-floating | Heavy Rectangular Sec. |

**Springs Front**—Semi-elliptic.
**Springs Rear**—Semi-elliptic, extra heavy.
**Carburetor**—Stromberg, M2.
**Cooling System**—Pump.
**Oiling System**—Splash and forced feed.
**Ignition**—High tension or dual system optional.
**Control**—Left drive, center control.
**Clutch**—Hartford cone.
**Transmission**—Selective, jaw clutch type, three speeds forward and one reverse.

| | | | |
|---|---|---|---|
| **Brakes** | Service, external contracting on drive shaft; Emergency, expanding on rear wheel drum | Service, external contracting on drive shaft; Emergency, expanding on rear wheel drum | Service external contracting on jackshaft; Emergency, expanding on rear wheel drum |

**Steering Gear**—Screw and nut, irreversible.
**Equipment**—Electric side and tail lights, storage battery, fenders, horn, seat with full upholstery, tool kit.

**Tire Equipment**—GOODRICH SOLID MOTOR TRUCK TIRES FURNISHED AS REGULAR EQUIPMENT.

Page 68

*This B. F. Goodrich advertisement, and the similar ad on opposite page, appeared in the 1917 issues of* Motor Trucks of America. *featuring Hewitt-Ludlow trucks.*

# HEWITT-LUDLOW TRUCKS

Manufactured by

HEWITT-LUDLOW AUTO CO., 901-951 Indiana St., San Francisco, Cal

## SPECIFICATIONS

| Model | 1500 | 1-ton | 1½-ton | 2-ton |
|---|---|---|---|---|
| Capacity | 1500 lbs. | 1 ton | 1½ tons | 2-2½ tons |
| Drive | Worm | Worm | Worm | Worm |
| Chassis Price | $1,650 | $1,800 | $2,250 | $2,350 |
| Motor | Buda | | | |
| Horse Power | 25 at 1500 R.P.M. | 25 at 1500 R.P.M. | 30 at 1200 R.P.M. | 30 at 1200 R.P.M. |
| Cylinders | 4 en bloc | 4 en bloc | 4 en bloc | 4 en bloc |
| Bore | 3½″ | 3½″ | 3¾″ | 3¾″ |
| Stroke | 5⅛″ | 5⅛″ | 5½″ | 5½″ |
| Wheel Base | 120″ | 126″ | 126″ | 140″ |
| Tread Front | 57″ | 57″ | 59″ | 59″ |
| Tread Rear | 57″ | 57″ | 59″ | 59″ |
| Tires Front | 34x3″ | 34x3″ | 36x3½″ | 36x3½″ |
| Tires Rear | 34x4″ | 34x4″ | 36x6″ | 36x7″ |
| Frame | Pressed steel, channel | Pressed steel, channel | Pressed steel channel section | Pressed steel channel section |
| Front Axle | I-beam section | I-beam section | Forged I-beam | Forged I-beam |
| Rear Axle | Semi-floating worm gear type | Semi-floating worm gear type | Semi-floating worm | Semi-floating worm |

**Springs Front**—Semi-elliptic.

**Springs Rear**—Semi-elliptic.

**Carburetor**—Stromberg with hot air attachment.

| | 1500 | 1-ton | 1½-ton | 2-ton |
|---|---|---|---|---|
| **Cooling System** | Thermo-syphon | Thermo-syphon | Centrifugal pump | Centrifugal pump |

**Oiling System**—Splash and positive plunger pump.

**Ignition**—Remy dual magneto and storage battery.

**Control**—Left hand drive, center control.

| | 1500 and 1-ton | 1½-ton and 2-ton |
|---|---|---|
| **Clutch** | Multiple disc, dry plate (both models) | Cone, leather-faced (both models) |
| **Transmission** | Selective, three forward and reverse | Selective, jaw clutch type, three forward and reverse |
| **Brakes** | Service, internal expanding on rear wheel drum | External contracting in driveshaft; Emergency, internal expanding on rear wheel drum, both sets equalized |

**Steering Gear**—Worm.

**Equipment**—Electric side and tail lights, storage battery, fenders, horn, seat and tools.

Note—1½ ton Model in chain drive $2,150; 1½ ton Model in worm drive $2,250; 2 ton Model in chain drive $2,250; 2 ton Model in worm drive $2,350.

**Tire Equipment**—GOODRICH MOTOR TRUCK TIRES FURNISHED WHEN SPECIFIED.

(See additional specifications on page 126)

SPRECKELS COMPANIES

CORONADO BEACH COMPANY
HOTEL DEL CORONADO
CORONADO TENT CITY
SAN DIEGO ELECTRIC RAILWAY COMPANY
SOUTHERN CALIFORNIA MOUNTAIN WATER CO.
CORONADO WATER COMPANY
SAN DIEGO AND CORONADO FERRY COMPANY
SAN DIEGO AND CORONADO TRANSFER COMPANY
UNITED LIGHT, FUEL AND POWER COMPANY
SAN DIEGO SOUTHERN RAILWAY COMPANY
SAN DIEGO AND ARIZONA RAILWAY COMPANY

GENERAL OFFICES
UNION BUILDING

GENERAL SUPERINTENDENT'S
OFFICE

J. D. SPRECKELS, PRESIDENT
W. CLAYTON, VICE-PRES. & MANAGING DIRECTOR
H. L. TITUS, SECRETARY, TREASURER & ATTY.
B. M. WARNER, GENERAL SUPERINTENDENT
A. H. KAYSER, GENERAL AUDITOR

SAN DIEGO, CALIFORNIA

March 2nd, 1917

Hewitt-Ludlow Auto Co.,
901 Indiana Street
San Francisco, Cal

Subject: S. D. & S. E. Ry, Co,
Gasoline Motor Car

Gentlemen:

I beg to advise that the gas motor car built by you for our Company has this day been accepted as per terms of contract. The car has fulfilled all requirements to our satisfaction.

We received the car on February 4th and started it on trial runs at once, having operated it practically every day since. On Feb. 23rd, the car went into regular schedule service and I am pleased to state that it has not only met with the approval of the officials of the Company but has been unanimously accepted by our patrons who have had the opportunity of riding on it. I wish to state that the acceptance or approval of a new transportation vehicle by the public means every thing to its existence and practically assures its success.

The contract called for a maximum speed of 35 miles per hour on level track but during several of our test trips the car developed 40 miles per hour. It takes our long grades, ranging from 3/4 to 2-1/2% at 25 miles per hour on the third gear or speed. It holds the rails well, in fact, our drivers do not find it necessary to slacken speed thru any of the curves on the main line. We have operated this car over the tracks of the San Diego Elec. Co., thru the business District of San Diego, going around curves of 55 feet radius and over all kinds of special track work with perfect ease.

While we have not operated this car long enough to arrive at operating costs, except fuel, I do not hesitate to fully endorse this type of car and recommend its use by any rail road having conditions similar to our own. The car is operating on straight distillate costing 9-1/2 cents per gallon and is giving about 5-1/2 miles to the gallon.

In conclusion, I must again congratulate your company for the splendid success of this "Little Car". I shall be pleased to furnish you with operating data as soon as possible.

Yours very truly,

B M Warner

Gen. Supt.

EDITOR'S NOTE: In 1916 the Spreckels Companies of San Diego, California, had need for a "gasoline motor car" to be operated on the railroad tracks of the San Diego Electric Company. Consequently, Spreckels commissioned the Hewitt-Ludlow Company to design and build a car that would fulfill their need. This letter of March 2, 1917, describes the favorable results of rail car tests that were conducted in downtown San Diego, California. Hewitt-Ludlow had built a unique passenger vehicle.

*Distillate railway car, designed and built by Hewitt-Ludlow in San Francisco, for the Spreckels Companies of San Diego. It was a "first" in this type of passenger transportation. This railway car had a seating capacity for 32 passengers and a driver. Edward and William Hewitt, fifth and sixth from left, 1917.*

# Hewitt-Ludlow Auto Co.

*San Francisco, California*

THE ELECTRIC RAILWAY JOURNAL of April 1917, reported that the San Diego & Southeastern Railway (later a branch of the San Diego & Arizona Eastern) placed in service on its San Diego-to-Santee branch a 10-ton, 25-foot-long oil engine car built by Hewitt-Ludlow of San Francisco, apparently a one-of-a-kind effort.

Built in February of 1917, the car, number 31, seated 32 passengers and could make 40 mph on the hilly, 18-mile branch. In downtown San Diego the car operated on regular streetcar tracks.

By some strange quirk of fate, this car was sold to the Arcade & Attica, a short line all the way across the country in upstate New York.

*Distillate railway car built by Hewitt-Ludlow in 1917 was a new entry into transportation engineering.*

HEWITT-LUDLOW
AUTO CO.

Transportation Engineers

Builders Distillate Railway Cars

901-951 INDIANA, near 22nd ST.

Tel. Mission 8129

San Francisco, Calif.,

*This specialized Hewitt-Ludlow letterhead of 1917 was used after the company's entry into the field of engineering for passenger transportation.*

HEWITT-LUDLOW AUTO CO.
901-951 INDIANA STREET
SAN FRANCISCO
CALIFORNIA

**1919 3½ TON GASOLINE CHASSIS**

144″ WHEELBASE
36″ X 3.5″ FRONT WHEELS 36″ X 7″ REAR WHEELS, SOLID TIRES
4-CYLINDER 4-CYCLE BUDA ENGINE 28.9 HP, 4.25″ BORE, 5.5″ STROKE
FLEXO RADIATOR
STROMBERG CARBURETOR
BOSCH IGNITION
HAND STARTING
BORG AND BECK CLUTCH, LEATHER FACED CONE TYPE
COTTA 4-SPEED GEARBOX
CHAIN DRIVE REAR AXLE
SEMI-ELIPTIC SPRINGS
CHANNEL SECTION, ALL-RIVETED FRAME
6V LIGHTING SYSTEM
CHASSIS PRICE $3,550

**RETAIL SERVICE GASOLINE TANKER TRUCK**

The vehicle has the maker's standard radiator, hood and driving compartment. The roof and side curtains are detachable for seasonal use.

The load carrying system of the truck is unusual. The main tank is divided into three compartments so that three different grades of fuel may be dispensed. The total capacity of the tank is 1,000 gallons. There are also two side-mounted 40 gallon tanks holding lubricating oil. Each container has a two-way outlet cock which may be padlocked.

An equipment box containing measures, cans, funnels and similar retailing hardware is situated at the rear of the main gasoline tank.

*Hewitt-Ludlow published information sheets giving specifications and special information to the trade. Vehicles fitted with this style of tankage were intended for direct sales of motor fuels and lubricants to automobile owners. Probably curbside sales were also made on occasion but in the days of cobbled streets, together with a multiplicity of iron-shod hooves striking sparks, and generally primitive safety attitudes, the hazards of these tanker trucks were enormous. It is likely that local legislative actions prohibited this method of carrying and selling motor fuels thus rendering this type obsolete by the early 1920s.*

CONDITIONAL SALE AGREEMENT

Hewitt-Ludlow Auto Co. Inc. San Francisco, Cal., December 14th 1921, hereinafter called the Seller, hereby agrees to sell at and for the agreed price of Forty six hundred Dollars, to Mattocks & Mattocks hereinafter called the Buyer, one automobile known as Hewitt-Talbot motor Truck, Low Bed Type Model 1921 4 ton Car No. 333 Engine No. 2606-94670 and said Buyer agrees to buy said automobile and pay said sum of Forty six hundred dollars ($ 4600.00) Dollars therefor as follows:

One thousand Dollars on the execution of this agreement, and the balance of Thirty six hundred ($ 3600.00) Dollars in payments evidenced by 18 notes bearing interest at the rate of 7 per cent. per annum from date, as follows:

| | | | | | |
|---|---|---|---|---|---|
| 1. $ 200.00 | on January 14th, 1922 | 7. $ 200.00 | on July 14, 1922 |
| 2. $ 200.— | on Feb. 14, 1922 | 8. $ 200.— | on Aug. 14, 1922 |
| 3. $ 200.— | on March 14, 1922 | 9. $ 200.— | on Sept. 14, 1922 |
| 4. $ 200.— | on April 14, 1922 | 10. $ 200.— | on Oct. 14, 1922 |
| 5. $ 200.— | on May 14, 1922 | 11. $ 200.— | on Nov. 14, 1922 |
| 6. $ 200.— | on June 14, 1922 | 12. $ 200.— | on Dec. 14, 1922 |

which notes are accepted as memoranda only and not as payment, and on the conditions and terms hereinafter set forth.

Mattocks & Mattocks

IN WITNESS WHEREOF, the Seller and Buyer have caused these presents to be duly executed the day and year first above written.

G. E. Mattocks
Stephen I. Smith

Hewitt-Ludlow Auto Co. Inc.
901 Indiana St. San Francisco Calif.
Seller.

Mattocks & Mattocks
Buyer.

Address 259 California St. San Francisco Cal.
Phone Kearny 3093

For value received, the above agreement is hereby sold, transferred, assigned and set over unto

and the undersigned hereby guarantees the payment and performance of each and all of the conditions therein mentioned, and further waives demand, protest and notice of nonpayment.

Dated: Dec. 30 1921
Witness:

Hewitt Ludlow auto Co
per Wm. A. Hewitt
Pres

*An example of a Hewitt-Ludlow conditional sales agreement, dated December 14, 1921. (Several long routine paragraphs have been omitted.) The interest rate in 1921 was seven percent.*

*A Hewitt-Ludlow furniture moving truck.*

*Uncle Bill Hewitt, at right, with a Hewitt-Ludlow truck, San Francisco.*

*Hewitt-Ludlow truck and trailer, San Francisco.*

*Stretched model of a Hewitt-Ludlow truck, San Francisco.*

*The handwritten note on this photograph calls attention to the "dust proof carburetor attachment" and the "distillate attachment."*

*Close-up of chain drive mechanism, which was popular on motor trucks before "worm" drive was developed.*

*Edward T. Hewitt at the wheel, 3½ Ton Worm Drive, 18-foot body.*

Edward T. Hewitt at the wheel.

EDITOR'S NOTE: Bob Keystone and I were classmates at Grattan Grammar School. His father was one of the Keystone Brothers, manufacturers of leather goods. See signs on display windows. Edward T. Hewitt, standing near entrance, circa 1918.

*Edward T. Hewitt at the wheel, San Francisco.*

*What appears to be a single large tank was actually several tank compartments for delivering gasoline, distillate and oil.*

*3½ Ton Vinegar Tanker. There must have been a lot of sauerkraut produced in San Francisco in those days.*

*At left, William A. Hewitt.*

*Mattei was an old, established California name in the San Francisco and Santa Barbara areas.*

*Hewitt-Ludlow 2½ Ton Worm Drive Sheriff's Van, San Francisco.*

*Cable-operated dump truck designed by Edward T. Hewitt for the California State Highway Department.*

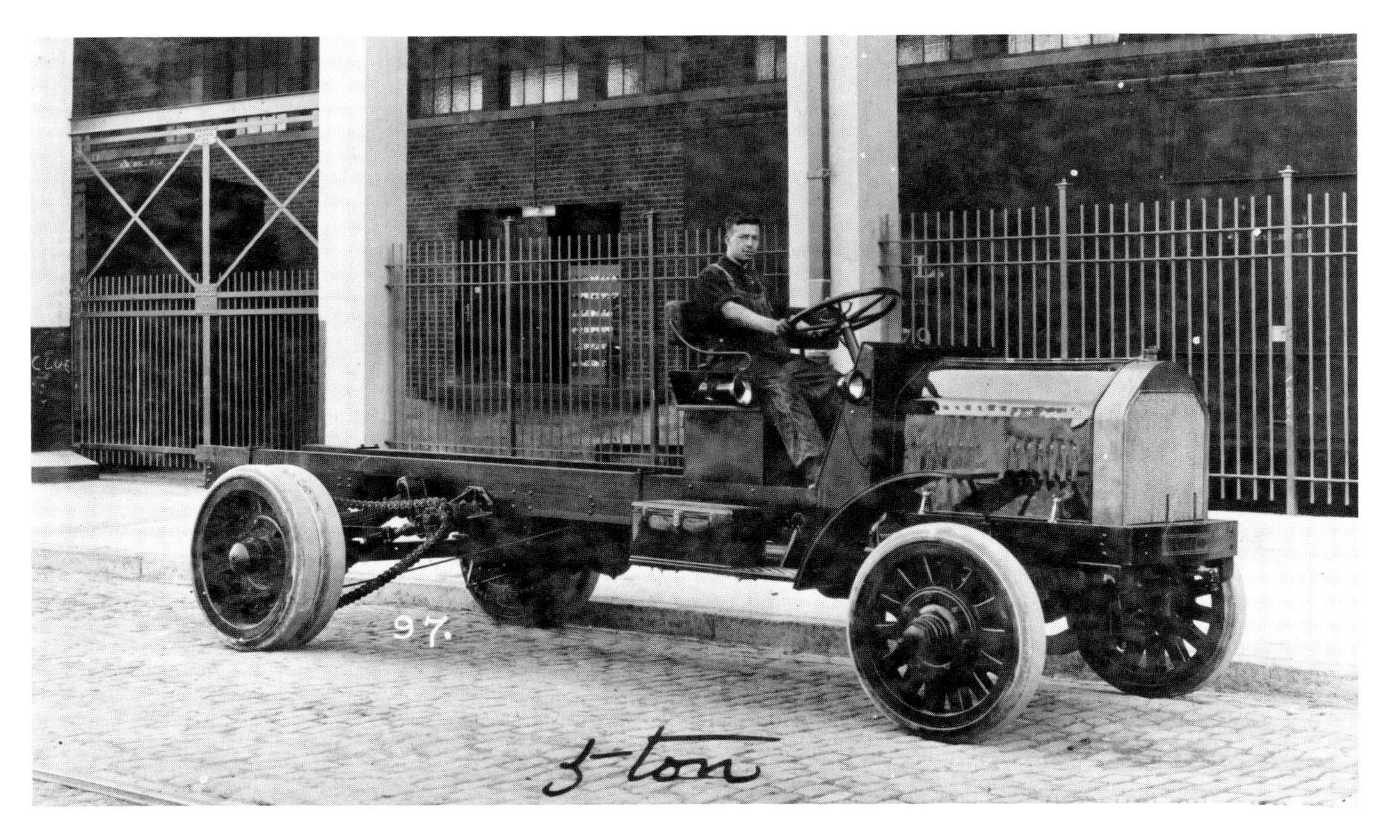


*"Chappie" Friend, Hewitt-Ludlow shop superintendent, at the wheel.*

*California was granted statehood on September 9, 1850. It was the 31st state to be admitted to the Union. This dazzling temporary arch was erected in San Francisco's Civic Center in 1925 as part of the celebration of California's Diamond Jubilee. Photograph by Edward Hewitt.*

EDITOR'S NOTE: Following World War I city-sponsored programs in San Francisco were used to stimulate local business. For example, this mobile business caravan in San Francisco's Civic Center was sponsored by companies such as Hewitt-Ludlow. The theme of the parade was "Support California Industries—Build California Payrolls—Give Employment To Our Heroes." Hewitt-Ludlow 5 ton truck was pulling three trailers displaying local products.

EDITOR'S NOTE: Hewitt-Ludlow trucks for Tubbs Cordage Co. delivered rope throughout California.

*Mother's Bread operated a fleet of Hewitt-Ludlow trucks as delivery vans for its products.*

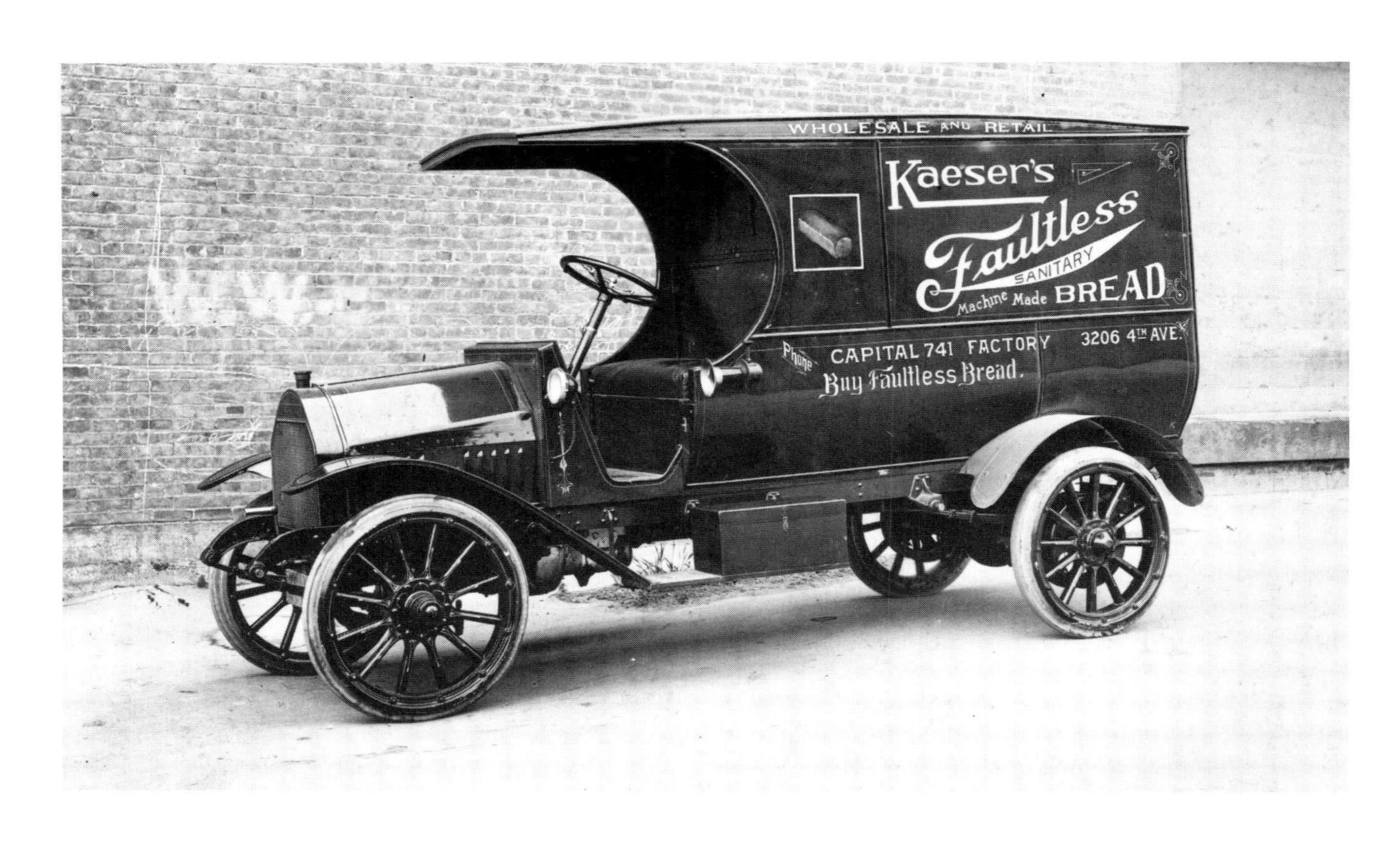

*Hewitt-Ludlow 2 ton truck used in parade promoting the Home Industry Show, 1919.*

*Top-of-the-line commercial trucks for Home Industry Show.*

*Special retail delivery truck customized for Hires Root Beer, 1914.*

*The Majestic Bottling Co. distributed a number of different soft drinks.*

*Picking up grain at a railroad siding for local flour mills.*

*Hewitt-Ludlow truck and trailer, manufactured at 901 Indiana Street, San Francisco.*

*Delivery truck from produce house hauling a load of sacked potatoes.*

*In front of the fire house of the Sausalito Volunteer Fire Department, Marin County. Hewitt-Ludlow fire engine, early 1920s.*

*Early 1920s Hewitt-Ludlow fire engine in Sausalito, California.*

*At right, Edward T. Hewitt, outside the Third and Townsend Street Railroad Station, San Francisco.*

*Fleischmann Co. 3½ ton delivery truck...might be carrying a load of more than 3½ tons.*

*Two ton Rainer Beer delivery truck, manufactured by Hewitt-Ludlow.*

*Hewitt-Talbot motor trucks followed the Hewitt-Ludlow line, early 1920s.*

*Hewitt-Talbot truck, San Francisco, early 1920s.*

*A Hewitt-Talbot truck built for Pope & Talbot Lumber Company. William A. Hewitt, standing at right. Photograph was taken in 1921 by Beaver Engraving Co. of Portland, Oregon.*

*William A. Hewitt, standing by a low-bed trailer, pulled by a Hewitt-Talbot chain drive tractor.*

*A Fordson tractor, adapted by Hewitt to pull a low-bed trailer which was easier to load than the standard high-bed truck. This was before elevated loading docks had been thought of.*

*Bill and Ed Hewitt, with a Fordson tractor, circa 1925, modified by Hewitt-Talbot. The company's plant, in background, was on 11th Street near Market, San Francisco.*

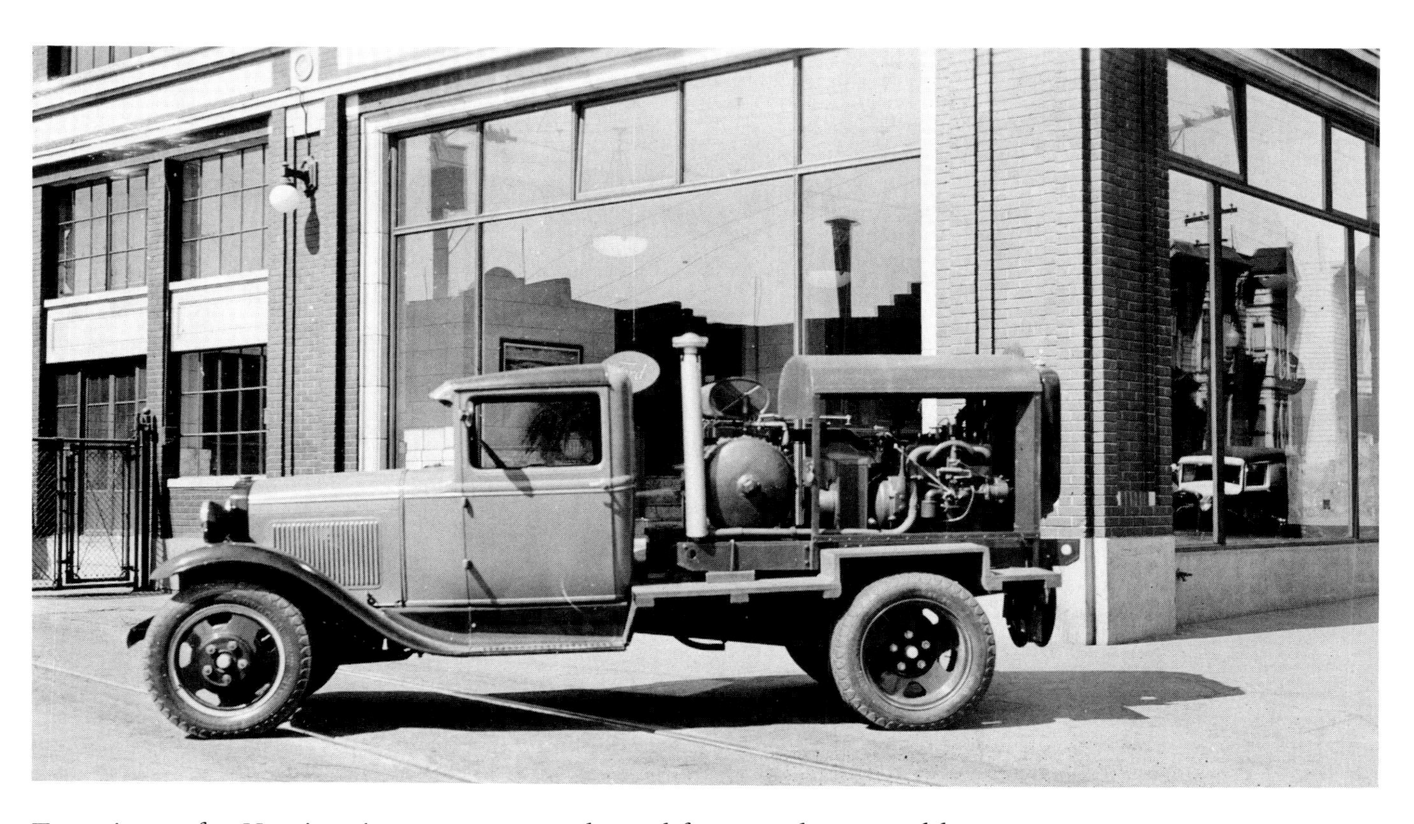

*Two views of a Hewitt air compressor, adapted from and powered by Ford engines, mounted on a Ford truck, 1932.*

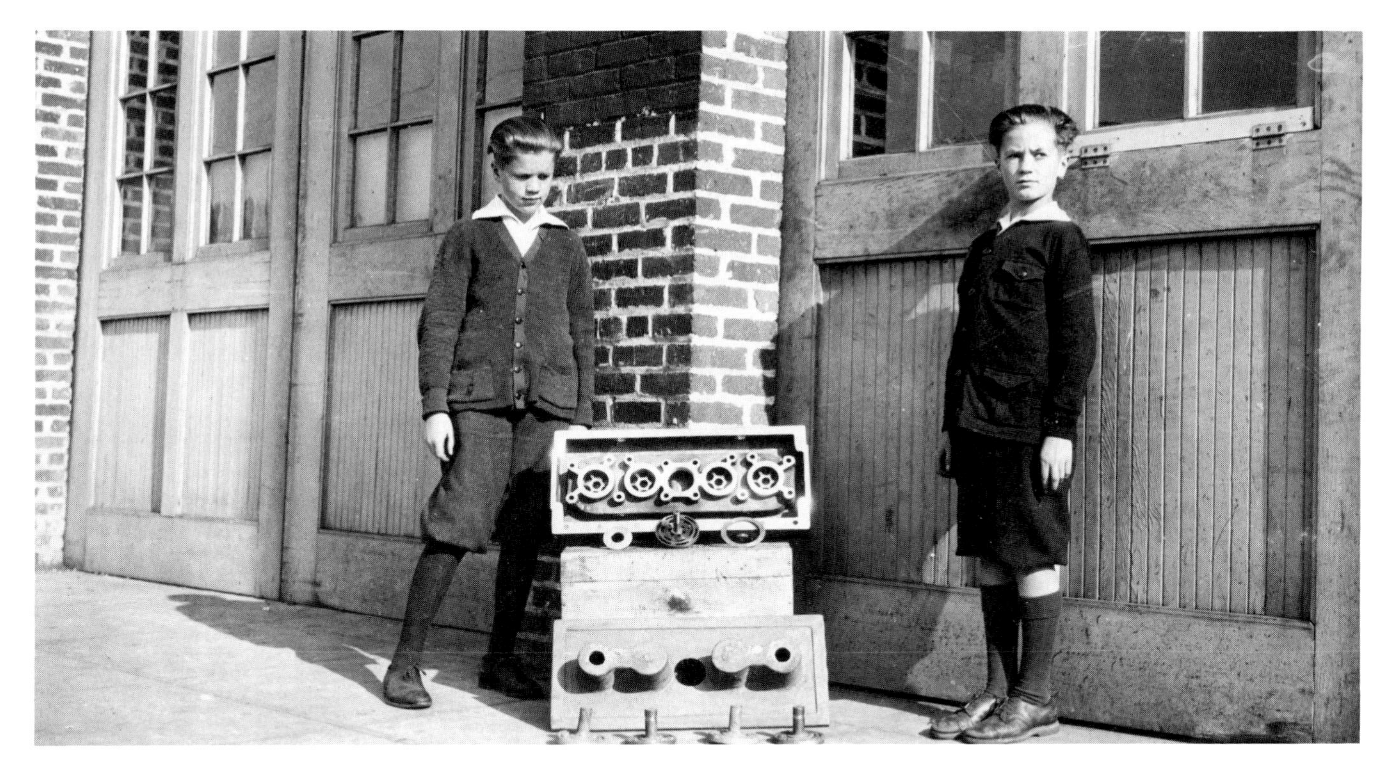

*Ed and Bill Hewitt in front of Hewitt-Talbot plant on 11th Street, San Francisco.*

*Hewitt air compressor, at a California gold mine. William A. Hewitt, at right, early 1930s.*

*Hewitt air compressor, mounted on a 2-wheel trailer, San Francisco, early 1930s.*

EDITOR'S NOTE: A small vignette of automotive history, published by *Motorland* (the American Automobile Association magazine) in 1959, shows part of a Hewitt-Ludlow exhibit in the right foreground in the Oakland Auditorium, early 1920s.

*The 1959* Motorland *caption for this photograph read: "San Francisco's own Hewitt-Ludlow trucks offered worm or chain drive in 6 sizes, and Henry Ford was still turning out his Model T's when this automobile show came to Oakland's huge auditorium in the 1920s."*

THE CALIFORNIA
SCHOOL OF MECHANICAL ARTS
FOUNDED BY JAMES LICK
SIXTEENTH AND UTAH STREETS

SAN FRANCISCO, May 15, 1930

Mr. Ed. T. Hewitt,
4724-17th Street,
San Francisco, Calif.

Dear Mr. Hewitt:

Will you kindly let me know in what year it was that you went to Los Angeles to supervise the inauguration of the shopwork in the Polytechnic High School of Los Angeles? The University of California is gathering information regarding the place of the Lick, Wilmerding and Lux Schools in the pioneer work of industrial education in California, and the fact that you went from this school to Los Angeles is a matter of interest to the University. The man who is preparing the material telephoned to me yesterday asking for this information. I thought that I could get it from our records, but they are not altogether clear and I want to be absolutely right, so that the information will check up with whatever the University may find by asking the Los Angeles people when their Polytechnic High School was established.

Yours very truly,

Geo. A. Merrill

Geo. A. Merrill,
Director.

EDITOR'S NOTE: As late as 1930 the California School of Mechanical Arts was corresponding with Edward T. Hewitt, who had completed his teaching duties at CSMA in 1906.

# HEWITT FAMILY PHOTOGRAPHS

*A rare, early photograph of our grandparents: Mary Rebecca Jones Hewitt (1841-1904) and William Alexander Hewitt (1838-1910). The pouting little boy, wearing a Victorian-style dress, is Uncle Bill Hewitt, who was born on August 7, 1870. The original of this photograph was by Taylor's Photographic Studio, Glasgow, Scotland.*

*A handwritten note on the back of the original of this photograph reads: "Rebecca Jones, June 1861." She married William A. Hewitt, our grandfather, four years later, on September 13, 1865.*

*Our grandmother, as a young woman, Mary Rebecca Jones (Hewitt). Photographed in England.*

The following eight photographs, taken in the first decade of the 20th century, include key members of two generations of the Hewitt family on whom this book is based.

Mary Rebecca Jones Hewitt—1841-1904
William Alexander Hewitt—1838-1910

and their six children:

Edward Thomas Hewitt—1868-1933
William Alexander Hewitt—1870-1950
Mary Hewitt—1872-1925
Arthur Hewitt—1874-1912
Margaret Kathleen Hewitt (McLeod)—1877-1946
Daisy Leo Hewitt (Hobart)—1881-1964

*Mary Rebecca Jones Hewitt, grandmother, San Francisco, circa 1902.*

*William Alexander Hewitt, grandfather, San Francisco, circa 1902.*

*Edward Thomas Hewitt, father, San Francisco, circa 1905.*

*Uncle William Alexander Hewitt, San Francisco, circa 1910.*

*Aunt Mary Hewitt, San Francisco, circa 1905.*

*Uncle Arthur Hewitt, San Francisco, circa 1908.*

*Aunt Margaret Hewitt McLeod, Portland, Oregon, circa 1908.*

*Aunt Daisy Hewitt Hobart. Photographed in Fresno, California, circa 1909.*

VIEW OF SAN FRANCISCO, FORMERLY YERBA BUENA, IN 1846-7
BEFORE THE DISCOVERY OF GOLD


EDITOR'S NOTE: March 26, 1847, Immanual Charles Christian Russ, with his wife, Christina, and their nine children, arrived in San Francisco aboard the U.S. Transport Loo Choo, from New York, via Cape Horn with Col. Stevenson's volunteers. The eldest of the nine children, Adolphus Russ, then 25 years old, was the great-grandfather of Viola Koster Hewitt, wife of Edward T. Hewitt, Jr. The Loo Choo is the third sailing ship from the right.

Note that caption 12 on the lithograph reads: "Residence of the Russ Family." The site of that house is now (1989) in the heart of San Francisco's financial district. San Francisco's first sky-scraper, 34 stories high, was built there in the 1920s, and it still stands. It was named the Russ Building. Viola Koster Hewitt's grandmother, Lilly Russ Bruckmann, was born in the house that originally stood on that site.

# Highlights of San Francisco History and Family Activities

1776-1906

(Note: The city was originally called Yerba Buena.)

| Dates | Family Happenings and Historical Events |
|---|---|
| June 19, 1776 | A military Presidio was founded in Yerba Buena |
| October 9, 1776 | Mission Dolores founded |
| 1826 | California becomes a part of Mexico |
| June 25, 1835 | First civilian building erected in Yerba Buena |
| October 1835 | W. Richardson draws first official plan for the Pueblo of Yerba Buena |
| 1845 | Grandfather, Jean Adolphe Brun, is born in Creuse, France |
| January 30, 1847 | Yerba Buena renamed San Francisco |
| | End of Mexican War; U.S. flag is raised above the plaza of Portsmouth Square in San Francisco |
| March 26, 1847 | Viola K. Hewitt's great-great-grandfather, I.C.C. Russ, with his wife and their nine children, arrive in San Francisco aboard U.S. Transport Loo Choo. Population of city is 200, living in 25 houses. |
| 1847 | Immanuel Charles Christian Russ purchases land on Montgomery Street and builds a house |
| Late 1847 | Portsmouth Square schoolhouse is the first public school in San Francisco |
| January 24, 1848 | Gold discovered on American River in the Sacramento Valley of California |
| 1848 | Treaty of Hidalgo; California is ceded by Mexico to the U.S. |
| February 2, 1848 | First Chinese arrive in San Francisco |
| Summer-Fall, 1848 | San Francisco booms as first Gold Rush crowds arrive |
| November 1848 | First post office opens |
| 1848-1849 | Russ family becomes the most extensive owner of real property in San Francisco |
| 1849 | Great-grandfather, Louis Mermoud arrives in San Francisco from Poliez Le Grand, near Lausanne, Switzerland |
| April 1, 1850 | Local government established in San Francisco County |
| April 15, 1850 | San Francisco is incorporated as a city |
| May 1850 | The city begins "planking" its streets |
| May 11, 1850 | Begin construction of first brick building in San Francisco |
| October-November 1850 | Cholera epidemic |
| End of 1850 | Population estimated 20,000 to 25,000 |
| May 4, 1851 | Fire destroys 18 square blocks of San Francisco, nearly three-quarters of city; $12 million in damages |
| 1851 | Adolphus Russ marries Frances Simon (Viola Koster Hewitt's great-grandparents) |
| 1852 | Lilly Russ is born, Viola Koster Hewitt's grandmother |

| | |
|---|---|
| 1852 | Woodward's What Cheer House hotel opens on Sacramento Street |
| | First stage line from North Beach to South Park |
| | Fourteen volunteer fire companies are active in San Francisco |
| 1853 | Population estimate: 50,000, of whom only 8,000 are women |
| July 17, 1853 | Construction begins on St. Mary's Church at California Street and Grant Avenue |
| November 1854 | First cobblestone paving is layed on Washington Street between Grant and Kearny |
| | Gas is introduced as a fuel, and gas flame street lighting is made possible |
| 1855 | Vicinity of Sacramento Street and Grant Avenue is called "Little China" |
| October 1855 | Customs House on Battery Street is completed; cost: $850,000 |
| 1856 | Maquire's Opera House opens |
| August 1856 | First high school in San Francisco enrolls 35 boys, 45 girls |
| 1857 | San Francisco Water Works opens |
| | Spring Valley Water Company purchases Chrystal Springs water shed |
| 1860 | Grandmother, Emma Mermoud (Brun) is born in San Francisco. Population: 56,802 |
| December 1860 | Work begins on Market Street Railroad |
| 1862 | Lick House hotel opens |
| 1863 | Population estimated: 115,000 |
| July 1863 | Water from Spring Valley Water Company enters San Francisco from Lake Honda |
| September 1863 | Railroad and ferry connections from San Francisco to Oakland start to operate |
| | First street rail cars are placed in service |
| 1864 | Land is appropriated for Golden Gate Park and city cemeteries |
| 1870 | Population of San Francisco: 149,473 |
| | Work on Golden Gate Park begins |
| August 2, 1873 | A cable car has first trial run on Clay Street between Kearny and Jones |
| 1874 | Jean Adolphe Brun settles in the San Francisco area (Napa Valley) |
| 1875 | Palace Hotel opens; city growth extends beyond Van Ness Avenue |
| 1880 | Population: 233,959<br>City growth pushing into Pacific Heights |
| | Emma Mermoud marries Jean A. Brun in San Francisco (our grandparents) |
| 1883 | William A. Hewitt, with his wife and six children, arrives from England to reside in San Francisco |
| | Sutro plants trees on Twin Peaks, to start Sutro Forest |
| January 12, 1888 | Population: 298,997 |
| April 18, 1906 | Earthquake and fire destroy much of San Francisco |

*Aunt Daisy Hewitt, left, listens as her sister, Margaret, plays the piano.*

*Uncle Bill and Aunt Sophie Hewitt (second and third from left, seated) having fun at a festive dinner with a group of friends, at the Bismarck Cafe, San Francisco, circa 1909.*

*At Uncle Ralph Hobart's residence, Fresno, California, 1910. Left to right: Mary Hewitt, Arthur Hewitt, Margaret Hewitt, Daisy Hewitt Hobart, Dr. Sophie K. Hewitt (sitting), Jeannette Brun Hewitt, Edward Hewitt, William A. Hewitt. The child is Cousin Mary Hobart.*

*At the Ralph Hobart residence, Fresno, California, 1910. Left to right: Mother (Jeannette Brun Hewitt), Aunt Sophie (Dr. Sophie K. Hewitt), Uncle Bill (William Hewitt) holding Cousin Mary Hobart, Aunt Mary Hewitt, Aunt Daisy Hewitt Hobart, Aunt Margaret Hewitt McLeod, Uncle Arthur Hewitt.*

*San Francisco street scene, at the intersection of Kearny, Market, Third and Geary Streets, circa 1906. Photograph by Edward Hewitt.*

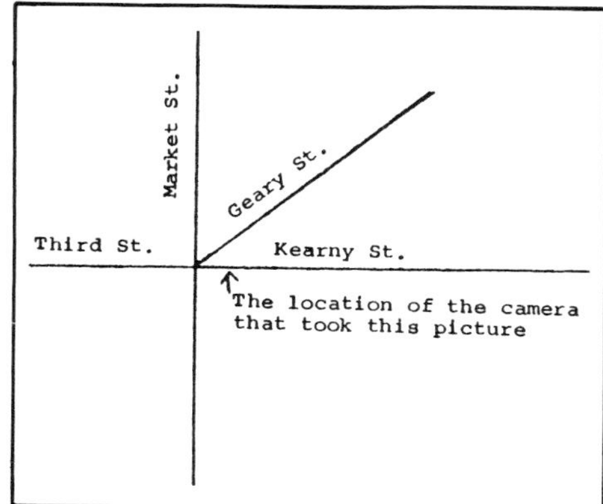

*Jeannette Brun Hewitt strolls past sidewalk flower vendors on Kearny Street, San Francisco, 1906. Photograph by Edward Hewitt.*

*Mission Dolores, San Francisco, was founded on October 9, 1776. Photograph by Edward Hewitt, 1905.*

*Early days of Fisherman's Wharf, San Francisco, before it was sheltered by breakwaters. Photograph by Edward Hewitt, 1910.*

*Stagecoach that transported William Hewitt to a mining camp in northern California, early 1900s.*

*William Hewitt (Uncle Bill), standing, center, at a California mining camp, early 1900s.*

*William Hewitt (Uncle Bill), standing directly behind the campfire, at a California mining camp, early 1900s.*

*Aunt Daisy, left, rear, and her sister, Margaret, somewhere in the California countryside, early 1900s. The driver and other passenger are not identified. Note: The carriage must have had more than a two-horse hitch because reins are visibly extending ahead of the pair of horses shown in photograph.*

*Grandmother Mary Rebecca Jones Hewitt and her daughters, Daisy and Mary, San Francisco, circa 1900.*

*Left to right: Delphine Brun, Daisy Hewitt, Julie Brun, Mary Hewitt, California, early 1900s.*

*Father, Edward T. Hewitt, San Francisco, early 1900s, in the brief period during which he wore a mustache.*

*Edward Hewitt, Sr., and son, Edward, Jr., San Francisco, 1912.*

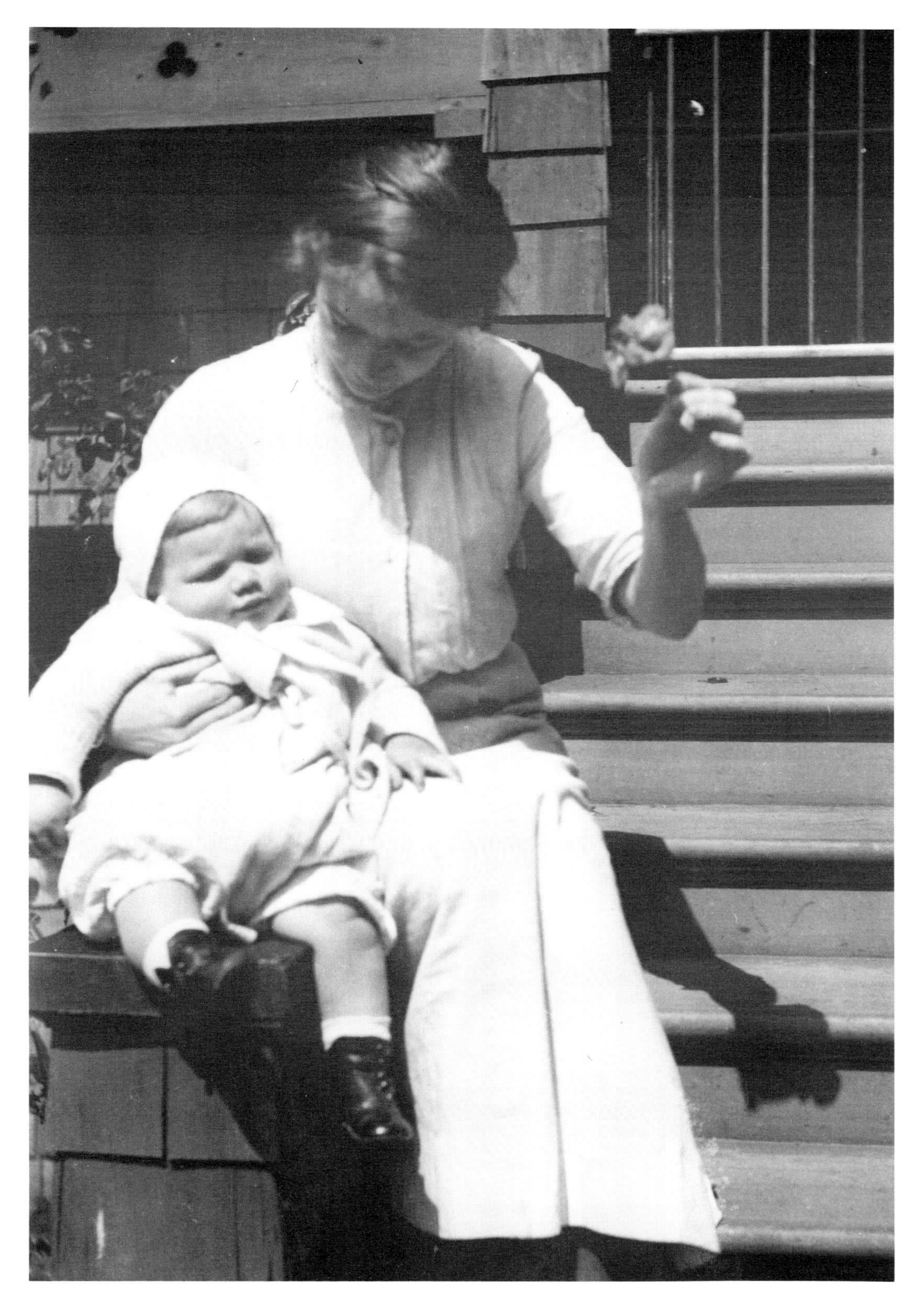

*Jeannette Brun Hewitt and her first son, Edward, Jr. (born April 5, 1912), San Francisco.*

*Christmas dinner at Uncle Bill Hewitt's house, 32nd Avenue at El Camino Del Mar, Sea Cliff, San Francisco, 1913. Left to right: Aunt Mary Hewitt, unidentified, Arthur's friend, Arthur Hewitt, Daisy Hewitt Hobart, Mary Hobart (Daisy's daughter), Uncle Bill Hewitt, unidentified, Dr. Sophie Kobicke Hewitt, Edward Hewitt with his young son, Ed, sitting on his lap, Jeannette Brun Hewitt, Ralph Hobart, unidentified.*

*William A. Hewitt and his brother, Edward T. Hewitt, ham it up behind a photographer's cardboard cutout, San Francisco, early 1900s.*

*Daisy Hewitt Hobart at top of pyramid; Delphine Brun, left, standing with friends, California, early 1900s.*

*Uncle Arthur Hewitt, a member of the Olympic Club wrestling team, San Francisco, circa 1900.*

*Sisters Mary and Daisy Hewitt, Fresno, California, circa 1910.*

*William A. Hewitt, left, Edward T. Hewitt, Sr., right, with their uncle, Edward Thomas Jones, brother of our grandmother, Mary Rebecca Jones Hewitt, in front of Eleventh Street plant where Hewitt-Talbot trucks were manufactured, San Francisco, mid-1920s.*

*Our Great-Uncle Edward T. Jones, San Francisco, brother of Mary Rebecca Jones Hewitt.*

Editor's Note: Ed, Deets and I were well acquainted with our Great-Uncle Edward Jones during the 1920s, but we never had the pleasure of meeting our Great-Uncle George Hewitt, who lived in Michigan.

*Edward T. Hewitt's Uncle George C. Hewitt, Port Huron, Michigan.*

*Daisy Hewitt Hobart and her daughter, Mary, Fresno, California, 1909.*

*Jeannette Brun Hewitt with her three children, Adrienne (Deets) born May 13, 1916, Ed and Bill, San Francisco.*

*Jeannette Brun Hewitt, with her children, Ed, Adrienne (Deets) and Bill, San Francisco, circa 1917.*

*Adrienne (Deets), Bill and Ed Hewitt, San Francisco, circa 1920.*

*Bill and Ed Hewitt, with Rodin's* Thinker, *Golden Gate Park, San Francisco, 1919.*

*Ed and Bill Hewitt, Golden Gate Park, San Francisco, 1919.*

*Over the years, Golden Gate Park offered many attractions to children growing up in San Francisco. It even offered Bill, Ed and Deets Hewitt an opportunity to get acquainted with a baby elephant.*

*Cousin John McLeod, as a young boy in Portland, Oregon, early 1920s.*

*Uncle Bill Hewitt in his new fig orchard, San Joaquin Valley, California, circa 1919. Inset: Cousin Betty Hobart in Uncle Bill's new orchard.*

*Ralph and Daisy Hobart and daughter, Mary, in front of their house in Fresno, California, circa 1910.*

*Uncle Ralph Hobart and daughter, Betty, Riverbank, California, circa 1920.*

*Cousin Mary Hobart, Riverbank, California, circa 1920.*

*Cousin Betty Hobart in her "Egyptian Period," circa 1921.*

*Left: Aunt Daisy Hewitt Hobart and husband, Uncle Ralph. Right: Margaret Hewitt and her brother, Edward, circa 1910.*

*Mary and William Hewitt, sister and brother, at a "children's party," San Francisco.*

*Bette Hobart, Topeka, Kansas. (Note new spelling of Betty.)*

*Uncle Bill Hewitt, The Gardener, circa 1915.*

*Standing: Edward Hewitt, Margaret Hewitt McLeod, Daisy Hewitt Hobart, Mary Hewitt, William Hewitt. Sitting: Ed Hewitt, Deets Hewitt, Cousin Betty Hobart, Bill Hewitt, San Francisco, circa 1922.*

*Jeannette Brun Hewitt with her son, Ed, in the tree, in Uncle Ralph Hobart's orchard near Riverbank, California, circa 1919.*

*Bill, Deets and Ed Hewitt, Mill Valley, circa 1919.*

*Ed and Bill Hewitt on the steam engine of the Tamalpias, Muir Woods Railway in Mill Valley, Marin County, California, circa 1919. It was affectionately called "The Crookedest Railway in the World" because its right-of-way up the mountain included so many curves, and almost no straight-away tracks.*

*Ed and Bill Hewitt, Mill Valley, California.*

*Ed and Bill Hewitt, ready to go to the top of Mount Tamalpias, Marin County. The passenger cars on the Tamalpias Railway were all open. (Note: The T-shirt was not yet invented.)*

*Waiting at the Mill Valley Station of the Northwestern Pacific Railroad. Uncle Ralph Hobart at the wheel, with Aunt Daisy in back seat. Deets Hewitt is between them; standing on pavement, Cousin Mary Hobart with Ed and Bill Hewitt, early 1920s.*

*Deets Hewitt, Uncle Bill, Ed Hewitt, Jeannette Brun Hewitt, Bill Hewitt, Mill Valley, circa 1920. Since Dad was almost always behind the camera, informal photographs of him were a bit rare.*

*Edward T. Hewitt, Sr., at the newly-opened Palace of the Legion of Honor, San Francisco, mid-1920s.*

*Edward T. Hewitt, Sr., San Francisco, circa 1927.*

*Uncle Bill Hewitt, left, Deets Hewitt, Aunt Ruth Brun, Grandmother Emma Brun at right in rear seat. Front seat: Bill Hewitt at wheel, with Ed; Aunt Ruth's father, Mr. Finnell, standing at right. In front of Uncle Bill's house, Sea Cliff, San Francisco.*

*Uncle Bill and Aunt Sophie, with a friend, in front of their house, San Francisco. The hills of Sausalito are in the background.*

*Left to right: Cousin Mary Hobart, Ed and Bill Hewitt, Cousin Betty Hobart, Deets Hewitt, at Uncle Bill's house, Sea Cliff, San Francisco, gathered on the lawn to watch the U.S. "Great White Fleet" sail through the Golden Gate, circa 1921. This view of the entrance to San Francisco Bay was perfect, before houses were built across the street (El Camino Del Mar).*

*At Uncle Bill's house. At left: Uncle Bill and his niece, Betty Hobart. Ed Hewitt in near front seat; Bill Hewitt, center front; and Mr. Finnell (Ruth Brun's father) at the wheel; Grandmother Emma Brun is in near back seat; Deets Hewitt, far side of back seat. Cousin Mary and Aunt Daisy are at top right of stairs; Aunt Sophie, center; Aunt Mary at left. (Note: Of the automobiles manufactured at that time, only the Pierce-Arrow had its headlights faired into the front fenders. It was a uniquely distinctive design.)*

*Ed and Bill Hewitt on the deck of a Sausalito ferry on San Francisco Bay, long before the Golden Gate Bridge was built.*

*Deets, Bill and Ed Hewitt with their mother on the shore line of San Francisco Bay, near Sausalito, California. Angel Island and a ferry boat are in the background.*

*Deets, Bill and Ed Hewitt on the Sausalito shore line of San Francisco Bay, early 1920s. One of the last active square-rigged sailing ships is in the background.*

*Bill, Deets and Ed Hewitt with their Uncle Bill, Mill Valley, California, 1921. Inset: William Hewitt with his sister, Daisy Hewitt Hobart, February 28, 1931.*

*Jeannette Brun Hewitt and her children, Deets, Bill and Ed, at Aunt Mary's house, Mill Valley.*

*Ed and Bill Hewitt, Aida de Veuve, Deets Hewitt, Aida's poodle, Sue and Ruth Brun, in Golden Gate Park, San Francisco, circa 1923. Aida and Deets are still very close friends in 1989.*

*Deets, Bill and Ed Hewitt, San Francisco, admiring flowers they arranged for their mother, circa 1924.*

*Ed Hewitt.*

*Bill and Ed Hewitt with Clifford Longfellow.*

*During long summer vacations in Marin County, one of the pastimes that Ed and Bill enjoyed most was sandlot baseball. They played it almost every day with boys who lived nearby.*

*Second from left, Bill Hewitt; fourth from left, Ed Hewitt.*

EDITOR'S NOTE: Swimming pools were scarce in Marin County in the 1920s, so Ed and Bill took a break from baseball once a week to swim at the San Raphael Public Swimming Pool.

*Family group: Jeannette and Edward Hewitt with their three children, Ed, Bill and Deets, San Francisco, mid-1920s.*

*Grattan Grammar School, San Francisco, 1922. Bill Hewitt in second row from top, second from right.*

*Grattan Grammar School, San Francisco, 1923. Top row: Fourth from left, Virgil Muller; fifth from left, Jane Fairweather; second row from top: first left, Bob Ridley; second from right, Harlow Williams; third row from top: third from left, Bill Hewitt; fifth from left, Hazel Reinhardt; bottom row: fourth from left, Wentworth Sankey; fifth from left, Ruth Zellars; sixth from left, Gordon Wayne; seventh from left, James Phelan.*

*Grattan Grammar School, San Francisco, 1925. Second row from top, fourth, fifth, sixth from left: Bill Hewitt, Bob Ridley, Bob Keystone.*

*Deets Hewitt's 1925 class picture at Grattan Grammar School.*
*Deets is sitting at the far right end of the bottom row.*

EDITOR'S NOTE: Our family's affectionate name for Adrienne was "Petite Soeur." As a small child Adrienne had difficulty in pronouncing those French words, so her familiar name became "Deets," a long lasting familiar name that evolved from her own lips.

*Grattan Grammar School Class of 1927. Top row, left to right: Robert Addicott, Bob Ridley, Raye Watts, Leo Murphy, Howard Markwart, Loretta Brady, Donald Hearst, Billy Johns; second row, left to right: Frances Simmons, Gordon Lee, Johanna Barman, Sarah Hamlin, Leslie Winant, Nancy Ringol, George Kurtz, Dana Kistler, Violet Davis; third row, left to right: Richard James, Phillip Warren, Joe Durkin, Martin Berizi, Emanuel Rosenblat, Norma Tyson; bottom row, left to right: Bill Hewitt, Earl Smythe, Edwin Miller, Dick Danford, Stanford Christian.*

*Ed, Deets and Bill Hewitt in front of their primary school, Grattan Grammar, San Francisco, mid 1920s.*

*Budding architectural buff, Bill Hewitt, with a "model house and garden" that he "built," San Francisco, early 1920s.*

*Ed, Deets and Bill Hewitt with their mother, San Francisco, early 1920s.*

*In July 1924, Ed and Bill Hewitt accompanied their father on a visit to HMS Hood, the largest battleship in the world, which was anchored in San Francisco Bay together with other British warships. In a letter from Edward Hewitt, Sr., to his sister, Daisy, he described his "mingled feelings of pride" to see such an important British battleship in company with U.S. warships.*

July 21/24

Larkspur, Marin County
Calif.
Until end of July

S.A. ans. July 21/24

My Dear Sister Daisy

Thought you would like some (6) snap shots of us boys on the good old battleship, H. M. S. Hood in San Francisco Bay recently.

It was with mingled feelings of pride to see such a ship in company with several other British Warships, and U. S. war ships I assure you. Well Billie, and Ed and yours truly managed to get aboard after all kinds of attempts to do so. Met the sailors and marines, saw all that we was permitted to see, and returned in the Admiral's private gig or launch, that pleased the boys immensely. They sat, one each side of a young officer in charge of the gig.

I will have to tell you all about it some time, its a real story I tell you. Hope you and your Dear family are jolly well dont you know, remember us to [nieces] cousins Mary Betty, and tell Ralph we hope the pictures will interest him also. Vacation time for the family is hurrying along, so they must enjoy it all possible now.

We all send you our love, affectionately your brother
Edward.

*Letter from Edward T. Hewitt to his sister, Daisy, July 21, 1924.*

*An Army officer on horseback observes the scene.*

*Crissy Field, in the Presidio of San Francisco, on the shore of San Francisco Bay, early 1920s. Bill and Ed Hewitt made their first flight in this ancient biplane, squeezed into one of the two open cockpit seats. The flight took them across the Golden Gate and back to Crissy Field. Ed's leather helmet was loaned to him by the pilot.*

*Round-the-world fliers land at Crissy Field, San Francisco Presidio in April 1924, on their way to Seattle for official start of flight. Photograph by Edward Hewitt, Sr.*

Editor's Note: The first round-the-world flight took place in 1924. Four Douglas World Cruisers, with interchangeable wheel and float landing gear, started from Seattle on April 6 and flew west via the Aleutians, Japan, India, Europe, Iceland, Greenland and the United States. Only two of the aircraft completed the trip, on September 28. There were no human casualties. Elapsed time for the 27,534 miles was 175 days, which included 15 days, 11 hours and 7 minutes flying time. The flight was sponsored by the U.S. Army. The pilots who successfully completed the round-the-world flight were Captain Lowell H. Smith and Lieutenant Leslie P. Arnold flying the *Chicago*, and Lieutenants Erick H. Nelson and John Harding flying the *New Orleans*.

*Bill, Uncle Bill and Ed Hewitt in Belvedere, Marin County. Tiburon is in the background, mid-1920s.*

*Bill, Deets and Ed Hewitt on San Francisco Bay near Tiburon. Corinthian Yacht Club in background.*

*Ed, Deets and Bill Hewitt on the small ferry boat that plied between Sausalito, Belvedere and Tiburon on San Francisco Bay, mid-1920s.*

*Deets and Ed Hewitt, sister and brother, Ocean Beach, San Francisco, mid-1920s. Dutch windmill pumped water into the lakes in Golden Gate Park.*

*Deets and Bill Hewitt with their father, Yosemite National Park, mid-1920s.*

*In front of their family residence at 4718 Seventeenth Street, San Francisco, Ed and Bill Hewitt, with their mother who designed the house. Early 1920s. Inset: The Hewitt house, photographed in its 80th year.*

*Deets, Bill and Ed Hewitt at 4718 Seventeenth Street, San Francisco, mid-1920s. The house was built by their parents in 1908.*

*Ed Hewitt, Jr., a member of the Lowell High School Symphony Orchestra, San Francisco, mid-1920s.*

*Ed Hewitt, Uncle Bill, Bill Hewitt, Betty Hobart, Deets Hewitt, Golden Gate Park, San Francisco, mid-1920s.*

*Ed and Bill Hewitt at the Ocean Beach end of Golden Gate Park, San Francisco. The small sailing ship was the GJOA in which Roald Amundson sailed from the Atlantic to the Pacific through the Northwest Passage. The GJOA was later shipped to a museum in Norway.*

*Deets and Bill Hewitt, Japanese Tea Garden, Golden Gate Park, San Francisco.*

*Bill, Deets and Ed Hewitt at De Young Museum, Golden Gate Park, before exterior remodeling made the building look naked. The remodeling "removed the frosting from the cake" as a precaution against potentional earthquake damage that might result if a strong tremor was to shake off the brittle external decor.*

*Bill, Ed and Deets Hewitt, Egyptian Museum, San Francisco, next to the De Young Museum, Golden Gate Park, mid-1920s. During recent years, this building was torn down to make space for a museum staff parking lot. Only the two sphinxes that guarded the entrance to the museum remain in place in 1989.*

*Ed, Adrienne and Bill Hewitt, at the Palace of Fine Arts, San Francisco, late 1920s. Inset: The Palace of Fine Arts was one of the principal buildings in the Panama Pacific International Exposition of 1915 in San Francisco. It was an exposition to celebrate the opening of the Panama Canal.*

*Edward Thomas Hewitt and his son, Ed, Jr., at Palace of Fine Arts, San Francisco.*

*Bill Hewitt, Yosemite National Park, California, circa 1930. Half Dome in background.*

*Lowell High School, Hayes Street at Masonic Avenue, San Francisco. Alma Mater of Ed, Bill and Adrienne Hewitt.*

*Part of Lowell High School ROTC Battalion on parade, San Francisco, 1926. Ed Hewitt is circled (under the Company E flag).*

*Ed Hewitt, fourth from left standing, with classmates at Lowell High School, San Francisco, circa 1928.*

*Junior class dance committee, Lowell High School. Bill Hewitt, standing at left end, 1929.*

*Edward T. Hewitt, Jr. Graduation photograph for Lowell High School yearbook, 1928.*

*Bill Hewitt's graduation photograph for Lowell High School yearbook,* The Red and White, *1931.*

*Adrienne Hewitt's graduation photograph for Lowell High School year-book, 1934.*

BENJAMIN IDE WHEELER
MEMORIAL LIBRARY

CALIFORNIA CHAPTER
OF ALPHA DELTA PHI
B E R K E L E Y
2401 RIDGE ROAD

*The Ex Libris of the Alpha Delta Phi house in Berkeley, where Bill Hewitt lived while a student at the University of California.*

*Annual photograph of members of Berkeley Chapter of Alpha Delta Phi, University of California, 1936. Top row, left to right: Harry Gibson, unidentified, unidentified, Bob Horton, Deming McClease, unidentified, Ted Ingham, John Cooper. Second row from top, left to right: Steve Smith, Bill Hewitt, Bill Briggs, John Selfridge, Ad Poett, Kirk Smith, Bud von Loben Sels, Murray Johnson, unidentified, Ron Matthews. Third row from top, left to right: Al Moffatt, Ted Atwood, Steve Goodspeed, Pete Burgess, Stan Johnson, Bob Bennett, Henry Thelen, Wally Haas, Jim Davis, Greg Stout. Bottom row, left to right: Bob Frick, Bob Law, Sam Stevens, Roy Tremereaux, Walt Krenz, Howard Allen, Ferrier Goss, unidentified.*

*Bill Hewitt at Carson Hill Mine residence of Pete Burgess' family, Melones, California, 1936. It was a gold mine in the foothills of the Sierra Nevada mountains that was a deep shaft, hard rock operation. It was a fascinating place to visit. Pete's father was superintendent of the mining operation.*

*Berkeley Chapter of Alpha Delta Phi, University of California, Class of 1937. Standing: Greg Stout, Steve Smith, Bill Hewitt, Wally Haas. Sitting: Pete Burgess, Henry Thelen, Will Goodwin, Stan Johnson.*

*Bill Hewitt, Spring 1937, at the Alpha Delta Phi House, University of California, Berkeley...a few months before graduation.*

*Horse-drawn hearse at Alpha Delta Phi House, University of California, Berkeley, 1936, en route to a parade on campus. Bill Hewitt is sitting on the box, holding Cala lilies. "Karl Marx and His Campus Red Hots" are about to be buried. Inset: Bill Hewitt sits next to the driver, while Ferrier Goss, dressed in red as the Devil, stands on top of the hearse.*

*Left to right: Will Goodwin, Steve Smith, Bill Hewitt, Greg Stout, Wally Haas, 1936. At Stan Johnson's family summer house on the Russian River.*

*Pete Burgess at the Carson Hill Gold Mine residence of his parents, Melones, California, 1935.*

*Dinner table at Alpha Delta Phi House, University of California, Berkeley, 1936.*

*Left to right: Greg Stout, Henry Thelen, Bill Hewitt, Stan Johnson, Steve Smith, Wally Haas, on lawn at Alpha Delta Phi House, University of California, Berkeley. It was a good place to live.*

*Bennet Skewes-Cox, one of Bill Hewitt's several roommates in the Alpha Delta house at Cal. Bennet was a freshman at that time and later became chapter president.*

*Left to right: Bob McNamara, Stan Johnson, Vern Goodin (Bill Hewitt classmates), on the University of California campus, Berkeley, Spring 1937.*

*Alpha Delts gathering for dinner following the 1936 initiation ceremony at the Berkeley Chapter House. Classmate Greg Stout, second from right, center.*

*Will Goodwin, getting ready to ski in New Hampshire during Christmas holidays from Johns Hopkins Medical School, 1938.*

*Classmate Henry Thelen was a warm-hearted friend, a Phi Beta Kappa, and a student philosopher with a sense of humor. He would have become an outstanding medical doctor, but sadly for us, he died of a chronic heart condition a few years after he graduated from Johns Hopkins Medical School.*

*Right, the Willard Incorporated sign caught our attention somewhere in the Southwest in 1938. Willard Goodwin (looking up at sign) and Bill Hewitt (standing) were driving from the East Coast to California at the end of the school year. Some of us wore funny hats in those days. Photograph by Bob McNamara.*

*Wally Haas busts a bronc named "Taxidermy's Triumph" in Wickenburg, Arizona.*

*University of California graduation exercises, Berkeley, California, Spring 1937, on the day Bill Hewitt received his AB degree from Cal's College of Letters and Science. His major was economics, with a minor in political science. The graduates are sitting on the football field. Families and friends are in the stands.*

*Bill Hewitt and his mother following University of California graduation exercises, Berkeley, 1937. Inset: Ed and Bill Hewitt taking an early look at the University of California campus during the mid-1920s. The Campanile is in background.*

*Two Alpha Delt legal eagles, Max Thelen and Stan Johnson, after graduation from Harvard Law School.*

*Bob McNamara, during our Christmas vacation from Harvard Business School, early 1938. Our holiday group also included Stan Johnson, who was at Harvard Law School, plus Will Goodwin and Henry Thelen from Johns Hopkins Medical School. All were classmates at the University of California, Berkeley.*

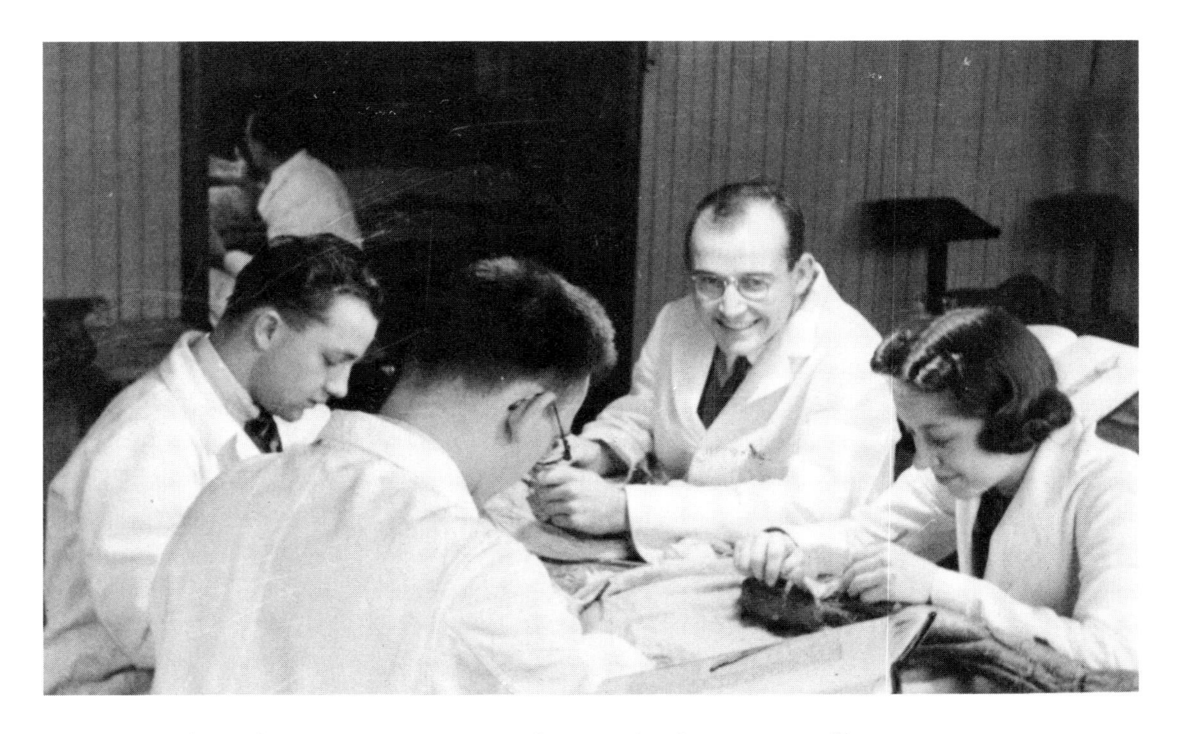

*Henry Thelen (facing camera) together with classmates, dissecting a cadaver, Johns Hopkins Medical School, 1938.*

*Top: Bill Hewitt on the rowing machine, Harvard University Boathouse, Cambridge, Massachusetts, 1938. Bottom: Bob McNamara on the rowing machine, with Bill observing. The Boathouse is on the Charles River.*

*In the French Quarter of New Orleans in 1938, Bill Hewitt, Bill Bethea and Bob McNamara were welcomed by Jean Lafite, center, the notorious French pirate. Photograph by classmate, Will Goodwin. The photograph of Will (right) was taken circa 1940, soon after he became Dr. Willard Goodwin at the Johns Hopkins Medical School.*

*Bill Hewitt and Bob McNamara, on the rim of the Grand Canyon, Arizona. A scenic stop while ferrying Wally Haas' Plymouth convertible from Harvard Business School to San Francisco. The next morning, together with Will Goodwin, we walked to the bottom of the Canyon (7½ miles) and then "climbed" out. It was easy for Bob and Will, but a struggle for me. It was like mountain climbing in reverse. The steepest part came last in the Grand Canyon. Inset: Bill Hewitt and Bob McNamara somewhere in the deep South, en route from Boston to San Francisco... dressed for eating watermelon without a fork or spoon.*

*Bill Hewitt's roommate at University of California, Berkeley.*

Could they both be Wally Haas?

*Bill Hewitt's roommate at Harvard Business School.*

*Wally Haas and Bill Hewitt on opening day of the Golden Gate Bridge, San Francisco, May 27, 1937. Only pedestrian traffic was allowed on the bridge between 6:00 a.m. and 6:00 p.m., and more than 200,000 people walked across it on that day. The main span between the two 746-foot-high towers is 4,200 feet. Total cost was $35 million. Addendum: The retail price of a pair of Levi jeans in 1937 was $1.45.*

*Bill Hewitt, left, with Munroe Deutsch, Provost of the University of California, Berkeley, at a Sunday lunch at Dan Koshland's house (Wally Haas' uncle) in Hillsborough, near San Francisco, 1937.*

*Early days in Stern Grove, San Francisco, circa 1939. Left to right, standing: Albert Bender, Peter Burgess, unidentified, Bill Hewitt, plus three distinguished guests. Sitting: Marjorie Powell and Mrs. Sigmund Stern (Wally Haas' grandmother) who always provided an elegant picnic lunch for her friends before each Sunday afternoon performance during the summer season.*

Form 348
Rev. 1-1-40

UNITED STATES OF AMERICA
CIVIL AERONAUTICS AUTHORITY
WASHINGTON, D. C.

C-6/22/40

AIRMAN CERTIFICATE NO. 46488-40

This certifies that WILLIAM ALEXANDER HEWITT is properly qualified and is physically able to perform the duties of PRIVATE PILOT
Address 4724 17th Street San Francisco, California

| DATE OF BIRTH | WEIGHT | HEIGHT | HAIR | EYES | SEX |
|---|---|---|---|---|---|
| 8/9/14 | 175 | 6'2-3/4" | Brown | Brown | Male |

THIS CERTIFICATE is of 60 days duration and, unless the holder hereof is otherwise notified by the Authority within such period, shall continue in effect indefinitely thereafter, unless suspended or revoked by the Authority, except that it shall immediately expire (1) at the end of each TWELVE months' period after the date of issuance hereof if the holder of this certificate fails to secure an endorsement by an authorized Inspector of the Authority within the last 45 days of each such period, or (2) at any time an authorized Inspector of the Authority shall refuse to endorse this certificate after inspection or examination.

Endorsement Refused:
Date:

Inspector, Civil Aeronautics Authority

Date of Issuance SEPTEMBER 29, 1940
By direction of the Authority:
Signature: W. R. McNulty
Title: Aeronautical Inspector

This certificate is not valid unless there is attached hereto the appropriate Rating Record bearing the above number. Any alteration of this certificate is punishable by a fine of not exceeding $1,000 or imprisonment not exceeding three years, or both.

(Over)

Signature of Holder: William A. Hewitt

*Pilot license issued to William A. Hewitt after the necessary ground instruction and required flight hours, at Mills Field in September 1940. Mills Field later became San Francisco International Airport.*

Form ACA 345
(Rev. 11-1-40)

UNITED STATES OF AMERICA
DEPARTMENT OF COMMERCE
CIVIL AERONAUTICS ADMINISTRATION
WASHINGTON

AIRMAN RATING RECORD NO. 46488-40

This Rating Record is not valid unless accompanied by the appropriate certificate bearing the above number.

Name WILLIAM ALEXANDER HEWITT
Address 4724 17TH STREET, SAN FRANCISCO, CALIFORNIA

RATINGS WITH LIMITATIONS

AIRPLANE SINGLE-ENGINE LAND 0-80 H.P.

By direction of the Administrator:

(Civil Aeronautics Inspector)

SEPTEMBER 29, 1941
(Date of Issuance)

Any change of address should be endorsed on reverse side hereof but only after written notice has been mailed to the Certificate Division, Civil Aeronautics Administration, Washington, D. C. Any alteration of this form may result in the suspension or revocation of the Certificate to which this form is attached.

(Over)

*Recertification was required every twelve months by the C.A.A. This renewal was issued two months before the Japanese attacked Pearl Harbor, December 7, 1941. Bill Hewitt wanted to become a Navy pilot in World War II, but he became a Navy line officer instead due to the fact that he did not have the 20-20 vision required to become a Navy pilot.*

*Viola Koster (Hewitt), second from left, standing, as a student at the Hamlin School, San Francisco, 1928.*

*Ed Hewitt and daughter, Pamela, at Glenbrook, Lake Tahoe.*

*Ed Hewitt and Viola "Cooks" Koster (Hewitt), Yosemite, 1931.*

*Ed Hewitt in the days when men wore hats, 1930s.*

*Ed and Cooks at their wedding rehearsal, St. Peter's Episcopal Church, San Francisco, 1935.*

*Cooks at Stinson Beach during Great Depression of the 1930s.*

*Cooks Koster Hewitt, after the economic depression of the 1930s.*

*Pamela Hewitt at the ranch of her grandparents, the Harold Kosters, near Boulder Creek, Santa Cruz County, California.*

*A Sunday morning in Golden Gate Park, San Francisco, 1946.*

*Bill Hewitt with his niece, Pamela Hewitt, and nephew, Rodger Gordon.*

Editor's Note: Whenever Ed was away on a business trip, while Cooks was expecting Tina, Uncle Bill came to the rescue by taking Pam on an outing to Golden Gate Park.

*Deets and Donald Gordon with their son, Marshall, San Francisco, 1942.*

*Marshall Gordon, one year old, 1942.*

*Rodger Gordon, San Francisco, 1945.*

*Rodger Gordon celebrates the Fourth of July in Mill Valley, 1945.*

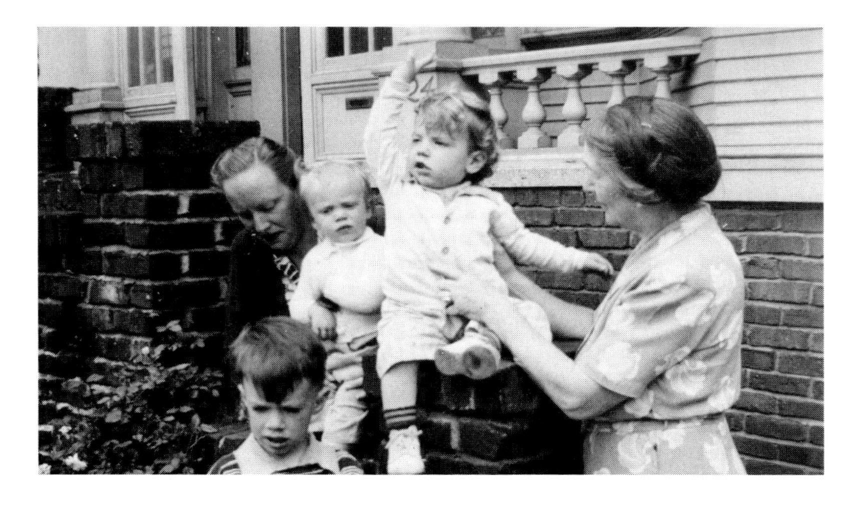

*Cooks and Pam Hewitt with Rodger Gordon and his grandmother, Jeannette Hewitt. Marshall Gordon in foreground, San Francisco, 1945.*

*Daisy Hewitt Hobart and her granddaughter, Katy Krieger, September 1942.*

*Charles and Bette Krieger and their daughter, Kathryn (Katy), June 1942.*

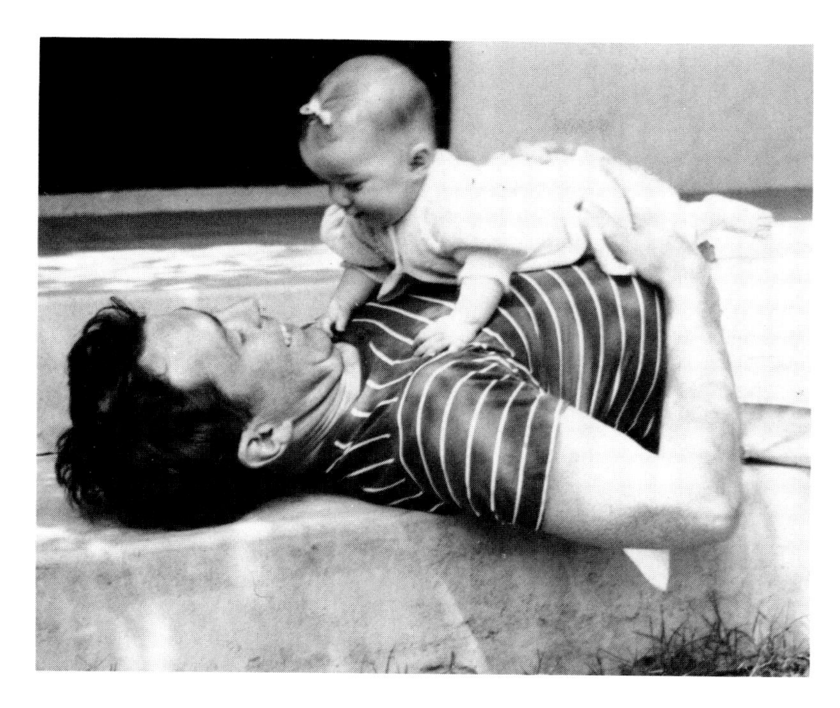

*Charles Krieger and daughter, Katy, age four months, June 1942.*

*Katy Krieger, Topeka, Kansas, April 1945.*

*Katy Krieger, center, with her cousins, Tina and Pam Hewitt, at Ed and Cooks' house for Christmas, Bronxville, New York, 1946.*

One man's experience throughout World War II, as recalled by Lt. William A. Hewitt, USNR

Honolulu Star-Bulletin 1st EXTRA

(Associated Press by Transpacific Telephone)
SAN FRANCISCO, Dec. 7.—President Roosevelt announced this morning that Japanese planes had attacked Manila and Pearl Harbor.

# WAR!

# OAHU BOMBED BY JAPANESE PLANES

SIX KNOWN DEAD, 21 INJURED, AT EMERGENCY HOSPITAL

Attack Made On Island's Defense Areas

Hundreds See City Bombed

Names of Dead and Injured

Schools Closed

Editorial

Honolulu Star-Bulletin 2nd EXTRA

# DEATHS OVER 400 ON OAHU, LATEST REPORT

TOKYO ANNOUNCES "STATE OF WAR" WITH U. S.

Japanese Raids On Guam, Panama Are Reported

Oahu Blackout Tonight; Fleet Here Moves Out to Sea

Four Waves, Start At 7:55, Oahu Hit In Many Places

Governor Proclaims National Emergency

Known Oahu Casualties

BULLETINS

Blackout For Oahu Ordered

Military Censorship On All Messages

Editorial



EDITOR'S NOTE: As described in the Introduction of this book, Bill Hewitt went directly to the Twelfth Naval District Headquarters in San Francisco on the morning of December 8, 1941, to seek active duty in the U.S. Naval Reserve. It was the same day on which President Roosevelt declared a state of war, the first day of World War II.

This effort resulted in Hewitt being commissioned as a Navy Ensign two months later. He was then immediately assigned to the Operations Office of the Twelfth Naval District.

During the ensuing months he sought sea duty, and in the fall of 1942 he was assigned to the USS St. Louis, a light cruiser. The day after that assignment, the St. Louis sailed from San Francisco to the Solomon Islands, with only one brief stopover in Noumea, New Caledonia. The action part of this story would soon begin.

*Official U.S. Navy photograph shows the USS California under attack in the shallow waters of Pearl Harbor, Hawaii, during the December 7, 1941, surprise attack by the Japanese. Eventually the California was raised, and fully repaired and modernized at Bremerton Navy Yard near Seattle. She was ready again for wartime duty in January 1944. Lt. William Hewitt served aboard the California from September 1943 until February 1946.*

*In late 1942, Ensign Bill Hewitt was assigned to the light cruiser, USS St. Louis. He served aboard that ship in the South Pacific until she was torpedoed in the Second Battle of Kula Gulf, in July 1943.*

*Here we see the USS Helena, sister ship of the St. Louis, at target practice, as photographed from the St. Louis. Note: The Helena was later sunk during the First Battle of Kula Gulf in the Solomon Islands, in July 1943, while in battle formation 1,000 yards ahead of the St. Louis.*

*Lt. JG. Bill Hewitt of USS St. Louis, on a beach walk, Espiritu Santo, New Hebrides, 1943.*

*Bill Hewitt and a friend, New Hebrides, 1943. Photograph by Lt. Barney Lewis, a shipmate.*

*Bill Hewitt of USS St. Louis explores a native village, Espiritu Santo, New Hebrides, 1943.*

*Japanese cruiser dead in the water and on fire after being hit by U.S. warships during First Battle of Kula Gulf, Solomon Islands, 1943. W. A. Hewitt was a gunnery officer aboard USS St. Louis in this surface action. Photograph taken from the St. Louis.*

*USS St. Louis in action against Japanese cruisers and destroyers during Second Battle of Kula Gulf, Solomon Islands, 1943.*

*USS St. Louis, firing her main battery at Japanese warships during Second Battle of Kula Gulf, Solomon Islands, 1943.*

U.S.S. ST. LOUIS
ORDERS OF THE DAY
Saturday, July 3, 1943

OFFICERS SEE THAT THESE ORDERS ARE PUBLISHED TO ALL HANDS AT THEIR BATTLE STATIONS.

ALL HANDS KEEP ESPECIALLY ALERT ON WATCH. GET ALL THE REST YOU CAN WHILE OFF WATCH. BE PREPARED TO MAN YOUR BATTLE STATIONS AT ANY TIME, TAKING FULL EQUIPMENT WITH YOU.

ALL HANDS HAVE BEEN FURNISHED WITH EYE SHIELDS FOR PROTECTION OF THE EYES AGAINST FLASH. THESE SHIELDS ARE PART OF THE NEW ANTI-FLASH OUTFITS AND ARE FOR USE BY EACH MAN REGARDLESS OF LOCATION OF HIS BATTLE STATION. THEY WILL BE USED BY ALL HANDS IN ACTION WHENEVER ORDERED BY PROPER AUTHORITY AND MAY BE WORN AT ANY TIME AT DISCREATION.

EACH MAN WILL BE ISSUED AN APPLE AND AN ORANGE AT THE EVENING MEAL, TO EAT DURING GENERAL QUARTERS. YOU MAY BE AT GENERAL QUARTERS FOR A LONG TIME, AND YOU ARE URGED TO KEEP THE APPLE AND ORANGE UNTIL AT YOUR BATTLE STATION. SANDWICHES WILL BE PASSED OUT IN THE MESSHALL JUST BEFORE GENERAL QUARTERS. EACH MAN WILL BE ISSUED TWO (2) SANDWICHES, ONE OF WHICH IS FOR ONE OF THE MEN ON WATCH AT YOUR BATTLE STATION. EAT YOUR SANDWICH WHEN YOU WANT, BUT BE SURE THAT YOUR SHIPMATE GETS HIS. SANDWICHES WILL BE SENT TO THE ENGINEERS, TURRETS 1 AND 4, SKY CONTROL, CONTROL FWD. AND BRIDGE PERSONNEL ON WATCH, BUT EVERY-ONE ELSE WILL DEPEND UPON A SHIPMATE FOR HIS SANDWICH.

0510 Reveille. Pass the word: "Stow all bedding in flame proof bags and place on lower bunks".
Bedding may be removed from bags during the day for use.
Each man will restow his bedding whenever he turns out.
0530 Sound General Quarters.
0634 SUNRISE. Set Condition of Readiness and Material Condition as ordered.
0650 Sweep down all decks and living compartments.
Commence burning trash at incinerator. Empty all trash cans.
0715 Mess gear.
0730 Pipe to breakfast.
0815 Turn to. Muster on stations.
Scrub wash and dry down all decks. No other routine ship's work will be scheduled. Keep decks swept down and do not allow trash to accumulate in compartments.

Reports certifying correction of defects noted at last Captain's Inspection will be due at 1600, Monday, July 5, 1943.

Make all preparations for entering port.
Prepare both boats for lowering. Boats will not be lowered unless specifically ordered.
Do not rig out boat booms on anchoring.
0815 Butcher Shop Working Party (5 hands from 4th Division) muster on the quarterdeck.
____ (WHEN ORDERED) Station Special Sea Details and Anchor Detail.
____ (UPON ANCHORING) Hoist out one plane.
The ship will get underway during the afternoon. Time will be announced.
(ONE HOUR BEFORE TIME SET FOR GETTING UNDERWAY) Officer-of-the-Deck carry out all routine preparations as prescribed in Ship's Order Book.

Set Condition of Readiness and Material Condition as ordered by Executive Officer at this time.
1500 Empty all trash cans at incinerator.
Secure all loose gear. Division Officers inspect their parts of the ship to see that all inflammables have been eliminated and that all gear and material is secured for battle in accordance with previously prescribed policies.

(OVER)

ORDERS OF THE DAY CONT'D

1645 All divisions check Material Condition Settings and make reports to the Damage Control Office.

____ SUNSET - Darken ship.

ONE HOUR AFTER DARKEN SHIP - Dump all unburnable trash and punctured cans over the fantail.

NOTES: (1) Security Officer - Lt.Cdr. McCORMICK.
(2) Duty Section - 1st.
(3) Working Division - 4th.
(4) Reports on correction of defects noted at Captain's Inspection will be due at 1600, Monday, July 5, 1943. If conditions warrant, further extension will be granted.
(5) Officers in need of canvas first aid pouches may obtain them at Sick Bay to-day.
(6) All hands requiring Identification Tags report to Sick Bay to have them made.
(7) "Hammocks" will not be sounded before ship secures from Condition I or Condition II. However, men desiring to obtain hammocks from nettings at the regular time (1850) may do so.

J.E. FLORANCE,
Commander, U.S. Navy,
Executive Officer.

EDITOR'S NOTE: Orders of the Day presented on these two pages were issued to all shipboard personnel to inform officers and crew of their responsibilities on a day during which combat was anticipated.

U.S.S. ST. LOUIS
ORDERS OF THE DAY
Friday, July 2, 1943.

OFFICERS SEE THAT THESE ORDERS ARE PUBLISHED TO ALL HANDS AT THEIR BATTLE STATIONS.

ALL HANDS HAVE BEEN FURNISHED WITH EYE SHIELDS FOR PROTECTION OF THE EYES AGAINST FLASH. THESE SHIELDS ARE PART OF THE NEW ANTI-FLASH OUTFITS AND ARE FOR USE BY EACH MAN REGARDLESS OF LOCATION OF HS BATTLE STATION. THEY WILL BE USED BY ALL HANDS IN ACTION WHENEVER ORDERED BY PROPER AUTHORITY AND MAY BE WORN AT ANY TIME AT DISCREATION.

0000 Commence pumping salt water ballast from wing fuel tanks.
0510 Sound Reveille. Call all hands.
Pass the word to stow bedding in flame proof bags.
0530 Sound General Quarters. During General Quarters, test Chemical Attack Alarm from Battle Two.
0631 SUNRISE - Light ship. Set Condition of Readiness and Material Condition as ordered.
0640 Turn to. Commence burning trash at incinerator. Sweep down and remove trash from all compartment.
Rig starboard side for fueling from tanker; to be in all respects ready by 0830.
0715 Mess gear.
0730 Pipe to breakfast.
0815 Turn to. Muster on stations.
Hold field day below decks in so far as practicable.
Thoroughly clean heads and washrooms.
General cleaning topside upon completion of fueling.
0815 Butcher Shop Working Party (5 hands from 3rd Division) muster on the quarterdeck.
____ (WHEN ORDERED) Sound Flight Quarters. Catapult plane for anti-submarine patrol.
1300 (IF FUELING COMPLETED) Turn to. Continue with field day where practicable until 1445.
1415 (IF FUELING COMPLETED) Hold Air Lookout instruction for 4th section Air Lookouts in Compartment B-316-L.
1445 Knock off work.
1500 Empty all trash cans at incinerator.
1650 All divisions check Material Condition Settings and make reports to the Damage Control Office.
SUNSET - Darken ship.
ONE HOUR AFTER DARKEN SHIP - Dump all unburnable trash and punctured cans over the fantail.

NOTES:
(1) Security Officer - Comdr. GILL.
(2) Duty Section - 4th.
(3) Working Division - 3rd.
(4) Too much outgoing airmail has been received at the Post Office, with insufficient postage. This mail has to be returned to the sender for additional postage, and only delays the mail. Postage for airmail is 6 cents per half ounce, and 6 cents for each additional half ounce. Airmail to foreign counties must be taken to Post Office to determine correct postage.
(5) Swabs will float in water and clog drains - they should be well secured in place with marline stops. All division leading petty officers and petty officers in charge of compartments take proper action.
(6) All Division Officers inspect their parts of the ship to see that there is no material adrift which might clog drains or submersible pumps.

J.E. FLORANCE,
Commander, U.S. Navy,
Executive Officer.

EDITOR'S NOTE: Orders of the Day emphasized precautions related to the ship's safety and welfare of the crew.

U.S.S. ST. LOUIS
ORDERS OF THE DAY
Sunday, July 4, 1943

OFFICERS SEE THAT THESE ORDERS ARE PUBLISHED TO ALL HANDS AT THEIR BATTLE STATIONS.

ALL HANDS KEEP ESPECIALLY ALERT THROUGHOUT THE DAY.

0520 Sound Reveille. Call all hands.
Pass the word to stow bedding in flame proof bags and place on lower bunks.
0540 Sound General Quarters.
(WHEN ORDERED) Station Repair Party Anchor Detail.
Make preparations for entering port.
0650 SUNRISE. Set Condition of Readiness and Material Condition as ordered.
0700 Turn to. Sweep down and remove trash from all compartments.
Sweep down all weather decks.
(WHEN ORDERED) Station the Special Sea Details.
UPON ANCHORING - Swing gig out at davit heads. Do not lower it unless ordered.
0715 Mess gear.
0730 Pipe to breakfast.
Special sea details and others in similar status go to breakfast in relays as they can be spared.
Turn to. Muster on stations.
Scrub, wash and dry down all decks. No other routine ship's Work will be scheduled. Keep decks swept down and do not allow trash to accumulate in compartments.

All hands are urged to rest and relax as much as possible during the day.

The ship will get underway during the day. Time will be announced.
0815 Butcher Shop Working Party (5 hands from 5th Division) muster on the quarterdeck.
(ONE HOUR BEFORE TIME SET FOR GETTING UNDERWAY) Officer-of-the-Deck carry out all routine preparations as prescribed in Ship's Order Book.

Set Condition of Readiness and Material Condition as ordered by Executive Officer at this time.
1500 Empty all trash cans at incinerator.
Secure all loose gear; Division Officers inspect their parts of the ship.
1700 All divisions check Material Condition Settings and make reports to the Damage Control Office.
____ SUNSET - Darken ship.
ONE HOUR AFTER DARKEN SHIP - Dump all unburnable trash and punctured cans over the fantail.

NOTES: (1) Security Officer - Lt.Cdr. CLARK.
(2) Duty Section - 2nd.
(3) Working Division - 5th.

J.E. FLORANCE,
Commander, U.S. Navy,
Executive Officer.

EDITOR'S NOTE: These Orders of the Day spelled out precautions that had to be taken to achieve battle readiness.

HUBBLE BUBBLE

Page 1 July 9, 1943

UNDATED PACIFIC WAR: American troops have landed at two points near the Japanese Air base at Munda on New Georgia Island Allied headquarters announced in the Thursday noon communique. The communique in an collaboration of the Naval battle in the Kula Gulf above New Georgia also announced that nine Japanese Crusiers and destroyers were sunk there. The landings near Munda which is the immediate objective of the Central Solomons offensive were at four miles northeast of Bosroko Boiroko and at Zanzna six miles east of Munda. At the other end of the 700 mile arc where Americans and Australians hold positions near Salamaua New Guinea Allied planes dropped more than 100 tons of boms on Japanese positions near Mumbo. The communique announced that the Japan has definitely lost nine ships in the Kula gulf Battle which occoured on the night of July 5, and in the predawn of July 6 increased the extent of the American victory. Yesterdays communique had reported a number of six ships probably were sunk and four damaged as against the loss on our side of one cruiser since disclosed to be the U.S.S. HELENA. In addition to reporting the aerial bomb bardment at Mumbo which is 12 miles below Salamaua the communique also announced the capture by Australians of an important hill there. The Japs continued to send more planes against Rendova Island seized in the central Solomons June 30th within artillery shelling distance of Munda. In the latest raid the Japs lost 12 bombers and fighters the communique siad. Jap plane losses in this sector alone now approximate 180 since the beginning of the offensive.

WASHINGTON: Warships of the North Pacific force poured hundreds of shells in to Japanese defenses on Kiska Island Tuesday night in an operation possibley preliminary drive to reconquer that Aleutian position. A Navy communique announcing the attack Wednesday afternoon gave no details except that enemy shore batteries failed to return the fire. It left no doubt that the bombardment was a heavy and prolonged raid into hundreds of shells. The assault came at a time when combined land, sea and air forces of the south and southwest Pacific commands are putting huge pressure on enemy positions in the Solomon Islands and New Guinea put Tokyo on notice that American offensive power in not limited to one sector of the Pacific front alone and that powerful new blow was to be expected at other points. The communique covering actions in the South as well as the North disclosed that American ship lost in the battle of Kula Gulp in the Central Solomons. July sixth was the sinking of the 9700 ton cruiser commanded by Capt. PURCERL of Louisville, Ky. Loss of life aboard the HELENA was not reported.

EDITOR'S NOTE: *Hubble Bubble* was the USS St. Louis' newsletter which apprised the crew of national and international events during the war. A portion of the newsletter, reproduced above, gives a vivid account of wartime activities in other parts of the world as well as in our own theatre of activity.

*USS St. Louis awaiting repairs in the harbor of Espiritu Santo, New Hebrides. A torpedo fired by a Japanese cruiser during an engagement with the "Tokyo Express" in the Second Battle of Kula Gulf, July 1943, severely damaged the bow of the St. Louis.*

*USS St. Louis receiving temporary repairs in Espiritu Santo, New Hebrides, before it sailed to California for major repair work at the Mare Island Navy Yard in San Francisco Bay.*

*Preparing for trip to California from the New Hebrides, 1943. Steel beams were welded to the foredeck of USS St. Louis for reinforcement, after the ship had been hit by a Japanese torpedo, 1943.*

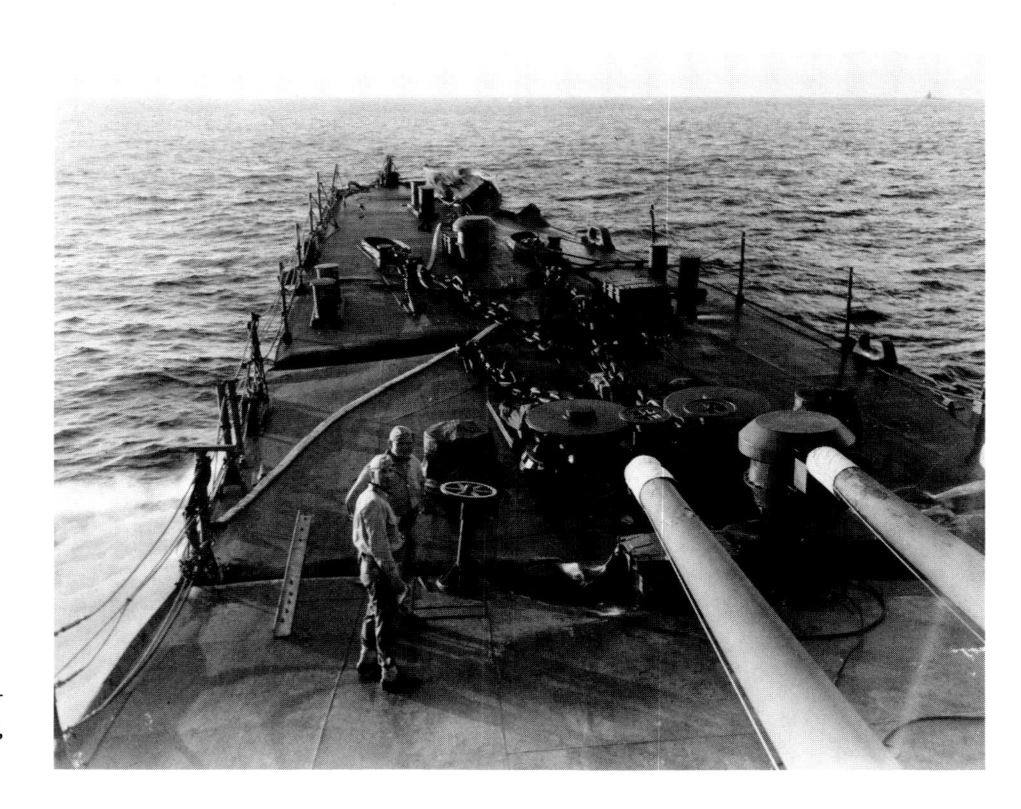

*Bow of USS St. Louis was buckled by a Japanese torpedo during a surface battle with Japanese warships in the Solomon Islands, 1943.*

*Espiritu Santo, July 1943, temporary patch-up job on bow of USS St. Louis enabled her to sail to Mare Island Navy Yard in San Francisco Bay for further repairs. The St. Louis had been hit by a Japanese torpedo during a surface battle in the "Slot" of the Solomon Islands, 1943.*

*USS St. Louis in the Pacific heading for California to have its bow straightened out after being hit by a Japanese torpedo in the Solomons, 1943.*

*The USS California, before she was sunk in Pearl Harbor on December 7, 1941. Note the tall slender stacks, and also the spotting planes atop turret three.*

*When the noise had subsided and the smoke had cleared, after the Japanese surprise attack on Pearl Harbor, the USS California was sitting on the mud bottom in very shallow water. Fortunately, it was feasible to raise the ship and restore its ability to participate effectively in combat with the enemy.*

*USS California, before Pearl Harbor, December 7, 1941. Note the tall, old style, cage masts that were designed to give officers and lookouts maximum opportunity to observe enemy ships from a high elevation. The tall masts also were a handicap because they gave the ship a high profile when it was a potential target. The advent of radar allowed the modernized USS California to have a much lower profile.*

*The modernized USS California, back at sea, after being raised and reconditioned following her sinking in Pearl Harbor on December 7, 1941. Note her lower profile, with only one wider and shorter stack.*

*Lt. W. A. Hewitt, USNR, USS California, San Francisco, 1944.*

*Lt. W. A. Hewitt, USNR, on the open bridge of the USS California during his watch as Officer of the Deck in the South Pacific, 1944.*

*Hewitt as Officer of the Deck, on the open bridge of the USS California.*

EDITOR'S NOTE: After the USS St. Louis was torpedoed, during the Second Battle of Kula Gulf in the Solomons, Lt. Hewitt was transferred to the USS California to serve as Radar Operations and CIC Officer.

*Bill Hewitt, Officer of the Deck, at the gangway of the USS California, 1944, in the South Pacific. When coming aboard, all naval personnel first salute the colors and the Officer of the Deck. Then they request, "Permission to come aboard, sir."*

Landing on Saipan

PLAN OF THE DAY
THURSDAY, 15 JUNE 1944

SENIOR DUTY OFFICER..........................Lt. Cdr. Ward.
WORKING DIVISION.............................6th division
RELIEF WORKING DIVISION......................7th division

DAILY ROUTINE
EXCEPT AT

0325 - Flight Quarters. Gas and prepare two planes for launching.
0330 - Reveille. Have coffee and food ready in General Mess and Wardroom.
0345 - Synchronize all clocks.
0400 - Turn to. Sweep down, remove all trash and inflammables. Stow loose gear.
0425 - (Twilight) Set Condition I.
0432 - Close all battle access routes. Anticipate Advance Transport groups approaching. transport areas 1 and 2 from north west (course 110 degrees True). Tractor groups A and B and screen approaching LST areas A and B from North( Course 155 degrees true).
0530 - Pass through point XXX (11000yds, 273 degrees True from Afetna Pt.) Cover advance of transports and tractor groups. When released proceed to close support station on flank of LST areas. Begin delivery of Main battery scheduled fire (170 H.C. range 1A and 1 B.)
0600 - Launch 2 planes.
0610 - Transports arrive transport areas 1 and 2.
0640 - Tractor groups arrive in LST areas A and B.
0700 - (H-90) Air strike. Cease fire.
0730 - (H-60) F.S.U.1 under command C.T. G.522 deliver 30 rounds C.B. fire from 3C and proceed to point K.
0800 - (H-30) Deliver 100 rounds H.C. from PtK.
0825 - (H-5) Air strike on beach. Continue fire.
0830 - H hour. MB lift fire when LVT wave 1000 yds from beach, 5" at 300 yds and move fire to 01 line.
0900 - Released by CTG 52.2. Establish communication with SFCP and continue call fire for remainder of day.
1230 - Set Condition "Zebra" Easy. Feed crew on station in accordance with battle messing bill.
XXXX - Recover and service aircraft. Notify Com FSU-1 and own SFCP when withdrawing.
1800 - Set Condition IE. Feed crew in sections in accordance with Messing bill.
1847 - Sunset. Darken ship.
2008 - End of evening twilight.
0119 - Moonrise.

To all hands: "WELL DONE"

BULLETINS

1. In case of injury to any ships personnel, Do not remove dog tag.
2. Officers are responsible that when battle rations are drawn no more than enough for personnel in Their charge are obtained. Adequate rations were provided for all hands yesterday but due to failure on the part of responsible individuals to follow this rule, the early hogs deprived some of their shipmates of food for several hours. Nearly 4000 rations were issued many of which are still lying about the ship. Officers must also supervise distribution, many outlying stations missed out today. Remember we are all on the same team and accept personal responsibility that proper action is taken.

F.R. BUNKER,
Commander, U.S.Navy.

EDITOR'S NOTE: When combat action was imminent, the ship's Plan of the Day outlined special procedures for engagement with the enemy. Above Plan of the Day was for "D-Day" at Saipan, June 15, 1944.

*"F" Division, USS California, operated the ship's Combat Information Center. It was the only division aboard BB-44 in which every enlisted man was a petty officer. Officer in Charge, Lt. W. A. Hewitt, USNR, seated in center of second row, May 24, 1945.*

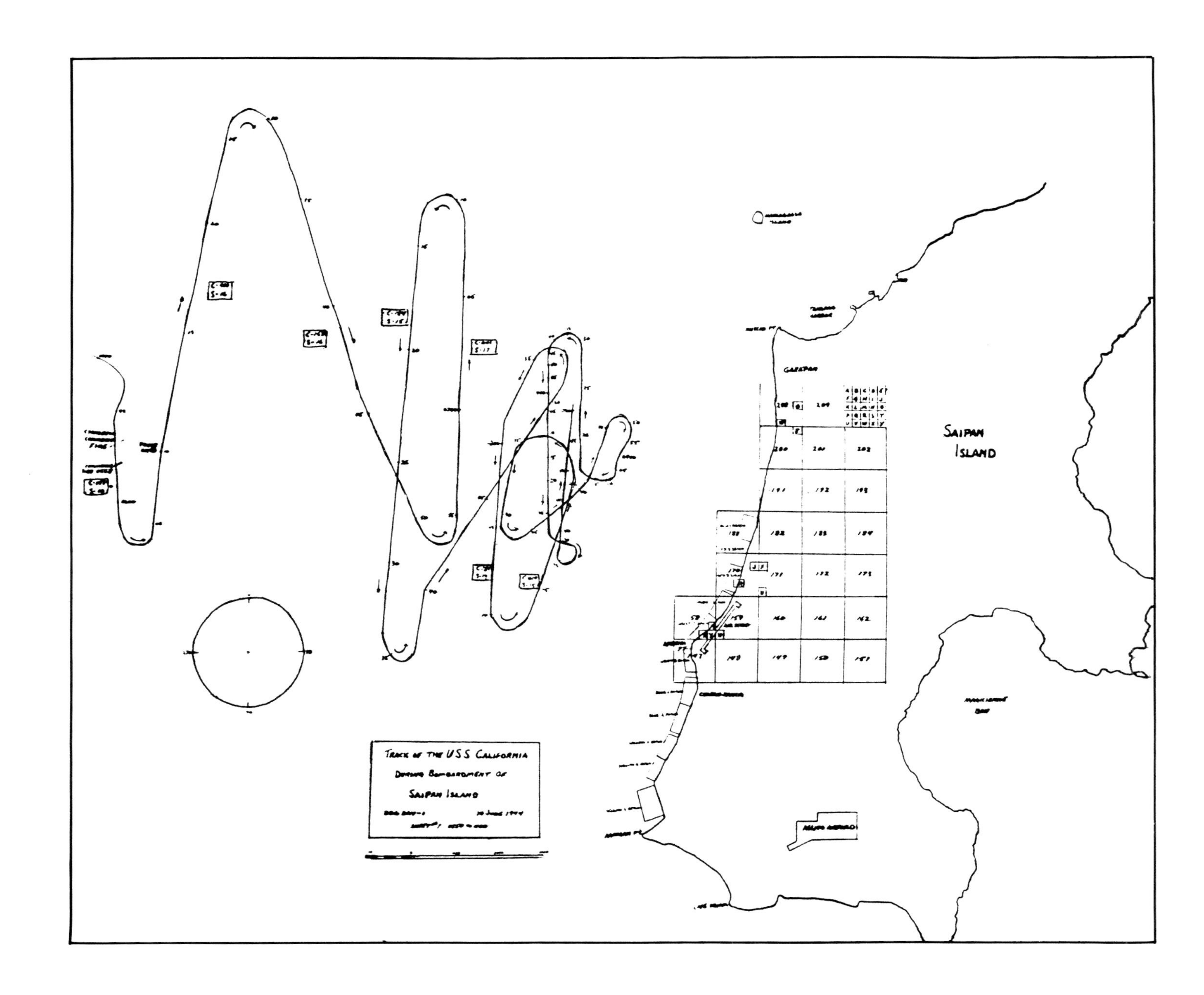


Editor's Note: Lt. William A. Hewitt was in charge of the USS California's CIC and radar operations. During naval combat, it was his responsibility to track the ship's course and speed in order to provide the range and bearing of enemy targets to the ship's gun control centers during bombardment operations and surface battles against enemy ships. The above track of the USS California during the bombardment of Saipan by the USS California was made by Hewitt in CIC on the ship's DRT table (dead reckoning tracer).

*The USS California carried two OS-2U spotting planes. It was customary to launch one of those planes before a bombardment so that the pilot could observe the accuracy of the ship's guns, and estimate the damage when they were shooting at designated targets. The pilot made his reports on his visual sightings by radio transmissions to the bridge, to the main battery fire control officer, and to the Combat Information Center.*

EDITOR'S NOTE: The USS California was severely damaged when her sister ship, the USS Tennessee, accidentally rammed her in September 1944. The collision occurred in total darkness at 3:30 a.m., while cruising in a large formation of U.S. warships that were heading for Espiritu Santo in the New Hebrides, after having bombarded Saipan, Guam and Tinian.

The incident began when the Tennessee's electric steering mechanism failed while the formation was zigzagging to evade Japanese submarines. When the Tennessee left the formation to make rush repairs, she sent a message over short-wave radio to the other ships in the formation: "We have a steering casualty and are leaving the formation. Disregard our movements until repairs are made." After repairs were made, and the Tennessee was returning to formation, she had an unexpected second steering casualty, and failed to report it by radio. The California continued to disregard her movements until it was too late. In spite of evasive action by the California, the Tennessee's clipper bow knifed into the port bow of the California and killed seven enlisted men who were sleeping in their bunks.

*The collision-damaged USS California in Espiritu Santo, before she entered the floating dry dock for repairs.*

*Inspection of damage to the USS California after she was rammed by USS Tennessee.*

*Here, the repair work had progressed to the point where all badly damaged parts of the port bow of the USS California had been cut away.*

*The force of the Tennessee's ramming of the California made a gigantic hole in her port bow, and buckled the edge of the foredeck (see upward curve of edge of the main deck).*

*USS California in the floating dry dock in Espiritu Santo, New Hebrides. All major repairs were made at this location after the California was rammed by her sister ship, the USS Tennessee. When repairs were completed, the California headed for Okinawa.*

EDITOR'S NOTE: The delay involved in making repairs in the New Hebrides was much shorter than it would have been had it been necessary to return to the United States for repairs. Still, the delay, such as it was, caused the California to miss participating in the bombardment of Iwo Jima. But we did catch up with the fleet in Okinawa.

*Senior officers of the USS California, below the level of department head. Top left: Gabriel Hauge, Bill Hewitt's cabinmate for two years. Gabe was in charge of the ship's secondary battery of five-inch dual purpose guns. Bill Hewitt was the Radar Operations Officer in charge of the Combat Information Center. After the war Gabe became Economic Advisor to President Eisenhower, and then Chairman of Manufacturers Hanover Bank in New York.*

*October 17, 1944. U.S. warships entering Leyte Gulf in the Philippines, to bombard Japanese shore positions prior to amphibious landings by U.S. Marines and Army units. Lt. Bill Hewitt was aboard the USS California, second ship in the column.*

*1944, "D-Day," landing at Leyte in the Philippines. After three days of bombardment of the beaches of Leyte by U.S. warships, countless landing barges shuttle Marines and soldiers ashore to secure the island for U.S. occupation.*

*Leyte Gulf, Philippines, November 1, 1944. Sinking of USS Abner Read (destroyer) by one of the first Japanese Kamikazes. Photographed from USS California which was tied up to an ammunition ship, replacing the projectiles and powder bags that had been expended in the bombardment of Leyte. The USS Tennessee was also tied to the ammunition ship. What a Kamikaze target we could have been.*

EDITOR'S NOTE: In Volume Twelve of his *History of U.S. Naval Operations in W. W. II,* Admiral Samuel Eliot Morison tells of: "Rough days in Leyte Gulf, 1-2 November 1944." During the morning of November 1, 1944, Lt. Hewitt was on duty aboard the USS California and observed the action described by Admiral Morison as follows: "...a pair of VALS were sighted from destroyer ABNER READ through a break in the clouds. As the leading plane nosed into a dive, prompt gunfire action shot away its port wing, but the fuselage crashed the deck and started a fire which exploded the destroyer's magazines, let in a flood of water, and gave her a list of 25 degrees. Abandon Ship was ordered at 1358 hours and, 17 minutes later, ABNER READ rolled over and sank stern first."

After describing other intermittent air attacks during the day of November 1, 1944, Admiral Morison continued with: "Rough as this day was in Leyte Gulf, it was but a foretaste of many worse days off Leyte, Lingayen and Okinawa that KAMIKAZES would provide. Not since Guadalcanal had the Navy experienced anything like this in the Pacific."

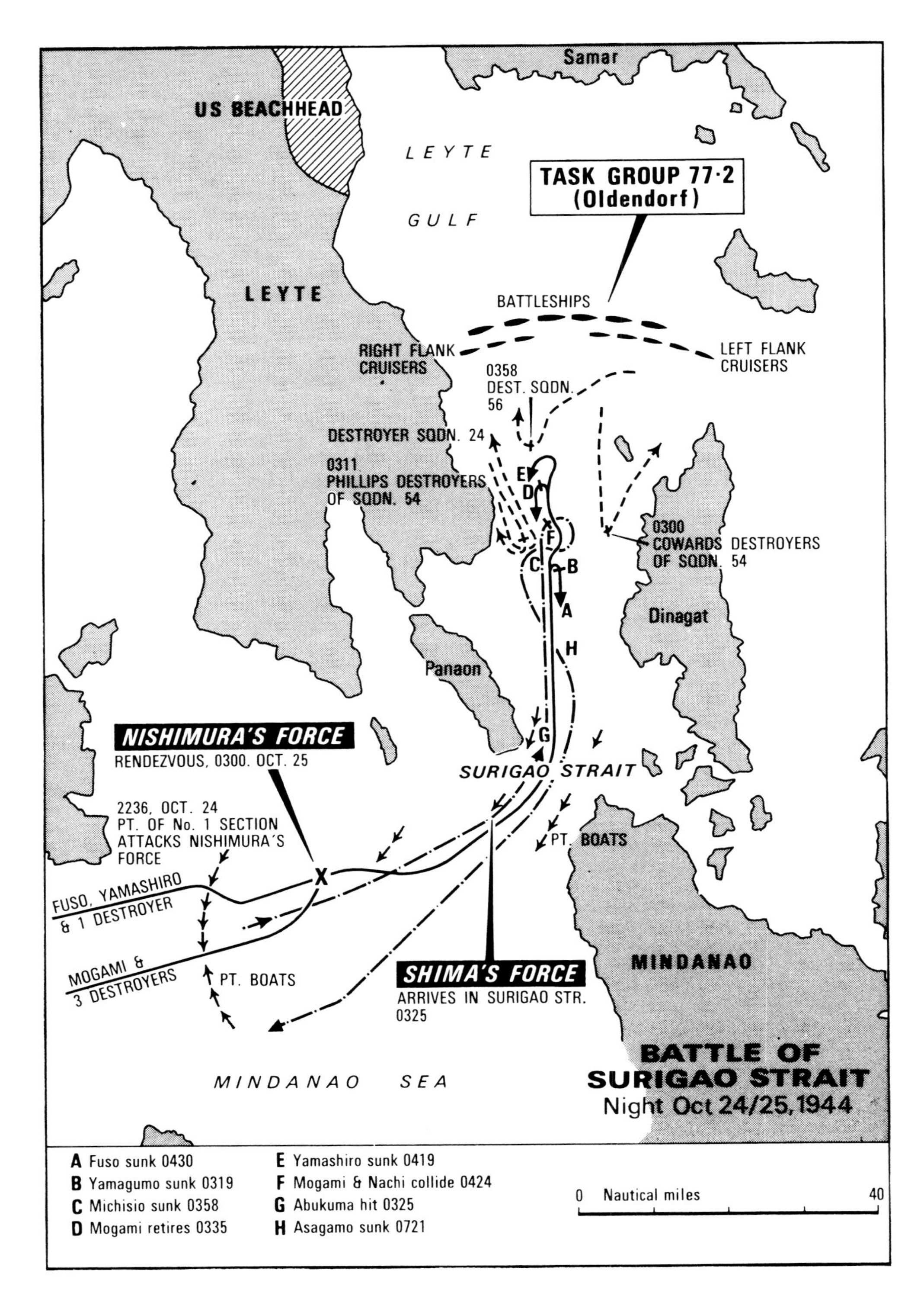


*This chart shows the positions of U.S. ships when they engaged the Japanese naval forces that attempted to penetrate Surigao Strait, with the objective of retaking the new U.S. beachhead in Leyte Gulf. The box at the bottom of the chart indicates the times and places where nine Japanese warships were sunk, damaged or retired. Only one U.S. destroyer was lost in the battle.*

Editor's Note: Of the two Japanese battleships that participated in the Battle of Surigao Strait, the Yamishiro was sunk at 0419 hours, the Fuso went under at 0430.

Both of those Japanese capital ships were hit repeatedly by broadsides from the West Virginia, California, and Tennessee, all of which were equipped with the latest design of centimetric fire control radar, which made their shooting devastatingly accurate. The other three American battleships in the battle line lacked that equipment and consequently were unable to distinguish clear targets.

The Pennsylvania did not fire at all; the Mississippi fired only two salvos; and the Maryland improvised by ranging on the splashes of the West Virginia.

Shortly after the Japanese heavy cruiser Mogami retired at 0335, it collided with Admiral Shima's cruiser flagship, the Nachi. Judging the Mogami to be stopped, the Nachi steered too closely across her bow, and was rammed, suffering severe damage to her stern, which reduced her speed to eighteen knots.

*The USS California is one of the ships firing a salvo during the Battle of Surigao Strait, near Leyte, 1944. This night engagement was one of the most important surface battles between U.S. and Japanese warships during all of World War II.*

EDITOR'S NOTE: This painting by Eldred Clark Johnson captures the principal action of the Battle of Surigao Strait in the Philippines, 1944. The painting was commissioned by Conrad Black of Toronto, Ontario, Canada.

The U.S. warships on the battle line are, from left, Maryland, Mississippi, Tennessee, California, and Pennsylvania. The ship with the tall pagoda-like superstructure, to the right of the West Virginia's aftermast, is the Japanese battleship, Yamashiro, which was about to sink due to the many hits scored by broadsides fired by several of the U.S. battleships, including the California.

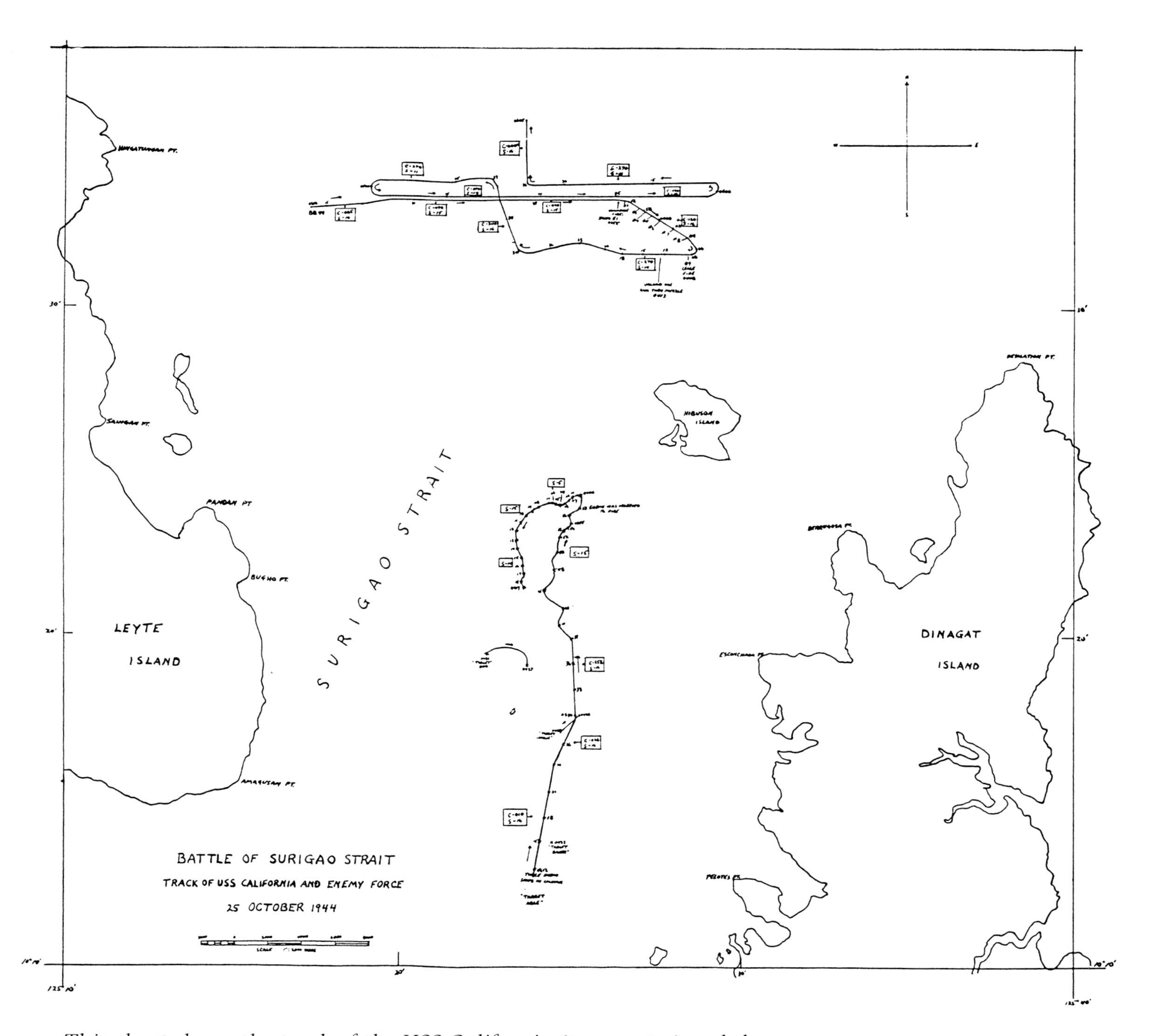


*This chart shows the track of the USS California (top, center) and the approaching enemy force during the Battle of Surigao Strait. It was made in the ship's Combat Information Center under the direction of Lt. W. A. Hewitt, October 25, 1944.*

*Several 20 mm antiaircraft guns aboard the USS California engage in target practice, while the 40 mm guns behind them await their turn.*

*A Japanese divebomber is shot down in flames by the USS California during the early daylight hours that followed the Battle of Surigao Strait, November 1944. The guns shown on the opposite page were part of the California's antiaircraft battery that shot her down.*

(AP) Wirephoto from U. S. Navy

**LINGAYEN EXPRESS—Before MacArthur's men landed on the shores of Lingayen gulf, the battlewagons of our Seventh Fleet opened up with their heaviest guns on the enemy's defenses. These are the battlewagons, steaming in line for the attack. Their timing and accuracy accounted in large part for the success of this Philippine landing.**

EDITOR'S NOTE: The USS California is fifth in this column of battleships. Lt. W. A. Hewitt was aboard. The date was January 6, 1945. The bombardment by these ships would soon be pounding Japanese shore positions, and the Kamikazes would soon be diving on U.S. ships from low altitude approaches.

*Officers from USS California at a baseball game, Samar Island, Philippines, 1944. W. A. Hewitt, lower right. Father Keneally, the ship's chaplain, is seated at left end of bench.*

EDITOR'S NOTE: One day, while the California was anchored in Leyte Gulf, 1945, I had occasion to go ashore. I liked the contrast between the native outrigger sailboat and our modern warship, so I recorded the scene. Incidentally, the Filipinos were very happy that the Americans were there.

*Cartoon of Lt. Bill Hewitt, Officer in Charge of Combat Information Center, USS California. Drawn in 1944 by one of the petty officers in Hewitt's Radar Operations Division, the cartoon was eventually presented to Hewitt who was delighted to receive it. The drawing is accurate, except for the cigarette holder.*

*Bill Hewitt (right), in the Sulu Sea of the Philippines, at the air plot table of the USS California, 1944. He was directing, by voice radio, fighter planes from distant aircraft carriers that were covering the naval task force of which the California was then a part.*

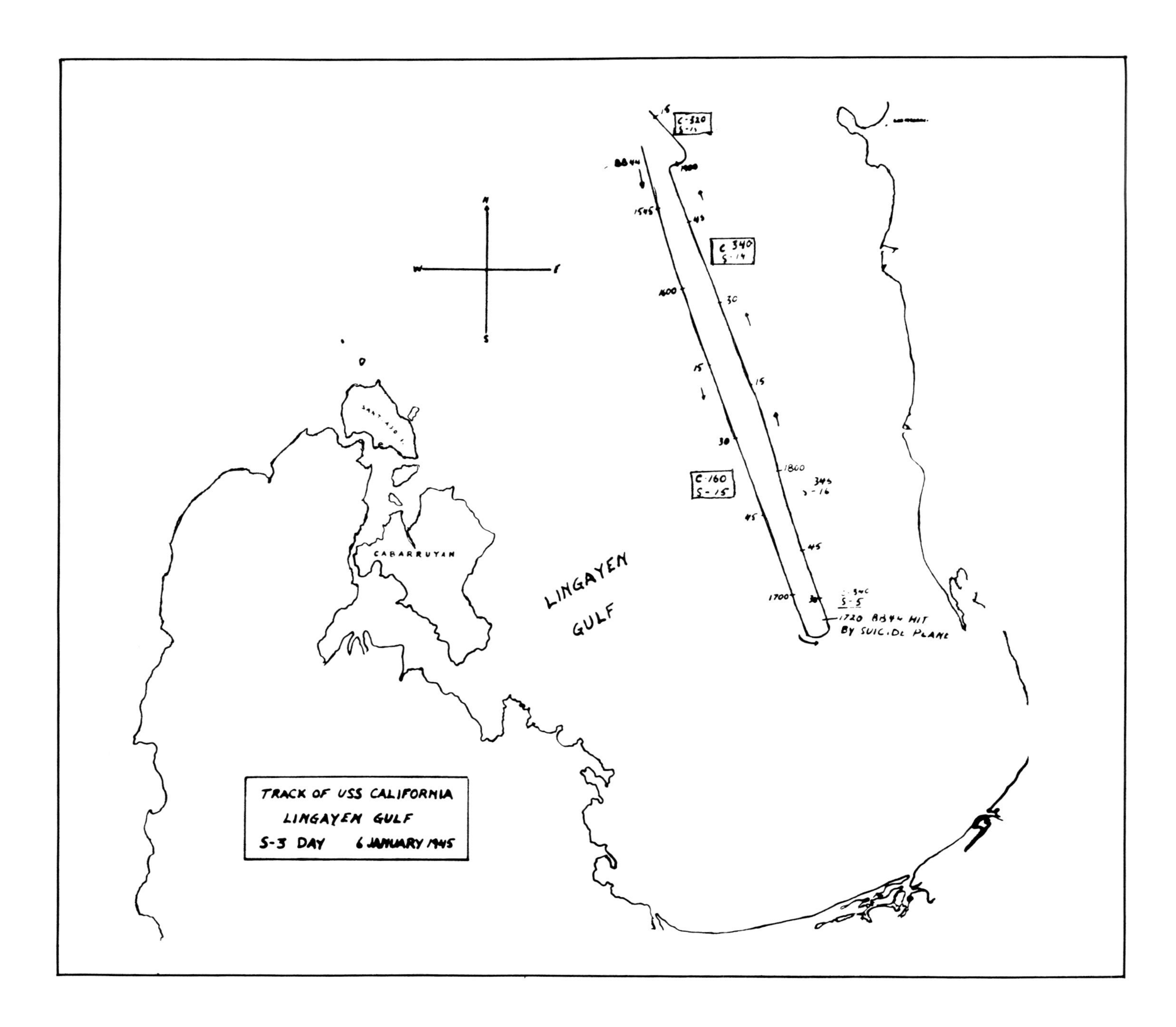


EDITOR'S NOTE: This chart and those on following pages are from official photographs (no longer classified) of large charts I made in BB-44's Combat Information Center during various bombardment actions in Lingayen Gulf, Philippines, January 1945.

The chart shown on this page is the afternoon chart of BB-44's sortie into Lingayen Gulf on January 6, 1945, which was the third day before the troops landed. The chart shows our ship's position when a Japanese suicide plane hit us at 1720 hours (5:20 p.m.). Note: C-340 means Course 340 Degrees; S-5 means Speed 5 Knots.

*Lingayen Gulf, January 6, 1945. USS California was hit simultaneously by a Japanese suicide plane and by a five-inch projectile from a U.S. destroyer. The destroyer did not cease fire soon enough while tracking the Kamikaze that crashed into the fire control tower of the California. Six officers and 26 enlisted men were killed outright. Three were reported missing. Thirteen others died later from injuries. The wounded numbered 155.*

*Part of the damage done by the Japanese Kamikaze that crashed into the fire control tower of the USS California, and then burst into flame. There were many casualties. Lingayen Gulf, January 1945.*

*A Navy bugler plays taps as the Marine Guard of the USS California stands ready to fire a final salute during burial at sea for officers and enlisted men who were killed during the action in Lingayen Gulf.*

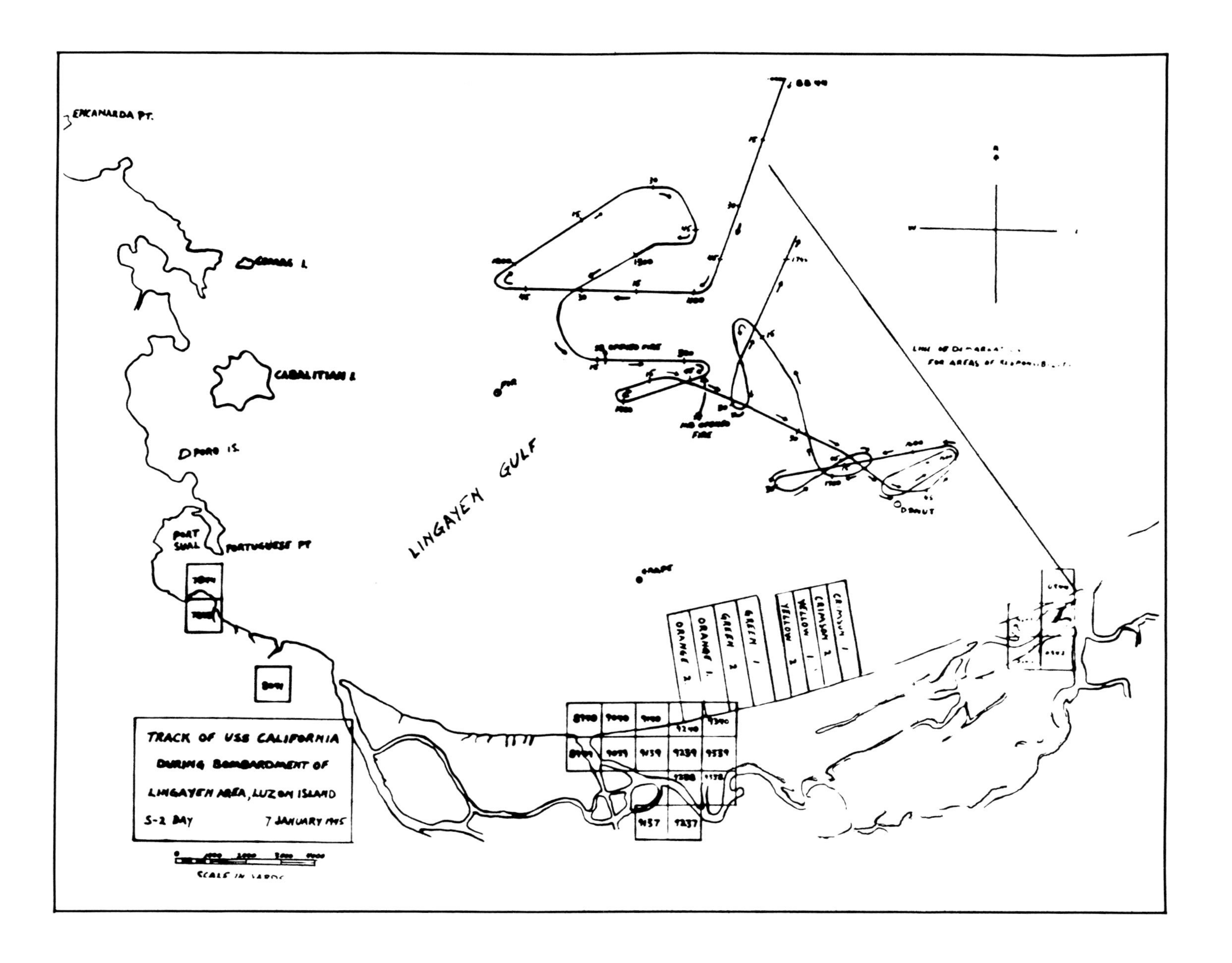


Editor's Note: The chart on this page records the action during our second day in Lingayen Gulf, January 7, 1945. The long rectangles marked with names of colors designate the various landing beaches. The squares represent the bombardment target areas. Charts were made by Lt. W. A. Hewitt.

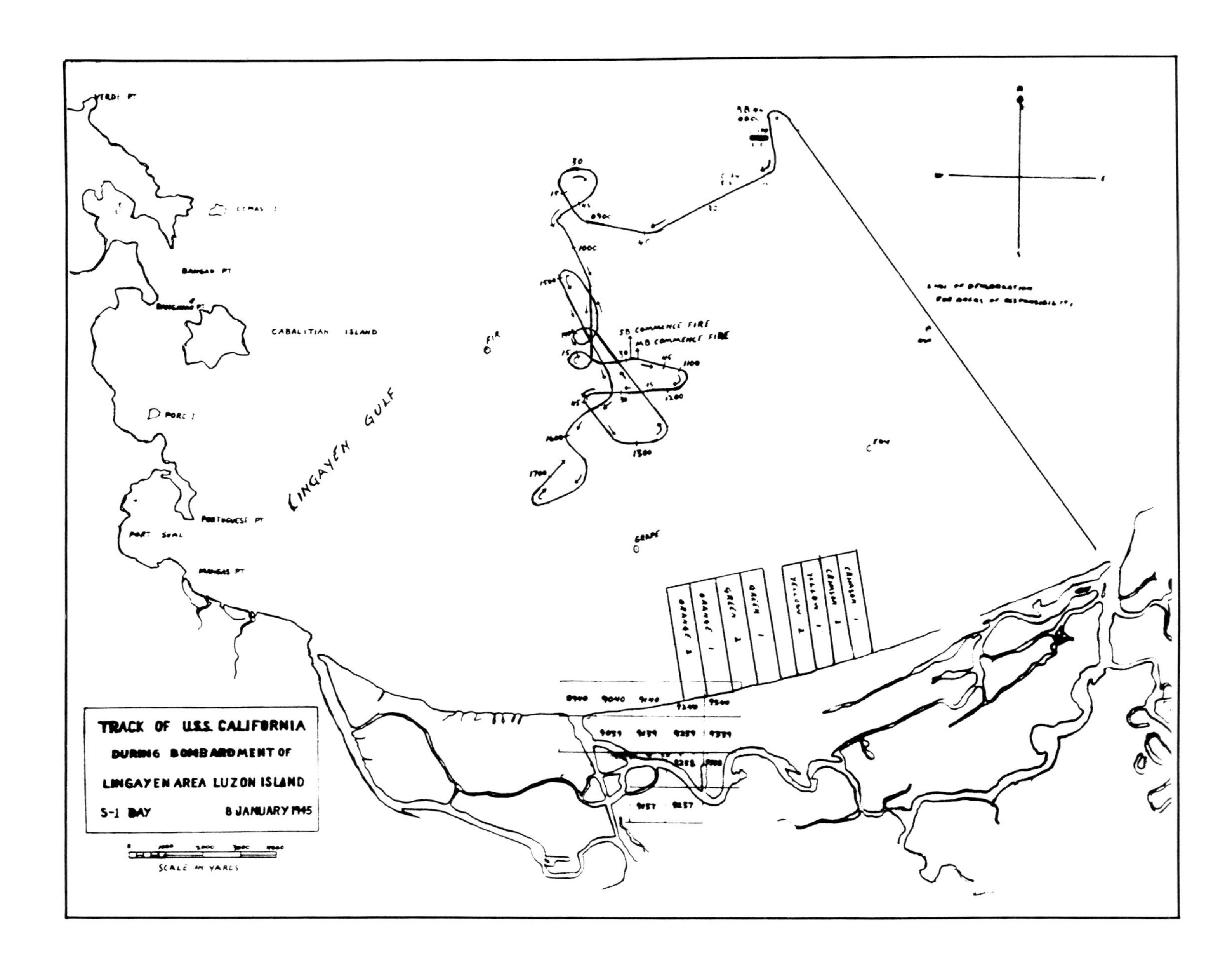


Editor's Note: Track of USS California on S-1 Day, January 8, 1945, which was the day before the scheduled landing of the U.S. Marines on Luzon Island. Our firing course for this engagement looks like a pile of pretzels.

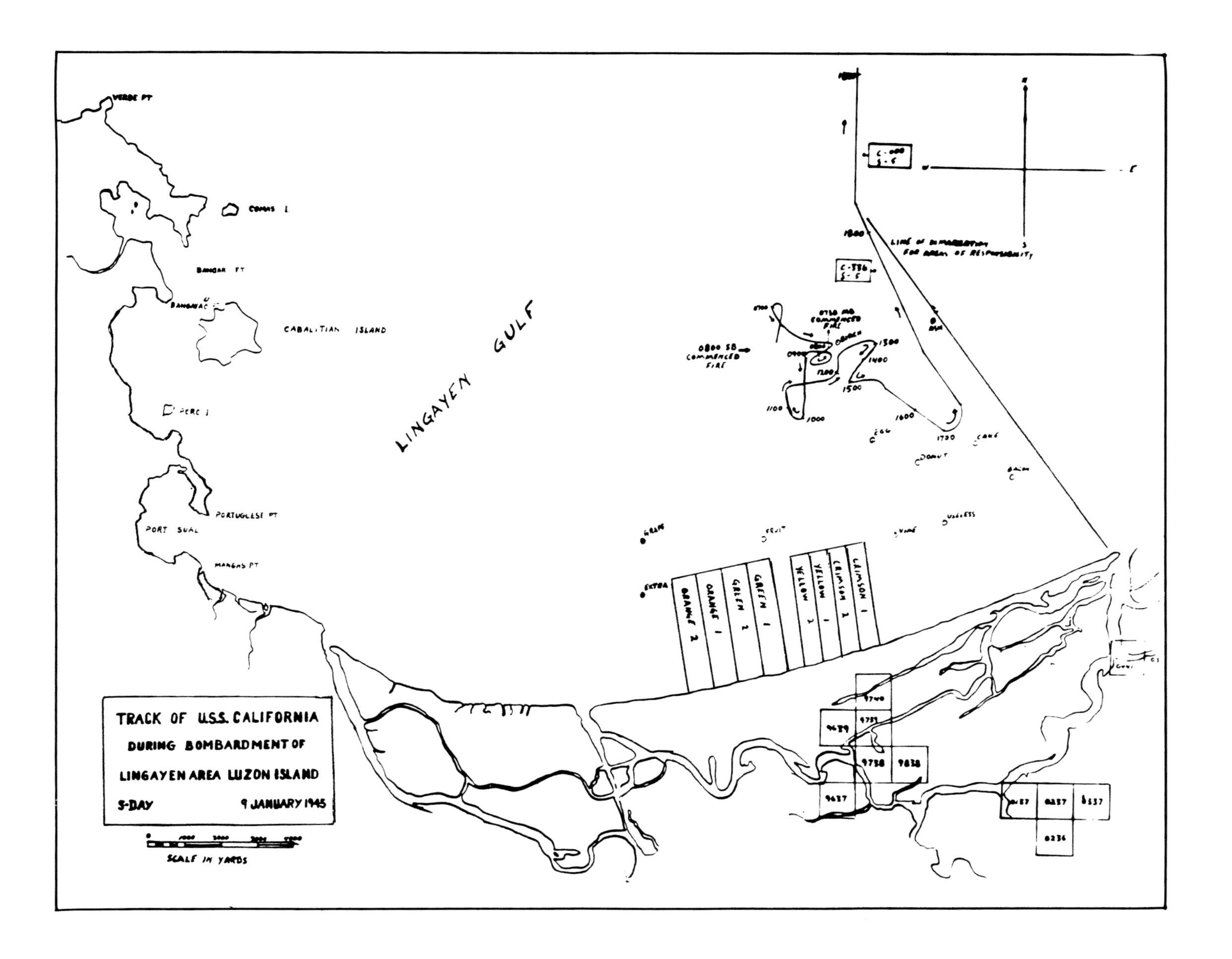


EDITOR'S NOTE: Track of BB-44 on Lingayen's D-Day, January 9, 1945. Note that the bombardment target areas have shifted but the landing beaches remain the same. The Marines landed.

*The aircraft is a Japanese Kamikaze on a suicide mission, diving on the light cruiser, USS Columbia. Puffs of smoke on starboard side of Columbia are from the guns of ships that are firing at other Japanese Kamikazes. This action was in Lingayen Gulf, in the Philippines, prior to our bombardment of Japanese shore positions.*

*Moment of impact, when the Japanese Kamikaze crashed onto USS Columbia, Lingayen Gulf, Philippines, January 1945. The Columbia was steaming in column formation immediately ahead of the USS California, from which the photographs on these two pages were taken. Later, another Kamikaze crashed into the USS California.*

*40 mm tracers from USS California antiaircraft guns during a night attack by Japanese aircraft.*

*Scoreboard of USS California indicates that she helped sink one Japanese battleship; downed seven Japanese aircraft; and participated in six major shore bombardments.*

*A gunnery officer, Lt. Leo Mack, and a gunner's mate inspect the 2,000 pound, 14-inch projectiles in the lower handling room of one of the USS California's four main battery gun turrets.*

*USS California, 1944, taking on fresh ammunition in Leyte Gulf, Philippines, after having expended almost all of our bombardment projectiles in softening up the beaches for MacArthur's landing. Also, most of our armor-piercing projectiles had been expended in the Battle of Surigao Strait. During this loading procedure a Japanese Kamikaze crashed into the destroyer USS Abner Read, which was anchored nearby, and sunk it. Hewitt witnessed that attack.*

*A damaged Japanese battleship (Fuzo class), Tokyo Bay, 1945. Photograph by W. A. Hewitt.*

*A U.S. Marine sentry on patrol on the quarterdeck of the USS California at anchor in the South Pacific.*

*Shipboard entertainment was available only when the ship was in port. It included movies, concerts by the ship's band and boxing matches. To make room for these events, the guns of turret four were swung outboard, and the crowd gathered on the quarterdeck.*

EDITOR'S NOTE: Petty Officer 2nd Class Hayes of Hewitt's "F" Division, the boxer in this photograph, was killed when the Kamikaze hit the USS California in Lingayen Gulf.

*Rest and recreation, Okinawa, 1945, waiting for the shore boats after liberty on the beach. Translation: Recreation meant two beers for each man.*

*Lt. Bill Hewitt, Okinawa, 1945. "Womb Tomb" in background. Many people in Okinawa believe that since man enters into the world from the womb, he should leave it, when he dies, by being buried in a womb-shaped tomb.*

128208 U.S.S. CALIFORNIA

15 June, 1945.

From: The Commanding Officer.
To: Lieutenant William A. HEWITT, (D)R, USNR.

Subject: PHILIPPINE LIBERATION RIBBON
*Authorization to wear.*

Reference: (a) AlNav No. 64-45.

1. You are hereby authorized to wear the *Philippine liberation ribbon* with *two bronze stars* in accordance with reference (a) for your service in Philippine waters for more than thirty days commencing 17 October, 1944, on board the U.S.S. CALIFORNIA during which period this ship participated in the initial landing operations on Leyte Island, P.I., and engaged enemy surface forces in The Battle of Surigao Strait.

2. A copy of this authorization has been forwarded to the Chief of Naval Personnel to be made a part of your official record in the Navy Department.

S.B. Brewer

S.B. BREWER.

EDITOR'S NOTE: Officers were notified by the ship's captain, after major actions, of battle stars and ribbons that were authorized.

"U.S.S. CALIFORNIA"

R-A-D-I-O P-R-E-S-S

1st Lt's. & Navgt's. Off. Page 1 8 August 1945

WASHINGTON:

The United States unleashed Monday the most terrible weapon in the history of war, an-Atomic Bomb- carrying the destructive power of 2000 Superforts, that crashed with annihilating force on a Japanese army base Washington announced. President Truman made the original announcement that American and British Scientists had unlocked the power of the atom and produced the Atomic Bomb. The President said the first Atomic Bomb had been dropped on the Japanese Army base of Hiroshima, some 16 hourse before. One bomb alone carried a more violent wallop than 2000 Superforts carrying the old type TNT bombs normally could hand an omeny city. War Secretary Stimson followed through with a report that the blast stirred a cloud of smoke and dust so impenetrable as to make an immediate observation of the results impossible. Stimson said the power of the bomb is such as to "stagger the imagination" and would prove a tremendous aid in shortening the war with Japan. The Japanese radio mentioned that Hiroshima had been bombed, but made no mention of the damage. President Truman noted the surrender ultimatum had been issued at Potsdam in an effort to spare the Japanese people from utter destruction. Mister Truman pointed out that the Japanese leaders had promptly rejected the ultimatum. Now said the President they "may expect a rain of ruin from the air, the like of which has never been seen on this earth". The President said the new bomb which draws its energy from the same sources as the sun, has a two thousand time blast power of the eleven ton British Grand-slam Bomb--the most concentrated bundle of destruction previously known on earth.

In fact, in evaluating the enormous power involved in the new weapon, the President had to reach beyond the limits of the earth for comparison. Said the President, "it is the harnessing of the basic power of the universe, The force from which the sun draws its power has been loosed against those who brought war to the Far East".

The announcement of the first use of the Atomic Bomb heralded an Anglo-American Victory in one of the grimmest battles of the war--the battle of laboratories--to unlock the secrets of the atom and yoke its energies to military use. The Germans were striving desperately to win this highly secret contest in the closing months of the European War. Thick secrecy still shrouds much of the Atomic Bomb work despite the intense excitement in usually staid Government Offices which attended Monday's startling announcement. The size of the bomb has not been revealed beyond the statement that the size of the explosive charge is exceedingly small. Nor was it told how the atoms are stored for the moment of explosion. The start of the project which the Government gave the code name of "The Manhatten Project", goes back before the War. For years Scientists had experimented with splitting the Atom--that is breaking off Electrons from the Atoms to see what would happen. They realized energy was released, but also that it would take literally billions of atoms--perhaps massed into the shape and size of a pea--to release enough energy to have a terrific explosive effect. But they know also that once they got it, they would have something unlike any force ever before released on the earth. In 1940, the United States and Britain pooled secret knowledge on Atomic Energy. It was agreed that the Scientific research would be concentrated in the United States, because of the facilities and greater safety from enemy action. Two great plants and many lesser ones were built and are now in operation. The total cost has been about two billion dollars. One of the plants is at Oakridge, Tennessee, another near Seattle, and a special laboratory near Santa Fe, New Mexico. What goes on in these plants is one of America's greatest secrets. It took one-hundred twenty five thousand persons to construct the plants and more than sixtyfive thousand are now employed in operating them, but only a handful know what happens. Many learned Monday for the first time the nature of the project on which they have been working.

EDITOR'S NOTE: From time to time, radio press releases were posted aboard the ship to inform all hands of important events related to the war. The long document reproduced on these three pages announced the epic dropping of the first atomic bomb ever used in combat. This message was radioed to all U.S. armed forces personnel immediately following the dropping of the bomb on Hiroshima.

(Cont'd. from page 1)

Exactly what the bomb is remains one to the mysteries. The Army considered releasing a picture of the bomb Monday and then decided not to. The President let it be known that the bomb is exceedingly small. How the bomb effects a target is another unanswered question; When TNT explodes it blows the air away from it with a great violence, creating a vacuum. Then there is a backward rush of air which often wrecks what the outrushing air failed to get. This works on a different principle. All that is known is that uranium enters into the manufacture of the explosive. Uranium is found chiefly in Canada and Belgian Congo. There is little in the United States and little in Germany.

The Atomic Bomb was previewed by scientists and military authorities on a desert in New Mexico, July 16th. The test bomb was set off from a steel tower. The explosion sent a huge ball of fire many times brighter than the mid-day sun billowing skyward. It set off a blast which rattled windows more than 250 airline miles away. The steel tower used in the test was vaporized. A huge sloping crater was left where the tower stood. Men outside the control center, more than 5 miles away, were knocked down by the heavy pressure waves. The test bomb was set off at 5:30 in the morning. An eye witness account said there was a blinding flash lighting up the whole area brighter than day. Then came a tremendous sustained roar and a heavy pressure wave which knocked down two men more than five miles away. Immediately thereafter a hugh multi-colored surging cloud boiled up to an altitude of over 40,000 feet. Clouds in the path disappeared. Two supplementary explosions of minor effect occurred in the cloud shortly after the main explosion. The blast from the test bomb caused consternation throughout Southwestern New Mexico and Southern Arizona. Forest Rangers more than 150 miles away thought there had been an earthquake.

The late President Roosevelt is officially credited by the British Government with pushing the development of the weapon. His backing of the project is said to have come at a time when the gamble of enormous expenditures and vitally needed scientific man power might have weakened the Allied war effort. Almost two billion dollars and work of 125,000 persons went into the development over a period of several years. Former Prime Minister Churchill has released a statement in London lauding the decision taken by Mister Roosevelt and advisors to go ahead with the plans to manufacture the world's greatest weapon of destruction despite the great risk of the venture. Churchill's statement was prepared before he was succeeded by Prime Minister Clement Attlee, who released it. The statement disclosed President Roosevelt had urged joint British and American efforts to beat the Germans in a race to manufacture a new type of bomb even before America's entry into the war. The statement says on October 11, 1941, President Roosevelt sent Churchill a letter suggesting any extended efforts on development of the weapon might usefully be coordinated or even jointly conducted. Accordingly all British and American efforts were joined and a number of British scientists concerned proceeded to the United States. In praising President Roosevelt and his war chiefs, Churchill says, "The whole burden of execution including setting up of the plants and many technical processes connected therewith in a practical sphere, constitutes one of the greatest triumphs of American or indeed human genius of which there is a record. Moreover, the decision to make these tremendous expenditures upon the project which however, hopefully established by British and American research remained nevertheless a heartshaking risk, stands to the everlasting honor of President Roosevelt and Advisors.

The Osaka Radio announced cancellation of various trains in the Hiroshima prefecture--the district in which President Truman disclosed the first Atomic bomb in the world had been dropped. The enemy broadcast did not refer to the bomb, or to any damage which might have resulted from it, however, no mention was made of any form of explosive. Hiroshima is around twenty miles from the Kuro Naval Base.

WASHINGTON(Cont'd from page 2)

President Truman has clearly indicated that scientists who have made the Atomic Bomb have done two things. One, they have created a monster which could wipe out civilization. Two, some protection against the Monster must be found before its secret is given the world. Said the President, "Under the circumstances it is not intended to divulge the technical processes of production or all military applications pending further examination of possible methods of protecting us and the rest of the world from danger of sudden destruction. We are now prepared to obliterate more rapidly and completely every productive enterprise the Japanese have above the ground in any city. Let there be no mistake; we shall completely destroy Japan's power to make war".

WASHINGTON:

A Japanese suicide plane crashed upside down into the Battleship CALIFORNIA at Lingayen Gulf on January 6th and damaged her severely, causing 203 casualties, but the old ship didn't even stop fighting.

The navy told the story of heroism, tragedy and seamanship in the Philippines action.

Six officers and 26 enlisted men were killed outright. Three were reported missing. Thirteen others died later from injuries. The wounded numbered 155.

The Lingayen Gulf action was the third in which the 24-year old battleship suffered major damages and casualties. Hit by two torpedoes at Pearl Harbor, she was raised from the mud to repay the Japanese with death and destruction at Guam, Saipan, Tinian and the Philippines.

At Saipan, on June 14th, 1944, a shell struck the upper deck after a fire control tower and penetrated deeply before it exploded. One man was killed and one officer and eight men were wounded.

Two planes attacked the CALIFORNIA'S formation January 6th at Lingayen Gulf. The first to make a run was shot down by A.A. fire. The second which had been hit, appeared to be passing the ship on the starboard side when it banked sharply and roared in upside down to crash against the tower.

Fire fighters and Damage Control personnel went to work while others began rescue work for gunners and other personnel trapped in the stricken area.

Using a portable voice amplifier, Lt. William J. KENEALLY, Chaplain Corps, helped fire-fighters locate the most dangerous areas despite heavy smoke which interfered with operations. The fires were extinguished in 12 minutes.

Although communications were disrupted and damage was done in other departments, the ship made temporary repairs while still underway and carried out her assignment at Lingayen. Her guns drove the Japanese out of the town of Lingayen and followed them inland with deadly accuracy. Aviators reported that Philippine natives finally put up signs saying "No Japs".

Several weeks later she returned to the Puget Sound, Washington Navy Yard for general overhaul and repair, which even then was much simpler than the gigantic modernization the same yard had given the vessel after Pearl Harbor.

In the Lingayen action, Pfc.R.A. Linday, U.S.M.C.R., 509 South Johnson St., Pocatello, Ida., extinguished fires in the clothing of an officer and returned to his gun station for action despite his own injuries from burns.

G.L. Weatherwax, Gunner's Mate Second Class, Chelsea, Mich., and Arthur Haney, Jr., Seaman First Class, Lawrence, Mich., were credited with preventing ignition of ammunition below deck when they fought fires from burning oil dripping through the main deck. William W. Church, BM1c, Compton, Cal., rescued men from a damaged gun until he collapsed with his own severe injuries. Marine Gunnery Sgt., R.W. Gunningham, 1516 N. Gordon St.; Chief Boatswains Mate H.H. Lane, 97 Lime Ave., Long Beach, Cal., were cited for outstanding work.

Twenty other officers and men also were commended for outstanding action.

LOS ANGELES:-

Major Richard Ira Bond, 24, America's ace fighter pilot in the South Pacific before returning to this country to become a test pilot, was killed today in the crash of a jet propelled P-80.

*Ship's crew is lined up for Captain's Inspection on the USS California, after peace was declared, 1945.*

*Admiral C. W. Nimitz signing Japanese peace treaty for the United States, aboard the USS Missouri, Tokyo Bay, September 1945. Standing, from left, General Douglas MacArthur and Admiral W. F. "Bull" Halsey.*

*Lt. W. A. Hewitt, USNR, Wakayama, Japan, October 1945. The Japanese children were both curious and shy, but always friendly.*

*Lt. W. A. Hewitt of USS California (kneeling) with two chief petty officers and Japanese children, one month after the Peace was signed, Wakayama, Japan, 1945.*

*Wakayama, Japan, October 1945. Lt. W. A. Hewitt, with sailors from USS California. Many young Japanese spoke English at that time because it was taught in their schools during the war years.*

*Tokyo, October 1945. The buildings still standing have been gutted by fire. During World War II, most of the buildings in Tokyo were made of wood, and were easily destroyed by fire bombs. The reinforced concrete buildings remained standing, but were severely damaged by fire.*

*U.S. sailors sightseeing in Tokyo, October 1945, a few weeks after the Peace was signed. The concrete building in the background still stands, but it was gutted by fire started by U.S. Air Force bombs. Photograph by Lt. W. A. Hewitt.*

*Lt. W. A. Hewitt with the ship's doctor of the USS California, 1945.*

*Lt. W. A. Hewitt, Tokyo, 1945, at Sacred Twin Bridges that span the outer moat that surrounds the Emperor's Palace.*

*Roommates aboard the USS California, Gabe Hauge and Bill Hewitt at one of the two moats that surround the grounds of the Emperor's Palace, Tokyo, 1945.*

*A cosmopolitan scene in Singapore, November 1945. A Chinese rickshaw man pulling two American sailors; several Indians walking down the street and a British sailor, wearing his flattopped hat. Photograph by Lt. W. A. Hewitt.*

*Six U.S. Navy destroyers escorting USS California and USS Tennessee from Tokyo to Philadelphia, 1945.*

*USS California at anchor in the harbor of Colombo, Ceylon, en route from Tokyo to the Philadelphia Navy Yard, via Singapore, Ceylon and Cape Town, November 1945. Photograph by Lt. W. A. Hewitt, who had a secondary duty as ship's photographic officer.*

*USS California in heavy seas, on a clear day, off Madagascar, en route from Tokyo to Philadelphia Navy Yard, after the Peace was signed.*

*USS California in heavy seas, near Madagascar, off the southeast coast of Africa. Photograph by Lt. W. A. Hewitt, USNR, late 1945.*

*Sailors aboard the USS California, mustering on the foredeck before going ashore on liberty in Colombo, Ceylon, November 1945.*

*When the USS California started to cross the equator in November 1945, en route from Japan to the Philadelphia Navy Yard, King Neptune emerged from the briny deep and came aboard with his retinue. Here we see Captain Mason welcoming the King on the open bridge. Tough guy, Davey Jones, is at the left, and the beautiful, but shy, Princess is sitting in the Captain's chair.*

*More of King Neptune's Purification by Salt Water Ceremony, aboard BB-44, as conducted by Davey Jones and his gentle lieutenants.*

*King Neptune and His Royal Court. Left to right: The Salty Chaplain, the King's Number One Sea Lawyer, a Lovely Girl (more or less), Davey Jones, King Neptune, the Royal Princess, the Heavenly Twins, Royal Undertaker, Royal General. Seated: Davey Jones' Law Enforcement Lieutenants.*

*King Neptune and His Royal Court aboard BB-44, crossing the equator.*

*Oops! This poor miserable polywog accidentally took one backward step too many.*

# USS California (BB-44)

Highlights from the ship's log
December 7, 1941 - December 1945

| | |
|---|---|
| December 7, 1941 | Sunk at Pearl Harbor |
| October 10, 1942 | Departed Pearl Harbor |
| October 19, 1942 | Arrived Bremerton |
| January 31, 1944 | Departed Bremerton |
| February 3, 1944 | Arrived Long Beach |
| March 31, 1944 | Departed Long Beach |
| April 1, 1944 | Arrived San Francisco |
| May 5, 1944 | Departed San Francisco |
| May 10, 1944 | Arrived Pearl Harbor |
| May 31, 1944 | Departed Pearl Harbor |
| June 5, 1944 | Crossed 180th Meridian |
| June 8, 1944 | Arrived Roi, Kwajalein |
| June 10, 1944 | Departed Roi, Kwajalein |
| June 14, 1944 | Arrived Saipan |
| June 22, 1944 | *Departed Saipan |
| June 25, 1944 | Arrived Eniwetok |
| July 16, 1944 | Departed Eniwetok |
| July 21, 1944 | *Arrived Guam |
| July 22, 1944 | Departed Guam |
| July 23, 1944 | *Arrived Tinian |
| August 2, 1944 | Departed Tinian |
| August 2, 1944 | Arrived Guam |
| August 10, 1944 | Departed Guam |
| August 12, 1944 | Arrived Eniwetok |
| August 19, 1944 | Departed Eniwetok |
| August 21, 1944 | Crossed Equator |
| August 24, 1944 | Arrived Espiritu Santo |
| September 18, 1944 | Departed Espiritu Santo |
| September 22, 1944 | Arrived Manus |
| October 12, 1944 | Departed Manus |
| October 17, 1944 | *Arrived Leyte |
| October 25, 1944 | **Battle of Surigao Strait |
| November 20, 1944 | Departed Leyte |
| November 25, 1944 | Arrived Manus, Admiralties |
| December 15, 1944 | Departed Manus |
| December 19, 1944 | Arrived Kossal Roads, Baobeltaob Island |
| January 1, 1945 | Departed Kossal Roads, Baobeltaob Island |
| January 6, 1945 | *Arrived Lingayen Gulf, having passed through Leyte Gulf, Surigao Strait, Mindanao Sea, Sulu Sea, Mindoro Strait and South China Sea |
| January 22, 1945 | Departed Lingayen Gulf |
| January 27, 1945 | Arrived Ulithi |
| January 28, 1945 | Departed Ulithi |

| | |
|---|---|
| February 7, 1945 | Arrived Pearl Harbor |
| February 8, 1945 | Departed Pearl Harbor |
| February 14, 1945 | Arrived Bremerton |
| April 29, 1945 | Departed Bremerton |
| May 2, 1945 | Arrived Long Beach |
| May 10, 1945 | Departed Long Beach |
| May 16, 1945 | Arrived Pearl Harbor |
| May 28, 1945 | Departed Pearl Harbor |
| June 9, 1945 | Arrived Ulithi |
| June 13, 1945 | Departed Ulithi |
| June 18, 1945 | Arrived Okinawa |
| June 20, 1945 | Departed Okinawa |
| July 25, 1945 | Cruised off Shanghai, China |
| August 7, 1945 | Arrived Okinawa |
| August 8, 1945 | Departed Okinawa |
| August 11, 1945 | Arrived Leyte |
| August 20, 1945 | Departed Leyte |
| August 23, 1945 | Arrived Okinawa |
| September 20, 1945 | Departed Okinawa |
| September 22, 1945 | Arrived Wakanoura Wan, Japan |
| October 2, 1945 | Departed Wakanoura |
| October 3, 1945 | Arrived Yokosuka, Tokyo Bay |
| October 7, 1945 | Departed Yokosuka |
| October 8, 1945 | Arrived Wakanoura |
| October 15, 1945 | Departed Wakanoura |
| October 23, 1945 | Arrived Singapore |
| October 26, 1945 | Departed Singapore, and through straits of Malacca |
| October 30, 1945 | Arrived Colombo, Ceylon |
| November 3, 1945 | Departed Colombo |
| November 15, 1945 | Arrived Cape Town, South Africa |
| November 19, 1945 | Departed Cape Town |
| December 1945 | Arrived Philadelphia, U.S.A. |

* USS California participated in naval shore bombardments prior to landing by U.S. troops.

** In this classic surface battle, U.S. ships "crossed the T" and helped sink a Japanese battleship.

EDITOR'S NOTE: These entries from the ship's log of the USS California list the ship's principal ports of call from December 7, 1941, to the end of its World War II tour of duty, December 1945.

# From Pearl Harbor

COCOON-LIKE coatings now envelop the potent guns of the *U.S.S. California*—for the famed battleship has been assigned to inactive reserve status. And it wasn't until the retirement ceremonies held recently in Philadelphia that the full story of the *California's* dramatic role in the war was told—a story that opened in the mud of Pearl Harbor and reached its climax in Tokyo bay.

The *California* was one of the victims of the sneak attack on Dec. 7, 1941. Japanese torpedoes sent it to the bottom. American determination raised the battered hull, refitted its armament and carried it through a string of victories that ended with the Japanese surrender less than four years later.

Every scene in this drama, from the disastrous sinking to the triumphant arrival in Tokyo bay, is graphically portrayed in a book prepared for the ship's personnel by Lieutenant William A. Hewitt '37. Filled with pictures, the book not only describes the naval enagagements, but also life on board the popular "Prune Barge"—nickname given the *California* following a generous gift from a state farmer.

The crew, including a number of California alumni, was largely untried when the refitted battlewagon headed revengefully west in May, 1944. But their trials came thick and fast. On June 13, the *California* helped soften up Saipan. Then she covered the invasion of Guam and rushed back to do a similar job at Tinian, thus aiding in acquisition of bases that put American B-29s within striking distance of Japan.

In October, the battleship joined the Philippines campaign and shot down its first Kamikaze. Under Rear Admiral J. B. Oldendorf, its task force successfully "crossed the T" in the night battle of Surigao strait with the *California* accounting for one Jap battleship. Death and damage struck the "Prune Barge" shortly after in a Kamikaze attack off the Lingayen gulf, but following repairs it rejoined the fleet off Okinawa and finally covered the landings of occupation troops in Japan—its mission gloriously completed.

# . . . To Tokyo Bay

California Monthly, *November 1946 issue published by the University of California Alumni Association.*

FROM THE hour it was sunk during the Japanese surprise attack at Pearl Harbor, until she steamed triumphantly into Japanese waters on September 22, 1945, the *USS California* was a symbol of American determination, aroused by the sneak attack on December 7, 1941. After being raised and refitted, the famed battleship performed with courage and distinction. Its scoreboard shows: one Japanese battleship, seven aircraft and six shore bombardments during actions in the Marianas, Philippines and Okinawa campaigns. Her potent 14-inch guns were effective. A number of University of California alumni served aboard the ship named after their state, including Lt. WILLIAM A. HEWITT '37 (left), Radar Operations Officer, and Lt. Cmdr. RALPH W. SAUER '41, Supply Officer.

## U. S. S. CALIFORNIA

*An account of the wartime cruising of the USS California from Pearl Harbor to Tokyo Bay.*

*7 December 1941* — *3 October 1945*

## DEDICATION

*To our Honored Dead . . . the Shipmates who did not sail home with us . . . who made the Supreme Sacrifice, in the Marianas, the New Hebrides, the Philippines . . . whose broken bodies are buried at sea or interred on Espiritu Santo . . . whose unbroken souls rest in peace with the Prince of Peace . . . whose abiding memory will forever light our lives . . . we Dedicate, with Affection and Reverence, this book.*

*Lt. William Hewitt, USNR, and Gunnery Sergeant Richard Cunningham, USMC, compiled and published a wartime history of their ship, the USS California, for presentation to each officer and crew member as a remembrance of his service. The book was authorized by the ship's captain, and 3,000 copies were printed. It was financed by profits from the ship's service store.*

*Since no one serving on board was allowed to have a camera for personal use during the war, there was great interest in the* USS California *book which contained 200 photographs of the ship's wartime activities, some of which are in this volume. The pictures were available through Hewitt's secondary responsibility as ship's photographic officer. The full text of the* USS California *appears on the following pages.*

## FOREWORD

☆ *The wartime story of the battleship* CALIFORNIA *is the story of the men who gave her their fighting spirit. The account in these pages is an attempt to fix on paper the feelings and actions of these men as each did his part in contributing to the American victory against the enemy, Japan.*

When the Japanese struck Pearl Harbor on that black Sunday in December, 1941, the CALIFORNIA was severely damaged by two aerial torpedoes and a bomb. She was left crippled and lying in the mud. With grim determination she was raised and rebuilt into a modern warship capable of deadly assault against the enemy. In the crucial amphibious campaigns in the Marianas, Philippines and Okinawa, and in the great Battle of Surigao Strait, the ship dealt heavy blows to the Japanese hope of conquest.

The final goal was reached when, early in the misty morning of 3 October 1945, the CALIFORNIA sailed into the heart of the enemy homeland, Tokyo Bay. Her wartime mission was accomplished. With its completion there came a sense of deep satisfaction in a job well done. Her ship's company was proud of her and the part she had played in the great enterprise that gave to men everywhere another chance to build a better world. The men of the CALIFORNIA are determined that the design of the new world shall be ample and noble and to that high endeavor they pledge their energy and their devotion.

## UNDERWAY

On 5 May, 1944, an entry in the CALIFORNIA's Plan of the Day read cryptically: "Make all preparations for getting underway." Underway! That was a big word to us then. It was a symbol, a symbol of the impossible finally achieved. It meant that we had taken 40,000 tons of messed-up steel from the bottom of Pearl Harbor, patched her up, brought the cripple back to Puget Sound Navy Yard, repaired the damage, modernized her throughout, trained a crew, and were on our way to carry the war to the enemy.

Ours is a story of the Pacific War from the Marianas through the Philippines and Okinawa to the occupation of Japan.

Our crew was typical of any wartime Navy crew. We had men who were with the ship during the blitz of December seventh and were coming out with her for a second try. We had men from other ships of the fleet, some of whom came aboard by routine transfer and others who came via the life raft. But to most of us who were fresh from training stations and shore duty it was all spanking new. We were farmers and clerks, laborers and school boys, mill workers, miners and lumberjacks. Some said, "You-all," and some said "Youse." You could hear the nasal twang of the Middle West and the baritone bragging from Texas, stories of cowboys from Wyoming, of pheasant hunting in South Dakota and of fishing for big cats in the Mississippi. The boys from Bawston told the guys from N'Awlins about the marvels of the East, and the boys from N'Awlins thrilled the Iowa farmers with stories of the Mardi Gras. We were a cross-section of all America.

The skyline of San Francisco faded into the gray fog that hovered over the building tops as we made our way down the bay, under the Oakland Bridge, through the Golden Gate and out to the open sea. Many, somewhat wistfully, stayed topside to watch California's rolling hills merge with the enveloping mist. We strained for those last few glimpses of Mount Tamalpais piercing the fog and then we shifted our gaze to the ship's wake and our escort of excited seagulls wheeling overhead. To reduce to words the feelings of a man as he watches the last dim outlines of the United States fade away, as he heads out where the boys play for keeps, is almost impossible. We knew that in the months to come we would go through the process which separates the men from the boys and then makes men out of the boys.

Six days later the crew turned out and manned the rail in an effort to catch its first glimpse of the land heaving into view over the western horizon. It was Hawaii. Old timers started talking about the last time they had seen the Islands and pointed out familiar landmarks as we approached Oahu. First there was Koko Head, then Diamond Head, Waikiki and the Royal Hawaiian. We passed Honolulu and proceeded on along the shore line to the entrance to Pearl Harbor. The water was a deep cobalt blue, but as we neared the channel entrance it changed through a series of lighter blues to green and then down to a milky jade. The ship tied up at "Fox 3," the very quay at which she had been sunk at the time of the Blitz in December 1941.

Pearl Harbor had the smell of something big in the wind. Here we saw a snarl of every type of vessel the Navy could muster . . . warships, supply ships, and loaded troop transports that looked ready to go. It was obvious that a big operation was in its last stages of preparation.

We made liberties into Honolulu, went swimming at Waikiki, and, like suckers, returned to the ship with arm-loads of junk from a thousand and one gift joints.

In a short time the mass of organized confusion began to unwind as ships of various units left for the forward area. After a week of shore bombardment rehearsal off Kahoolawe Island we got underway, 31 May, 1944, for an undisclosed destination.

## SAIPAN

On our way to meet Mr. Tojo's team we crossed the 180th Meridian which made us Golden Dragons. We bumped over the line to the accompaniment of something new aboard, sunbathing. Before the day was finished the crew managed to stage a waterfight which bordered on bloodshed and acquired a dose of sunburn that verged on catastrophe.

We stopped at Kwajalein in the Marshalls, where we refueled, took on stores, and shoved off. The ship was still full of rumors as to our destination and the nature of the coming operation. Finally, all the scuttlebutt was laid low by the Executive Officer, Commander F. R. Bunker, who read a message over the public address system. The message was from the Skipper, Captain H. P. Burnett, and it informed us that we were headed for Saipan, the key to Japan's outer defense. A number of top personnel were taken down to the Admiral's Cabin to see the amazing collection of battle plans, topographical maps, charts and information of all sorts which had been supplied by Naval Intelligence. Until you have seen such material spread out before you, you cannot begin to realize the magnitude of detail which goes into the planning of a great amphibious operation, especially when the territory has been held by the enemy for many years.

The night of June thirteenth was one which none of the green hands will ever forget. It was the kind of night that millions of men have experienced during the past few years. Although many will tell you that nothing happened inside themselves, the honest ones confide a different story. It was the last night before action with the enemy. We showered and shaved, put on clean underclothes, laid out clean dungarees, and turned in. The attention to immaculate cleanliness was intended to prevent infection in case we were wounded. With this pleasant thought we lay down and attempted, or rather pretended, to sleep.

An hour before dawn on the fourteenth, reveille sounded and like automatons we made up our bunks, pulled on our clothes and went to the mess deck for chow. Everyone was pretty quiet that morning and the chow lines moved swiftly. We put out our hands for that paper cup of beans, the piece of cornbread, took another paper cup of coffee, and moved off into little groups to eat in near silence. Most of us were already at our stations when General Quarters sounded and the word was passed to man our battle stations.

At dawn the old Prune Barge rounded the northern tip of Saipan. Our two "Quarterdeck Messerschmidts" were catapulted into the air and headed in the direction of a huge fire on the beach. We moved down the coast to the capital city, Garapan, and maneuvered into a position that would bring our guns to bear on Jap batteries, supply dumps, pill boxes and various other targets. This was the moment towards which we had been working for better than two years. The main battery was trained out, the directors were on the target, the ship was buttoned up and all hands were on station. The standby buzzer sounded in the turrets, and then SALVO! The heavies and the five-inch opened up and American shells crashed home.

At first it was like a training course. After a short period of bombarding the men began laughing and wise-cracking about the "rice-merchants" over on the beach. All this was before there was a splash on the port side, then one on the starboard side and then several all around us. The last one wasn't a splash. There was a dull thud up in the foretop and pieces of gear floated out of the Skipper's sea cabin. Men glanced at each other with a sort of surprised look. Fire call was sounded and the damage control crews went to work with fire hoses. An officer came down from the bridge with a puzzled look and with blood oozing from his forehead, his clothing torn. A marine passed up a stretcher and then a litter was lowered from the tops with a man strapped in. His clothing was ripped and burned and one of his legs was mangled. He was dead. The war was now a serious business. The day dragged on and the heavies and the secondary battery kept tossing slugs into the beach. Finally, late in the afternoon, our two spotting planes came home to roost and we headed out to sea for the night.

The next morning at dawn we were back at business as usual, but this morning was another one of those firsts. Out of the horizon we could see the masts of the invasion fleet. On this second morning we moved to a new target area, the town of Charon Kanao. There we spotted a sugar mill with a tall smoke stack which we used to good advantage as a base sight in the preparatory softening of the beach. As the minutes of the morning passed the invasion fleet grew larger until it was just a few hundred yards away. Then it squatted down and gave birth to all kinds of landing craft which growled around in circles waiting for their cue. Our guns put a methodical rain of projectiles down on the beach for the first hour and then, as the landing teams prepared to go in, we turned loose with a vengeance.

There is no sight like a beachhead just before H-Hour, D-Day. Warships of all sizes concentrate on pouring what sounds like millions of tons of shells onto the beach. The deafening roar rolls up and up like thunder of all of the gods of war. Your main battery fires a broadside. There is a flash of yellow flame, a pall of brownish smoke and the ship shudders and rolls. You watch the tracers of your projectiles drift into the beach and disappear in a cloud of dust and smoke and flame. Then you hear the rammers and the mechanical noises of turrets as a new salvo is loaded into the guns. The landing teams pass in assault boats, weighed down with the tools of war. Many of the Marines who are about to land have their faces painted like Indians. Some wave to us as they go past but most of them stare straight ahead, their faces tense. As we watch we can't help commenting on how much guts those guys have and we hope and pray that they won't be battered around like our gang at Tarawa.

While the first wave of landing craft was approaching the beach the warships stepped up their bombardment to rapid fire. It was an all-out concentration of fire power in a final effort to completely devastate every enemy position in the landing area. The deluge continued until the boats were within a thousand yards of the beach, whereupon three flares were shot into the air as a signal to cease fire. The troops were now on their own until they had established their beachhead. This was the end of act one, and the first part of our job was done.

We waited and watched and wondered. It was mighty hard to watch a lot of guys move into the oblivion of a beachhead and wonder how they were making out. We wanted reports. We heard the crackle of small arms fire and saw splashes in the water around the advancing landing craft. Our guns were quiet, waiting for the word to let go at the beach with some more of our five- and fourteen-inch. The smoke started clearing away. Reports came filtering in. "Red Beach is tough as hell and the first wave is being torn to pieces." Another beach is moving along OK and our amphtracks are on solid ground. "A barrage of five-inch is needed over here." The second and third waves are reorganizing on a beach to the south. "Casualties are way up." As soon as radio communications were established with the Shore Fire Control

Party we commenced fire again in support of the advancing troops.

In the late afternoon we recovered our spotting aircraft and started out to the open sea. Towards evening we looked back over the fantail and saw the invasion ships sending up a cone of tracers at an attacking plane and strained our eyes for any bogies in our vicinity, but none got to us.

The days dragged on, and things went slower and slower for the fleet. Bombarding became a routine pastime and men came up from below decks to watch the secondary battery lob shells into the targets. One wiseacre even described the bombardment as being: "A Navy sponsored farm project that simultaneously plows the fields, prunes the trees, harvests the crops and adds iron to the soil."

On our last day at Saipan we refueled tincans and in the afternoon got underway for Eniwetok. Our first job was done. We had emptied our magazines into an enemy island and had received laurels from our troops on the beach for accuracy. We had shot down our first enemy plane since Pearl Harbor, had buried our dead, transferred our wounded and were on our way to a rear area to refuel, rearm and reprovision for the next phase of the Marianas operation.

## GUAM-TINIAN

Eniwetok was our first stop at a Pacific atoll. An atoll is a string of coral based sand piles, more or less circular in shape forming a lagoon, which affords an excellent anchorage for the fleet. Foliage is optional, depending on the intensity of the previous bombardment required to take the atoll away from the "rice-merchants."

Here we had our first advance-base liberty and swimming calls off the forecastle. The liberty was "wonderful." Recreation parties formed on the port quarterdeck and were taken on self-propelled pontoon barges, called sea mules, to Runit Island. Runit seemed to be about 80 feet long and 12½ feet wide and accommodated close to 12,000 sailors and marines on liberty.

Each man was allowed two cans of warm beer and all the freedom the mob on the island would permit. It was a picturesque little spot. There was razor-edge coral on either side of the strip of terra (there wasn't enough of it to be firma) that petered out into a mound of sand, which was covered with a dingy undergrowth and young coconut palms. The beach was lovely with its hundreds of beer cans, broken bottles, and empty beer cases. The main event in these liberty parties was to swim out to a half-sunk Japanese ammunition lugger and get quantities of ammunition to bring back to the ship as souvenirs; that is, until the Executive Officer heard about it. At any rate it was fun while it lasted.

But our stay at Eniwetok didn't last long and soon we got underway again, loaded for bear. Guam was our objective and we reached it on the afternoon of 18 July. There is no doubt that we set some sort of precedent here, for as we steamed in we could watch other ships bombarding Jap positions while our band was holding a swing session for the crew on the forecastle.

The next morning was William-Day minus one and we went in and assisted with the preparatory bombardment on the northwestern coast of the island.

William-Day was the occasion for another of those amphibious landings which starred the Marines. The general feeling was that those guys on the beaches were among the hottest outfits we had. This time a new weapon was used in the final five hundred yards of the assault. When the gunfire of the navy ships was lifted, rocket-firing landing craft went up almost to the beaches and poured out a holocaust of explosives into the Jap defenses. Before the dust had settled the Marines were ashore beginning their push to regain this American territory which had been stolen by the Japs. On the evening of William-Day we ceased firing, recovered our aircraft and headed north for Saipan.

At Saipan, we rearmed for a new assault, this time on the Japanese island of Tinian. On Jig minus one day we steamed down to the central west coast of Tinian and started the day by leveling off targets in

Tinian Town. We encountered no return fire and did our job in more or less leisurely fashion. Actually this was not the point where our troops were to land, but rather a feint to divert the Japanese forces to that section so that we could land more easily at the scheduled point further north. Evidently it worked because the next morning when a diversionary bombardment group returned with a fleet of empty LST's to complete the ruse, one of the battlewagons tangled with a Jap shore battery and absorbed twenty-seven hits before she silenced the challenger. The actual landing, further north, was made unopposed.

After the assault we worked down the east coast giving gunfire support to the Marines as they advanced on the island. For the ships this operation was a push-over. The CALIFORNIA'S radios carried the conversation between tank and infantry teams and gave us all an inside look at the boys on the beach and the cool methods they used in slaughtering the Japs.

The last day of the operation was the most impressive. The Japs were making a final stand on the high ground of Tinian's southern tip. The boys on the beach asked for a hand from the fleet. In the early morning all of the ships of our group formed a ring around the southern end of the island and waited for the green light on our pulverization plan. The sky was gray and a drizzle set in. The barrels of the heavies shone as though they had been polished by the rain that fell on them. The word was passed, the main battery trained out and the guns began to speak their pieces. We had an assigned target area and simply laid down a box barrage which had an effect similar to plowing before spring planting. Every ship turned to with a violence that the defenders of Tinian had seen before on nearby Saipan. Finally our fire was lifted and the Marines moved forward to spend the next two days flushing what was left of the Tinian garrison out of its caves.

With Tinian under our belts we moved south again to Guam to relieve fire support units there. We lay off the northwest coast and advanced with the Marines to the north day by day until the end of the campaign. It had been rather slow going because the Jap retreat was aided by the concealment offered by the thickness of the jungle. In fact, our part of the campaign became so dull that on several occasions our 5″ battery was in Condition ONE on the port side waiting for a call fire mission while on the starboard side we were holding a field day. During our last days at Guam we were able to get the ship fairly well painted and cleaned up before returning to Eniwetok.

## FROM POLLYWOGS TO SHELLBACKS

Our second visit to Eniwetok meant only rearming, provisioning and refueling. As soon as these tasks were accomplished we got underway for the south in company with a small task force of battlewagons, cruisers, and destroyers. On August 20th the Commander of our task group sent a message to all ships present, saying that it would be permissible to hold equator-crossing ceremonies. That afternoon our ship divided into two camps, pollywogs and shellbacks, and prepared for entrance into the realm of Neptunus Rex. This realm is a pathological kingdom, entered by all those unfortunate enough to cross that mythical line via a rugged procedure classed as fun and called an initiation. The shellbacks held council and made their diabolical plans. By dusk preparations were in full swing.

On the morning of the 21st, King Neptune set up his royal Court on top of Turret One and the lowly pollywogs passed in judgment all day long before the Ruler of the Deep. They were given fancy haircuts by the Royal Barber and strange remedies prepared by the Royal Doctor. Then they had to kiss the Royal Baby's belly, were warned not to flirt with the Royal Princess and finally were ordered to climb down a Jacob's ladder that was hung over the side of the turret. While the unfortunates were coming down the ladder they were practically drowned with salt water from a fire hose. When they came within range of the deck, they were whacked unmercifully on their posteriors with canvas shillelaghs. After once reaching the deck the pollywogs ran between two rows of shillelagh-wielding shellbacks to the other side of the deck where they got down on their hands and knees and crawled through a nylon AA target sleeve. The sleeve was held open by wire hoops and when a pollywog came out of the bitter end he was greeted by another fire hose, this time in the face. At the same time he was pummeled by a merry group of shellbacks who shouted, "What are you?" The idea was to say, "Shellback," but it usually took a few minutes for this to sink in and during the interim the pollywogs consumed a few gallons of salt water and stuttered, "I'm a sailor." For this there was another hail of blows until the battered mind squeezed out the idea that shellback status had been achieved.

This was great fun and it took us only two or three days to get the graphite, grease, saltwater soap and vinegar taste out of our mouths. By the time the black and blue marks had cleared up and our hair had started growing back we got our certificates proving that we were bona fide seadogs and shellbacks.

When we arrived in the New Hebrides we heard that the back country in those islands was still a home for head hunters. However, none of us ever heard any more about the story. We did, though, meet the semi-civilized natives of the islands. Each afternoon while we were on liberty a group of the local gentry used to paddle down to the recreation area in crude outrigger canoes to sell us trinkets.

This group of uneducated natives that we more or less looked down on used to return to their homes nightly with a roll of cabbage that would choke a horse. These poor illiterate cannibals picked up sea shells in wholesale lots and came down each afternoon to take the suckers for a ride. They couldn't savvy our talk and just grinned at us whenever we said anything. However, when you pointed at several shells and picked them up you could see the unenlightened minds of the natives fall into order like the tumblers in a combination lock. Just hand them a twenty and watch how uneducated they were. Out would come a bag stuffed full of dough and before you could figure the total cost this one-time cannibal was handing you back your change, grinning and nodding his head in thanks.

Of course they knew many points of sales psychology such as indifference to the customer and eye appeal to get you up to the spot where they made the kill. They achieved eye appeal by coming down to our area in native sport clothes which consisted of a string secured about the midriff which held a loincloth in place. Their skin was so dark that the blue tattooing they wore on their arms, faces and chests was hardly noticeable. Sometimes they would carry native bows but no arrows. That helped to attract a crowd. While we examined their stock of shells, they would stand in their naturally bad posture, flat-footed as infantrymen, and eye us quizzically. Occasionally they would bring one of their children along, naked as a Jay bird, as another attraction in their sales scheme. Then, when the recreation party was ready to go back to the ship the natives would leave the area, some on foot and others in outrigger canoes. We often wondered what model Cadillac they drove home in after we were out of sight.

## ASSAULT ON THE PHILIPPINES

After several weeks at Santo we got underway and steamed northwest to the Admiralty Islands. We had enjoyed our stay in the New Hebrides with their low foliage-smothered hills and sultry days but every island gets tiresome and we looked forward to seeing the Admiralties. On our way we passed New Guinea with its steep jungle-covered mountains pushing up out of the sea. Here and there we could see smoke rising where the Aussies were flushing the Japs from their positions. We gazed at New Guinea for about half a day and then it faded into the horizon.

At that time the harbor at Manus was still more or less empty with only two or three hundred ships present. After a few days at anchor, other ships began streaming in. The port filled almost to overflowing. Each day brought more war vessels, more cargo ships, LST's and amphibious craft. The troops this time were Army and our objective was in the Philippines. We wondered which island we would hit.

After a seemingly endless period that familiar bugle call, a single note, was sounded and we were on our way again to make the Philippines unfit for Jap habitation. As we passed through the sub nets at Manus the various ships of our force took up their positions in column. Just after the column had formed, it made a 90 degree turn to port. Being in the rear of the formation we saw each ship as it came up to the turning point. As we watched we engaged in the old pastime of naming ships as they turned in order to get a composite picture of who was with us. There was the PORTLAND with the Flag aboard and the MINNEAPOLIS with her destroyer-like camouflage job, the TENNESSEE, our sister ship, and the PENNSYLVANIA, which was an asset to any outfit.

The days passed slowly as we steamed northwest. Our officers gave us a general idea of what to expect in the way of trouble in this operation against the Philippines. We were told that there was a large number of Jap PT boats active in the islands and that there were several hundred airfields within a 300-mile radius of our specific objective, the island of Leyte.

When not standing watches, we spent most of our time preparing for another big show. The gunner's mates worked for hours on their guns making sure that everything was 4.0 before going in. Two days from our objective watches tightened up and a sharper lookout was kept for aircraft. Then on the morning of October 17th, after dawn GQ, we caught our first glimpse of the Philippines. We could see a misty looking pile of sharp pointed hills holding up the masses of clouds that are forever resting on the Visayas.

At first we thought we were going in immediately to start our bombardment, but instead we circled around outside the entrance to Leyte Gulf while a final sweep was made of the mined area inside. While circling we must have looked like a gang of boys milling around, building up courage before making a raid on a neighbor's apple tree. Finally the PENNSYLVANIA dropped from the formation with a group of smaller supporting craft and went over the fence into the orchard to get the apples.

We maneuvered outside the entrance of Leyte Gulf most of the day, then late in the afternoon the PENNSYLVANIA sent us word that the coast was clear and to come on in. We formed column and steamed through a marked channel that had been swept clear of mines that morning.

We made quite a picture as we steamed into the Gulf. We were in about the center of the column and by looking either forward or aft we could see a string of battleships and cruisers cutting their way through the water toward the objective. Because of the possibility of mines all ships went into the Gulf with paravanes rigged. This handy little device, designed to cut mines free from their moorings, probably saved us from a number of casualties and a first class hole in the bow. Our starboard paravane cut one mine free and after it bobbed up to the surface it floated past our side close enough so that we could see the horns, rust cakes, and green moss on top. Having never seen an enemy mine most of the crew on the starboard side of the quarterdeck ran over to the lifelines to get a good look, which might well have been their last had the thing bobbed in the wrong direction.

We got the word on our way in that we were going to be brave and remain in the Gulf during the night, which brought on dire predictions about being slaughtered in our sleep by stealthy Jap PT boats. Eye strain was at its peak on the gun watches but when dawn came there had been no PT boats, no trouble, just sore eyes. We steamed to within 8,000 yards of the beach and started our familiar refrain on another enemy held island.

D-Day in the Philippines was not the D-Day that we had seen on operations in the Marianas. We started our pre-invasion bombardment on schedule just before dawn, and the main batteries of the multitude of battlewagons, cruisers, and destroyers raked the landing beaches thoroughly. Evidently previous experience had proven to the enemy that the price paid to resist a landing within range of naval gun fire support was not worth it, for the Army troops hit the beach at H-hour with negligible resistance. Even the expected air raids did not materialize immediately, and it was evident that the Japanese had chosen to make their stand later. The landing forces were welcomed enthusiastically by hundreds of Filipinos, who appeared from nowhere as soon as the bombardment ceased. After it was assured that we had secured a strong beach-head, General of the Army Douglas MacArthur, broadcasting from his flagship, the Cruiser NASHVILLE, broke the news that the world had long been waiting to hear; he had fulfilled his three-year-old promise, U. S. forces had returned to the Philippines.

That day at dusk we had an air attack. There were hundreds of transports and cargo vessels in close to the beach and when "Flash Red" was announced a smoke screen was laid over the transport area. But in spite of the smoke, a Jap plane got through and launched a torpedo which hit the cruiser HONOLULU, while another Nip crashed his plane into the Australian flagship, HMAS AUSTRALIA, killing the Commodore as well as her Captain on the bridge. For a period of about an hour reports came to us about the HONOLULU. At first it was believed she was sinking. Then they were going to beach her, but some beautiful work by our tincans kept her afloat until she could patch up her damage.

This was the first of a series of seemingly endless air attacks. On that same evening a destroyer escort that had struck a mine and had been beached at the entrance to the Gulf was subjected to a merciless strafing attack. But by the end of our first week in that area everyone had become accustomed to the alerts and began to say, "The show is over for us." The sure indication of this was that the CPO's had set up their game of grommets, or ring toss as the USO calls it, out on the starboard quarterdeck.

This attitude of the show being over changed in just one evening. We were at battle stations steaming along in formation with no indication that there were any hostile aircraft in our immediate vicinity. Suddenly one of the 20mm. group control petty officers stuttered into his phone that there was a plane diving on us out of the clouds. Before he could finish his report 12 or 15 guns had opened fire.

The plane was a Zeke and it seemed to be heading directly for our stack or foremast. All of the 20mm. guns and several 40mm. quads turned loose a deluge of slugs into the attacker. The sheer weight of machine-gun fire forced the plane off its centerline course and deflected it to our starboard side where it crashed into the sea near the forecastle. There was a terrific flash of yellow flame when it struck. The explosion blew the pilot out of his cockpit, opened his parachute and suspended him in the air up a hundred feet or so. We watched the mangled body float down, drop into the sea, and drift past the ship.

The Captain sent down a "Well Done" from the bridge to the light machine-gun battery. The Admiral in command of our task force said that he had never before seen such a heavy concentration of accurate 20mm. fire from one ship. The part we couldn't understand was that the Jap hadn't attempted to strafe us and we could see that he was carrying no bomb. We learned the answer in days to come. Our ship had been attacked by one of the first Kamikaze planes.

## BATTLE OF SURIGAO STRAIT

Each evening during our first days in Leyte Gulf the battleships of our force cruised down to a point of land that jutted out near the town of Abuyog. There we would lie-to all night long, as though waiting in ambush. There was some talk about it among the crew but it didn't mean anything until the night of October 24th. On the afternoon of that day at about four o'clock we received word from the Flag to prepare for a surface engagement. Up to that time we had more or less considered ourselves a shore bombardment group. This assumption proved entirely incorrect. Immediately after the word had been received we made our preparations. Fire hoses were faked down, unnecessary topside gear was secured and the lifelines and their stanchions were taken down and stowed. The stern crane was lowered and secured on deck and our aircraft were catapulted and sent to the Leyte beachhead to sit it out. Many an envious eye was cast on the airdales as they got into their planes and hauled off to the safety of the beach.

Soon after the final intelligence reports the Captain gave the Chaplain permission to put out the word over the PA system on the coming engagement. An enemy force of two battlewagons, two heavy cruisers, two light cruisers and ten tincans had been sighted in the Sulu Sea. It had been attacked by our aircraft but was still coming. The Padre also told us to be sure to shower and put on a clean change of clothing to prevent infection in case we were wounded. He closed with a prayer.

For the first few minutes after we got the dope we talked anxiously to one another and listened to men who had been shot off ships in the battles off Guadalcanal. Then, after a short interval, we came back to normal. Everything went off like clock-work as we readied ourselves for this new test. Of course, there was the regular Jap air attack at dusk, but it was secondary compared to what was in store for us later in the evening. We watched the LOUISVILLE, which was carrying Rear Admiral J. B. Oldendorf, send out a deluge of visual messages to ships of our task force. Her superstructure looked like an electrical advertising sign as her signal lights blinked on and off. It was one of the few times that we had seen a ship showing lights after sundown. We formed for battle at the Leyte entrance to the Surigao Strait and as the sky darkened we were able to see stars only now and then. There was a low ceiling of clouds drifting overhead which made the night as black as the pitch in the deck seams.

After we secured from AA defense that evening we went below to wash up and change clothing as advised and turned in as soon as we could to get as much sleep as possible. In the tropics a large part of the crew sleeps topside on the decks and when we came up that night we could barely make out the other battlewagons in the column. There was a cool breeze and after a few minutes we dropped off to sleep.

At 0130 on the morning of the 25th of October, the General Alarm was sounded and the crew manned battle stations. Picket ships had spotted the Japanese task force and it was definitely coming our way: The picture was something like this: Surigao Strait is a narrow passage between the Mindanao Sea and Leyte Gulf. Our six battleships were stationed at the top of the Strait, steaming back and forth in battle line. Further down the Strait, on each side, were our cruisers, destroyers and PT boats, in that order. The Jap ships entered this trap in column formation, steaming at 20 knots at right angles to our battle line. It was a setup for us.

As the suckers steamed in our search radar picked them up at 42,000 yards and, as they kept coming, down, down, down went the range until we wondered if we were ever going to open fire. Then we saw the first indication that the Japs knew we were there. They fired starshells into the air like a man in the dark striking matches to try to see where he is.

The starshells were the first visible sign that our attack had been launched. The PT boats and tincans went in on torpedo runs to harass and cripple the enemy. As soon as their fish had been launched the signal was given for the cruisers to open fire, and they turned loose with everything they had except the contents of their spud lockers. Then came the final blow when the battlewagons let go with their 14- and 16-inch guns to make the kill.

A night surface engagement is a weird sort of thing. You fire into the darkness at a target that you can't see and it fires back. There is that first terrific rolling roar when your main battery cuts loose at the enemy. Then there is a moment of silence followed by the noise of an air blast clearing the gun barrels of inflammable gases. Next come all of the whirring mechanical noises of reloading. Powder and projectiles are hoisted up, rammers and elevating gears grind away; then the standby buzzer sounds and another blinding flash of yellow lights up the sky so brightly that you can see the other ships of your force. Another moment of silence is followed by a third flash and so on as rapidly as possible until the enemy is sent to the bottom or gets away.

On that red-letter night of the 25th of October our Jap target did not get away. We poured sixty-three 1500-pound projectiles into a battleship of the Fuso class and sent it to the bottom. It was breathtaking to watch the sky light up with each salvo and then see the tracers streak through the darkness toward the target. Only sixteen minutes after our first salvo we ceased fire because of a lack of targets.

Our task force commander, Rear Admiral J. B. Oldendorf, had successfully crossed the "T", a maneuver which is the dream of every naval tactician. As a result we had divided Surigao Strait with the Nips. We took the top half and they took the bottom. Admiral Oldendorf's comment was, "Never give a sucker an even break." We hadn't.

We had remained at battle stations throughout the engagement and just about the time it was determined that the show was over those unpredictable grandsons of Heaven sent in an air attack which kept us at the guns for another hour or so. To get even with the Jap for this imposition our 5-inch battery shot down a Val-type divebomber. Just before securing from the alert word came that there were more Jap ships about 60 miles northeast of us outside the entrance to Leyte Gulf. In company with two other battleships, three cruisers and a group of cans we started out to get them.

Morale was high throughout the ship that morning for, though we hadn't eaten, we had been through a surface engagement and won, we had just shot down a plane and there wasn't anyone who could whip us. We were going out to plaster some more Jap battlewagons. The men were crummy with burnt powder and cork and the sun, as usual, was hotter than the hubs of hell. While heading toward this new threat to our beachhead we took our first "Stand Easy." We started to gripe about not having had breakfast and beat our chests over the affair of a few hours before.

Soon the mess cooks were secured for a short while and went down to get corn bread, coffee and beans for the gun crews topside. They came back up with the paper cups, the old blue enameled coffee pitchers and the chow. At the moment it was better than anything we had ever tasted before, but later on it was good ground for a lot of gumbeating.

The Padre went on the PA system again and gave us the dope on the anticipated engagement. It seemed that the Japs had sent two forces into our area; one was supposed to enter Leyte Gulf through Surigao Strait and the other through the eastern entrance. We had erased the Surigao Strait threat, but the other group had started working over a force of our jeep carriers and tincans just east of Samar.

These six CVE's, with only one five-inch gun each, put up a heroic fight against the Jap task force of 5 battleships, 8 cruisers, and 13 destroyers. Admiral Sprague, in charge of the jeeps, tincans and DE's used smoke screens to out-maneuver the Japs and, as an additional insult, sent part of his tincan escort against the enemy formation for torpedo runs. The action lasted for more than two daylight hours and during that time the mighty Japanese Navy sank one CVE, three tincans and damaged four carriers. For supposedly first-class naval warriors this was a miserable showing and probably grounds for much hara-kiri around Imperial Japanese Naval Headquarters. Planes from the CVE's had also joined the attack on the second enemy force, so by the time our task unit reached the eastern entrance to Leyte Gulf the Japs had broken off the action and were in full retreat. They had too much of a head start for us to catch them.

During our first two weeks at Leyte we had participated in a shore bombardment, a night surface battle and had set Condition ONE in our anti-aircraft batteries fifty-one times. Here we had met our first Kamikazes and had sunk a Jap battleship in one of the most important naval engagements of the war.

## CHRISTMAS IN THE PALAUS

In early December we were underway again from Manus where we had returned from Leyte in late November. On this business trip we were not going directly to our destination. We were to stop at Kossol Passage in the Palaus before the final push. This anchorage is formed partly by coral reefs and partly by the island of Babelthuap, which at the time was still in Japanese hands. It was the first port where sentries had to be posted on deck as a precaution against boarding parties. In two instances of desperation Japs had boarded small craft to take much-needed food. However, this situation didn't bother us sufficiently to interfere with movies on the quarterdeck in the evenings and each morning and noontime we could go up on the forecastle and watch the Marine Corsairs from Peleliu make their milk runs against enemy positions on the island.

This was the spot where we spent Christmas. Christmas isn't much out in this country—it is just another day. For two months previous to December 25th and for two or three months afterwards, we received packages from home. For some reason people seemed to think that we were starving to death and sent large quantities of food.

There is nothing in any cook-book that can describe a South Pacific Christmas delight. Yet it's really very simply made. First you get someone in the States to send you a fruit cake. By the time it gets to you it has traveled a good 12,000 miles. It is a sure thing, since it is second class mail or parcel post, that it has been lying for at least a month in a mail bag at some spot like Manus or Leyte where it rains every day. During that period the South Pacific part comes in. It comes in through every crevice in the package and lays eggs of all flavors and denominations and, helped by the dampness and the heat, it works up into something that the sender would never recognize. Mail call sounds, the recipient rushes up and grasps his package, unwraps it, anticipating a thousand pleasures, and when he finally tears off the last wrapper, all the mosquitos, flies, ants, beetles, cockroaches, larvae, pupae and spiders each hold up a crumb and in their best Micronesian shout, "Merry Christmas."

However, we were fortunate because we were in a port and not out on an operation. We were able to have a whale of a lot better celebration than our friends fighting in the mud on Leyte or Mindoro and we had a good supply of holiday chow aboard, which is about the biggest thing in the advanced area.

On Christmas Eve our main deck messing compartment, port side, was closed off with signal flags hung from the overhead. An altar was set up and a High Mass was conducted, followed by a General Service. At the conclusion of the services most of the men had that faraway look that comes when they are thinking about home and all of the things that went to make up their lives before the war. It's an odd look, a sort of preoccupied stare.

Christmas Day meant turkey dinner with trimmings and that strange thing called "holiday routine," an event that occurs about as often as a total eclipse. For Christmas night a Happy Hour had been scheduled. During the afternoon it began to rain and up until a few minutes before the show was due to begin the drizzle hung on. Then, as if by a prearranged signal, it stopped. The boxing ring was rigged on the quarterdeck and all hands rallied round. The band climbed into the ring, put on an hour show and then gave way to the boxers and the movies. It was a swell show but after the movie was secured we turned in feeling rather down in the dumps because in spite of anything you can do to celebrate Christmas in the tropics, 8,000 miles from home, it just does not hit the mark.

The next few days passed quickly and brought us up to a sober, painless and uneventful New Year's Eve. On New Year's Day we left Kossol Passage for another crack at the Philippines. Scuttlebutt had it that we were going to attack Manila or some point on the east coast of the island of Luzon. This time the dope was better than usual, because they did guess the right island, which was closer than any of the scullery strategy had been before.

## LINGAYEN

On our way to Lingayen we passed through our old stamping grounds, Leyte Gulf and Surigao Strait, and then into the Mindanao Sea, through the Sulu Sea, past Manila and up the northwest coast of Luzon, where we witnessed a few Hashi Krashi attacks and the sickening loss of the CVE, OMMANEY BAY.

On the afternoon of the 5th of January, 1945 we passed Manila and during the early evening we were off the entrance to Lingayen Gulf. The plan was to steam north of the Gulf in order to lead the Japs to suppose we were going to attempt a landing further up the coast. But early in the morning of the sixth we doubled back so that by dawn we were again at the entrance to the Gulf. About an hour and a half before daybreak the force was picked up by enemy aircraft. An occasional flare was dropped and in that period a destroyer-minesweep was sunk.

The Lingayen operation was carried out according to the Navy's well-tested invasion formula. About an hour before sunrise we manned our battle stations after a cornbread and beans breakfast. By the time the sun was up over the horizon we had catapulted our "lame ducks" and were ready for the shooting.

The bombardment went off with considerable ease during the morning. Our targets were on Santiago Island on the western side of the entrance to the Gulf. The terrain was fairly low, tending to be hilly with a heavy growth of trees and foliage. Things were so quiet that by noon men were secured in small groups from their gun stations to go below to the mess deck for dinner.

After the noon meal our ship joined forces with the rest of our task group and formed a column to enter the Gulf. Our mission was to give support to the minesweeps, to draw fire from any heavy shore installations and to bombard the beach in the vicinity of Lingayen Town.

Being the flagship for this operation we headed the formation. There were tincans on either side of us with battleships and cruisers astern. It was one of those impressive sights, a force of warships pushing through enemy waters and within range of shore batteries on three sides. We had the Task Force Commander, Vice Admiral J. B. Oldendorf, aboard and as his signal flags were hoisted one could look back and see the entire line of ships break out their bunting. We were plowing ahead into a light breeze taking in the entire sight, the high mountain range to port, the low impossible looking cone-shaped hills to starboard and, dead ahead, the San Fernando Valley.

That was the picture on the afternoon of January 6, 1945, when suddenly a plane was reported bearing 170 relative at zero degrees elevation, coming in. We opened fire. The whole starboard side turned loose with everything it had. The plane made its run parallel to a tincan in order to blank our fire and then headed in for us after crossing the can's bow. In the few firing seconds we had, smoke from our salvos covered almost our entire starboard side but the plane was identified as a Zeke 52, the new Zero. It kept coming through a wall of fire, heading directly for our bridge. The smoke increased as did the terrible pounding of every gun we could bring to bear. The gunners and loaders swung with the target as it came streaking in. Then at the last instant, the Jap pilot turned his plane in a vertical bank and came roaring through the tracers and smoke to smash in a violent cloud of billowing yellow flame against our after fire control tower.

The plane's motor and a shower of debris were thrown over the port side into the water. Steel fragments from the explosion tore chunks out of the decks 35 feet below, killed men at their gun stations, smashed into splinter shields and tore a sizable piece out of the ship's bell. The whole anti-aircraft control area, known as Sky Aft, was ablaze with burning gasoline. The only thing that broke the silence for some time after the crash was the crazy, maddening, blare of the cease-firing claxons that had been shorted out at their control switches in Sky Aft. The men didn't seem to talk, their lips just moved and the claxons went on and on. One man yelled, "Cut the sonofabitches off." Someone tore a wire loose and there was silence. Other sounds then became audible. Some men directed rescue parties, while others remained dazed and milled about aimlessly. One man broke out a fire hose on the quarterdeck and just stood with a blank stare, not moving. Another yelled down from above, "Get that damn hose away from him and bring it up here quick." The man didn't hear and someone went down and took it away from him. There was another sailor lying on the quarterdeck with a badly torn-up leg asking men as they passed in their feverish work if they thought he would lose the leg and if he was all right.

You could look down from above and see the dead at their gun stations. The 20mm.'s had their cradle bolts loosened and those guns where men had died were pointing skyward with the gunners in their harnesses holding the barrels vertical like so many grave markers. There was the steady sputtering of the water from the fire hoses on the hot steel of the superstructure and little streams poured through the holes in Sky Aft down to the decks below. The damage control parties worked quickly and methodically. Sixty-three men of the 20mm. groups and two 40mm. quads were wiped off the slate as casualties, either killed or wounded, and in a matter of minutes emergency crews were made up as replacements. Men were sent from the turrets, lookout stations and other gun positions to assist in manning the AA guns that had suffered casualties. The majority of the wounded were able to make it unaided to the battle dressing station in the CPO Mess.

The members of the medical department worked quickly and skillfully in tending the wounded. The first man to reach the CPO Mess was from five-inch mount No. 4. He opened the door, staggered in and said, "Well here I am," and died. His right arm was torn off at the shoulder and he died from the shock. Then the overwhelming collection of wounded poured in. There were shrapnel wounds, burns, shock cases, fractures and hysteria. The corpsmen went to work and for three days scarcely stopped for a breather. Some of the men they tended were horribly burned, their faces and torsos absolutely black, and others had raw skin showing through torn clothing and burned shreds of flesh hanging down. The worst cases needed plasma in considerable quantities, as well as morphine, before the doctors could work on them. The Chaplain moved among the men lying on litters and cots, giving comfort and last rites.

It is difficult to describe the scenes about the ship that day. One must have lived all of it to understand what it means to be steaming along with flags flying and majestic white clouds piled around the horizon against a brilliant blue sky when suddenly there is a terrific roar of guns and a crash and you look around to see a shipmate hanging in a gun harness with his back broken and his torso contorted so that his head is on the deck between his feet. It takes guts and devotion to go where the wounded are and where you have to be careful of your balance on the blood-slippery deck.

By eight o'clock darkness had set in. The stars were out and the moon was a slight crescent. Our day was nearly over. Word was passed that the condition watch was being set and we could secure from our General Quarters battle stations. When new men came to the guns to relieve us, most of us just sat down thinking, "I can't believe it has finally ended."

On the morning of the 7th before we went to General Quarters we were able to bury some of our dead in a fittingly simple ceremony. Here we had no caissons, no muffled drums, no guard of honor, no black drapes nor stately procession. What we had was the real thing; the only ones present were the truly close friends of those that had gone; no sightseers, just a flag-draped litter and a chaplain in a khaki uniform with a helmet close by reading the ceremony in the near-dark. Ours were fortunate men. When they had to leave they left with friends on all sides and when they were buried there were no hypocrites, only those who loved and fought with them and wanted to be there as a final tribute instead of a final duty.

The operation proceeded as planned. During the next two days we lobbed five- and fourteen-inch projectiles at Jap targets. On the morning of the 9th came another D-Day and we started in towards the beachhead again throwing everything but spuds into the rice paddies. Transports came in with our soldiers. The rocket-firing LCI's blasted the beaches as did the air strikes. In this operation the Army used Australian transports and assault boats as well as our own. We could distinguish them by their trim dark paint jobs and large white numerals and the iron Kelly-type helmets their crewmen wore. We waved as the landing boats went by and the soldiers waved back as though they weren't very worried about this beachhead. We hoped they would move fast in occupying the air strip, so we could base our own planes there soon. They did.

The landings were successful and the casualties light. Before noon heavy construction equipment and engineers were leaving the transports and were heading for the beaches. The advances were encouraging and the resistance was light in this first phase of the fight.

To our relief after lying around the Gulf for several days we moved out to sea with our carrier task force and patrolled northwest of Lingayen until we were recalled to load ammunition. After rearming we headed back out to sea and steamed with the force through some wonderfully rotten weather. A low ceiling, frequent rain and a first-class storm for two or three days did wonders in cooling off the ship as well as giving us good cover.

It was a great feeling when finally on the afternoon of January 22nd, we left Lingayen Gulf behind. We watched the hundreds of ships grow hazy against the background of the San Fernando Valley; we passed those impossible cone-shaped hills that marked the spot where we had taken our hit and then we were out into the open sea and steaming south on our way to Ulithi.

The day after we arrived at Ulithi was the first Sunday since our departure from Kossol Passage during which religious services could be held topside. It was on this Sunday that we had our memorial services for those shipmates whom we had lost on January 6th.

An altar was set up on the fantail and instead of an actual casket, a large oblong box was covered with a black cloth and draped with the flag to serve as a symbol of all our dead. The crew sat on mess benches which extended as far forward as deck space would permit. The ship's band and an honor guard of sailors and marines flanked the catafalque. It was a beautiful day for the tribute we paid our men. The sun was brilliant, casting its thousands of sparkling reflections over the water and a slight breeze on our starboard beam rippled the colors flying from the stern. The Chaplain read a Requiem Mass.

It was the kind of ceremony that you see only during wartime. There was the silence of the sea with the barely audible slapping of waves against the ship's side, and the far off sounds of bugles calling this and that ship to church. There were the impressive words with which the souls of the men we lost were committed to God and the sea. Finally, there were the volleys of fire saluting our dead. We left the quarterdeck slowly, carrying with us thoughts that will live in our memories always.

## HOME ON LEAVE

The next day saw us underway again and this time for Pearl Harbor. Men started shining shoes and getting ready for real liberty. Then the scuttlebutt got started and burned through the ship like a prairie fire. "We're going back to the States," or "I saw Lieutenant so and so taking his blues to the tailor shop." But the Skipper didn't put out any dope except to caution us not to count our chickens before they were hatched. So we started sweating it out.

The morning we arrived in Pearl Harbor the crew was nearly crazy. There were a lot of rumors about what day we would reach the States while others claimed that we wouldn't go there at all. However, all speculation was quickly ended when, next morning, we left Pearl Harbor and set our course east. East, what a beautiful word! It meant that in five days we would see that mystical piece of real estate called the United States. The crew was at a fever pitch getting gear ready for that first liberty and leave back in God's country.

On the morning of February 14th we saw the snow-capped peaks of the Olympics and were met by a flock of the first sea gulls we had seen since we had left 'Frisco nearly a year before. The air was cold and it chilled the thinned-out blood we had acquired in the South Pacific. But it was wonderful. It was the first time we had been really cool since we left in May, 1944.

All morning long, as we passed through the Straits of Juan de Fuca, men would run out for a few minutes from their work to take another look at those beautiful mountains. We steamed up through Puget Sound, passed Port Angeles and Seattle and cut back in towards the Navy Yard at Bremerton. The hook was dropped in the channel opposite the Yard and shortly afterward mail was brought aboard. All that first night there was mail call. It included Christmas packages that had been all over the Pacific gathering entomological collections; also magazines and newspapers and all of the stuff that had been missing for weeks.

The morning of February 16th was cold and foggy and the men going on leave fell in on deck and fidgeted around while waiting for the ferry that was coming alongside. We waited from 0800 until about 0930 before we finally got aboard and were on our way down Puget Sound towards Seattle. We laughed and made cracks about each other and looked out the windows just to make sure it was all real. The ferry ride took about an hour, but it seemed like a lifetime. Finally the gangplank dropped and the various leave parties waiting in ranks rushed off in the fashion of an orderly mob through the ferry terminal and out onto the streets of Seattle.

Here we split into groups and marched to the various railroad and air terminals where we were scheduled to get our transportation. Some of the groups didn't leave until later that afternoon and evening, so they proceeded to get well organized. In fact there were a couple of men who never got out of Seattle. They just spent 21 days there letting off the steam that had been building up during the ten months they had been away.

This period in the Navy Yard was practically all one could ask for. We had our leaves and furloughs and got to see all of the people we had talked about for the last ten months. Some of us got married, others divorced; we danced, went to the movies, had picnics, bowled, fished, and did just about everything in the book in the way of good living. One of the big events of the Yard period was the ship's dance, a success all the way around. We took five thousand bucks out of the ship's welfare fund and threw a wing-ding in Seattle that will take the proprietors some time to forget. We rented the entire Melody Lane Night Club for two successive nights and jammed it each time with a thousand sailors and their partners.

A Navy Yard period is hard to describe. First the ship goes into a drydock and half of the crew goes home on leave. Then come the hundreds of Navy Yard workers, who, to the novice, seem to be tearing the ship to pieces rather than doing anything in the way of bettering its condition. They install the worst conglomeration of hoses, pipes and electrical wiring that it is possible to imagine. It can be called only one thing, "organized confusion." However, during the last few days things started to look up. We were in better shape than ever and ready for sea again.

After clearing Bremerton, we made trial runs for several days before getting underway for Long Beach, California. Here we went into drydock for a minor repair job and then out to sea for training and shakedown. This meant a few more precious liberties in the States.

## BACK TO THE WARS

On the afternoon of May 10, 1945, we made preparations for getting underway. At 1630 the hook was heaved in and we were leaving again, leaving for the forward areas. It's not so bad when you go the second time. You know by then what it's all about and what to expect. The only catch is that you've been back home; you've had a taste again of what it is like to spend those intimate hours that mean so much more than ever after you are nine thousand miles from your wife, or family, or girl friend, and the people you love. Now that you know the score you wonder how you will make out this second time. As war novels might put it, you've beaten fate once and are going back to be dealt in for a second hand.

Once again we tied up at Fox-Three in Pearl Harbor. We made liberties in Honolulu but this time we were not the wide-eyed suckers from the mainland that we had once been. We were savvy to the rackets and did only what spending was necessary. We heard through the underground that we were going to stay there quite a while and get some work done by the Navy Yard at Pearl Harbor. But shortly we were underway for Ulithi.

Ulithi in June was not nearly as crowded as when we had come through in January. The straight dope from the forward head was that we were standing by to go into the fight at Okinawa. That was precisely right, for after fueling and provisioning we cleared the anchorage and steamed northwest for Okinawa.

On arriving at Okinawa we anchored in Hagushi Bay. We received a much anticipated welcome from the Come Acrazys during our first evening there. A Flash Red alert brought us to our battle stations. Once again the protective smoke was laid over the harbor area. We were on the edge of the smoke screen and one minute we would be enveloped in the blanket and the next we would be sticking out like a sore thumb. We could see the moon and the stars break through the thin cover and our foremast created a sizable pylon that floated above the cloud like a damning finger pointing us out.

We waited in the smoke straining for some sound of a plane. We kept a sharp lookout in all directions and moistened our lips. Then off the starboard quarter we heard and felt the crump of two explosions and the smoke reflected a yellow flash. No one knew what had happened. If we could only see! Finally the alert ended and we came down from our gun stations. We went back to them later but the second time there was no show, just the waiting for one of those crazy sons-of-heaven to streak in through the screen and try to lay one on us. The next morning we found out that the Japs had dropped bombs the night before and had hit a small amphibious landing craft in which several men lost their lives.

The next day we left Hagushi Bay and went down the coast of Okinawa to bombard the remnants of the enemy force still holding out on the southern part of the island. The day was uneventful as we lobbed our five-inch slugs into the beach. Late that afternoon we returned to our anchorage for another evening of Flash Red.

About a week later we left Okinawa on a security patrol to guard the newly acquired island from possible Japanese fleet action. After about a week of this duty we returned to Okinawa Gunto for fuel and provisions. This time we anchored in Kerama Retto, a group of small islands close to Okinawa. As we left that afternoon the ships in the harbor were making smoke in preparation for the usual evening air attack.

This routine of patrolling, fueling and provisioning continued until our task force was assigned the job of covering a minesweeping operation in the East China Sea. During this period we were in company with a group of aircraft carriers which were providing air cover for the minesweeps up ahead of us. The area being swept lay between Formosa, Okinawa and the China Coast. It was a long and tedious job for which we later received a "Well Done" from Vice Admiral J. B. Oldendorf, Commander of Task Force 95.

## VICTORY

August 8th was a big day. At that time we were on our way to Leyte for refitting and recreation when the first news of the atomic bomb was broadcast by Radio Okinawa. The information we received at first was hazy and unbelievable, but as time passed we learned all of the details and even the ordinarily gabby guys were at a loss for words.

During this same trip we also learned of Russia's entry into the war against Japan and on the night of August 10th at 2117 the first word came through that the Japanese had offered to surrender. The majority of the crew had turned in their bunks and most of the others were on watch with the exception of the men on the main mess deck drinking coffee. When the Skipper passed the word over the public address system, the ship turned into a wild mob of shouting, back-slapping, hand-shaking, laughing sailors and marines. The main mess deck looked like Times Square on New Year's Eve.

The gedunk stand was thrown open with "cokes on the house for all hands." The Skipper told us that it was not official and that it might be a trick so we shouldn't let down in our vigilance but should wait for definite word from official sources. So we did. When the official news finally did come to us, it was an anti-climax compared with our first "V-J" Night.

The next morning we entered Leyte Gulf and dropped the hook. This stop was for liberty and recreation and the accomplishment of maintenance jobs not possible underway. We made our liberties at the Osmena Beach Fleet Recreation Center on the island of Samar. There was no swimming, but beer was available and we had a couple of ball games.

At the recreation center the natives set up a counter a quarter of a mile long, put a thatch roof over it and divided it off into partitions about five feet long. During the day, while the recreation parties were ashore, these shrewd folk would come down from their homes and sit behind the counters which they loaded with all kinds of native weaving, souvenir money, sea shells and trinkets. The place was a bedlam of shouts of "Hey Joe, Two Dolla, Five Dolla, Faw Dolla."

The crafty young American sailor would slip up to the counter and inquire, "How much?" The poor uneducated man behind the counter would say, "Faw dolla Joe," and smile. Then the sailor would say, "Nope, two dollars is all I'll give you for that knife." The native would look hurt and say, "Three Dolla Joe, OK?" "I'll take it," says this brilliant white hat and hands out the three skins to the little fellow behind the counter. Now they are both happy. The sailor runs off to tell his friends of the hard bargain he has driven and how he got the merchandise for practically nothing and the Filipino turns to his wife and tells her how he just sold a knife that cost him fifty cents to a sucker for three bucks. We were "taken" but we liked it. We bought Japanese money which was worthless for two bucks a shot and bought Philippine money which is worth just half what ours is for twice its value. Our liberty parties came back loaded down with slippers, hats, mats, knives, shells, foreign money and all manner of junk to shower on the folks back home.

Finally we received the official news that the Japs had accepted the Allied surrender terms. The announcement was made by the Captain and the ship staged another demonstration, which turned out to be desultory compared with the first. The ship's band broke out its gear and paraded around the ship in single file with part of the crew serpentining behind. They finally drew up to a halt on the port quarterdeck and put on a spontaneous concert that lasted for an hour and then we went back to work.

That evening we had an organized celebration on the fantail. Turret Four was trained out on the beam and the mob crowded into every available corner to see the show. The ship's band together with its regular entertainers put on an hour and a half performance, the best we had had out there. After the Happy Hour a movie was shown and that wound up our victory celebration.

One good feature was that the next morning no one had a hangover and there was no one in the brig as a result of overdoing the "three cheers for us" routine. However, there were sad faces the next day when we read of celebrations in the States. What we wouldn't have given to have been there! In the whole fleet there is no better mob of liberty commandos than in our ship. If we had been on the mainland perhaps the Skipper would still be hearing the mast reports.

## MISSION ACCOMPLISHED

Early on the morning of September 20th, the ship got underway from Okinawa and steamed north. Two days later we turned west to pass between the islands of Shikoku and Honshu. It was a cold, rotten day with an intermittent drizzle and not at all the kind of day for our first view of Japan. To both port and starboard we could make out the dim forms of land. This was Japan!

When we anchored on the morning of September 22nd in Wakanoura Wan the shore line was barely visible through the rain. In the days that followed, the weather cleared and we were able to see what we looked at. Off our port bow was the industrial city of Wakayama with its large steel mills and to starboard was the resort town of Wakanoura with a scattering of hotels and fishing villages on either side. All of this was set in a background of heavily wooded, rugged hills that sloped steeply into the sea.

Our reason for being in this port was to cover the landings of the Sixth Army occupation troops scheduled for September 25th. However, plans progressed so smoothly that on the 25th we sent a sightseeing party to Wakanoura and it arrived there at about the same time that the occupation forces hit their beaches a few miles up the coast.

So, after nearly four years of war, we were on Japanese soil. We were a little surprised at the apparently friendly attitude of the people. At worst some regarded us coolly. We gawked at this oriental town and its strange houses and shops. Our B-29's hadn't hit the town itself but its buildings were badly in need of paint and minor repairs. The people looked as though they needed to be retreaded. Most of the men wore various sorts of uniforms which, for the most part, were ragged. The women had doffed peacetime kimonos and wore wartime rompers. Leather shoes were practically nonexistent. Wooden clogs or fibre sandals were worn instead. The local gentry all looked as though they could stand a square meal.

After six days we left Wakayama, steamed north, and entered the anchorage at Yokosuka Naval Base, Tokyo Bay. From our berth there we could see one of Japan's key naval centers and the gutted Jap battlewagor NAGATO. On October 4th, half the ship's company embarked aboard an LSM for Tokyo proper, twenty-five miles up the bay. This was our big day. At last we were going to see the spot we had been talking about for better than three years.

All the way up the bay we could see the shore line on our port hand. The Yokosuka Naval Base seemed to melt into Yokohama and Yokohama into Tokyo with no dividing line between them. Although the day was misty we could see an almost continual line of smokestacks and waterfront buildings. We were impressed by the contrast between Japan's highly developed industrial regions on one hand and her antiquated modes of living that prevailed in such places as Wakanoura.

Of course, by the time we docked it had begun to rain. The waterfront where we landed was in good condition and we asked about all the devastation that our air force had heaped on the city. It didn't take us long to find out. Several blocks in towards town we entered the bombed areas. Tokyo was once the third largest city in the world but as we neared the central business district we realized that it had been vastly reduced. Great sections of the city had been leveled to ash heaps and hundreds of buildings made of brick or concrete remained only as burned-out shells.

Before we left the ship we had exchanged American dollars for yen at the rate of one to fifteen. So with Japanese money in our pockets we were able to go souvenir hunting once more. Various merchants had set up shop on the sidewalks or at temporary counters in their shattered stores. As usual, we returned to the ship loaded with junk.

In Tokyo we saw what Sherman meant when he defined war. We saw a people that were punch drunk, on the ropes, living in dugouts and shanties built in rubble heaps. They were clothed in anything they could find. Their great metropolitan city was a hollow shell of shabbiness and devastation. We returned to the ship that evening with a bad taste in our mouths.

The next day liberty was cancelled because of a typhoon, so the second half of the crew waited until the sixth for their trip to the hub of the Japanese Empire.

And so our story for this book ends in Tokyo Bay. It had taken us three years and ten months to fight our ship from the bottom of Pearl Harbor to the heart of Japan. But now that we have actually seen U. S. sentries, with rifles and fixed bayonets, standing guard at the gates to the Imperial Palace we know we have reached our wartime goal.

In a few days our duty in Japan will be complete and the CALIFORNIA in all her glory will sail back to the good old U.S.A. Our route will be via South Africa and thus a round-the-world trip will be added to the ship's log of achievements. Perhaps we will be home for Christmas. That is our fond hope. But the hope that lies deepest in our hearts is that God will grant each of us the vigilance and strength to put forth as much courage and devotion towards keeping the Peace as we did in winning it.

*GUNNERY SERGEANT RICHARD W. CUNNINGHAM, USMC*

*LIEUTENANT WILLIAM A. HEWITT, USNR*

*USS California, entering Wakanoura Wan, Honshu, Japan. BB-44 was among the first U.S. Navy ships to reach Japan after the World War II Peace was signed in October 1945.*

## STATISTICAL SUMMARY OF U.S.S. CALIFORNIA (BB 44)
## WAR SERVICE

(A) Number of operations against the enemy: Six (6).

(B) Number of days in combat areas for each operation:

| | |
|---|---|
| SAIPAN | 11 days |
| TINIAN & GUAM | 21 days |
| LEYTE | 36 days |
| LINGAYEN | 24 days |
| OKINAWA | 5 days |
| OKINAWA - CHINA COAST AREA | 48 days |
| TOTAL | 145 days |

(C) Number of days in Pacific areas not classified as combat areas:

Completed modernization on 16 January 1944, and after training and shakedown period proceed via Pearl Harbor to Roi (Kwajalein Atoll) arriving 8 June 1944. Departed Roi for Saipan on 10 June 1944.

| | |
|---|---|
| ENIWETOK | 34 days |
| ESPIRITU SANTO - MANUS - KOSSAL PASSAGE AREAS | 88 days |
| Departed ULITHI for United States on 27 January 1945. Arrived ULITHI from United States on 9 June 1945. | 136 days |
| Grand Total | 403 days |

D) Number of aircraft shot down or enemy ships destroyed:

Seven (7) enemy aircraft shot down.
Assisted in the destruction of _?_ enemy aircraft.
Assisted in the destruction of one (1) FUZO Class battleship.

(E) Amount of ammunition fired against the enemy:

14″/50 - 3,239
5″/38 - 14,567
40 mm - 12,928
20 mm - 31,052

—1—

EDITOR'S NOTE: This two page document is a summary of the USS California's war service prepared by Captain S.B. Brewer at the close of the war in the Pacific.

## STATISTICAL SUMMARY OF U.S.S. CALIFORNIA (BB 44)
## WAR SERVICE (CONT'D)

---

(F) Number of times own ship damaged by enemy aircraft or enemy fire:

SAIPAN - Direct hit apparently from a Japanese mortar or howitzer shell which struck the fire control platform and penetrated three decks.

LINGAYEN - After side of mainmast tower struck by suicide plane (Zeke 52).

(G) Miles steamed during each war year and total:

Calendar year 1944 —41,487
Calendar year 1945 —40,704
(to 28 August 1945)

Total —82,191

(H) Number of personnel casualties:

SAIPAN - 1 man killed
2 seriously wounded
1 officer & 7 men—minor wounds

LINGAYEN - 5 officers killed
1 officer died of wounds
26 men killed
13 men died of wounds
3 men missing
7 wounded

(I) Other information of interest:

The U.S.S. CALIFORNIA (BB 44) participated in the Battle of Surigao Strait.

—2—

*1944, a destroyer escort collides slightly with the USS California while refueling at sea.*

*October 31, 1944, Cousin John McLeod and "Jimmy" James. They married at the end of World War II.*

EDITOR'S NOTE: John served aboard a destroyer escort similar to the ship shown on opposite page.

# Jones-Hewitt Family Tree

1775-1989

The names and dates covering the period 1801-1881 in the first three sections are from the Family Bible of Edward Thomas Jones of Coalbrookdale, Shropshire, England

(Compiled by William A. Hewitt, 1989)

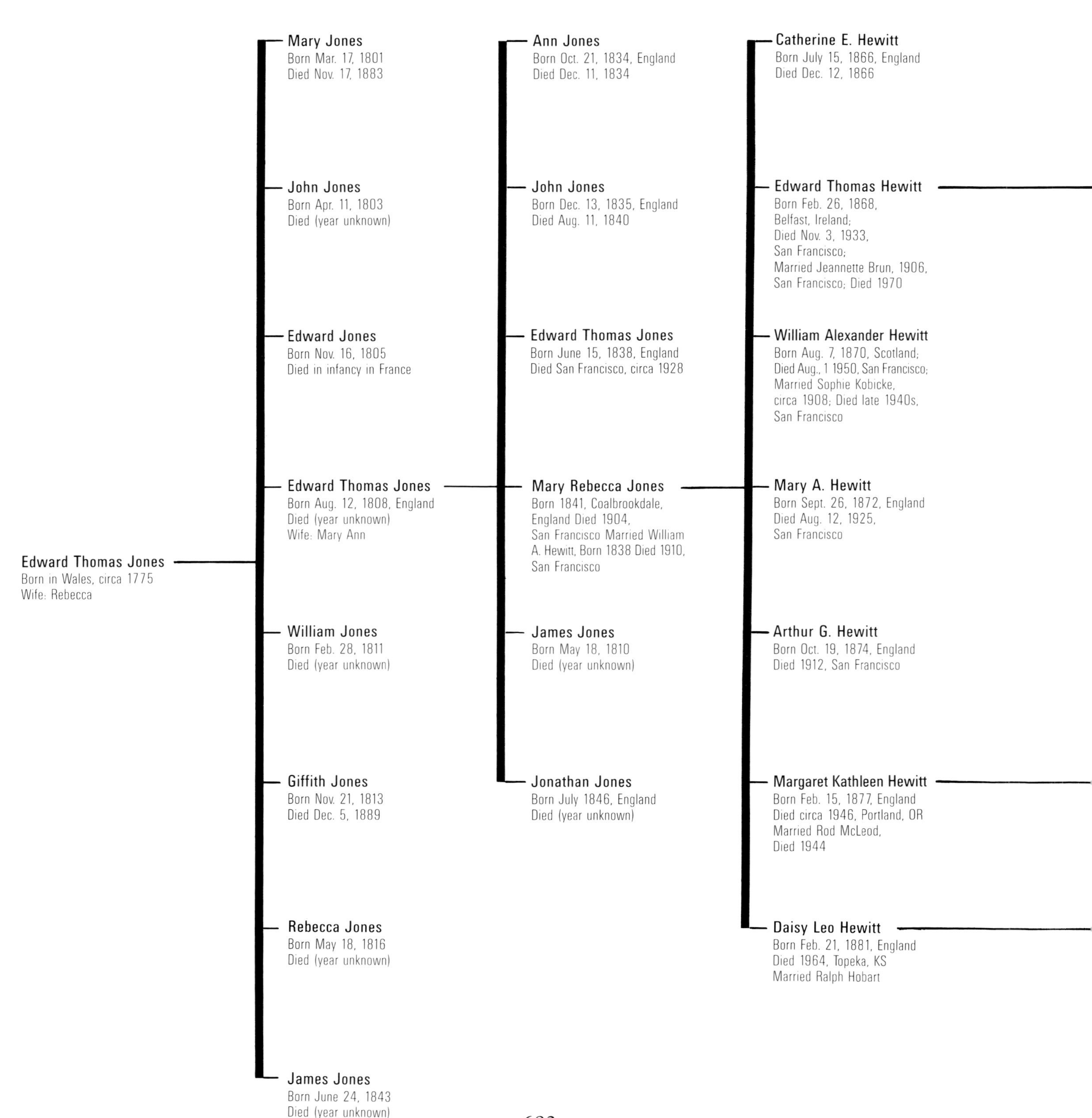

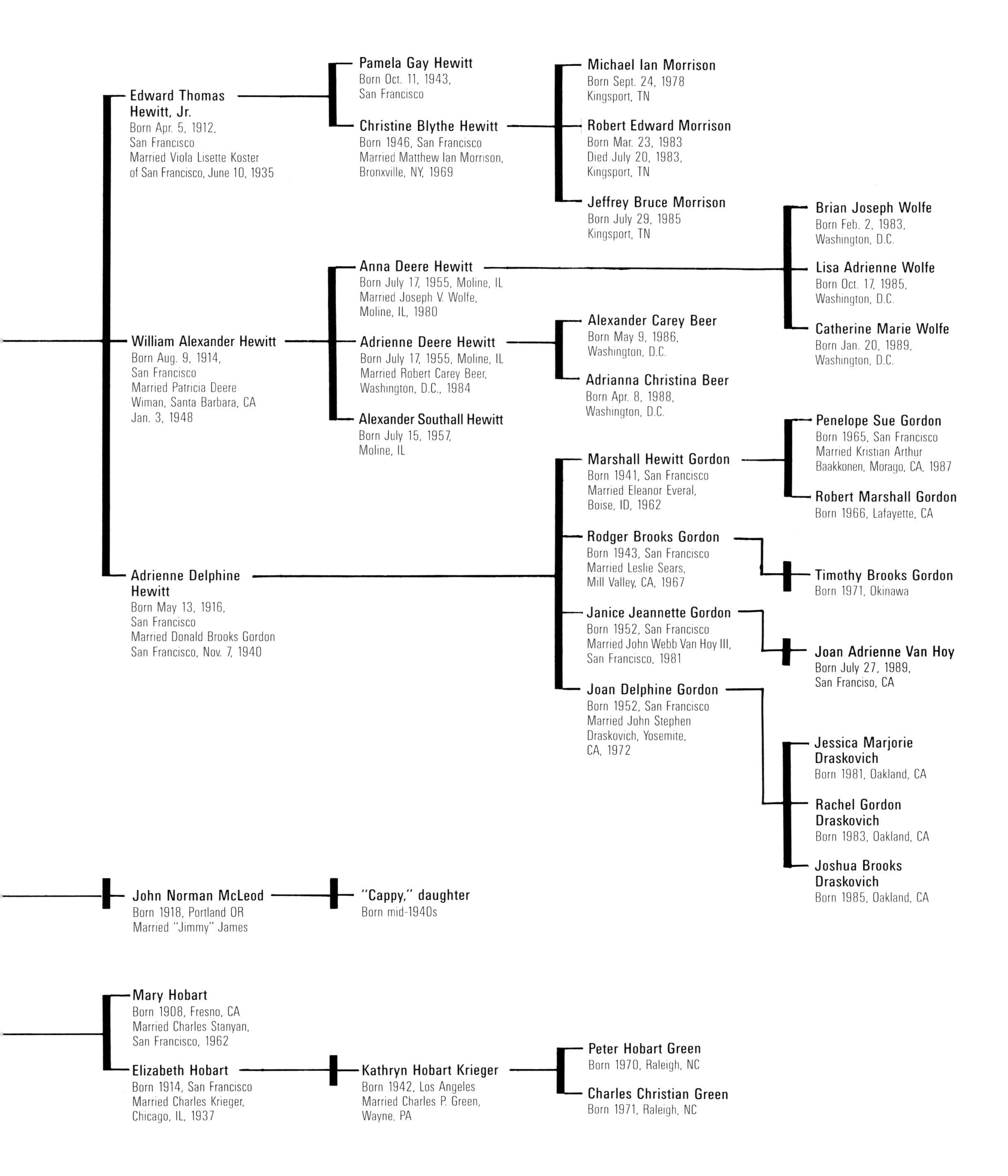

Edward Thomas Hewitt, Jr.
Born Apr. 5, 1912, San Francisco
Married Viola Lisette Koster of San Francisco, June 10, 1935
Pamela Gay Hewitt
Born Oct. 11, 1943, San Francisco
Christine Blythe Hewitt
Born 1946, San Francisco
Married Matthew Ian Morrison, Bronxville, NY, 1969
Michael Ian Morrison
Born Sept. 24, 1978
Kingsport, TN
Robert Edward Morrison
Born Mar. 23, 1983
Died July 20, 1983,
Kingsport, TN
Jeffrey Bruce Morrison
Born July 29, 1985
Kingsport, TN
William Alexander Hewitt
Born Aug. 9, 1914, San Francisco
Married Patricia Deere Wiman, Santa Barbara, CA Jan. 3, 1948
Anna Deere Hewitt
Born July 17, 1955, Moline, IL
Married Joseph V. Wolfe, Moline, IL, 1980
Brian Joseph Wolfe
Born Feb. 2, 1983, Washington, D.C.
Lisa Adrienne Wolfe
Born Oct. 17, 1985, Washington, D.C.
Catherine Marie Wolfe
Born Jan. 20, 1989, Washington, D.C.
Adrienne Deere Hewitt
Born July 17, 1955, Moline, IL
Married Robert Carey Beer, Washington, D.C., 1984
Alexander Carey Beer
Born May 9, 1986, Washington, D.C.
Adrianna Christina Beer
Born Apr. 8, 1988, Washington, D.C.
Alexander Southall Hewitt
Born July 15, 1957, Moline, IL
Adrienne Delphine Hewitt
Born May 13, 1916, San Francisco
Married Donald Brooks Gordon San Francisco, Nov. 7, 1940
Marshall Hewitt Gordon
Born 1941, San Francisco
Married Eleanor Everal, Boise, ID, 1962
Penelope Sue Gordon
Born 1965, San Francisco
Married Kristian Arthur Baakkonen, Morago, CA, 1987
Robert Marshall Gordon
Born 1966, Lafayette, CA
Rodger Brooks Gordon
Born 1943, San Francisco
Married Leslie Sears, Mill Valley, CA, 1967
Timothy Brooks Gordon
Born 1971, Okinawa
Janice Jeannette Gordon
Born 1952, San Francisco
Married John Webb Van Hoy III, San Francisco, 1981
Joan Adrienne Van Hoy
Born July 27, 1989, San Franciso, CA
Joan Delphine Gordon
Born 1952, San Francisco
Married John Stephen Draskovich, Yosemite, CA, 1972
Jessica Marjorie Draskovich
Born 1981, Oakland, CA
Rachel Gordon Draskovich
Born 1983, Oakland, CA
Joshua Brooks Draskovich
Born 1985, Oakland, CA
John Norman McLeod
Born 1918, Portland OR
Married "Jimmy" James
"Cappy," daughter
Born mid-1940s
Mary Hobart
Born 1908, Fresno, CA
Married Charles Stanyan, San Francisco, 1962
Elizabeth Hobart
Born 1914, San Francisco
Married Charles Krieger, Chicago, IL, 1937
Kathryn Hobart Krieger
Born 1942, Los Angeles
Married Charles P. Green, Wayne, PA
Peter Hobart Green
Born 1970, Raleigh, NC
Charles Christian Green
Born 1971, Raleigh, NC

Hewitt Family Burial Plot
Cypress Lawn Cemetery
in Colma, a suburb of San Francisco

| | |
|---|---|
| Mary Rebecca Hewitt | 1841-1904 Mother |
| William A. Hewitt | 1838-1910 Father |
| Arthur Hewitt | 1874-1912 Son |
| Mary Hewitt | 1872-1925 Daughter |
| Edward T. Hewitt | 1868-1933 Son |
| Ralph W. Hobart | 1868-1944 Son-in-Law |
| William A. Hewitt | 1870-1950 Son |

## Sources of Research Material

*St. Helena Star*
*Napa Register*
*Napa Reporter*
*San Francisco Merchant*
*Directory of Grape Growers, Wine Makers & Distillers of California*
*The Vineyards of Napa County*
Board of State Viticulture Commissioners
*Napa Daily Journal*
*Wine, An Introduction for Americans*
*Fine Wine of California*
*Story of Wine in California*
Napa Valley Grape Growers Association
County Supervisors Association of California
Recorder of Deeds, Napa County, California
Registrar of Land Records, Napa County, California
California Historical Society
American Wine Society, New York
Gomberg, Fredrickson & Associates, San Francisco
*Wine in California*
*Wines & Vines*
*Ghost Wineries of California*, Irene W. Haynes, Calistoga
Napa Valley Vintners Association
Arthur Schmidt, Oakville, California
Gunther R. Detert, San Francisco, California
Leon D. Adams, Sausalito, California
Ted Lemon, St. Helena, California
William A. Heinz, Sonoma, California
Kevin Tikker, San Francisco, California
Jim Sullivan, Sullivan Vineyards Winery, Rutherford, California
Anne G. McWilliams, Villa Mt. Eden, Oakville, California
Bonny Myer, Silver Oak Cellars, Oakville, California
Phyllis Van Kriedt, Mill Valley, California
Francis DeWavrin, Woltner Estates, Ltd., St. Helena, California
Reverdy Johnson, Johnson Turnbull Vineyards, Oakville, California
William Garnett, San Francisco, California
Professor Donald Wood, San Francisco State University
United States Navy
*California Monthly*
Smithsonian Institution
Reńe Rondeau, San Francisco, California
Sally Taylor, San Francisco, California
Clive Jones, Edmonton, Alberta, Canada
Jean Claude Hiron, Paris, France
Art Toucher, Tuxedo Park, New York
Ralph Dunwoodie, Sun Valley, Nevada
John B. Montville, Poughkeepsie, New York
Society of Automotive Historians
American Truck Historical Society
Antique Automobile Club of America
Antique Truck Club of America
Father John Brenkle, St. Helena, California